STATECRAFT

STATECRAFT

Strategies for a Changing World

MARGARET THATCHER

HarperCollins*Publishers*

HarperCollins books may be purchased for educational, business, or sales promotional use. For information, please write: Special Markets Department, HarperCollins Publishers Inc., 10 East 53rd Street, New York, NY 10022.

First published in the United Kingdom in 2002 by HarperCollins Publishers.

FIRST EDITION

Library of Congress Cataloging-in-Publication Data is available upon request.

ISBN 0-06-019973-3

02 03 04 05 06 RRD 10 9 8 7 6 5 4 3 2 1

This book is dedicated to Ronald Reagan
To whom the world owes so much

Contents

List of Illustrations ix

List of Maps xi

List of Tables xiii

Acknowledgements xv

Introduction xvii

1 Cold War Reflections 1

2 The American Achievement 19

3 The Russian Enigma 63

4 Asian Values 111

5 Asian Giants 151

6 Rogues, Religions and Terrorism 207

7 Human Rights and Wrongs 248

8 Balkan Wars 282

9 Europe – Dreams and Nightmares 320

10 Britain and Europe – Time to Renegotiate 360

11 Capitalism and its Critics 412

Postscript: Runnymede 467

Index 473

Illustrations

With Ronald Reagan at the Reagan Library, California, February 1991. *(The Ronald Reagan Presidential Library Foundation)*

With Ronald Reagan at his Los Angeles office, February 1995. *(The Ronald Reagan Presidential Library Foundation)*

Receiving the Presidential Medal of Freedom from George Bush Sr at the White House, March 1991. *(Official White House Photograph)*

Greeting Mikhail Gorbachev at Prague Castle, November 1999. *(Photograph © Karel Cudlin)*

With Vaclav Klaus at the unveiling of Churchill's statue in Wenceslas Square, Prague, November 1999. *(Photograph © Tomáš Jubánek)*

At Air Force Plant 42, Palmdale, California, March 1991. *(Personal collection)*

Meeting students as Chancellor of the College of William and Mary, Virginia, February 2001. *(Courtesy College of William and Mary)*

Receiving an honorary doctorate at Brigham Young University, Utah, March 1996. *(Personal collection)*

Walkabout with Boris Nemtsov, Nizhny Novgorod, July 1993. *(The Office of Boris Nemtsov)*

With Lee Kuan Yew, Singapore, September 1993. *(The Office of the Senior Minister, Singapore)*

At the launch of *Ever Result* at the Mitsubishi shipyard in Kobe, October 1994. *(Personal collection)*

Being met by Li Peng, Beijing, September 1991. *(Personal collection)*

With Jiang Zemin in Beijing, September 1991. *(Personal collection)*

Meeting Lee Teng Hui, Taipei, September 1992. *(Courtesy Ministry of Foreign Affairs, Taiwan)*

Graffiti in Kuwait City, November 1991. *(Personal collection)*

Talks with Yitzhak Rabin, Israel, November 1992. *(Personal collection)*

Visiting Vukovar hospital, September 1998. *(Personal collection)*

Paying respects to British war dead at San Carlos Water in the Falklands, June 1992. *(PA Photos)*

Visiting General Pinochet and his wife Lucia at the Wentworth Estate, Surrey, in March 1999. *(Popperfoto)*

With Silvio Berlusconi in London, February 2001. *(Courtesy Office of Prime Minister Silvio Berlusconi)*

Maps

Potential reach of ballistic missiles in Libya and Iraq   56
Russia and the former states of the USSR   66–7
The Caucasus and Central Asia   98–9
Japan and North and South Korea   113
South-East Asia   116
China   156–7
The Indian sub-continent   195
World religions   218–19
The Middle East   224
Middle East oil and natural gas reserves   238
The Balkans   284–5
Bosnia – political divisions   289
EU members, EU candidate states and non-EU members   378–9

Tables

NATO Defence Expenditure   42
Free Countries   250
Government Spending and Unemployment   332
International Labour Costs   387
Overseas Investment   402
Trade Blocs   407
Freedom and Prosperity   437
Fertility Rates   446

Acknowledgements

In the course of writing this book I have run up many debts of gratitude and it is a pleasure to acknowledge them. In the first place, my thanks are due to Robin Harris whose robust instincts and intellectual vigour have been a bracing presence over the years. This is the third volume on which we have worked together, and once again Robin provided indispensable help and sure advice at every stage. Without his assistance, I would not have begun and I could not have completed this work. Nile Gardiner acted as my indefatigable and always cheerful researcher. His dexterity in untangling the World-Wide Web made certain that no question went unanswered and no source was left untapped. Mark Worthington, as director of my office, ensured that the whole project ran as smoothly as the ups and downs of political life allowed – still more, he ensured that we met our deadlines.

I benefited from the help of a number of experts distinguished in their respective fields. Martin Howe and Patrick Minford generously gave up their time to read and offer invaluable comments upon several chapters. I am enormously grateful to them. I am also extremely grateful to Mark Almond, Christopher Booker, Sir John Boyd, Cynthia Crawford, John Gerson, Allister Heath, Brian Hindley, Andrew Roberts, Julian Seymour, Ronald Stewart-Brown and David Tang.

The responsibility for the opinions conveyed in these pages is, of course, mine alone. But the opinions themselves were developed, challenged and refined in the course of many conversations with old friends and new acquaintances. I would particularly like to mention: Robert Conquest, Chris Cviić, Steve Forbes, Frederick Forsyth, Gerald Frost, John Hulsman, Gary McDowell, Noel Malcolm, Boris Nemtsov, Gerald P. O'Driscoll, John O'Sullivan, Richard Perle, Peter G. Peterson, Lord Powell of Bayswater, Justice Antonin Scalia, Lord Skidelsky and Sir Alan Walters.

Finally, I would like to thank Michael Fishwick, James Catford, Robert Lacey and all those at HarperCollins whose professionalism ensured that this book now reaches the reader in such good order.

Introduction

For as long as there have been states, there has been discussion of statecraft or statesmanship.* The emphasis has changed over the centuries, as ideas of the state itself have changed – from the Greek city-state (or *polis*) with its narrow (and naturally all-male) citizenship; to the vastness of the Roman Empire with its enthronement of law; to the idealised, if not always idealistic, rulers of medieval Christendom; to the rumbustious politics of Renaissance Italy, home to Machiavelli's *Prince*; to the absolute monarchies of the seventeenth and eighteenth centuries, the ages of Richelieu and Frederick the Great; to the French Revolutionary Wars and Napoleon, the clashing European empires, and the competing nationalisms of the nineteenth century; and to the democratic concepts and the welfare state of the twentieth century. To plot the course of statecraft over so long a period would require skills that I, for one, do not possess.† Yet just the sense of so much history lying behind the tasks and goals of statesmen today is sobering and provides perspective.

---

* Statecraft and statesmanship are, according to the dictionary definition, interchangeable. But the former has a more practical ring to it, emphasising activity rather than rhetoric, strategy not just diplomacy. All too often, statesmanship turns out simply to be political action of which we politicians approve – frequently our own.

† But Henry Kissinger does, as he reveals in his magisterial study *Diplomacy* (New York: Simon and Schuster, 1994). The opening section of Dr Kissinger's book provides an account of statesmanship as it has evolved since the seventeenth century.

The early twenty-first century also has its distinctive features that govern the nature of statecraft now. These can conveniently, if not altogether satisfactorily, be summed up by the expression 'globalism'. In the course of the rest of this book I shall examine, test and explore the realities behind that term in its application to strategy, international interventions, justice and economics. And I shall do this for different countries and continents.

I must start, though, with the state itself. If you were to heed some commentators you would believe that globalisation spells the end of the state as we have known it over the centuries. But they are wrong: it does not. What it actually does is to prevent – in some degree – the state from doing things which it should never have been doing in the first place. And that is something rather different.

A world of mobile capital, of international integration of markets, of instant communication, of information available to all at the click of a mouse, and of (fairly) open borders, is certainly a long way from that world favoured by statists, of whatever political colour, in the past. It is nowadays, as a result, more difficult for governments to misrule their peoples and mismanage their resources without quickly running into problems. Unfortunately, though, it is still not impossible. Many African governments get away with kleptocracy. Several Asian governments get away with disrespect for fundamental human rights. Most European governments get away with high taxation and over-regulation. Bad policies inflict damage on those who practise them, as well as those on whose behalf they are practised, but bad government is still eminently possible.

That somewhat gloomy reflection should be balanced, though, by three much more positive ones. States retain their fundamental importance, first, because they alone set legal frameworks, and having the right legal framework is enormously important – probably more important than ever – for both society and the economy. Second, states are important because they help provide a sense of identity – particularly when their borders coincide with those of a nation – and the more 'globalised' the world becomes the more people want to hang on to such identity. Third, states alone retain a monopoly of legitimate coercive power – the power required to suppress crime at home and to maintain security against threats abroad.* This final coercive function of the state, although it may in practice involve a degree of contracting out to private enterprise, can and must never be yielded up. The state is something different from society; it is ultimately the servant not the master of individual human beings; its potential for inflicting horrors remains as great as ever. All these things are true. But we need states and we always will.†

It is on the state's role in the maintenance of international security that I concentrate in this book. This, in itself – at least until the events of Tuesday, 11 September 2001 – was slightly unfashionable. Today's politicians, at least in the democracies, had become almost exclusively interested in domestic politics. Of course, in one sense that was understandable. In a democracy we first have to win the votes of the electorate before we strut the world stage – unless we are European Commissioners. As Disraeli once put it, a majority is the 'best repartee', and he might have added the 'best basis for diplomacy'. But the fact remains that the great issues of war and peace which traditionally commanded the attention of statesmen down the ages should again command them today – and to a greater extent than they have in recent years. Riots, epidemics, financial crashes – all can be very frightening and disruptive. But war is still the most terrifying and destructive experience known to man.

Foreign and security policy, though, concerns much more than the two opposing poles of war and peace. It concerns the whole range of risks and opportunities which the far-sighted statesman must appreciate and evaluate in the conduct of his craft. Above all, foreign and security policy is about the use of power in order to achieve a state's goals in its relations with other states. As a

---

* These arguments are developed at greater length in a stimulating essay by Martin Wolf, 'Will the Nation-State Survive Globalization?', *Foreign Affairs*, January/February 2001.

† It might be argued that the attacks on America by Osama bin Laden and his network suggest that power has passed from states to terrorists. But even 11 September 2001 shows how important is the role of states: bin Laden could not have functioned effectively if he had not first been provided with bases and protection by the Taliban regime in Afghanistan.

conservative, I have no squeamishness about stating this. I leave it to others to try to achieve the results they seek in international affairs without reference to power. They always fail. And their failures often lead to outcomes more damaging than pursuit of national interest through the normal means of the balance of power and resolute defence would ever have done. It is, indeed, a recurring theme in Western liberal democracies, this mixture of naïve idealism with a distaste for power – and we should be on our guard against it.*

One example. In 1910 Norman Angell, the Nobel Prize-winning economist, wrote a celebrated book called *The Great Illusion*. In this he argued that because of global economic interdependence – particularly between the great powers – and because the real sources of wealth that lie in trade cannot ultimately be captured, warfare conducted for material advantage is always pointless. There is a small kernel of truth in this. Peace, not war, promotes commerce, and commerce is the driving force for prosperity – other things being equal. But in the real world other things are quite often not at all equal. Aggression may make perfect sense to a tyrant or a well-armed fanatic in certain circumstances. It may even appeal to a whole nation. Trade protectionism, which stops countries from having access to the commodities they need for their industries, may also lead political leaders to launch 'rational' wars. In any of these conditions there is precious little point in either victims or onlookers protesting that everyone would be better off without war. The only alternatives on offer are to fight, or to raise the white flag. Concerns for a safer world and attempts to secure it are admirable. But when, as in the case of Norman Angell, they lead a writer to believe, four years before the most terrible conflict the world has known, that 'it is absolutely certain – and even the militarists . . . admit this – that the natural tendencies of the average man are setting more and more away from war' – then something is badly wrong.†

---

* For a further example – that of the League of Nations – see p. 29.

† Norman Angell, *The Great Illusion: A Study of the Relations of Military Power in Nations to their Economic and Social Advantage* (London: William Heinemann, 1910), p.301.

It is sometimes suggested, or at least implied, that the only alternative to such dangerous high-mindedness as this in foreign policy is the total abandonment of moral standards. The thought behind Sir Henry Wotton's well-known definition of a diplomat as 'a good man sent abroad to lie for his country' has been applied more widely.* Yet I am not one of those who believe that statecraft should concern power without principle. For a start, pure *Realpolitik* – that is, foreign policy based on calculations of power and the national interest† – is a concept which blurs at the edges the more closely it is examined. Bismarck, its most famous practitioner, once remarked over dinner that conducting policy with principles would be like walking along a narrow forest path while carrying a long pole between one's teeth. But even the Iron Chancellor had principles of a kind: after all, he accepted without demur that his loyalty was to his royal (and later imperial) master rather than to the German people – a large section of whom he left excluded from the Reich.‡ He upheld the system and the values of the Prussian state, not those of a liberal democratic Germany. Whatever you think of this policy, it was not mere pragmatism.

Moreover, in the age of democracy the pursuit of statecraft without regard for moral principles is all but impossible, and it makes little sense for even the most hard-nosed statesmen to ignore this fact. Since Gladstone's Midlothian Campaigns in 1879 and 1880 – launched on the back of denunciations of Britain's foreign policy as 'immoral' – politicians who try to appeal exclusively to national interest have repeatedly run into trouble with national electorates. And the rise of America, as a great power with an easily troubled conscience, has confirmed that trend.

The years of the Cold War also had a deep and lasting effect.

---

* Sir Henry Wotton (1568–1639), poet and diplomat. He wrote this cynical inscription on the flyleaf of a book, while on a mission to Augsburg in 1604; it was subsequently made public. Wotton's indiscretion displeased his superiors and he lost preferment as a result. But he finished his days as Provost of Eton.
† The definition here – and there are other possible definitions – is Henry Kissinger's, from *Diplomacy*, p.137.
‡ Bismarck's unification of Germany in 1870 excluded Germans living under Habsburg rule, as part of his policy of ensuring that the German state was based on Prussia not Austria.

In that period, when the world was divided into two armed blocs with opposing ideologies – capitalism and socialism – the upholding of national interest and the upholding of political principles were for most of the time a seamless web. And though much has been questioned since the end of the Cold War, there have been few attempts to suggest that considerations of national interest are *all* that matter in weighing up foreign policy choices.

For my part, I favour an approach to statecraft that embraces principles, as long as it is not stifled by them; and I prefer such principles to be accompanied by steel along with good intentions. I accordingly suggest three axioms which the statesman would do well to bear in mind today.

First, the extension of democracy through every country and continent remains a legitimate and indeed fundamental aspect of sound foreign policy. There are many practical reasons for this: democratic states do not generally make war on each other; democracy generally promotes good government; democracy generally accompanies prosperity. But I do mean true democracy – that is a law-based state with a limited government, in which the tyranny of the majority no less than that of a minority is banished. Furthermore, as I shall explain, I entertain deep reservations about some initiatives taken in the name of human rights and democracy, on grounds of both practicality and of legitimacy.* And I would also caution against making the best (perfect democracy) the enemy of the good (imperfect democracy).† Commonsense must always temper moral zeal.

Second, a sound and stable international order can only be founded upon respect for nations and for nation states. Whatever the flaws of particular nationalisms, national pride and national institutions constitute the best grounding for a functioning democracy. Attempts to suppress national differences or to amalgamate different nations with distinct traditions into artificial states are very likely to fail, perhaps bloodily. The wise statesman will celebrate nationhood – and use it.

Third, whatever stratagems of international diplomacy are

---

* See Chapter Seven.

† See, for example, the discussions on pp. 124–6.

deployed to keep the peace, the ultimate test of statesmanship is what to do in the face of war. Deterring wars, and being in a position to win wars that are forced upon one, are two sides of the same coin: both require continuous investment in defence and a constant and unbending resolution to resist aggression. Our present age is one in which even the thought of war has become anathema. Yet at any one time wars of varying intensity are being fought around the globe. For example, in 1999 alone there were civil wars of one kind or another taking place in nineteen countries around the world.* In addition there were four international armed conflicts between governments over sovereignty and territory: the Kosovo conflict (and subsequent NATO intervention); the war between Ethiopia and Eritrea; the clash between India and Pakistan over Kashmir; and the Arab–Israeli conflict in Southern Lebanon. Most such conflicts are in places remote from the daily concerns of Western electorates and politicians. But in today's world, with its widely available weapons of mass destruction, its ethnic and religious fault-lines, and its propensity for international interventions, distant wars easily pose present dangers.

The first draft of this book was completed before the terrorist attacks on America of Tuesday, 11 September 2001. Any study of events always runs the risk of being overtaken by them.† This happened to *Statecraft*. In fact, so traumatic and far-reaching have been the consequences of that day's vile outrages that an author may be tempted to follow some commentators in concluding that only entirely new approaches are relevant to an entirely different world.

But I resisted that temptation. Instead, I set about reconsidering my thinking and revisited my conclusions in the light of what we

---

* Afghanistan, Algeria, Angola, Azerbaijan, Burma, Burundi, Chad, Colombia, Democratic Republic of Congo, Indonesia, Iran, Iraq, Kosovo, Mexico, Rwanda, Somalia, Sudan, Turkey and Uganda (International Institute for Strategic Studies, *Strategic Survey 1999/2000*).

† This, for example, was true of Henry Kissinger's superb study entitled *Does America Need a Foreign Policy?* (New York: Simon and Schuster, 2001). Dr Kissinger's book contains only three references to terrorism – so much have perspectives changed, and so fast.

now know about the scale of the threat posed by Islamic terrorism. I also reflected upon how the requirements of the global war against terrorism, which President Bush and his allies have declared, altered the way in which we should handle relations with other world powers like Russia, China and India. I weighed up the case for a radically different approach to the Middle East. I tried to assess whether the crisis altered Britain's role in Europe or Europe's role in the Western Alliance. In fact, I sought to test everything.

On some questions I did indeed find myself altering my emphasis. In giving priority – as we now must – to beating terrorism, we inevitably give less attention to other issues. We have to achieve a somewhat different balance between individual liberties and the safety of the public at home. Abroad, our attentions will also be refocused. In forging a coalition to defeat one enemy we may have, at least temporarily, to deal more closely with unsatisfactory regimes which we have otherwise been right to criticise. But then, having a conservative rather than a liberal view of foreign and security policy, I agree with Winston Churchill, who once remarked of his alliance with the Soviet Union to defeat Nazi Germany: 'If Hitler invaded Hell I would at least try to make a favourable reference to the Devil.' Thankfully, we are not confronted with allies like Stalin, and the Devil's hand is clearly recognisable in the works of Osama bin Laden and his al-Qaeda network.

Yet, all that said, I do not in fact find myself altering my analysis in any very significant respect. And this is not mere stubbornness on my part. Let me explain why.

In the wake of America's tragedy, we heard it said again and again that Tuesday, 11 September was 'the day the world changed'. The headlines proclaimed it. The newscasters repeated it. The politicians, with a few exceptions, echoed it. It is easy to understand why the statement came to be made. What happened that day was the worst ever terrorist outrage. Westerners in general, Americans in particular, never felt more vulnerable or less prepared. The scale of the grief and the depth of the anger simply have no equivalent.

For those who mourn, of course, reality had changed – for

ever. In time, perhaps, they will find new lives, new sources of consolation, blessed forgetfulness; but nothing politicians or generals do can recapture what they have lost.

But in a different way the world has stayed the same: it is just that years of illusion have been stripped away. Ever since the end of the Cold War, the West had come to believe that it was time to think and speak only of the arts of peace. With one great enemy – Soviet communism – vanquished, it was all too demanding and unsettling to think that other enemies might yet arise to disturb our prosperous calm.

So we heard more and more about human rights, less and less about national security. We spent more on welfare, less on defence. We allowed our intelligence efforts to slacken. We hoped – and many were the liberal-minded politicians who encouraged us to hope – that within the Global Village there were only to be found good neighbours. Few of us were tactless enough to mention that what makes good neighbours is often good fences.

Yet, the world we all view so much more clearly now, with eyes wiped clean by tears of tragedy, was in truth there all along. It is a world of risk, of conflict and of latent violence. Democracy, progress, tolerance – these values have not yet taken possession of the earth. And the only sense in which we have reached the 'end of history' is that we have gained a glimpse of Armageddon.*

We now know that bin Laden's terrorists had been planning their outrages for years. The propagation of their mad, bad ideology – decency forbids calling it a religion – had been taking place before our eyes. We were just too blind to see it. In short, the world had never ceased to be dangerous. But the West had ceased to be vigilant. Surely that is the most important lesson of this tragedy, and we must learn it if our civilisation is to survive.

---

* For the phrase 'the end of history', see p. 30.

XXV

CHAPTER 1

Cold War Reflections

PICTURES AT AN EXHIBITION

At the time of writing these lines I have just learned that my portrait has been moved from the 'Contemporary' to the 'Historical' Room of London's National Portrait Gallery. This is perfectly fair. After all, eleven years have passed since I left Number Ten Downing Street. The world has, as they say, 'moved on' in all sorts of respects.

For example, in 1990 we could not have foreseen the huge impact which the information revolution would have upon business, lifestyles and even war. We could not have imagined that the mighty Japanese economy would have stalled so badly, or that China would have risen so fast. We could not have envisaged that perhaps the most chilling threat to Man's dignity and freedom would lie in his ability to manipulate genetic science so as to create, and re-create, himself. Nor, needless to say, would even the most far-sighted statesman have predicted the horrors of 11 September 2001.

But it is always true that the world that is can best be understood by those conversant with the world that was. And 'the world that was' – the world which preceded today's world of dot.coms, mobile phones and GM food – was one which saw a life-and-death struggle whose outcome was decisive for all that has followed.

Of course, just to speak of the 'Cold War' nowadays is to refer back to an era which seems a lifetime, not a mere decade and a half, ago. In truth, as I shall argue at many stages in this book, the underlying realities have changed rather less than the rhetoric. But changes there have been – and, on balance, ones of enormous benefit to the world.

DEBATES IN PRAGUE

People will continue to argue about the significance of the collapse of communism for as long as there are books to write and publishers to print them. But on Tuesday, 16 November 1999 a number of the main actors in those dramatic events – myself among them – met in Prague to put our own interpretations. It was ten years since the Czechoslovak 'Velvet Revolution' had led to the fall of one of the most hardline communist governments in Europe and its replacement by democracy.

I had not participated in the celebrations a few days earlier in Berlin held to mark the tenth anniversary of the fall of the Berlin Wall. I would have felt uneasy doing so. This was not because I felt any nostalgia for communism. The Wall was an abomination, an indisputable proof that communism was ultimately a system of slavery imposed by imprisoning whole populations. President Reagan had been right in 1987 to demand of the Soviet leader: 'Mr Gorbachev, tear down this wall!'

But nor could I then or now regard Germany as just another country whose future was a matter for Germans alone to decide, without involving anybody else. A united Germany was bound to become once again the dominant power in Europe. It would doubtless be diplomatic, but it would also be culpably naïve, to ignore the fact that this German drive for dominance has led in my lifetime to two terrible, global wars during which nearly a hundred million people – including of course nine million Germans – died. The Germans are a cultured and talented people; but in the past they have shown a marked inability to limit their ambitions or respect their neighbours.

Awareness of the past and uncertainty about the future led President Mitterrand and me, with not very effective assistance from President Gorbachev, to try to slow down the rush to German unification. In the end, we failed – partly because the United States administration took a different view, but mainly because the Germans took matters into their own hands, as in the end, of course, they were entitled to do. It was good that German reunification took place within NATO, thus avoiding the risk that it might have constituted a dangerous non-aligned power in the middle of Europe. It was also good that Germans were able to feel that they had won back control of their own country – as a patriot myself I certainly do not deny anyone else the right to be patriotic. But it would be hypocritical to pretend that I did not have deep misgivings about what a united Germany might mean. So I had no intention of going to Berlin in October 1999 to spoil the party.

Prague, though, was a different matter entirely – this was one party I hoped to enjoy. The Czechs, of course, have suffered the brunt of both Nazism and communism. And, having been failed by the democratic powers in the face of both totalitarian aggressions, they know a thing or two about the need for vigilance.

My favourite European cities all lie behind the former Iron Curtain – St Petersburg (for its grandeur), Warsaw (for its heroism), Budapest (for its leafy elegance). But Prague is quite simply the most beautiful city I have ever visited. It is almost too beautiful for its own good. In 1947 the historian A.J.P. Taylor asked the then Czech President Edvard Beneš why the Czech authorities had not put up stronger resistance to the seizure of Czechoslovakia by Hitler in 1939. Beneš might, I suppose, have replied that the Czechs were taken unawares, deceived by German promises. Or he could have answered that the Czechs were outnumbered and so resistance was useless. Instead, to Taylor's surprise, he flung open the windows of his office overlooking the irreplaceable glories of Prague and declared: '*This* is why we did not fight!'

The Czech Republic has been one of the more successful post-communist countries, thanks mainly to the visionary economic policies of its former Prime Minister, my old friend and Hayekian *extraordinaire*, Vaclav Klaus. But he could not have succeeded as he did had the Czechs not retained an instinctive understanding of how to make a civil society and a free economy work. They gained these insights through the historical memory ingrained in their culture – it is, after all, worth remembering that before the Second World War Czechoslovakia enjoyed an income per head equal to that of France. The Czechs are a people who have never forgotten how to combine knowing how to live with knowing how to work. So, for all these reasons, when I was invited to Prague with George Bush Sr, Mikhail Gorbachev, Helmut Kohl, Lech Walesa and (representing her late husband) Mme Danielle Mitterrand, I eagerly accepted.

Our host was President Vaclav Havel. Czechoslovakia had been immensely fortunate in 1989 to have Mr Havel – someone of total integrity and enjoying near-universal respect – to symbolise popular resistance and eventually become its leader and the nation's president. President Havel is the sort of leader you could not imagine coming to power in ordinary circumstances – which some people may consider quite a recommendation. He is a considerable playwright, an intellectual, a combination of gentleness and courage – he spent over five years in jail for his views. He speaks quietly but forcefully, no orator in the ordinary sense but with something of the preacher's ability to convey moral certainty and to communicate inspiration.

Mr Havel's office in the presidential wing of Prague Castle, where we met that afternoon, looks out onto the river and the old city beyond. The furnishing has doubtless changed since Beneš's time. A large Egyptianesque nude female statue stands by his desk: for the President's tastes in art, like his politics, are not altogether mine.

President Havel's anti-communism is not in doubt. But he is a man of the left and his view of the world reflects this. As he would put it in a speech the following day: 'The present calls for a new perception of the contemporary world as a multi-polar, multi-cultural and globally interconnected entity, and for a consistent reform of all international organisations and institutions in order that they might reflect this new understanding.' This kind of utopian language, even from one so eloquent, worries me.

Mr Havel and I, though, agree entirely, I think, about what was wrong with communism – a system which (to quote him again) was 'based on lies, hatred and coercion'. My first engagement on Wednesday morning allowed me to gauge how the President's fellow countrymen thought. I was to unveil a new statue of Sir Winston Churchill – a life-size copy of that which stands in front of the Palace of Westminster in London. Also due to speak were Vaclav Klaus and Sir Winston's nephew, Rupert Soames.

It was very cold indeed; a bitter wind cut through me to the quick. I had decided on a black wool suit with fur trim and black hat, but had rejected advice to wear a thick coat and quickly regretted it. Prague's Churchill Square is quite large, but it was packed. Some seven thousand people stood there and more were hanging out of overlooking windows to get a better view. I made my speech:

> Each time I come [to Prague] I seem to enter a world of majestic churches, mighty palaces and evocative sculpture. But I confess that I am very glad that you have found a place for this new statue. It will remind you here, as every generation has to be reminded – and amid all this beauty – that the price of freedom can be high, and that it may indeed require the sacrifice of 'blood, toil, tears and sweat'. This statue of Sir Winston Churchill will also remind you, as it reminds me, of something else – that liberty must never be allowed to perish from the earth, it must endure for ever.

The reception was tremendous. Some applause has a special quality that you remember for a lifetime. This had it. Finally, the Czech national anthem was played by the band and sung with passion by the crowd. I could only imagine what it meant – for the old people who recalled the Nazi invader, for the younger ones who had suffered under communism, for the very young who knew, without having experienced either of these totalitarianisms, what freedom truly was.

By now I had been standing completely still for almost an hour, and I was frozen. As we left the platform a Czech veteran who had served with the British in the last war stood forward to request an autograph. My hands were shaking so much that I could barely write. The almost illegible signature he has is certainly unique and will in future years probably be denounced by the experts as a fake.

It was apparent from the panel discussion that afternoon in Prague Castle's huge, gilded baroque ball room, that whatever chord I struck with the Czech people evoked less harmony from some of my fellow guests, above all from Mikhail Gorbachev. The discussion was tactfully chaired by the historian Timothy Garton Ash, who had himself played a distinguished role in the events of ten years earlier. To his left sat Mme Mitterrand, George Bush, myself and Helmut Kohl. To his right were Vaclav Havel, Mikhail Gorbachev and Lech Walesa. The theme of the discussion was 'Ten Years After'.

Interestingly, written down like that, the title looks strangely unfinished. Ten years after . . . what? The obvious reply, of course, is 'Prague's Velvet Revolution'. But it is not the only reply. One might say instead 'the collapse of communism', or 'the triumph of freedom', or – even more controversial for some – 'the West's victory in the Cold War'. It was a fundamental difference about these other possibilities that underlay the disagreement that followed.

All those present (with the exception of Danielle Mitterrand) had played a considerable part in securing the outcome ten years earlier. Lech Walesa's leadership of the Polish Solidarity trade union was crucial in the fight for Polish freedom (I well remembered my visit to the Gdansk shipyard in November 1988 and my – as it turns out – successful attempts to persuade General Jaruzelski to negotiate with Solidarity*).

Mikhail Gorbachev began the reforms in the Soviet Union that opened the way – albeit unintentionally on his part – for the fall of communism. But perhaps the decision for which he should be given most credit is a decision not to do anything at all – when he allowed the Eastern Bloc countries to break free of Soviet control without sending in the tanks.

Helmut Kohl, for all the criticism that has since been made of him, must be ranked with Bismarck and Adenauer as one of Germany's most successful statesmen. He showed great political courage in resisting the threats and blandishments of a Moscow that was desperate in the 1980s to drive a wedge between Europe and America. And, though I did not appreciate his tactics at the time, he also showed cunning and bravura in securing his country's unity and freedom in 1989–90.

---

* See *The Downing Street Years*, pp.777–82.

6

George Bush – looking drained from an overlong tour of European cities, but as always supported by Barbara – was also present. We are very different people, from different backgrounds and with different instincts. But I have always warmed to his decency and patriotism. He took over where Ronald Reagan left off, and then finished the job – combining sticks and carrots to induce the Soviets along the path of reform and then negotiating the reunification of Germany within NATO.

I have written elsewhere of my own part in the affairs of that time: without Britain's wholehearted support for the Reagan administration I am not sure that it would have been able to carry its allies along the right path. I also think that the fact that Ronald Reagan and I spoke the same language (in every sense) helped convince friend and foe alike that we were serious.

All of our contributions were quite sufficiently substantial without needing exaggeration or distortion. But human nature being what it is – and academics, like politicians, being on this score quite especially human – a certain amount of revisionism had set in. In particular, the role of Ronald Reagan had been deliberately diminished; the role of the Europeans, who, with the exception of Helmut Kohl, were often all too keen to undermine America when it mattered, had been sanitised; and the role of Mr Gorbachev, who failed spectacularly in his declared objective of saving communism and the Soviet Union, had been absurdly misunderstood.

I was conscious of all this as I prepared my thoughts for the panel. But I tried to be diplomatic. I declared that 'everyone on this platform was marvellous'. But I also said that it was America and Britain with their deep, historic commitment to the values of liberty which had been crucial in bringing about freedom. I added that what interested me now was to extend the rule of liberty everywhere:

> We've got the greatest opportunity we've ever known to extend liberty and the rule of law to those countries that have never known them, and that's what I think we should get on with. I trust I make myself clear!

I certainly had, it seems, to Mr Gorbachev, who became really quite angry and delivered an energetic and lengthy rebuttal. He denied that there had been any victor in the Cold War, accused people like me of having a 'superiority complex', asserted that no single ideology – 'neither the liberal, nor the communist, nor the conservative nor any other' – had all the answers, and informed us that 'even the communists wanted to make the world a happier place'.

It followed, of course, that since no side had won (or, doubtless more important to Mr Gorbachev, no side had lost) and no single ideology was sufficient for the needs of the world today, the search for solutions must go on. And, not surprisingly perhaps, it was through resort to all the most fashionable nostrums that this search should be pursued – by turning (as he put it) to 'new methods, a new philosophy, a new thinking that can help us understand one another and the conditions of the globalising world'.

Mr Gorbachev is lively, engaging and a great talker – a subject on which I am a good judge (on this occasion he spoke for about a third of the conference). But his remarks in Prague seemed to me, to say the least, of doubtful validity.

Yet nor should they be lightly dismissed. They represent the articulation of a strategy, common to the left in many countries, of seeking to escape all blame for communism and then going on to take credit for being more pragmatic, modern and insightful about the world which those who actually fought communism have created. It is a pressing necessity to expose and defeat both distortions.

Revisionism about the Cold War has taken various guises. But underlying them all is the assertion that the policies of Ronald Reagan towards the Soviet Union were, as you prefer, superfluous, dangerous or even counter-productive. It was not just loyalty towards my old friend that irritated me about this. It struck me – and still strikes me – as potentially disastrous, because learning the wrong lessons could still result in adopting the wrong responses.

With all this in mind, on the same evening in Prague I put to good use a short speech of thanks when I and the other distinguished guests received the Czech Order of the White Lion. I said:

Belief in the unique dignity of the human person, in the need for the state to serve and not to dominate, in the right to ownership of property and so independence – these things were what the West upheld, and what we fought for in the long twilight struggle that we call the Cold War. In the ten years that have elapsed since communism fell, much has been written of that great conflict. There has even, at times, been a little revisionism at work. But truth is too precious to become the slave of fashion.

As I receive this award today, I would like to refer to the man who more than any other – and more than me – can claim to have won the Cold War without firing a shot – I mean, of course, President Ronald Reagan. The fact that he cannot be here, for reasons that are well-known,* reminds us also of so many others who can't be here – because they perished in prisons and by torture.

In the joy we now feel that Europe is whole and free let us not forget the terrible price that was paid to defend and to recover liberty. As the poet Byron wrote of another such prisoner of conscience:

> Eternal spirit of the chainless mind!
> Brightest in Dungeons, Liberty! thou art,
> For there thy habitation is the heart –
> The heart which love of thee alone can bind;
> And when thy sons to fetters are consigned –
> To fetters, and the damp vault's dayless gloom,
> Their country conquers with their martyrdom,
> And Freedom's fame finds wings on every wind.

I wanted to remind the politicians present – the ordinary Czechs needed no reminding, as the reception they gave me had demonstrated – that the Cold War was a war for freedom, truth and justice. And we anti-communists won it.

---

* This was, of course, a reference to the fact that since 1994 President Reagan had withdrawn from public life because of the onset of Alzheimer's disease.

THE WEST WON

Above all, Ronald Reagan won it. Only when (and if) the full, undoctored records of the Soviet Union are released and studied will a full correlation be possible between the actions of the Reagan administration and the reactions of the Kremlin. But it is already possible to show that President Reagan deserves to be regarded as the supreme architect of the West's Cold War victory. This is, surely, the deduction to be made from the remarks of the last Soviet Foreign Minister, Alexandr Bessmertnykh, at a fascinating conference reflecting on Soviet–American relations in the 1980s.*

Among Mr Bessmertnykh's observations are the following:

On America's deployment in the autumn of 1983 of Cruise and Pershing II missiles in Europe in the face of both the previous deployment by the USSR of its SS-20s and a fierce barrage of propaganda and threats –

> ... the decision was definitely a great disappointment ... [T]he situation had tremendously deteriorated as far as Soviet interests were concerned. But looking back from today's position, I think that the fact itself ... helped to facilitate and to strongly concentrate on solutions.

On President Reagan's announcement earlier that same year of his plans for the Strategic Defense Initiative (SDI) –

> ... I would say that one of the major moments when the strategists in the Soviet Union started maybe even to reconsider its positions was when the programme of SDI was pronounced in March of 1983. It started to come ... to the minds of the [Soviet] leaders that there might be something very, very dangerous in that.

And, finally, on the relationship between the Reagan defence build-up (which both the deployment of intermediate range

---

* I am grateful to the Woodrow Wilson School of Public and International Affairs at Princeton University for making this material available to me.

nuclear weapons in Europe and the decision to go ahead with SDI
signified) and the internal weakness of the Soviet Union –

> ... When Gorbachev came to power in Moscow, the economic
> statistics already indicated that the economy was not doing so
> good. So when you were talking about SDI and arms control, the
> economic element ... was sometimes in my view the number one
> preoccupation of Gorbachev, *especially when we were preparing
> ourselves for Reykjavik.* [Emphasis added]

The October 1986 Reykjavik summit, to which Mr Bessmertnykh here alludes, was – as I have written elsewhere – the turning
point in the Cold War.* Mr Gorbachev already knew from earlier
discussions with President Reagan how passionately committed
he was to SDI, which he saw as not just practically necessary but
morally right – a programme aimed at the defence of lives and
one which did not rely only on a balance of nuclear terror. But
the Soviet leader also knew from all the information available to
him that the Soviet Union, with its stagnant economy and its
technological backwardness, could not match SDI. He had to stop
the programme at all costs. So he tempted President Reagan with
deep cuts in nuclear weapons, before springing on him the condition – that SDI must stay 'in the laboratory'.

Mikhail Gorbachev won and Ronald Reagan lost the public
relations battle in the wake of the consequent breakdown of the
talks. But it was the American President who had effectively just
won the Cold War – without firing a shot. In December 1987 the
Soviets dropped their demands for the abandonment of SDI and
agreed to the American proposals for arms reduction – notably
the removal of all intermediate range nuclear weapons from
Europe. Mr Gorbachev had crossed his Rubicon. The Soviets had
been forced to accept that the strategy they had pursued since the
1960s – of using weaponry, subversion and propaganda to make
up for their internal weaknesses and so retain superpower status
– had finally and definitively failed.

I still find it astonishing that even the left should try to deny

---

* See *The Downing Street Years*, pp.469–72.

all this. It is, of course, not a crime to be wrong. But it is not far short of criminal to behave as some of them did when they thought that the Soviet Union was on the winning side. These people were blind because they did not want to see, and because they were intoxicated with the classic socialist fantasy of believing that state power offers a short-cut to progress. Thus the American journalist Lincoln Steffens observed after visiting the Soviet Union in 1919: 'I have seen the future; and it works.'

At the height of the famine of 1932, the worst in Russia's history, the visiting biologist Julian Huxley found 'a level of physique and general health rather above that to be seen in England'. Similarly, George Bernard Shaw wrote that 'Stalin has delivered the goods to an extent that seemed impossible ten years ago, and I take my hat off to him.' H.G. Wells was equally impressed, reporting that he had 'never met a man more candid, fair and honest ... no-one is afraid of him and everybody trusts him'. Harold Laski considered that Soviet prisons (stuffed full of political prisoners in appalling conditions) enabled convicts to lead 'a full and self-respecting life'.*

Sidney and Beatrice Webb were similarly overwhelmed by the glories of the Soviet experiment. Their 1200-page book, which faithfully parroted any Soviet propaganda they could pick up, was originally entitled *Soviet Communism: A New Civilization?*: but the question mark was removed from the second edition, which appeared in 1937 – the height of the terror.†

The capacity of the left to believe the best of communism and the worst of anti-communists has something almost awe-inspiring about it. Even when the Soviet system was in its economic death throes, the economist J.K. Galbraith wrote of his visit in 1984:

That the Soviet system has made great material progress in recent years is evident both from the statistics and from the general urban scene ... One sees it in the appearance of well-being of the people

---

* These examples are drawn from Paul Johnson's *Modern Times* (London, 1992), pp.275–6.
† Robert Conquest, 'Academe and the Soviet Myth', *The National Interest*, spring 1993.

on the streets ... Partly, the Russian system succeeds because, in contrast with the Western industrial economies, it makes full use of its manpower.*

Professor Galbraith was one of the exponents of the once fashionable notion of 'convergence', according to which the capitalist and socialist models were destined to become ever more similar to one another, resulting in a social democracy that reflected the best of each without the disadvantages. One large problem with this theory was that those who held it had constantly to be trying to find advantages in a Soviet system which had none that were apparent to Soviet citizens. As the former dissident Vladimir Bukovsky once remarked – referring to the Russian proverb to the effect that you cannot make an omelette without breaking eggs – he had seen plenty of broken eggs, but never tasted any omelette.

A similar error – which I discuss in a later chapter – was made by those Sovietologists who tried to analyse and predict events in the Soviet Union in terms of doves and hawks, liberals and conservatives, left and right† (I am still perplexed as to why we should be expected to call hardline communists 'conservative' or anti-Semite fascists 'right wing' – except that it is a useful device of the liberal media to embarrass their opponents). For the advocates of 'convergence' and for certain advocates of *détente* it was assumed that a particular action by the United States would draw forth a parallel reaction from the Soviets.‡ Thus if we wanted peace we should not prepare for war, if we wanted security we should not threaten, and if we wanted cooperation we should

---

* Originally from 'A Visit to Russia', *New Yorker*, 3 September 1984; quoted in Dinesh D'Sousa, *Ronald Reagan: How an Ordinary Man Became an Extraordinary Leader* (New York, 1999), p.4.

† See p.70.

‡ Henry Kissinger defends his conception of *détente* in 'Between the Old Left and the New Right', *Foreign Affairs*, May–June 1999. Dr Kissinger powerfully argues: 'In the early 1970s, the option of what later became the highly effective Reagan policy did not exist. The obstacle to such a policy was not the Nixon or the Ford administration but the liberal Congress and media.' But he also concedes: 'Reagan proved to have a better instinct for American emotions.'

compromise. This approach was entirely wrong – at least while the Soviet Union remained a superpower with an expansionist ideology, which it did until some time in the mid-to-late 1980s.

The proof of this is clear. While the United States was led by administrations (Nixon, Ford and Carter) which were intent on compromise with the Soviets, the Soviet Union expanded its military arsenals and intensified its military interventions around the world. But once there was an American President who openly proclaimed his aims of military superiority, systemic competition and the global roll-back of Soviet power, the Soviet Union cooperated, disarmed and finally collapsed. President Reagan's former critics, in their desperation to find someone else to credit for an end to the Cold War, summoned up Mikhail Gorbachev as a kind of *deus ex machina* who transformed everything. And indeed Mr Gorbachev's role was positive and important. But what President Reagan's revisionist detractors fail to explain is (to use the words of Professor Richard Pipes) 'why, after four years of Reagan's relentlessly confrontational policies the Soviet Union did not respond in kind . . . by appointing a similarly hard-line, belligerent First Secretary, but settled on a man of compromise'.*

To be so wrong quite so often does not, it seems, in the post-Cold War world constitute any impediment to promotion. Far from it. Yesterday's critics of the strategy which so triumphantly destroyed the Soviet Union were then trusted to manage relations with its successor. Mr Strobe Talbott, in his previous career as a journalist on *Time*, variously attacked the Reagan defence build-up, dismissed SDI, mocked the idea that external Western pressures could be effective, described the Cold War as a 'grand obsession' which diverted the world from other more important matters and described NATO's continued existence as 'at best a stop-gap'.† Mr Talbott went on to become President Clinton's Deputy Secretary of State.

And, yes, all this *does* matter now. If so many influential people

---

* R. Pipes, 'Misinterpreting the Cold War: The Hard-Liners had it Right', review of Raymond Garthoff, *The Great Transition: American–Soviet Relations and the End of the Cold War* (Washington, 1994), *Foreign Affairs*, winter 1995.
† 'Rethinking the Red Menace', *Time*, 1 January 1990.

have failed to understand, or have just forgotten, what we were up against during the Cold War and how we overcame it, they are not going to be capable of securing, let alone enlarging, the gains that liberty has made.

The Cold War has sometimes been portrayed as a struggle between two superpowers, the United States (and its allies) on the one hand, and the Soviet Union (and its puppets) on the other. The term 'superpower' was not one that I relished at the time, because it always seemed to suggest a moral equivalence between the two political poles. Of course, at one level this was, indeed, a competition for advantage between broadly equivalent powers. But the equivalence reflected might not right. Much more important, and significant for us today, the Cold War was a struggle between two sharply opposing systems, encapsulating two wholly contradictory philosophies, involving two totally different sets of objectives.

The Soviet communist system was, in a sense, simpler. Its central purpose was to achieve domination over the world in its entirety by an ideology, Marxism-Leninism, and by the Communist Party, which was that ideology's supreme custodian and unique beneficiary. That purpose was, in the eyes of its proponents, subject to no moral constraints – the very notion of which appeared absurd. Communism recognised no limits except those posed by the power of its enemies. Within such a system individuals were only of value in so far as they served the role allotted them. Similarly, the expression of ideas, artistic endeavour, all kinds of 'private' activity, were judged and permitted according to whether they advanced 'the Revolution', which in practice increasingly meant the interests of the old men of the Kremlin. The pursuit of world revolution was at times largely suspended. At other times, notably in Soviet relations with China, disagreements broke out between the proponents of the great socialist 'idea' about its pace, conduct and immediate goals. But the objective of creating worldwide a fully socialist society, consisting of radically socialist citizens, remained.

Against this stood America and its allies. What we call in shorthand 'the West' was a reality as complex as 'the East' (in communist terms) was simple. First of all it consisted not of one power but of many. Within NATO, the institutional embodiment of Western defence resolve, individual states pursued constantly shifting policies, reflecting their own interests and the democratic decisions of their own peoples. America led; but America had to persuade its friends to follow. This reality reflected a fundamental philosophical difference. The very essence of Western culture – and the heart of both the strengths and weaknesses of Western policy during the Cold War years – was recognition of the unique value of the individual human being.

Put like this, it is easy to see why knowledge of the Cold War experience is important today. Still more important, though, is the fact that the struggle between two quite different approaches to the political, social and economic organisation of human beings has not ended and will never end.

Neither the fall of the Berlin Wall, nor victory in the Gulf War, nor the collapse of the Soviet Union, nor the establishment of free markets and a measure of democracy in South-East Asia – none of these has resolved the tension between liberty and socialism in all its numerous guises. Believers in the Western model of strictly limited government and maximum freedom for individuals within a just rule of law often say, and rightly, that 'we know what works'. Indeed, we do. But equally there will always be political leaders and, increasingly, pressure groups who are bent on persuading people that they cannot really run their own lives and that the state must do it for them. And, sadly but inevitably, there will always be people who prefer idleness to effort, dependency to independence, and modest rewards just as long as nobody does better. There is always a danger that, as Friedrich Hayek put it in his *Road to Serfdom*, 'the striving for security tends to become stronger than the love of freedom'.* It mustn't.

Otherwise we will find ourselves in the circumstances of which that far-sighted French observer, Alexis de Tocqueville, warned, when considering how democracies might incrementally lose their liberty:

---

* F.A. Hayek, *The Road to Serfdom* (London: Routledge and Kegan Paul, 1979), p.95.

Over [the citizens] stands an immense, protective power which is alone responsible for securing their enjoyment and watching over their fate. That power is absolute, thoughtful of detail, orderly, provident, and gentle. It would resemble parental authority if, father like, it tried to prepare its charges for a man's life, but on the contrary, it only tries to keep them in perpetual childhood ... Why should it not entirely relieve them from the trouble of thinking and all the cares of living? Thus it daily makes the exercise of free choices less useful and rarer, restricts the activity of free will within a narrower compass, and little by little robs each citizen of the proper use of his own faculties. Equality has prepared men for all this, predisposing them to endure it and often even regard it as beneficial ...

I have always thought that this brand of orderly, gentle, peaceful slavery which I have just described could be combined, more easily than is generally supposed, with some of the external forms of freedom, and that there is a possibility of its getting itself established even under the shadow of the sovereignty of the people.*

Only if we remain convinced that freedom – the freedom for which we strove in those Cold War years of struggle with socialism – is of abiding value *in its own right* will we avoid wandering down the inviting but dispiriting cul-de-sac which de Tocqueville describes.

That is why my old sparring partner, Mikhail Gorbachev, was wrong in what he said in Prague about the alternative to communism which the West offered in the past and which we still have to offer today. The politics and economics of liberty are not a kind of lucky dip from which one treat may be drawn out and enjoyed without tasting the others.

In truth, the Western model of freedom is something positive and universally applicable, though with variations reflecting cultural and other conditions. The theologian Michael Novak has

---

* Alexis de Tocqueville (ed. J.P. Mayer and Max Lerner, trans. George Lawrence), *Democracy in America* (New York: Harper and Row, 1966), p.667. Alexis de Tocqueville (1805–59), political philosopher, politician and historian.

christened that system 'democratic capitalism'.* It is a good phrase, because it emphasises the link between political and economic liberty. And it is significant that it comes from someone whose profession is more associated with supernatural doctrines than political programmes. Later in this book I shall try to describe the Western model of liberty more fully.† But perhaps its most important defining feature is that it is based upon truth – about the nature of Man, about his aspirations, and about the world he can hope to create.

---

* Michael Novak, *The Spirit of Democratic Capitalism* (London, 1991).
† See Chapter Eleven.

CHAPTER 2

The American Achievement

MY AMERICA

The America that I encountered on my first speaking tour after the terrorist attacks on New York and Washington was more sombre, reserved and intense than the America I had known. Six weeks after the outrage, with the war against al-Qaeda and the Taliban entering a new phase, there was only one issue on everyone's minds, only one message it was imperative to convey:

> In Britain we know how much we owe to America. We understand how close our countries are. America's cause is, and always will be, our cause. The message I bring to you today is that Britain is united with America in the war against terrorism.*

I have now been paying regular visits to the United States for more than thirty years. But there is something more subtle and less explicable than mere experience that binds me to America. I have reflected upon what this 'something' is.

Charles de Gaulle famously remarked that he had 'a certain idea of France'.† In fact, more accurately, he said that he had 'created for himself' that idea. To have an idea of a country is not necessarily to have a distorted view of it. It is, if the idea is a

---

* Speech in Fort Worth, Texas, 19 October 2001.
† 'Toute ma vie, je me suis fait une certaine idée de la France.' Charles de Gaulle, *Mémoires de guerre: l'Appel, 1940–1942* (Paris, 1954), p.1.

true one, to gain an insight into the mystery of a nation's identity.

I too have a certain idea of America. Moreover, I would not feel entitled to say that of any other country, except my own. This is not just sentiment, though I always feel ten years younger – despite the jet-lag – when I set foot on American soil: there is something so positive, generous and open about the people – and everything actually works. I also feel, though, that I have in a sense a share in America. Just why is this?

There are two reasons. First, in an age of spun messages and fudged options I am increasingly conscious that Winston Churchill was right about this – as about other things – in his famous speech in Fulton, Missouri in 1946:

> We must never cease to proclaim in fearless tones the great principles of freedom and the rights of man which are the joint inheritance of the English-speaking world and which through Magna Carta, the Bill of Rights, the Habeas Corpus, trial by jury, and the English common law find their most famous expression in the American Declaration of Independence.

Consciousness of the underlying commonalities of that 'English-speaking world' and of its values has never been more needed.

But the second reason for my sense of belonging to America is that America is more than a nation or a state or a superpower; it is an idea – and one which has transformed and continues to transform us all. America is unique – in its power, its wealth, its outlook on the world. But its uniqueness has roots, and those roots are essentially English. Already at the time of their foundation, the settlements across the Atlantic were deeply affected by religious, moral and political beliefs.

This fact is unforgettably recalled by the words of John Winthrop delivered in 1630 upon the deck of the tiny *Arbella* off the coast of Massachusetts to his fellow pilgrims:

> We must be knit together, in this work, as one man. We must entertain each other in brotherly affection. We must be willing to abridge ourselves of our superfluities, for the supply of others' necessities . . .

We shall be as a city upon a hill. The eyes of all the people are upon us so that if we shall deal falsely with our God in this work we have undertaken, and so cause him to withdraw his present help from us, we shall be made a story and a byword throughout all the world.

The pilgrims were in search of freedom to worship as they chose, but, as Winthrop's words demonstrate, they were by no means relativists or liberals. They were imbued with a deep sense of individual and collective responsibility. They practised self-discipline and lived according to a dogged, undoubtedly severe spirit of community. The pilgrims were Calvinists, whereas my own upbringing was against the somewhat less forbidding background of Methodism. But in and around my old home town of Grantham there were preachers who spoke in the tones of Winthrop, and we all lived in a not dissimilar atmosphere. So I feel that I understand the pilgrims, who symbolise for me one aspect of the American character, one feature of the American dream.

But America was not just the new Jerusalem. It could not have been made by the saints alone, or if it had been it would not have prospered. As the years went by more and more people left their homes in the Old World to seek a life in the New for straightforward material reasons. And they are not to be despised for that. They wanted better prospects for themselves and their families and they were prepared to make enormous sacrifices to achieve them. These men were fearless, tough, dynamic. They too, whatever their origins, their destinations or their hopes, are a vital part of the American story. They represent the risk-taking, the enterprise and the courage which endured every danger, natural and man-made, to bring virgin forests and open prairies into productive use. Whether trappers, farmers, traders or (later) miners, these are the men whose spirit underlies American individualism in all its manifold forms today.

A sense of personal responsibility and of the quintessential value of the individual human being are the twin foundations of orderly freedom. In the years before the American Revolution the colonists, because of circumstances, developed such awareness to a high degree. But the political culture from which the American colonies sprang – that is English political culture – had always been imbued with it too.

One American scholar, Professor James Q. Wilson, has listed the following factors as important in shaping English (later British) freedom: physical isolation (which helped protect us from invasion); a deep-rooted and widespread commitment to private property; ethnic homogeneity (which helped create a common culture) and a tradition of respect for legality and the rights it guaranteed.* The Founding Fathers of the United States of America inherited all this. Their thinking about the rights of the subject and the purposes of a constitution were developments of what had occurred over more than five centuries in the country whose yoke they were determined to break.

I advanced this thesis in the course of a speech I delivered on my investiture as Chancellor of William and Mary College in Williamsburg, Virginia in February 1994.†

> The historical roots of our [Anglo–American] relationship are many. A shared language, a shared literature, a shared legal system, a shared religion, and a finely woven blanket of customs and traditions from the very beginning, that have set our two nations apart from others. Even when the founders of this great Republic came to believe that the course of human events had made it necessary for them to dissolve the political bands that connected them to Britain, and to assume among the powers of the earth the separate and equal station to which the laws of nature and of nature's God entitled them, it was from our Locke and Sidney, our Harrington and Coke, that your Henry and your Jefferson, your Madison and Hamilton took their bearings.‡

---

* James Q. Wilson, 'Democracy for All?', American Enterprise Institute, April 2000.

† In 1693 King William III and Queen Mary granted a charter to establish a college of the same name in today's Williamsburg, Virginia. It is the second-oldest college in the United States.

‡ John Locke (1632–1704), English liberal philosopher; Algernon Sidney (1622–83), English statesman and leader of the Whig opposition to King Charles II; James Harrington (1611–77), English political philosopher; Sir Edward Coke

These considerations are not just of academic importance. Their significance lies in the fact that they allow us to grasp an important truth about America – namely that it is the most reliable force for freedom in the world, because the entrenched values of freedom are what make sense of its whole existence.

That is why I felt equally entitled in another lecture on the same theme some two years later to make the following claim:

> The modern world began in earnest on July 4th 1776. That was the moment when the rebellious colonists put pen to parchment and pledged their lives, their fortunes, and their sacred honour in defence of truths they held to be self-evident: 'That all men are created equal, that they are endowed by their Creator with certain unalienable rights ... and that to secure these rights governments are instituted among men deriving their just powers from the consent of the governed.' Henceforth patriotism would not simply be loyalty to the homeland, but a dedication to principles held to be both universal and permanent.*

Similar claims have, of course, been made for other revolutions. But they cannot ultimately be sustained. The French Revolution sacrificed Liberty to Equality – Fraternity never really mattered at all – and then Equality quickly gave way to centralised dictatorship. Today the only constructive results of that upheaval are to be found in the administrative reorganisations which succeeded it. The Bolshevik Revolution can be seen in retrospect to have been a reversion to the most odious kind of age-old tyranny, supplemented by the technological apparatus of totalitarianism. And it had no constructive results whatever.

(1552–1634), eminent English judge and compiler of the law; Patrick Henry (1736–99), American statesman and orator; Thomas Jefferson (1743–1826), third President of the United States and author of the Declaration of Independence; James Madison (1751–1836), fourth President of the United States and 'Father' of the Constitution; Alexander Hamilton (1757–1804), American statesman and principal author of *The Federalist Papers*.

* The James Bryce Lecture, Institute of United States Studies at the University of London, 24 September 1996.

23

The American Revolution, however, was not a revolution in either of these senses. It was successful through war, but its intentions were to secure peace and prosperity. It broke the political link with Britain, but it contained no programme of social or cultural transformation. Its novelty was at once more limited and more radical, for on the basis of English thinking about the rights of the subject, the rule of law and a limited government, it pronounced a doctrine that would be the basis of democracy.

On frequent occasions, especially when I have a speech to make in the United States, I take in my handbag a well-thumbed little yellow volume – a *Bicentennial Keepsake Edition of the United States Constitution*, given me by President George Bush Sr and signed by the members of the United States Supreme Court. In the introduction to it, the late Warren Burger, one of the great American judges and the nation's longest-serving Chief Justice, notes: 'The [US] Constitution represented not a grant of power from rulers to the people ruled – as with King John's grant of the Magna Charta at Runnymede in 1215 – but a grant of power by the people to the government which they had created.'

And this really sums up what the American Revolution means to the world – and America to me.

These reflections lead me to certain conclusions about the conduct of international politics.

- **America alone has the moral as well as the material capacity for world leadership**
- **America's destiny is bound up with global expression of the values of freedom**
- **America's closest allies, particularly her allies in the English-speaking world, must regard America's mission as encompassing their own.**

JUST ONE POLE

As I have argued in the previous chapter, however you look at it, it was the West which won the Cold War. But among the victors the United States emerged supreme. Because America is uniquely

24

equipped to lead by its historic and philosophical identification with the cause of liberty, this is something I welcome. But many others neither welcome nor accept it.

As the jargon of the experts in geopolitics has it – and in such matters a certain amount of jargon must be permitted – we have moved with the end of the Cold War and the implosion of the Soviet Union from a 'bipolar' to a 'unipolar' world. Today America is the only superpower. No earlier superpower – not even the Roman, Habsburg or British Empires in their prime – had the resources, reach or superiority over its closest rival enjoyed by America today. Nor is this simply to be explained, negatively, by the outcome of the Cold War. It is also to be understood, positively, as the result of the dynamism inherent in the American system.

The Caesars, the Habsburgs and the British were in their day heartily disliked by those envious of their power: such is generally the fate of those who bestride the globe. America, by contrast, has until quite recently escaped such odium. This is because, at least outside its own hemisphere, it has refused the temptations of territorial expansion. Indeed, the potential of America has until the present day always exceeded its actual power.

The United States, as befits the world's greatest democracy, is a reluctant warrior. In the two great wars of the twentieth century it was a late entrant. Even during the Cold War America was, it is sometimes overlooked, for much of the time far from aggressively anti-Soviet. The very doctrine of containment, which exercised greater influence than any other upon American foreign policy during those years, was at heart a defensive doctrine, aimed not at rolling back communism but rather at preventing its rolling remorselessly forward. For all these reasons, America has been a rather well-liked power.

But Americans have recently had to take more seriously the hostility which the United States faces from powerful forces outside its borders. The opponents of the American superpower do not, at present at least, have much in common except their shared hatreds. The more moderate or most discreet of them – in Continental Europe (especially France), Russia and China – express their opposition to America's superpower status in terms of an alternative doctrine of 'multi-polarity'. Thus President Jacques Chirac of France has evoked a new 'collective sovereignty' to check American power, and his Prime Minister, Lionel Jospin, has complained that 'the United States often behaves in a unilateral way and has difficulties in taking on the role to which it aspires, that of organiser of the international community'.* Beijing is particularly fond of such language. In April 1997 then-President Boris Yeltsin and President Jiang Zemin embraced a Sino–Russian 'strategic partnership' aimed at those who would 'push the world toward a unipolar order'. The following month the ever-obliging French President agreed with his Chinese host that there was need of an international order with 'power centres besides the United States'.† Most recently, the Swedish Prime Minister, host to the chaotic EU–US Summit at Gothenberg, extolled the EU as 'one of the few institutions we can develop as a balance to US world domination'.‡

Very different in tone – and intent – from such grumblings from peevish statesmen have been the threats levelled against America and Americans from the proponents of Islamic revolution. Well before 11 September 2001 the Islamic terrorist supremo Osama bin Laden had left us in no doubt about his (and many others') objectives:

> We predict a black day for America and the end of the United States as the United States, and it will become separate states and will retreat from our land and collect the bodies of its sons back to America, God willing.§

Bin Laden and his associates were even then well advanced in their plans to fulfil those threats.

In the face of such hostility, any great power faces two temptations. The first, which has been much talked about, is isolationism.

---

* Quoted by Jeffrey Gedmin in *The Weekly Standard*, 29 March 1999.
† Quoted by Josef Joffe, 'How America Does it', *Foreign Affairs*, September–October 1997.
‡ *New York Times*, 15 June 2001.
§ Interview with John Miller of ABC News, reproduced in *Middle East Quarterly*, December 1998.

In fact, to judge from much of the rhetoric used about America one would easily think that the drawbridge had already risen. President Clinton, for example, described the Senate's (entirely correct) decision in October 1999 to oppose the nuclear test ban treaty as 'a new isolationism'. This was part of a broader campaign to portray the Republican Party as a whole as insufficiently committed to America's world role. It is in this context worth recalling perhaps that the great majority of Democrats in Congress voted *against* the Gulf War of 1991. It is equally relevant that it was President Clinton's own party in Congress which denied him fast-track negotiating authority on trade agreements. By contrast, President George W. Bush in his election campaign proposed an approach to American foreign and security policy which he termed 'a distinctly American internationalism' that involved 'realism in the service of American ideals'. He affirmed that 'America, by decision and destiny, promotes political freedom – and gains the most when democracy advances'. It was difficult to detect isolationism in any of that. Nor has there been any isolationism in the actions of the new administration, which has reaffirmed its commitment to the defence of Europe, proposed expansion of NATO to include the Baltic states, sought a new realistic relationship with Russia and advanced the idea of a vast free trade area covering North and South America. And in pursuit of the war against terrorism, President Bush has invested huge efforts and demonstrated great skill in assembling an international coalition to achieve America's objectives.

What most of the conservative critics of America's overseas engagements in the Clinton years were concerned about was the need to place national interest alongside, or ahead of, wider objectives. I disagreed with some of these critics on specific matters; but they were right to be concerned, and nine out of ten of them could not fairly be labelled 'isolationist'.

I too was anxious about the second temptation that faced – and must always face – American foreign policy-makers, namely that of ubiquitous intervention in pursuit of ill-defined goals. My concern was not, of course, that America would become too powerful, but rather that it might dissipate its power, and eventually lose the essential popular mandate for the use of power.

How, where and on what criteria should the American super-power and its allies intervene? We should resist pressure to set out inflexible rules in these matters: one of the marks of sensible statecraft is to recognise that each crisis is qualitatively different from another and requires its own response. But acknowledging that fact makes clarity of strategic thinking even more important: it is in unknown territory that you most need a compass. This is amply borne out by experience of the interventions which America and her allies have undertaken since the end of the Cold War.

The Gulf War against Iraq, in whose preparation I was involved, seemed to many at the time to represent the shape of things to come. Saddam Hussein's invasion of Kuwait in the early morning of 2 August 1990 would probably never have occurred at the height of the Cold War. Moscow would have prevented such reckless adventurism by any of its dependants. But it is equally certain that there would never during the Cold War years have been a unanimous decision of the UN Security Council to back the use of force against Saddam, particularly when 'force' involved a US-led operation in the Middle East.*

These were the circumstances in which President George Bush Sr delivered an address to a joint session of the US Congress on 11 September, which introduced a new expression to the lexicon of international policy analysts. The purpose of the President's speech was to rally support for the operation in the Gulf and its objectives, which he spelt out as follows:

> Iraq must withdraw from Kuwait completely, immediately and without condition. Kuwait's legitimate government must be restored. The security and stability of the Persian Gulf must be assured. And American citizens must be protected.

So far so good – indeed, excellent.
But the President went on:

> A new partnership of nations has begun and we stand today at a unique and extraordinary moment. The crisis in the Persian Gulf,

---

* For my own role in these events see *The Downing Street Years*, pp.816–28.

as grave as it is, also offers a rare opportunity to move toward an historic period of cooperation. Out of these troubled times ... *a new world order* can emerge. A new era – freer from the threat of terror, stronger in the pursuit of justice and more secure in the quest for peace. An era in which the nations of the world, East and West, North and South, can prosper and live in harmony. [Emphasis added]

So the 'New World Order' was born.

As I have already noted in the context of remarks by President Havel, this sort of stuff makes me nervous. President Bush, like any leader in time of war, was justified in raising the rhetorical temperature. But anyone who really believes that a 'new order' of any kind is going to replace the disorderly conduct of human affairs, particularly the affairs of nations, is likely to be severely disappointed, and others with him.

In fact, one of the first purposes to which I committed myself in the period after I left Downing Street (and after Saddam Hussein was left in power in Baghdad) was to throw some cold water on the ambitious internationalism which the Gulf War spawned. So, for example, speaking to the Los Angeles World Affairs Council in November 1991, I did not dispute that a new state of affairs had emerged as a result of the fall of Soviet communism and the advance of democracy and free enterprise – I did not even quibble with the expression 'New World Order'. But I also urged caution. I recalled the eerily similar language about 'New World Orders' which characterised diplomatic discussions between the two World Wars, and I quoted General Smuts' epitaph on the League of Nations: 'What was everybody's business in the end proved to be nobody's business. Each one looked to the other to take the lead, and the aggressors got away with it.'

Had I been less tactful, I might have added that Saddam Hussein also 'got away with it' – at least to the extent that he was still causing trouble in Baghdad while President Bush and I were writing our memoirs.

There were important lessons to be learned from the Gulf War, but only some were absorbed at the time, and some wrong conclusions were also drawn. In one important way, the campaign against Saddam turned out to be untypical of post-Cold War conflicts. The degree of consensus about military action was the result of a temporary and fortuitous series of conditions. Once Russia and China became more assertive, the UN Security Council was unlikely to be an effective forum for dealing with serious crises. Equally untypical was the fact that Saddam Hussein had managed to unite most of the Muslim nations against him. Much as he tried, he was thus never able to rely on anti-Western feeling to provide him with useful allies. Saddam was a blunderer. But as a rule in the post-Cold War world it was more likely that events would follow Samuel Huntington's thesis of a 'Clash of civilisations', where opposing religions and cultures wrestled for dominance, than Francis Fukuyama's forecast of 'the End of History', where democracy was the inevitable global victor.*

The real lessons of the Gulf had nothing to do with New World Orders but a lot to do with the fundamental requirements for successful interventions. It was the decisiveness of American leadership under President Bush and the superiority of American military technology which ensured the defeat of Saddam. America's allies – particularly Britain and France – helped. Diplomatic efforts to keep the coalition together were also valuable. But American power and the resolution to apply it won the war – and they could have won the peace too, if excessive concern for international opinion had not prevented America's demanding the complete disarmament of Iraqi forces.

What the Gulf War really demonstrated was the necessity of American leadership. But this was not to everyone's liking – not even, one suspects, entirely to the liking of the US State Department. Multilateralism – in effect, the use of force only under the authority of the United Nations and for international purposes – became almost an obsession in the years that followed.

It is worth recalling just how much of a contrast this was with earlier American interventions. Under President Reagan the actions against the regimes in Grenada in 1983 and Libya in 1986

---

* Francis Fukuyama, *The End of History and the Last Man* (London: Hamish Hamilton, 1992); Samuel P. Huntington, *The Clash of Civilizations and the Remaking of World Order* (New York: Simon and Schuster, 1996).

were unashamed exertions of American power in defence of American and broader Western interests.* Nor had President Bush shown before the Gulf War any inclination to break away from this formula. When on 20 December 1989 the United States overthrew the government of General Noriega in Panama it acted decisively against a drug-trafficking thug who had apparently been planning attacks on American citizens and who was implicitly threatening vital American interests in the Panama Canal. It was a large operation involving twenty-six thousand US troops and it provoked an international outcry – I was almost alone among other heads of government in voicing strong support.

But with the emergence of the doctrine of the New World Order such robustness was diluted in the search for international consensus. The intervention in Somalia was the high – or perhaps low – point of this subordination of US national interests in favour of multilateralism. In December 1992 President Bush authorised the deployment of up to thirty thousand US troops to safeguard food supplies for the Somali population, suffering starvation largely as a result of the chaotic conditions that followed the overthrow of the previous President Muhammad Siad Barre in January 1991. President Bush justified his action to the nation in a televised address:

> I understand the United States cannot right the world's wrongs, but we also know that some crises in the world cannot be resolved without American involvement, that American action is often necessary as a catalyst for broader involvement of the community of nations. Only the United States has the global reach to place a large security force on the ground in such a distant place quickly and efficiently, and thus save thousands of innocents from death.

In fact, Somalia was the first of the 'humanitarian interventions'. Later under President Clinton the multilateralist doctrine was pressed to its limit and beyond. In May 1993 the UN took control of the operation. Five thousand of the twenty-eight thousand

---

* My own involvement in these matters is described in *The Downing Street Years*, pp.326–32 and 441–9.

troops were American: this was the first time that American soldiers had served under UN command – a radically new departure. Thus far eight Americans had been killed in combat in Somalia. But as opposition among the Somali warlords – particularly the most powerful of them, Muhammad Farah Said – grew, the situation deteriorated. In the end more than a hundred peacekeepers (including thirty US soldiers) were killed and more than 260 (including 175 Americans) were wounded. Six months after a gun battle that left eighteen American dead in October 1993, the US officially ended its mission in Somalia. By the time the United Nations operation was wound up a year later it had cost the UN itself $2 billion and the US some $1.2 billion in addition. The well-intended intervention left behind it chaos as bad as ever it found. Its legacy was also much agonised heart-searching about the components of a fiasco which had dented American prestige and rendered American public opinion extremely wary about other such ventures.

The Somalia intervention exemplifies all the classic features of what not to do. Its objectives were insufficiently thought out; it suffered from 'mission creep' – the tendency to expand involvement beyond what is originally envisaged, and beyond what available resources permit; and, finally, lines of command were blurred.

I suspect that the Bush and Clinton administrations had been keener to respond to the sufferings in Somalia by 'doing something', because since the late autumn of 1991 they had been doing little to prevent or remedy the sufferings in Croatia and Bosnia. (I deal with these and subsequent Balkan matters in a separate chapter, because they are so interlinked and because they contain their own lessons.*) But we should recall that until the Washington Agreements of March 1994, which ended the Croat–Muslim conflict, the US had been studiedly absent from the former Yugoslavia, arguing that this was a European problem for Europe to solve. And only in August 1995 was European-led diplomacy finally abandoned, as NATO bombing in support of Croat–Muslim ground forces established a new balance of power and paved the way for a kind of peace.

---

* See Chapter Eight.

The intervention in the autumn of 1994 in Haiti marked the beginning of a gradual shift back towards an American foreign policy that reflected American national interests. More than sixteen thousand Haitian refugees had been intercepted by the US Coast Guard in the months preceding the US mission. These were mostly economic migrants, but undoubtedly the corrupt, authoritarian military government in Haiti had made things worse. Accordingly, the UN Security Council sanctioned an American-led military intervention to restore President Jean-Bertrand Aristide to power. In fact, negotiations led by former President Jimmy Carter resulted in a peaceful handover by the Haitian military regime to a force of over fifteen thousand US troops, who then ensured the return of Aristide. The operation, code-named 'Operation Restore Democracy' and hailed by President Clinton as a 'victory for freedom around the world', was unfortunately in truth much less than either. Aristide was no democrat, but rather an extreme left-wing authoritarian, and Haiti has since made little progress under him or his chosen successor towards legality, honesty or stability. America has spent $3 billion in Haiti but the place is still plagued by ignorance, poverty and corruption, and is an active centre of drug-trafficking. The best one can say of the intervention in Haiti is that it was a modestly useful venture in US immigration control.

Since Haiti, it has been the situation in the Balkans that has dominated debate about the means, scale and objectives of international intervention. Sixty thousand US and European troops were deployed in Bosnia in the wake of the 1995 Dayton agreement and, despite Congress's misgivings and the present administration's evident impatience, there has so far been no large-scale withdrawal.

On top of the continuing commitment to enforce and maintain the peace in Bosnia came the NATO operation in Kosovo in spring 1999. That campaign signified three important further developments in the conduct of interventions.

First, military action was taken without clear authorisation by the UN Security Council. Admittedly, several earlier UN resolutions, which talked of the need to act to prevent a destabilising catastrophe, could be used to provide a degree of legal cover.* Kosovo was, however, different in that no attempt was made to gain UN Security Council authority for the use of 'all necessary means' (i.e. force) before the operation. In this regard, it marked a major departure from the approach adopted in the Gulf in 1990. Similarly, NATO, which had hitherto been considered a defensive alliance without an ability to act 'out of area', was the organisation in whose name the war was conducted. Thus there was a quite different legal and institutional framework for intervention to that in the Gulf.

Secondly, and consequently, the Kosovo campaign was described and justified from the outset as a 'humanitarian intervention'. There was, of course, at one level a rather disingenuous reason for this: emphasis upon humanitarianism rather than the use of force avoided awkward questions about the need for explicit UN authorisation (which was not, in fact, forthcoming because of Russian and Chinese obstruction). Moreover, the notion of a humanitarian tragedy leading to a threat to international peace and stability, and thus to legitimate international intervention in a sovereign state's affairs, had been evoked already in recent years in Somalia, Haiti and Bosnia. But coercive humanitarian intervention, which had hitherto been a novel doctrine of uncertain scope and fuzzy legality, now began to be declared the basis of a revived if undeclared New World Order.

Above all, the doctrine was warmly embraced and loudly proclaimed by such enthusiasts for assertive internationalism as Britain's Prime Minister, Tony Blair. In his speech to the Economic Club of Chicago in April 1999, Mr Blair claimed to be 'witnessing the beginnings of a new doctrine of international community'. He noted that 'we cannot refuse to participate in global markets if we want to prosper' – which is true. He added that 'we cannot ignore new ideas in other countries if we want to innovate' – which is not strictly true at all, though an unexceptionable piece

---

* Notably, UNSC Resolution 1160 condemned Serbia's repression of the Kosovars and recognised that the situation created by this and the reciprocal violence of the Kosovo Liberation Army (KLA) constituted a threat to international peace and security. Similarly, Resolution 1199, adopted six months before NATO's action, expressed the Security Council's alarm at the impending humanitarian catastrophe.

of flannel. But his final thought, that 'we cannot turn our backs on conflicts and the violation of human rights within other countries if we want still to be secure', is patently an oversimplification.

We *may* believe that it is right to intervene to stop suffering inflicted by rulers on their subjects, or by one ethnic group on another: I am sure that it sometimes was, and is. And we *may* believe that we should be prepared to intervene in order to preserve our security, or in defence of an ally: I am convinced that we have to show resolution in doing so. But to pretend that the two objectives are always, or even usually, identical is humbug. The danger of swallowing it is even greater for America as a super-power with global interests than for a medium-sized military power like Britain. This doctrine of 'international community' *à la* Blair is a prescription for strategic muddle, military overstretch and ultimately, in the wake of inevitable failure, for an American retreat from global responsibility.

The third and last feature of the Kosovo operation that I want to mention here does indeed directly concern America's capability to launch and carry through successful interventions: this was the degree of reliance upon advanced military technology, not just as a source of superiority over the enemy but also as a means of avoiding NATO casualties. Rightly or wrongly, most leading US politicians judged that American public opinion was not prepared to face the risk, let alone the reality, of losses in Kosovo.

This may not, in fact, have been true. And if it was true it may have reflected poor leadership, or uncertainty about the declared (and undeclared) war aims. Or again it may, paradoxically, have been the effect of the enormous importance of television coverage in modern crises. By making so vivid the suffering of people in distant lands, television greatly increases pressure for intervention. But at the same time, by dramatising even more the grieving of the families of servicemen who are lost, it undermines national resolve to fight and to risk casualties.

America's commitment to the world's security is so extensive, and the sacrifices it makes so considerable, that it ill behoves America's allies to complain about reluctance by American families to sustain losses in other people's wars. But American leaders should recognise that this reputation, however unjustified, has given encouragement to America's enemies. This is all the more poignant when, as in Kosovo, the refusal to risk the loss of allied aircraft, and so to envisage operations below fifteen thousand feet, dented our effectiveness in preventing the ethnic cleansing of a civilian population we were committed to protect.

By contrast, the technological dominance of America, which had been such a factor in the Gulf, was by the time of Kosovo eight years later still more evident. In the Kosovo operation, however, it was less America's superiority over the Yugoslav army, which actually proved quite adept at protecting itself, but rather America's superiority over her NATO allies that was now most remarkable. The facts here speak eloquently for themselves.

Although all nineteen members of NATO made some contribution to the operation, that of the United States was overwhelmingly dominant. America paid for 80 per cent of the cost – Britain and France made up most of the rest. The US supplied 650 of the 927 aircraft that took part in the air campaign. The US flew two-thirds of the strike missions. Almost every precision-guided missile (PGM) was launched from an American aircraft. The US was alone in contributing long-range bombers, which dropped about half the bombs and missiles used in the campaign.

The cause of this imbalance was not generally, with the notable exception of the Greeks, any lack of commitment by the rest of NATO, and certainly not by Britain. The problem was rather that America's allies had neither the quantity nor, above all, the quality of weaponry required to be effective partners of the US. Thus while the British flew more than a thousand strike missions, three-quarters of the munitions we dropped were unguided. When poor visibility interfered with PGMs that relied on laser-designation or optical guidance, only the Americans had the technology (in the form of the Joint Direct Attack Munition) which allowed them to attack targets in all weathers. Finally, it was US intelligence which identified nearly all of the bombing targets in Serbia and Kosovo.

Is Kosovo, then, the shape of things to come? In one respect, at least, it should not be. We should be extremely wary of the doctrine of humanitarian interventionism as the main, let alone the only, justification for the use of force. There is, after all, a far more traditional alternative. Sovereign states have a right of self-defence which precedes the United Nations Charter and is not dependent on it, or on votes in international forums. Other states have a right to come to the aid of countries which are the victims of aggression. That is what military alliances like NATO are about. The habit of ubiquitous interventionism, combining pinprick strikes by precision weapons with pious invocations of high principle, would lead us into endless difficulties. Interventions must be limited in number and overwhelming in their impact.

There is always a risk in attempting to make observations about conflicts that are still underway, as is the case of that against bin Laden and the Taliban at the time of writing. On the other hand, if broad conclusions about the conduct of interventions are to be of practical value they must also be applicable in special cases – even one as special as that which now confronts America.

Moreover, the experience of recent years does indeed help, if only in knowing the pitfalls to avoid. The action against bin Laden and his network and the state that has harboured them is morally just, legitimate and necessary. America does not require anyone's agreement to act in self-defence against an unprovoked attack on its own people. It needs the support of countries whose territory or airspace are required for the conduct of operations. It may also find it valuable to receive practical help from its allies: Britain has been particularly active, for which the British Prime Minister, Tony Blair, deserves much credit.

But it is important not to allow ever wider coalition-building to become an end in itself. As we saw in the Gulf War of 1990, international pressures, particularly those exerted from within an alliance, can result in the failure to follow actions through and so leave future problems unresolved. So far, though, I am heartened by the fact that President Bush seems to have concluded that this is an American operation, and that America alone will decide how it will be conducted.

When democracies go to war, it is natural that they invoke the highest moral principles. That is always especially true of America's wars. And such principles are indeed truly involved in the present conflict. It is not mere rhetoric to state that democracy, liberty and tolerance are all under threat from violent Islamist fanatics embracing terrorism. But winning wars requires more than moral fervour: it demands clear thinking about targets and timetables, accurate estimates of the enemy's strength and intentions, pre-emptive action to minimise risks and guard against consequences. That is all the more so in this war against terrorism, because we are primarily dealing with distant lands and, in large part, unknown conditions.

In such circumstances, the conclusions I drew above about the need to limit the aims of interventions, while maximising their effect, are especially germane. It is doubtless true that the West should have done more in earlier years to prevent Afghanistan becoming a political powderkeg. And we should now supply humanitarian aid. But I would caution against open-ended attempts at nation-building. What matters, above all, is to neutralise the threat which resulted in the outrages of 11 September. That means taking out the terrorists and their protectors, and not just in Afghanistan but elsewhere too – a large enough task even for a global superpower.

America's action against bin Laden and the Taliban also demonstrates one other feature about interventions, which we should not overlook. The American people immediately understood that what happened on 11 September was an act of war against them. They responded accordingly. The military commitment by the United States and the willingness of its citizens to sacrifice their lives are testimony to how nations behave when their very survival appears at stake. They remind us that in the modern world only nation states will fight wars at sufficient cost in blood and treasure to achieve lasting victory.

The question of whether to act in Afghanistan was unusually clear-cut. But, more generally, knowing when and how to intervene is as much a matter of instinct as of reflection, although one does of course also need to reflect. The interesting arguments over foreign policies based on moral imperative versus those based on pragmatic national interest are really in the end only that – interesting. The greatest statesmen in the English-speaking world – men like Winston Churchill and Ronald Reagan – adopted policies that always contained both elements, though in different measures at different times. I should therefore prefer to restrict my guidelines to the following:

- Don't believe that military interventions, no matter how morally justified, can succeed without clear military goals
- Don't fall into the trap of imagining that the West can remake societies
- Don't take public opinion for granted – but don't either under-rate the degree to which good people will endure sacrifices for a worthwhile cause
- Don't allow tyrants and aggressors to get away with it
- And when you fight – fight to win.

MILITARY PREPAREDNESS – MATÉRIEL

Whatever cosy euphemisms we may want to adopt, defending our interests in battle is what our armies, navies and airforces ultimately exist to do. They are not well-suited to act as policemen, aid workers or civil engineers, and they should not be required to do so, except under extreme and temporary circumstances. They need the weapons to deter and destroy any enemy they may be called upon to face. They need to be well-trained, well-disciplined and well-led. And they need to be able to rely on wise and determined governments to see that the financial and other conditions under which they operate are conducive to these goals.

Democracies are actually quite good at fighting wars – as a series of dictators over the years have learned to their cost. Where democratic political leaderships are weak, however, is in their capacity for continuous military preparedness. Such weakness leads to unnecessary conflicts, because it undermines the will, and can exclude the means, to deter aggression. It also leads to wars being longer and more costly than they would otherwise be, because it takes years to build up the military might required to defeat an aggressor.

The end of the Cold War was in these respects more typical than the end of the Second World War. The defeat of the Axis powers evoked a huge sigh of relief. But it also brought the West to the very edge of a new conflict with the Soviet Union. Once it was known that the Soviets had the atomic bomb, it was clear to all but the very foolish and the fellow-travellers that military preparedness was the precondition for the West's survival.

The end of the Cold War was quite different. International utopianism became the rage. As at the end of the Great War, there was a marked preference for butter not guns.

The figures for defence spending show this.* They demonstrate that America cut too far and that Europe was even worse. The West as a whole in the early 1990s became obsessed with a 'peace dividend' that would be spent over and over again on any number of soft-hearted and sometimes soft-headed causes. Politicians forgot that the only real peace dividend is peace.

America's defence budget decreased every year from the end of the Cold War until 1998–99. It now stands at about 60 per cent of its peak of 1985. And this occurred during a period in which public expenditure on all other sectors of the federal budget rose. As a result, American active and reserve military forces in 2000 were more than a million below the levels reached in 1987. The Clinton administration reduced the number of active army divisions to ten, from the eighteen divisions under the Reagan administration. It reduced the airforce by almost half from the Reagan levels. And it reduced the number of naval ships and aircraft carrier battle groups by almost 45 per cent. Moreover, there was a severe shortfall in recruitment of service personnel – the US Navy missed its recruiting goal by nearly seven thousand in 1998.†

This steep decline in US military spending was more than mirrored elsewhere in NATO. Germany, Spain and Italy spend less than 2 per cent of their GDP on defence, while America spends 3 per cent. Put another way, the United States spent $296 billion on defence in 2000, compared with the European NATO members' total contribution of just $166 billion. The Europeans have cut defence by 22 per cent in real terms since 1992, and they are still cutting.

Furthermore, as the International Institute for Strategic Studies

---

* See Table, p.42.

† These and other figures are taken from the Heritage Foundation, *Issues 2000*, Chapter 14, 'National Defense: Restoring US Military Strength', compiled by Baker Spring, Jack Spencer and James H. Anderson.

notes in its 1999/2000 *Strategic Survey*: 'Much of what is spent by European governments goes not towards new technology or better training, but towards the costs of short-term conscripts, pensions and infrastructure.' European countries are not going to be able to match the United States at the cutting edge of military technology. (That is, of course, a further reason why they are not going to have the ability to field an effective European Union defence force.) But at least they can stop wasting resources on maintaining conscript armies that are inadequately trained and lack all credibility as fighting forces.

In America the dangers of underfunding defence have now been widely understood. Already under President Clinton (and also under pressure from the Republican-controlled Senate) the administration had begun to increase defence expenditure once more from the beginning of fiscal year 2000. In 1999 Congress also approved the first major increase in military pay since 1982 in order to improve recruitment. The new administration's strong commitment to increasing America's defence capability will doubtless also lead to further improvements. And doubtless lessons will be learned from the operations in Afghanistan.

By contrast, the European countries still demonstrate little or no sense of responsibility for upgrading the Alliance's defence effort. Wealthy European Union countries like Germany and Italy have been cutting, not increasing, their already low levels of military expenditure.

Military planners always have a thankless task. In peacetime they are accused of dreaming up unnecessarily ambitious war-fighting scenarios, and then demanding the money to pay for them. But when dangers loom, they are criticised for insufficient foresight. Moreover, a global superpower's military planners have a special problem. This is that a major threat to stability in *any* region is by definition a threat to the superpower's own vital interests. And the nightmare is that several serious regional conflicts may occur simultaneously. To the question of what precise overall capabilities, and thus exactly what levels of defence spending, are necessary to cope with such scenarios I can only answer: 'More than at present – and possibly much more than you think.'

NATO DEFENCE EXPENDITURE

DEFENCE EXPENDITURE OF LEADING NATO COUNTRIES, 1992–2000

	92	93	94	95	96	97	98	99	2000
USA	361	345	327	308	294	293	285	287	296
Canada	12.8	11.9	10.8	10.0	9.2	8.3	8.2	8.6	8.1
France	53.3	49.4	50.4	52.9	50.3	44.2	42.0	38.6	35.0
Germany	49.6	43.1	41.2	45.6	42.3	35.3	34.5	31.8	28.8
Greece	5.2	4.7	4.9	5.6	6.1	5.9	6.1	5.3	5.6
Holland	9.3	8.2	8.1	8.9	8.5	7.3	7.1	6.9	6.2
Italy	29.5	23.8	23.1	21.5	25.4	24.1	24.4	23.1	21.0
Spain	10.7	9.6	8.4	9.6	9.3	8.1	7.8	7.4	7.2
Turkey	7.3	8.2	6.0	7.3	8.1	8.6	9.1	9.9	10.8
UK	51.2	40.6	39.5	37.5	36.7	36.7	38.7	37.1	34.5

Figures in constant 2000 US$ billions

DEFENCE EXPENDITURE OF LEADING NATO COUNTRIES, 1992–2000, AS A PERCENTAGE OF GDP

	92	93	94	95	96	97	98	99	2000
USA	4.8	4.5	4.1	3.8	3.5	3.3	3.1	3.0	3.0
Canada	1.9	1.9	1.7	1.6	1.4	1.2	1.3	1.3	1.2
France	3.4	3.4	3.3	3.5	3.3	3.0	2.8	2.8	2.6
Germany	2.1	1.9	1.8	2.0	1.8	1.6	1.5	1.5	1.6
Greece	4.5	4.4	4.4	4.4	4.7	4.6	4.8	4.8	4.9
Holland	2.5	2.3	2.1	2.2	2.3	1.9	1.7	1.8	1.8
Italy	2.1	2.1	2.0	1.8	2.1	2.0	2.0	2.0	1.7
Spain	1.6	1.7	1.5	1.7	1.4	1.3	1.3	1.3	1.3
Turkey	3.7	3.8	3.5	3.9	4.1	4.4	4.4	5.2	5.2
UK	4.1	3.7	3.4	3.0	2.9	2.6	2.7	2.5	2.4

Source: International Institute for Strategic Studies, London

So I conclude:

- The West as a whole needs urgently to repair the damage that excessive defence cuts have done
- Europe, in particular, should sharply increase both the quantity and the quality of its defence spending
- The US must ensure that it has reliable allies in every region
- Don't assume that crises come in ones or even twos
- Don't dissipate resources on multilateral peacekeeping which would be better husbanded for national emergencies
- Whatever the diplomats say, expect the worst.

MILITARY PREPAREDNESS – MORALE

Western politicians have also been failing our armed forces in another important respect. They have either championed, or at least failed to counter effectively, pressures to alter fundamentally the traditional military ethos.

The tasks of war are different in kind, not just degree, from the tasks of peace. This does not, of course, mean that the laws of commonsense – or indeed Parkinson's law – are suspended in military matters.* Defence procurement programmes must be efficiently managed. Functions which can sensibly be contracted out should be. Unnecessary non-military assets should be sold. Reviews and scrutinies will be necessary to remove duplication and waste. These concepts were ones which I sought to ensure were applied when I was Prime Minister, and they are of universal application. But, for all that, it has also in the end to be recognised, I repeat, that the military is different.

One very obvious reason is that the defence budget is one of the very few elements of public expenditure that can truly be described as essential. The point was well-made by a robust Labour Defence Minister, Denis (now Lord) Healey, many years ago: 'Once we have cut expenditure to the extent where our

---

* 'Parkinson's law', it will be remembered, was coined by the late Professor C. Northcote Parkinson. It states that 'work expands to fill the time available'.

security is imperilled, we have no houses, we have no hospitals, we have no schools. We have a heap of cinders.'* For this reason, if the Chief of the Defence Staff (or his equivalent) declares that without certain military resources the country cannot be adequately defended only a fool of a politician refuses to listen.

But the military is also different because service life is different from civilian life. The virtues which must be cultivated by those who may be called upon to risk their lives in the course of their duties are simply not the same as those required of a businessman, a civil servant – or, indeed, a politician. Above all, courage – physical courage – is vital.

Servicemen need to develop a much higher degree of comradeship with their colleagues. They must be able to trust and rely on one another implicitly. Soldiers, sailors and airmen are still individuals – one has only to read their biographies to understand that. But they cannot be individualists. For those who live under discipline it is duties not rights that are the focus of their lives. This is why the military life is rightly considered a noble vocation, and also why over the years many of those who leave it for civilian careers find it difficult to adjust.

Soldiers also generally need to be physically strong. It is not enough to be clever – though to be cunning is certainly useful. No front-line forces can afford to have even a small proportion of their number who are not up to whatever tasks they may be called upon to perform.

So I am opposed to current attempts to apply liberal attitudes and institutions developed in civilian life to life in our armed forces. Programmes aimed at introducing civilian-style judicial systems, at promoting homosexual rights, and at making ever more military roles open to women are at best irrelevant to the functions that armies are meant to perform. At worst, though, they threaten military capabilities in a way that is actually dangerous.

The feminist military militants are perhaps the most pernicious

---

* Speech in the House of Commons, 5 March 1969, Hansard Col. 551. Denis Healey was Secretary of State for Defence from 1964 to 1970, and Chancellor of the Exchequer from 1974 to 1979.

of these 'reformers'. The fact that most men are stronger than most women means either that women have to be excluded from the most physically demanding tasks, or else the difficulty of the tasks has to be reduced – something that is evidently easier in training than in combat. But it is, of course, this second course which the feminists demand should be adopted. And all too often their agenda is being accepted.

When it was recognised that women cannot throw ordinary grenades far enough to avoid being caught in the explosion, the answer was not to let men take over but rather to make lighter (and less lethal) grenades. When it was discovered that women on board warships require facilities that men do not, the US Navy had to 'reconfigure' their ships to provide them – on the USS *Eisenhower* alone that cost $1 million. And when most women (rightly in my view) choose not to take combat roles, the answer, according to one professor at Duke University, is for the military to get rid of traits like 'dominance, assertiveness, aggressiveness, independence, self-sufficiency, and willingness to take risks'.* Women have plenty of roles in which they can serve with distinction: some of us even run countries. But generally we are better at wielding the handbag than the bayonet.

And warfare will always involve the use of bayonets, or their equivalents. It is unrealistic to expect that wars will ever be fought without physical contact and confrontation with the enemy at some stage.

With these considerations in mind, our political and military leaders should:

---

* The absurdities to which feminism in the military is leading – and the consequences that will result – are investigated by Kate O'Beirne, 'The War Machine as Child Minder: The Integration of Women into the US Armed Forces', in *Not Fit to Fight: The Cultural Subversion of the Armed Forces in Britain and America*, ed. Gerald Frost (The Social Affairs Unit, 1998), and by Stephanie Gutmann in *The Kinder, Gentler Military: Can America's Gender-Neutral Fighting Force Still Win Wars?* (New York: Scribner's, 2000). In Britain, too, the army is reported to have decided to change its fitness programme because of the number of training injuries suffered by women (*The Times*, 7 June 2001).

- Show some backbone in resisting the lobbies of political correctness that are out to subvert good order and discipline in our armed forces
- Make it plain that life in the services cannot take as its model the behaviour, legal framework, or ethos that prevail in civilian life
- Refuse to put liberal doctrine ahead of military effectiveness
- Demonstrate a little commonsense.

RMA

That said, we have reached one of those points in military history when the role of technology in fighting wars has taken on an altogether new importance. The Revolution in Military Affairs (RMA) is a real revolution. The term refers mainly to two developments: the power of instantly available, networked information, and the large-scale use of precision firepower. One of the foremost experts on the strategic implications of RMA, Professor Eliot Cohen, has graphically described its reality:

> Satellites beaming fresh pictures of targets to pilots in jet aircraft, tanks communicating their locations to computerized command posts, generals peering remotely over the shoulders of company commanders through the cameras of orbiting unmanned aircraft – these are all phenomena of today, not the military dreams of tomorrow.*

America is and will remain far ahead of any of her rivals in the use of these technologies – as long as she keeps on investing in them.

But RMA is not without its drawbacks. I have already referred to one of these – a feeling that technology can make war casualty-free. A more tangible danger is what (in the jargon) are called 'asymmetric threats'. By these are meant threats posed by powers which, although generally lagging well behind America militarily,

---

* Eliot A. Cohen, 'War: At Arms', *National Review*, 24 January 2000.

are able to concentrate their resources upon and exploit American vulnerability in one particular aspect of warfare. Thus China has on its own admission been developing plans to use networks and the Internet to cripple America's banking system and disrupt its military capability.* Information- or Cyber-warfare has leapt from the television screen to the centre of the Pentagon's preoccupations. That is absolutely right. It is a rule as old as warfare itself that every advance in military technology provokes countermeasures. And history is full of rich and technologically advanced civilisations which fell before a more primitive enemy who had seen and exploited a systemic weakness.

That is why we have to:

- Give top priority to investing in and applying the latest defence technologies
- Be alert to the dangers that America's technological sophistication could be undermined by asymmetric threats from a determined enemy
- Never believe that technology *alone* will allow America to prevail as a superpower.

'REMEMBER PEARL HARBOR'

Before, during and after my time as Prime Minister I have paid many visits to American military bases and other sites, but none like that which I made to the USS *Arizona* Memorial in Pearl Harbor on the morning of 11 May 1993. A tender took us out to the ship, upon whose shattered hull a special structure has been erected. For the last forty years, the colours have been raised and lowered each day in honour of the 1177 members of the *Arizona*'s crew who died in the Japanese air force's attack of 7 December 1941. Some of the bodies were recovered, but the remains of nine hundred still lie in the depths of the water that now fills the ship. Standing over a square opening that leads down to the ocean, I lowered a bouquet of flowers. The petals drifted across the surface

---

* *Washington Times*, 17 November 1999.

and I thought about the sailors who died in such terrible circumstances so that the rest of us could live in peace and freedom.

The USS *Arizona* should not only, however, be a place of pilgrimage: it should be a place of reflection. The immediate consequence of the Japanese bombing of Pearl Harbor was, of course, to bring America into the Second World War. So it was, in that sense, the day the Axis powers began to lose. The circumstances of the attack swung an earlier sceptical American opinion behind the war effort. 'Remember Pearl Harbor' became the title of America's most popular war song. Those words should also serve as a warning to us.

On that Sunday morning sixty years ago, just before eight o'clock, 353 Japanese aircraft began their devastating attack. Some three thousand military personnel were killed or wounded, eight battleships and ten other naval vessels were sunk or badly damaged, and almost two hundred US aircraft were destroyed in the space of just three hours. What made the attack on Pearl Harbor so shocking was the fact that it was entirely unexpected. Tension between America and Japan had been rising. But there was no suspicion of what the Japanese were planning and there had been no declaration of war. The inquiries launched after the event found that errors had been made by the US naval and army commanders in the Hawaii region. But the fact remains that what happened at Pearl Harbor reflected far more broadly on the unpreparedness of America for an attack coming (literally) 'out of the blue'.

The colours raised over the *Arizona* on the day of my visit were given to me when I left by the Commander-in-Chief of the US Pacific Fleet. They are now framed in my office in London. They serve as a constant reminder. What troubles me, however, is that America and her allies now face a similar threat, and we have been doing too little to guard against it.

MISSILES AND MISSILE DEFENCE

The lessening of superpower rivalry in the final stage of the Cold War also resulted in a loosening of superpower disciplines. On the one hand, Soviet political satellites were released to seek their own irregular and eccentric orbits. On the other, as the Soviet Union itself crumbled, its weapons stockpiles were dispersed and plundered, new clients were found for weapons production, and existing experts with knowledge of advanced military technologies abandoned a state that could no longer pay its bills.

Saddam Hussein's aggression against Kuwait in 1990 occurred a little too early for him. He had not quite been able to acquire the weaponry he needed to strike back at the West – his plans to develop the nuclear weapon having been seriously set back by Israel's pre-emptive attack in June 1981. But if Saddam had been in a position credibly to threaten America or any of its allies – or the coalition's forces – with attack by missiles with nuclear warheads, would we have gone to the Gulf at all? Just posing that question highlights how fundamentally the reality of proliferation can affect the West's ability to exert power beyond our shores.

Subsequent experience in dealing with Saddam Hussein should also bring home to us the difficulty of trying to maintain a united front against proliferators – even against a rogue whom everyone in public characterises as a pariah. The recent book by Richard Butler, former head of UNSCOM, the body commissioned to inspect and eliminate Saddam's weapons capability, provides new insights into how China, and in particular France and Russia, have played fast and loose with their international obligations. The Russians clearly still view Iraq as their gateway to the Middle East and the Persian Gulf, while the French have huge commercial interests in the Iraqi oil industry. All three powers have been driven by what Mr Butler calls 'a deep resentment of American power in the so-called unipolar post-Cold War world'.* If this is a precedent for international cooperation in such matters it would be better to pursue other channels.

The more general, and even more important, lesson from experience in dealing with Saddam is that it is extremely difficult to prevent states that are determined to acquire weapons of mass destruction (WMD) from doing so. If it is so hard to monitor and

---

* Richard Butler, *Saddam Defiant: The Threat of Weapons of Mass Destruction, and the Crisis of Global Security* (London: Weidenfeld and Nicolson, 2000), p.117.

control the activities of a country like Iraq, which has been defeated in war and subjected to repeated threats, sanctions and punishment, what chances are there of preventing the proliferation of WMD among states that are much less subject to scrutiny?

In fact, proliferation has proceeded, often assisted by the failure of the West to check the outflow of technologies. Nor have international arms control agreements helped much in this respect. The Biological Weapons Convention has been unsuccessful in preventing the development of this particularly horrible weapon, because its provisions are for all practical purposes unverifiable. The same is true of the Chemical Weapons Convention.

These agreements, though, are at least more or less neutral in their effects. The same cannot be said, however, of the Comprehensive Test Ban Treaty, which the United States Senate rightly refused to ratify. The fundamental truth here is that the nuclear weapon cannot be disinvented. A world without nuclear weapons is thus quite simply a fantasy world. The realistic question, therefore, is whether the West and America wish to stay ahead of potential nuclear competitors or not. If we do not, we hand power over regions where our interests are at stake to the Saddams and Gadaffis and Kim Jong Ils.

Faced with that prospect it is easy to see why America's nuclear deterrent must be completely credible, which means that it has to be tested and modernised as necessary. We should have learned by now that no weapons technology ever stands still. For every idealistic peacemaker willing to renounce his self-defence in favour of a weapons-free world, there is at least one warmaker anxious to exploit the other's good intentions. All those who shelter beneath the American nuclear umbrella should have been praising Senator Helms and his colleagues who defeated the CTBT – not having tantrums.*

Moreover, in the end nuclear weapons will probably be used. That is a terrible thought for everyone. It is also a novel thought for many who argued, as I did, during the 1970s and 1980s for an up-to-date deterrent as a means of keeping the peace.

---

* Senator Jesse Helms (Republican, North Carolina) was then Chairman of the US Senate Committee on Foreign Relations.

During the Cold War's 'balance of terror' it was always possible to argue that because both sides had powerful nuclear arsenals this provided an important stabilising factor, preventing not just nuclear but conventional war, at least in Europe. In truth, there was never any cast-iron guarantee against a nuclear exchange. *We* knew that *we* would never initiate a war of any kind against the Warsaw Pact. And we had good reason to believe that the Soviets would be too cautious to launch a *nuclear* war against the West. But we could never altogether rule out the possibility of miscalculation or technical error precipitating an exchange.

Since the end of the Cold War, it has been possible to cut back nuclear arsenals substantially, and it may be possible for America and Russia to cut back still further. But we should not forget that the START II and the proposed START III treaties, like earlier arms control (and, as in these cases, arms reduction) agreements, do not in themselves actually make us more secure. What they do is reduce the cost of our security, by lowering expenditure on surplus weaponry, and they arguably help ease tensions and mistrust. The last point is about all that can be said for agreements about the targeting of missiles – which can always be re-targeted.

With the end of the Cold War we entered what one leading expert has provocatively termed 'the second nuclear age'. Among the fallacies which Professor Colin S. Gray lists as afflicting Western strategic policy planners today are that 'a post-nuclear era has dawned', 'nuclear abolition is feasible and desirable', and 'deterrence is reliable'. He has also warned that 'the less strategically attractive nuclear weapons appear to the United States, the greater the attraction of those weapons and other WMD to possible foes and other "rogues"'.* And he is right.

The most important threat of this sort today does indeed come from the so-called 'rogue states'. This category usually refers to medium-sized (or even quite small) powers in the grip of an ideology (or of an individual) that shuns the existing international order, and is bent on aggression. The usual candidates are Iraq, Iran, Libya, Syria and North Korea, all of which should certainly

---

* Colin S. Gray, *The Second Nuclear Age* (Boulder and London: Lynne Rienner Publishers, 1999).

be included, as in the light of recent events should Afghanistan.*
But we should not disregard either the chilling remark of a senior
Chinese official made in 1995 at the height of confrontation
between China and Taiwan. The official noted sarcastically that
Beijing could take military action against Taipei if it wished, without worrying about US interference, because America's leaders
'care more about Los Angeles than they do about Taiwan'. Perhaps
the Chinese too remember Pearl Harbor.

We also have to guard against the idea that the desire of non-
nuclear powers to become nuclear is somehow irrational. Incon-
venient and even dangerous it may be, but irrational it is not.
After all, was Colonel Gadaffi unreasonable to draw conclusions
from Libya's inability to react to the punitive action that America
took against him in 1986 when he said: 'If [the Americans] know
that you have a deterrent force capable of hitting the United States,
they would not be able to hit you. Consequently, we should build
this force so that they and others will no longer think about an
attack'?†

By his own lights Gadaffi was talking sense – the folly is ours in
letting him think he could get away with threatening us in this way.

But it is not just fanatics and revolutionaries who make this
calculation. Every state that retains nuclear weapons makes it
too. This is something that the utopian New Left internationalists
simply refuse to grasp. Let me start close to home. Without
Britain's nuclear deterrent we would not be powerful enough to
have acquired our status as a Permanent Member of the UN Security Council. And I have no hesitation in affirming that it is a matter
of vital national interest that we retain both the weapon and the
international standing it secures. If the present British government
doesn't understand that, they should – it is the main reason why
the rest of the world takes notice of us.

Similarly, I fully understand India's – and, in response, Pakistan's – desire to demonstrate to the world that they too are nuclear
powers. India has China on her doorstep and Pakistan has India.
President Clinton was quite simply wasting his time when he

---

* I investigate the 'rogues' at greater length in Chapter Six.
† Gadaffi on Tripoli television, 19 April 1990.

advised India in the wake of its nuclear tests in 1998 to define her 'greatness' in 'twenty-first-century terms, not in terms that everybody else has already decided to reject'.* But we haven't left nuclear weapons behind, and if *we* did others wouldn't.

The arms control treaty that undoubtedly does most harm and makes least sense – and was accordingly regarded by the Clinton administration as 'the cornerstone of strategic stability' – is the Anti-Ballistic Missile (ABM) Treaty. The ABM Treaty had some rationale when it was signed in 1972, though in retrospect not much. It prevented either the United States or the Soviet Union from deploying a strategic missile defence system capable of defending the entire national territory. It also prohibited the development, testing or deployment of anything other than a limited, fixed land-based system. The original treaty allowed for the deployment of two sites for such a system, though a protocol reduced this to one each in 1974.

The philosophy behind the treaty was that contained in the doctrine of Mutually Assured Destruction (otherwise and rightly known as MAD). Essentially, the belief was that as long as each superpower was totally vulnerable to nuclear attack it would not be tempted to start a nuclear war. Practice never entirely followed this theory. The Soviets cheated by secretly building an early-warning station at Krasnoyarsk. NATO, through its doctrine of 'flexible response' – that is a graduated conventional and nuclear response rather than total nuclear war – also inched away from MAD. Not even the Cold War froze strategy entirely.

But there was, in any case, a deeper and more pervasive logic at work. The history of warfare, viewed from a technical perspective, is that of an unrelenting competition between offensive and defensive weapons and strategies, with progress in the development of one being countered by corresponding improvements in the other. Thus swords were countered by armour, gunpowder generated new techniques of fortification, tanks were opposed by anti-tank weapons and the bomber – known at the time as 'the ultimate weapon' – led to the development of radar systems capable of tracking its flight and the use of anti-aircraft guns and

---

* Reported in the *Washington Post*, 14 May 1998.

fighter planes to shoot it down. It was, therefore, written into the essential nature of warfare that exclusive reliance on that other 'ultimate weapon', the nuclear deterrent, could not last indefinitely: at some point the technology of defensive weapons would catch up. The ABM Treaty could not ultimately prevent that.

The treaty was also, of course, meant to contribute to arms control, because assured vulnerability should, the theory went, make it less necessary to build ever-increasing numbers of long-range missiles. On this point too it failed. The only time the Soviets slowed down the arms race was once they knew they had lost it.

The Anti-Ballistic Missile Treaty is a Cold War relic. It is, therefore, rather surprising that today's liberals show such misplaced affection for it. In fact, the best international lawyers tell us that the treaty has in any case lapsed, because one party to it, the Soviet Union, has ceased to exist. (Even if one takes a contrary view of the present legal position, it is clear from the treaty itself – Article XV, paragraph 2 – that either side is able to withdraw from it, giving six months' notice.) Whatever purpose the ABM Treaty had has certainly ended, now that an increasing number of unpredictable powers can threaten us with weapons of mass destruction.

This consideration also bears upon the frequently heard assertion that discarding the constraints of the ABM Treaty and building missile defence would precipitate a new arms race. I argued in a speech to a conference of experts on missile defence in Washington in December 1998 that such fears were groundless. On the contrary, a failure to deploy a ballistic missile defence system (BMD) would provide an incentive for the leaders of rogue states to acquire missiles and develop weapons of mass destruction. Conversely, the deployment of a global BMD would dampen the desire of the rogues to stock up their arsenals – because the likelihood of their missiles getting through would have greatly diminished. I concluded that seen in this light such a system actually had a 'stabilising potential'.*

Two broader objections, though, can and doubtless will be raised against my advocacy of missile defence.

---

* Speech to a Conference on Missile Defence organised by the National Institute for Public Policy, Washington DC, 3 December 1998.

The first is that I am exaggerating the threats. But I am not. I base my arguments on the work of acknowledged experts. And all the experience of recent attempts to assess these threats is that the experts have consistently been inclined to *underrate* them. For example, the US administration's 1995 National Intelligence Estimate, while taking current developments in missile proliferation seriously, concluded that the US would be free of threat for at least another fifteen years. Other evidence was, however, already by then emerging that caused me and my advisers to doubt whether this (relatively) comfortable judgement was soundly based.

Accordingly, in 1996 I warned in a speech at Fulton, Missouri – the site of Churchill's famous 'Iron Curtain' speech fifty years earlier – that there was a 'risk that thousands of people may be killed in [a ballistic missile] attack which forethought and wise preparation might have prevented'. The seriousness of the danger was highlighted when in April the following year the Japanese Foreign Minister spoke of reports that North Korea had deployed the Rodong-1 missile, with a range of 625 miles, and was therefore able to strike any target in Japan. Other reports highlighted the fact that proliferating rogue states were cooperating with each other – that Rodong missile was believed to have been financed by Libya and Iran. The Iranians were reported to have tested components of a missile capable of striking Israel, and Russia had been selling them nuclear reactors.

These ominous signs could still be discounted by those who chose to do so. But 1998 was the year in which much harder evidence emerged.

The authoritative report of the Rumsfeld Commission, appointed by Congress to assess the threat posed by ballistic missiles to the US, woke even the sleepiest doves from their dreams. Donald (now US Defense Secretary) Rumsfeld noted that, apart from Russia and China, countries like North Korea, Iran and Iraq 'would be able to inflict major destruction on the US within about five years of a decision to acquire such a capability, ten years in the case of Iraq', adding that for much of that time the United States might not know that such a decision had been taken. He concluded that the threat was 'broader, more mature and evolving more rapidly' than reported by the intelligence services,

POTENTIAL REACH OF BALLISTIC
MISSILES IN LIBYA AND IRAQ

——— Potential reach of missiles based in Libya
- - - Potential reach of missiles based in Iraq

Source: Heritage Foundation, *Defending America*, March 1999

whose ability to provide such warnings was in any case 'eroding'.

Simultaneously, events were lending further gravity to the report's conclusions. Although neither country poses any threat to the West, India's and Pakistan's nuclear tests in May 1998 took American intelligence by surprise, showing just how little we can expect to know about the new nuclear powers' capabilities and intentions. Still more seriously, in July Iran test-fired a nine-hundred-mile-range missile and was discovered to be developing a still longer-range missile, apparently based on Russian technology. This constituted a threat to Israel, America's closest ally in the Middle East. Most serious of all, in August North Korea took the world by surprise by launching a three-stage rocket over Japan. This represented a direct threat to America's most important ally in the Pacific, to American forces stationed there, and indeed by implication to the American homeland. One of Thatcher's laws is that the unexpected happens: but I doubt whether we can really still consider a missile attack as unexpected.

The second objection to my argument is quite the opposite of the first: it is that nothing we do will make any difference. This is turn comes in several variants. That most often heard today, especially since the terrorist attacks on New York and Washington and the later fears of biological terrorism, is the suggestion that an aggressor does not need to acquire missiles in order to attack us. He can rely on other means closer to hand – whether passenger aircraft loaded with fuel, or anthrax, or a smuggled-in so-called 'backpack' nuclear weapon. In these circumstances, it is argued, missile defence is a waste of time and money.

But this argument is flawed at several levels. The first is at the level of basic logic. It does not follow that because we have been shown to be vulnerable to one threat we should simply accept vulnerability to another. Second, no one argues that BMD offers a substitute for other measures. We need a layered defence so that we are able to guard against a range of threats. Of these the danger posed by an incoming missile is only one. But, third, it is by no means the least of the dangers we face; indeed, the likelihood that it will be employed against us must have increased as a result of the events of 11 September. Although we must avoid complacency, it is surely much less likely that hijacked aircraft will again be used as a means of mass terrorism against the West. In response to all that has happened, security has already been increased; a range of further measures will doubtless be adopted; air crews will be more alert; passengers will be less compliant; suicidal terrorists will find fewer collaborators to dupe; in short, the chances of a successful hijack will diminish. The attraction to terrorists or to a rogue state of an attack by the alternative means of a long-range missile has accordingly grown.

Moreover, that attraction was always considerable, for reasons that are often overlooked. We can never be sure that some fanatic may not seek to detonate a small nuclear weapon in a Western capital. We can, though, take some comfort from the fact that such acts of terrorism are not much favoured by the leaders of rogue states who want to use their weapons to maximum political effect. Ballistic missiles are attractive to them because they are designed to ensure that the weapon remains, from the moment of its launching until its impact, within the sole control of the power that fired it.

But in answer to the broader objection, I would simply say that no system is guaranteed perfect. I was never as optimistic as President Reagan seemed to be that even a fully-fledged Strategic Defence Initiative (SDI) would render nuclear weapons obsolete. But in the post-Cold War age we are, after all, most unlikely to be faced with a full-scale nuclear exchange with a major power. Far more probable is that a rogue state may fire one or more missiles with nuclear or chemical warheads at one of our major cities. Another ever-present possibility is that an unauthorised launch could occur. In such cases, missile defence offers the only protection we have – though I certainly would not rule out pre-emptive strikes to destroy a rogue state's capabilities.

The truth is that the global system of ballistic missile defence, which I am proposing, is by far the best chance we have of preventing missiles and their warheads reaching our cities. This is because unlike other less comprehensive systems a global ballistic missile defence system has the ability to target and destroy missiles in each of their three phases of flight – the boost phase, mid-course, and the terminal phase. The first phase, directly after launch, is naturally the best from the point of view of the intended victim – and the worst from that of the aggressor, on whom the warhead's destructive elements fall.

I believe that the best way to achieve such a global system is probably along the lines suggested by the excellent and authoritative report of the Heritage Foundation's Commission on Missile Defense. This would be based upon a combination of a sea-based missile defence system and a space-based sensor system. By contrast, it seems highly unlikely that a single land-based system, or indeed any system which accepts the constraints of the ABM Treaty, could provide America with an effective defence.*

I also believe that the British Missile Proliferation Study Report

---

* *Defending America*, Report of the Heritage Foundation's Commission on Missile Defense, chaired by Ambassador Henry Cooper, March 1999.

was right to underline the effect that restricting America's missile defence in that way, as proposed by the Clinton administration, would have on the rest of the Alliance. Britain, as America's closest ally and most effective military collaborator, would be particularly vulnerable to missile attack from a rogue state if we were not within the defensive shield.* The British and other European governments should be pledging their full support to those in America who wish to create an effective global ballistic missile defence. America's NATO allies should also be prepared to bear a fair share of the burden of the expense: so far there is little sign of this happening.

Though you would not guess it from President Putin's well-publicised objections, Russia too has a strong interest in America's building such a system. Its cities are closer to the potential threats than are most of the West's. For its part, America by offering to protect Russia has the potential to achieve the visionary goal of President Reagan who saw SDI as a benefit to share.

I was delighted that George W. Bush, in the course of his US presidential campaign, made his position on this matter so clear, saying:

> It is time to leave the Cold War behind, and defend against the new threats of the twenty-first century. America must build effective missile defences, based on the best available options, at the earliest possible date. Our missile defence must be able to protect all fifty states – and our friends and allies and deployed forces overseas – from missile attacks by rogue nations, or accidental launches . . . A missile defence system should not only defend our country, it should defend our allies, with whom I will consult as we develop our plans.†

As President, Mr Bush energetically set about honouring this pledge. I hope that Congress will see fit to support his endeavours. I also trust that America's allies, above all Britain, will take full

---

* *Coming into Range: Britain's Growing Vulnerability to Missiles and Weapons of Mass Destruction* (London, 2000).
† Speech in Washington DC, 23 May 2000.

advantage of the President's proposal to protect our populations too. And no one should pretend that the events of 11 September made effective missile defence any less important, or its acquisition any less urgent.

So I conclude that:

- We must recognise that the threat from ballistic missiles carrying nuclear or other WMD warheads is real, growing and still unanswered
- We should acknowledge that diplomatic and other means aimed at curbing proliferation will have little effect
- Politicians should stop talking as if a world without nuclear weapons were a possibility and begin to accept that nuclear weapons need to be tested and modernised if the nuclear shield is to be maintained
- They should recognise that though political conditions make proliferation and the threat of missile launches more likely, the advance of science has made coping with them more possible
- The only way to do this is to build a system of global ballistic missile defence.

TAKING THE STRAIN

Given leaders of resolution and foresight, and with the support of her allies, the American superpower has the material resources to prevail. But does it have the moral resources? I predict that this question will come to be asked even more frequently in the wake of the terrorist onslaught of 11 September. That outrage was aimed directly at the heart of America's culture, values and beliefs.

Osama bin Laden once described Americans as 'a decadent people with no understanding of morality'.* His contempt for America's fighting spirit has already been shown to be misplaced. But what of his and his fellow fanatics' scorn for our kind of liberal society?

---

* Interview with al-Jazeera Television in 1998, reproduced in the *Sunday Telegraph*, 7 October 2001.

It should be said at once that remarkably few Westerners view all that constitutes Western society today as perfect. Indeed, with us self-criticism is second nature. We worry openly about family breakdown, the dependency culture, juvenile delinquency, drug abuse and violent crime. We are all too conscious that a rising standard of living has not always brought with it a higher quality of life.

But at this point the critics and the enemies of our society part company. What conservative-minded Westerners want to see is the strengthening of personal responsibility in order to make our free society work. What our enemies demand is altogether different: it is the imposition of a dictatorial system in which neither freedom nor responsibility is valued, one where all that is required of individuals is obedience.

The Founding Fathers believed that although the form of republican government they had framed was designed to cope with human failings, it provided no kind of substitute for human virtues. For them American self-government meant exactly that – government by as well as for the people. James Madison knew that democracy presupposed a degree of popular virtue if it was to work well. In Number 55 of the *Federalist Papers* he wrote:

> As there is a degree of depravity in mankind which requires a certain degree of circumspection and distrust, so there are other qualities in human nature which justify a certain portion of esteem and confidence. *Republican government presupposes the existence of these qualities in a higher degree than any other form.** [Emphasis added]

The Founding Fathers and those who came after them had different religious beliefs, and sometimes none. But they were convinced that the way to nourish the virtues which would make America strong was through religion.

It is beyond my purpose to describe the complicated and still-evolving story of relations between Church – however defined –

---

* James Madison, Alexander Hamilton and John Jay, ed. Isaac Kamnick, *The Federalist Papers* (London: Penguin, 1987), p.339.

and state in America.* But when Alexis de Tocqueville wrote in 1835 that Americans held religion 'to be indispensable to the maintenance of republican institutions' he was recording a very wise observation.

Whenever I go to America I am struck by the unembarrassed way in which the divinity keeps making an appearance in political discourse. And this reflects the fact that so many Americans are so deeply religious. Surveys have shown that two-thirds of Americans say that religious commitment is either the most important or a very important dimension of their lives, and America, far more than Britain or Continental Europe, is a church-going country.† And the natural, collective response of Americans to the tragedy of 11 September was to fill the nation's churches. America's faith, including its faith in itself and its mission, is the bedrock of its sense of duty.

That is yet another reason why we non-Americans can make our own the words of the poet Henry Longfellow:

> Thou, too, sail on O Ship of State!
> Sail on, O Union, strong and great!
> Humanity with all its fears,
> With all the hopes of future years,
> Is hanging breathless on thy fate!‡

---

* In any case the story has been told superbly by Paul Johnson in 'God and the Americans', *Commentary*, January 1995.
† These data come from Patrick F. Fagan and Joseph Loconte, *Religion: Building Strong Families and Communities*, Heritage Foundation, Issues 2000.
‡ 'The Building of the Ship' (1849).

CHAPTER 3

The Russian Enigma

A VISIT TO NIZHNY NOVGOROD

Russia is so large that its overall conditions at any one moment almost defy generalisation. Indeed, it may be that the only way to understand the reality of Russia is to experience just a little of it at a time. Certainly, the impressions I gained from the visit I made in July 1993 have proved as instructive as anything I have read before or since.

I had been invited to receive an honorary degree from the Mendeleev Institute in Moscow, which specialises in chemical engineering and is one of Russia's leading scientific institutions. My own early background as a research chemist meant that the invitation was of special interest to me. But I was also impatient to see for myself how much progress Russia, after almost two years of Boris Yeltsin and his reforms, was making. There were so many contradictory reports in the West that it was difficult to know quite what to think. Sir Brian Fall, one of Britain's very best Ambassadors, had therefore prepared a programme that took in something of the old and the new. But even I was really not quite prepared for the resulting contrast.

On the afternoon of my first day in Moscow (Wednesday, 21 July) I was taken around a run-down shopping centre in one of the suburbs of Moscow. There was food on the shelves. But I could see that the choice was very limited and the quality, particularly of the fresh produce, was poor. The surroundings were as dreary as only socialist architecture can be. The locals were friendly, but half an hour of this was enough. Returning to the British Embassy for a working supper I reflected that though there were no evident shortages, neither was there much materially to show for reform. I had expected better, and I learned from the experts round the table that evening that a lot of Russians shared my view.

The following day I had another, more uplifting, rendezvous with the past in the form of several hours' enjoyable conversation with Mikhail and Raisa Gorbachev, at the palatial Gorbachev Foundation (whose purpose I have never altogether understood) and then over lunch at the Residence. I was glad to see that both were in good form, though still somewhat shaken and embittered by the circumstances of Mr Gorbachev's removal from power. Raisa told me about the discomforts of their three days of 'exile' in Crimea during the abortive coup in August 1991. There had apparently been little or no food, and she was lucky to have some sweets in her handbag to give to her granddaughter. In fact, I later learned that the mental pressure of the time had caused Raisa to have a stroke.*

After lunch we all went to the Mendeleev Institute. The ceremony was splendid. There were speeches. In mine I referred to the close relationship between science, truth and freedom. This relationship was, in fact, far from theoretical in the old Soviet Union, where independent-minded scholars of integrity often took refuge in the natural sciences, which were somewhat less contaminated and distorted by Marxist dogma.

An orchestra accompanied some wonderful Russian singing to round off the occasion. I could not though avoid noticing that the Gorbachevs were ignored by many present. Beneath the celebration political wounds ran deep.

At dinner that evening I had my first opportunity to discuss the Russian government's reform programme with one of its main proponents and activators, the immensely able economist Anatoly Chubais. His ideas sounded admirable. But I could not quite forget the previous day's dismal supermarket. Which was Russian reality? More importantly, which was the future?

Early next morning I and my party – which included Denis and

---

* Sadly, Raisa Gorbachev died on 20 September 1999 after a long illness.

our daughter Carol, who had shrewdly arranged to cover the trip for the *European* newspaper – left by plane for the city of Nizhny Novgorod. Under communism it was known as Gorky and was a closed city dedicated to secretive nuclear weapons research. Its very existence had long been concealed as far as possible from prying Western eyes. Indeed, the British crew of the private jet we were using had to take on board a Russian navigator in order to locate the airport, which did not appear on any of the usual maps.

But Nizhny Novgorod, I was aware, once symbolised a very different tradition in Russian history. In 1817 the city hosted its first trade fair, which quickly established itself as the most success-ful in the whole of Russia. The Russians, who are the world's most adept inventors of popular proverbs, used to say that Moscow was Russia's heart, St Petersburg her head and Nizhny Novgorod her pocket. With the end of the Cold War had also come an end to reliance on the defence budget to provide employment. The 'pocket' rapidly emptied. So there was every reason for the citi-zenry to return to their old entrepreneurial ways in order to earn a living.

Successful entrepreneurship is ultimately a matter of flair. But there is also a fund of practical knowledge to be acquired and, of course, the right legal and financial framework has to be provided for productive enterprise to develop. I had heard back in London that the Governor of the province, Boris Nemtsov, was someone who understood all this and that he was committed to a radical programme of what some call Thatcherism but what I had always regarded as commonsense. So I had decided to see for myself, and our Embassy made the arrangements.

Nizhny Novgorod's saviour was, I found, frighteningly young (in his mid-thirties), extraordinarily energetic, extremely good-looking and gifted with both intelligence and shrewdness (which do not always go together). He was a good talker and spoke fluent English. His background was in physics, on which he had written some sixty research papers. He was extremely self-confident, and with good reason.

Indeed, as we sat in his offices in the Nizhny Novgorod Kremlin building, the more I listened to Mr Nemtsov's account of his reforms the more impressed I was. He explained to me that he

RUSSIA AND THE FORMER USSR

had been using his powers as Governor to promote a real free-enterprise economy. At that time the Russian Duma had still not passed a law to create secure title to private property, but in Nizhny Novgorod he had already decreed a local law on private ownership of land. The soil, as I would later see for myself, was rich and well-cultivated. The prime difficulty was not therefore in growing crops – in fact, Nizhny Novgorod was already more than self-sufficient in grain – but rather in selling the produce. Under communism, decisions about distribution and marketing had, naturally enough, been left to the Party bureaucrats. But once that system collapsed, networks which in the ordinary conditions of capitalism would have evolved over time had to be created all at once from scratch. Mr Nemtsov had made it quite clear to the local farmers and traders that it was they who now had to fend for themselves: the state offered no answers. But he had made a large contribution to solving the problem by auctioning off the entire fleet of government-owned lorries – later that afternoon I visited one of the privatised transport firms and was extremely impressed with all I saw, not least the enthusiasm of the manager and his staff.

It was now time to gain some further information and some exercise, as amid what seemed a large proportion of the population of Nizhny Novgorod, the Governor and I took a walk down Bolshaya Pokrovskaya street. All the stores here were privately owned. Every few yards we stopped to talk to the shopkeepers and see what they had to sell. No greater contrast with the drab uniformity of Moscow could be imagined. One shop remains vivid in my memory. It sold dairy produce, and it had a greater selection of different cheeses than I have ever seen in one place. I ate samples of several and they were very good. I also discovered that they were all Russian, and considerably cheaper than their equivalents in Britain. I enthusiastically expressed my appreciation. Perhaps because as a grocer's daughter I carry conviction on such matters, a great cheer went up when my words were translated, and someone cried, 'Thatcher for President!' But the serious lesson for me – and for my hosts – was, of course, that in this one privately owned shop in this distant Russian city, a combination of excellent local products, talented entrepreneurs and laws favourable to enterprise applied by honest and capable political leadership could generate prosperity and progress. There was no need of a 'middle way' or of special adjustment to Russian conditions. In that cheese shop was proof that capitalism worked. The doubters would have been astonished.

THE PERILS OF PREDICTION

But then, Russia has always had a unique capacity to surprise. Every prediction about it should be hedged around with qualifications if whoever makes them would be secure from embarrassment. And before going any further I would like to make my own modest contribution to the current wave of apologising. For I too was wrong – about some things.

I never had any doubt that the communist system was doomed to fail, if the West kept its nerve and remained strong. (On occasion, of course, that seemed a very large 'if'.) I believed this simply because communism ran against the grain of human nature and was therefore ultimately unsustainable. Because it was committed to suppressing individual differences, it could not mobilise individual talents, which is vital to the process of wealth creation. It thus impoverished not just souls but society. Faced with a free system, which engages rather than coerces people, and so brings out the best in them, communism must ultimately founder.

But when? We did not know how desperately incompetent, indeed how near total breakdown, the Soviet system was in the 1980s. Perhaps that was for the best. Had some in the West been aware just how limited and over-stretched were the Soviet Union's resources the temptation would have been to drop our guard. That could have been fatal, for the USSR remained a military superpower long after it had become a political and economic fossil. I would, though, never have predicted that within a decade of my becoming Prime Minister the countries of Central and Eastern Europe would be free, let alone that two years later the Soviet Union would itself have crumbled.

I must also confess to being at least half-wrong about another important aspect of the Soviet Union in my time, namely its durability. I was never attracted by the idea of deliberately trying to hold the Soviet Union together. Such strategies were, in any case, bound to fail because we in the West lacked the knowledge and means to give effect to them. As I have related elsewhere, I was thus alone in opposing an attempt by the then President of the European Commission to have the EEC 'guarantee' the integrity of the USSR in the face of independence movements by the Baltic states.*

But like just about everyone else, I underestimated the fundamental fragility of the Soviet Union once the Gorbachev reforms had begun. A non-communist Soviet Union, which was what we at that time wanted to see, even though we did not put it like that, was actually an impossibility. This was because what held the USSR together was the Communist Party.

The Sovietologists, with their subtle analyses of Soviet society, were wrong: the dissidents with their emphasis on the role of a monolithic party ideology were right. Communism was, in fact, like a parasite, occupying merely the shells of state institutions. These institutions were thenceforth effectively dead and could not be revived.

In the period which has elapsed since those dramatic events, other confident predictions have exploded, though not I think any of mine. Some economic liberals were, for example, led astray by too much confidence in the prescriptions of their own 'dismal science'. It was not actually, as I shall explain, that the prescriptions were wrong. Rather, they took insufficient account of non-economic factors. The liberal economists assumed that with the Communist Party shattered and Western-style 'reformers' in the Kremlin it would be quite easy to instal the institutions of a free economy with rapid benefits for the Russian population. There appeared to be encouraging parallels with Poland, another former communist state where precisely such a crash programme of economic reform, masterminded by Leszek Balcerowicz in the early 1990s, had brought positive results within two or three years. But Russia was not Poland.

On the other hand, the gloomiest predictions about Russia have

---

* See *The Downing Street Years*, p.767.

also been largely – though it is premature to say permanently – disproved. Some foresaw a new Russian imperialism set on achieving by force the recreation of a Russian-centred Soviet Union. So far, at least, this has not happened. Tensions remain between Russia and her neighbours. But there have been no large wars, no use of weapons of mass destruction, no return of communism, no turn towards fascism. It is right that among the many criticisms which can be made of Western policy such important if negative achievements should also be acknowledged.

In truth, the story of Russia over the last decade is not one of progression or even regression along a clear path, rather it is a tale of twists and turns, accelerations and occasional derailments, of integration countered by disintegration, of reform and reaction, all alternately or even simultaneously in play. We have to try to understand what has happened and why, because only by doing so can we predict, let alone influence or steer, what happens in the future.

And that is important. Russia cannot and must not be written off. Personally, I feel this with a conviction bordering on passion. The Russian people suffered so much in the twentieth century – and they were so frequently left to their unhappy lot by those Westerners who lied and collaborated with their oppressors – that we must be indignant at the state in which they remain. In the Cold War the West's greatest allies were always the ordinary Russian people. They now deserve better.

But taking Russia seriously today is also a matter of calculation. When ex-President Yeltsin went to Beijing in December 1999 and reminded us undiplomatically that Russia still had a formidable nuclear arsenal, he was only telling the truth. Whether weak or powerful, an opportunity or a headache, Russia matters.

THE BURDEN OF HISTORY

The best analyses of the Soviet Union were by and large those of historians rather than Sovietologists, because the historians had the benefit of perspective, while the Sovietologists had to glean most of their material from the turgid and mendacious statements of one or other Soviet authority. With Russia's recent return to an older shape and identity, history is even more important as a basis for our assessments.*

It has been well-said that 'of all the burdens Russia has had to bear, heaviest and most relentless of all has been the weight of her past'.† Russia might have developed differently. The course of history is not inevitable. But it is unarguably irreversible. One would have to go far back through the centuries to find a glimmer of any indigenous Russian tradition that might have spawned liberalism of the kind that has flourished in the West. From the late Middle Ages the tsars ruled their vast expanding domains in a fashion which explains much about modern Russia.

First, they recognised no property rights except their own, because they treated all their realm as if they owned it, and they regarded all secular lords as their tenants in chief. With no private property – above all, no private land – there could be no law, other than the tsar's autocratic decrees. With no law, there could be no flourishing middle class, because there was lacking the security required for the accumulation of wealth, for the continuation of commerce and for the development of enterprise. Russian towns remained accordingly few, backward and small.

Secondly, the tsars admitted no institutional or even theoretical checks upon their power. They did not need to seek the consent of their subjects in order to raise revenues. Late-nineteenth- and early-twentieth-century Russian representative institutions thus had little resonance with most of the populace and were treated with scant respect by the tsar.

Thirdly, the tsars established an odd symbiotic relationship with the Russian Orthodox Church. On the one hand, the tsar exercised total control over it: the traditions of Orthodoxy – inherited from practice in Byzantium – were highly conducive to this, recognising no clear division between the ecclesiastical and political spheres.

---

* Over the years I have benefited from many discussions with two fine Russian scholars (and good friends), Professors Robert Conquest and Norman Stone. I draw on their thoughts as well as on the work of Richard Pipes and the late Tibor Szamuely among others in what follows.

† Tibor Szamuely, *The Russian Tradition* (London, 1974), p.12.

On the other hand, Russian Orthodoxy, claiming Moscow as 'the third Rome', deeply infused the whole Russian state with attitudes which were viscerally anti-Western.

These three elements combined uniquely with a fourth – the way in which Russia's development as a state more or less coincided with its acquisition of an empire. Both were intricately connected for, to quote one leading authority, 'since the seventeenth century, when Russia was already the world's largest state, the immensity of their domain has served Russians as psychological compensation for their relative backwardness and poverty'.*

Westerners who visited tsarist Russia immediately knew that they had to deal with something utterly alien and un-European. More open-minded than those intellectuals who a century later made their pseudo-pilgrimages to the Soviet Union was the Marquis de Custine, who wrote his recollection of a visit to Russia in 1838. He went there as a sympathetic admirer of Russia; he returned an outraged critic:

> The political state of Russia may be defined in one sentence: it is a country in which the government says what it pleases, because it alone has the right to speak. In Russia fear replaces, that is paralyses, thought ... Nor in this country is historical truth any better respected than the sanctity of oaths ... even the dead are exposed to the fantasies of him who rules the living.†

If this reads like a description of the Soviet communist dictatorship, that is more than coincidence; for it was grafted onto a Russian police-state tradition that was already well-established.

Custine's picture of backwardness and repression is not, though, the whole story. The depredations which communism later made upon Russia – and even from its political coffin still makes – went

---

* Richard Pipes, 'Is Russia Still an Enemy?', *Foreign Affairs*, 76/5, September/October 1997, p.68.

† The Marquis de Custine (1790–1857) was a French travel writer made famous by his *Letters from Russia* (1839). The quotation comes from Szamuely, *The Russian Tradition*, pp.3–5.

far beyond anything devised by the tsars. Furthermore, economically at least, things had begun to change well before the Bolshevik Revolution. Russia's belated but dynamic industrial revolution took off with a vengeance from the last decade of the nineteenth century. Indeed, as Norman Stone points out:

> By [the eve of the First World War], Russia had become the fourth industrial power in the world, having overtaken France in indices of heavy industry – coal, iron, steel. Her population grew from just over sixty millions in the middle of the nineteenth century to a hundred millions in 1900 and almost 140 million by 1914; and that was counting only the European part, i.e. west of the Urals. Towns, which contained only ten million people in 1880, contained thirty million by 1914.*

Russia lacked the social and political institutions to cope with the strains of such rapid economic change. Moreover, the empire was about to enter a terrible war which exposed its weaknesses, and which led first to anarchy, then revolution, and finally to the imposition by the Bolsheviks of the most total dictatorship that the world has known.

THE LEGACY OF COMMUNISM

The system was as much the work of Lenin as of Marx. The wordy, flawed analyses of the German were applied with ruthless violence by the Russian, who already lived and breathed the repressive atmosphere of the tsars.

The Soviets took the traditional tsarist hostility towards alternative sources of authority, towards freedom of thought, towards private property and towards a rule of law much further. While the tsar had demanded that he be treated as God's representative, the Party actually usurped the place of God Himself. Communism's war against religion – even one so politically amenable as

---

* Norman Stone, *Europe Transformed 1878–1919*, second edition (Oxford, 1999), p.144.

Russian Orthodoxy – was pursued with the same aim as that against the richer peasants and against all the habits and ties of private life: the state must seize, possess, and ultimately absorb all.

For seventy years this system was imposed on the Russian people. Of course, like all that is human, it had its less bad moments. In time, the frenzied campaign against religion abated, to be replaced under Stalin by an uneasy *modus vivendi* between Church and state, because the latter found the former's influence useful. Similarly, after Stalin's purges a certain stability descended on the Soviet system, which became more bureaucratic, stratified and corrupt – this was the period of the emergence of what Milovan Djilas called the 'new class'.* The monster of communism mellowed a little as sclerosis set in. Under Khrushchev, the errors of Stalin were admitted. Under Gorbachev, the conduct of Lenin was eventually debatable. In the last few years of the Soviet Union the pressure for free speech and free elections grew and – to his credit – Mr Gorbachev responded.

There was also talk of economic reform. But it never came to anything. This was essentially because, for communists – from Lenin to Gorbachev – 'reform' simply meant making the Marxist-Leninist system more efficient, not adopting a different system. Perhaps the last moment at which such an approach could have yielded positive results was under the intelligent Yuri Andropov (1983–84), who at least understood the economic abyss before which the Soviet Union tottered. But he was too sick – and his successor Konstantin Chernenko (1984–85) was both too sick and too dull – to make any impact. By the time that Mikhail Gorbachev took over in 1985 any attempt to reform the system was bound to fail and likely to result sooner or later in its dissolution.

And this, of course, is what happened. Mr Gorbachev's programmes of *glasnost* (openness) and *perestroika* (restructuring) were intended to be complementary, but that is not how they worked out. Openness about the failures of the system and of the people, past and present, who were responsible, was immensely

---

* *The New Class: An Analysis of the Communist System* (London: Thames and Hudson, 1957).

liberating for the Soviet citizenry who had for so long been denied the chance to debate the truth. But restructuring the ramshackle institutions of the state, let alone replacing the mediocrities who battened on them, was really out of the question. In any case, the basis of the Soviet Union was still the Communist Party (which also controlled the military-industrial complex and the security apparatus), and the Party would not meekly yield up the one thing it valued above all – power.

This fact also explains the personal tragedy of Mikhail Gorbachev, who was fêted by the West – and justly so – but who was rejected and reviled by his own fellow-countrymen. For all his talk of the need for 'new thinking', in the end he just could not practise it. Faced in 1991 with a choice between continuing along the path of fundamental change on the one hand and a return to repressive communism on the other, he dithered. I do not believe, though this has sometimes been said, that he secretly supported those hard-line communists who temporarily seized power in July 1991. But he had himself appointed them to their positions. And even when he returned to Moscow he proclaimed himself a communist. So for all my admiration for his achievements, my sympathy for his predicament, indeed my liking for him as a man, I am sure that his replacement by Boris Yeltsin was right for Russia.

The deep hostility between these two men who between them have done more for their country's freedom than any other Russians was doubtless partly to be explained simply by political rivalry. But it also, I am convinced, represented something deeper. Mr Yeltsin knew in his heart that the system in which he had risen and then fallen, only to rise again, was fundamentally wrong – and not just because it failed to give people a reasonable standard of living, but also because it was based upon a structure of lies and wickedness. This, I think, is why Mr Yeltsin looked so large as he stood on that tank in central Moscow when he led the heroic battle for Russian democracy. And it is why Mr Gorbachev looked so diminished as he returned three days later from his Black Sea coast retreat in the Crimea. Cameras often lie, but this time they told the truth: not just a tale of two Russians, but also a tale of two Russias.

The collapse of the August 1991 coup provided the opportunity for a triumphant Boris Yeltsin to order the banning of the Communist Party and to oversee the orderly dissolution of the Soviet Union. In recent years it has become the fashion to scorn Mr Yeltsin's weaknesses, which were doubtless real enough. But they were more than matched by astonishing courage and large reserves of political wiliness. And had bravery and cunning not also been accompanied by a typically Russian ruthless streak he could never have scored victory after victory against the communists who wanted to drag Russia back to its Soviet past.

Boris Yeltsin's shoulders were broad. But history's burden was still too heavy for them. The habits, instincts and attitudes developed by Soviet communism made the transformation of Russia into a 'normal' country immensely difficult. This has been glaringly apparent in the growth of lawlessness.

Long before the end of the Soviet era, Russians had come to regard the state itself as their enemy. For those who chose to proclaim their individuality it was an oppressor. But for many more the state was essentially a thief.

There was, of course, no law in a Western sense in communist society. Indeed, though there were rules and regulations at every turn there was no concept of equity, according to which a single set of obligations based on what each was due as a human being was applied to all equally. As the writer and dissident Alexandr Zinoviev strikingly put it: 'In Communist society a system of values prevails which is founded on the principle that there should be no general principles of evaluation.'*

In fact, the only dominant principle was that of predatory egotism. Such habits die hard, or not at all. It is important to stress that although the scale and violence of Russian crime have snowballed since the end of the USSR, its psychological and systemic roots were planted under communism. In the last years of Leonid Brezhnev's presidency corruption in high places became notorious. But from the mid-1980s, crime became fully institutionalised, not least through the activities of the KGB which, according to a senior CIA source,

---

* Alexandr Zinoviev, *The Reality of Communism* (London, 1984), p.117.

sold cheaply acquired Soviet commodities abroad at world prices, putting the proceeds into disguised foreign accounts and front companies . . . [Its] lines of business came to include money laundering, arms and drug trafficking and other plainly criminal activities.*

There was, understandably, little confidence that this disordered state of affairs would change under the new dispensation: most Russians had grown so accustomed to it that criminality appeared the ordinary way in which things were done. How could it be otherwise when so many of the same people who had held high positions under communism re-emerged under capitalism as the new masters?

Russia has accordingly become a notoriously criminal society. It is thought that between three thousand and four thousand criminal gangs operate there. The Russian Ministry of Internal Affairs says that organised crime controls 40 per cent of the turnover of goods and services; some estimates are higher. Half of Russia's banks are thought to be controlled by criminal syndicates. Not surprisingly, the European Bank for Reconstruction and Development (EBRD) considers Russia the most corrupt major economy in the world. Public opinion polls have suggested that Russians despair of honest effort as the means to advance. Instead, 88 per cent listed 'connections' and 76 per cent dishonesty as the best ways to get ahead.†

Estimates of the size of the black economy – always difficult to gauge – put it at between a quarter and a half of Russia's national income. Much of this is, of course, a matter of unpaid or badly paid Russian workers trying to earn a decent income; much of the rest reflects the chaotic circumstances in which all enterprises have to operate. But it is still a recipe for extortion and gangsterism.

In such circumstances violence has become a tempting method of settling scores, instilling fear, and deterring both competition

---

* F.W. Ermarth, 'Seeing Russia Plain: The Russian Crisis and American Intelligence', *The National Interest*, No. 55, spring 1999, p.10.

† *The Economist*, 28 August 1999; Grigory Yavlinsky, 'Russia's Phony Capitalism', *Foreign Affairs*, May/June 1998; Stephen Handelman, 'The Russian Mafiya', *Foreign Affairs*, March/April 1994.

and criticism. Russia's murder rate is now probably the highest in the world. Those who speak out against abuses in high places must expect to be targeted.

Such, for example, was the fate of that brave and principled lady, Galina Starovoitova. I first met her in London during the 1991 attempted coup, when she and I discussed how to help rally support for Boris Yeltsin. Mrs Starovoitova was a leading figure in the biggest political party at that time, 'Democratic Russia'. She became a personal adviser to President Yeltsin on inter-ethnic issues – a position she relinquished because of her opposition to the Chechen War. She was later elected as a member of the Duma representing St Petersburg, where she denounced the anti-Semitism and corruption which had become unpleasant facets of the life of that great city. She also proposed a draft Law of Lustration intended to prevent high-level former Communist Party and KGB members from occupying high state positions. This, though, was rejected by the communist majority in the Duma.

Galina Starovoitova was murdered on the night of 20 November 1998 as she climbed the stairs to her apartment. It was a well-prepared assassination with what her family later told me had all the marks of the old KGB style. I was horrified by this and wrote to President Yeltsin. But her murderers have never been brought to trial. She is a martyr to the ideal of the Russia most Russians long to see. It is impossible to have much confidence in the Russian authorities' promises to stamp out crime while her, probably well-connected, murderers remain at large.

ECONOMIC REFORM AND THE IMF

Lawlessness in all its forms has impinged on attempts to reform the Russian economy. And this should be remembered as a background to the agonised debates which have taken place since the crash of August 1998 on the theme of 'Who lost Russia?' In fact, the question is badly put for three rather obvious reasons: first, Russia is not necessarily lost; second, it was certainly not the West's to lose; and third, the loss for which the International Monetary Fund (IMF), senior politicians and advisers *should* be required to answer is that of billions of dollars by Western tax-payers in futile bail-outs.

Elsewhere, I consider more fully what might constitute a proper role for the IMF.* But it is worth rehearsing the arguments for and against its deep and costly involvement in Russia. The main argument for relying on an international organisation rather than, say, the Group of Seven (G7) major economic powers to help Russia out of the mess it inherited from communism, was that the IMF allegedly had the expertise to undertake the task and the neutrality to avoid outraging Russian sensitivities about the country's sovereignty.

In fact, things have not worked out that way. The IMF's decisions were increasingly politically motivated, clearly intended to keep President Yeltsin in and the communists out of power; and it found itself increasingly pilloried by Russians as an agent of malign Western intervention. Of course, the prior question is: did such massive programmes of assistance make sense in the first place?

The argument against the provision of loans and other aid to insolvent sovereign borrowers is well-known: it mirrors in many respects the problem involved in lending to insolvent individuals. Quite apart from whether the money will be repaid – which may not be the first consideration – such action creates what is called 'moral hazard'. This means that it is assumed by the recipient of the aid – or by others who benefit from it indirectly, or may wish to benefit in the future – that irresponsibility will not be penalised. And that, of course, increases the likelihood of its recurring.†

Taken to its extreme, this argument would suggest a policy of rigid international non-intervention in Russia's economic affairs. It should be said at once that this argument has its merits. Insofar as the West's billions of dollars have helped shore up a structurally unreformed economy and a corrupt plutocracy they have done harm not good. But the fact remains that Russia is too great a potential danger to her neighbours and the world to be allowed to fail entirely. In these circumstances, the needs of politics will

---

* See pp.462–5.
† See pp.435–47.

always tend to override the requirements of economics. The practical challenge is to ensure that intervention is correctly timed, targeted, monitored – and known to be limited. Unfortunately, with Russia this has not been the case.

Looking back, there was only a very narrow window of opportunity for the West and the IMF to act decisively. The Soviet Union was in discussions with the IMF as early as 1988. Two years later the Fund produced its recommendations for fundamental economic reform. President Gorbachev was presented with a number of possible reform programmes, but he had little understanding of economics and his preoccupations were mainly with his own and the Soviet Union's survival. From the beginning of 1991 the Soviet administration actually moved away from political and economic reform, a course which culminated in the August 1991 putsch.

Perhaps more could have been done in this initial period. I was very keen to see Mikhail Gorbachev rewarded and encouraged. That is why I wanted to see the Soviet Union/Russia associated with the G7 economic powers, in spite of its difficulties.* I was not keen to see open-ended credits supplied, which would just build up more debt. Instead, I believed that Sir Alan Walters (my old friend and economic adviser in government) had been right to argue for the setting up of a currency board to stabilise the rouble by backing it with dollars. I also thought that Western companies might be invited to use their expertise to reform a whole sector of the collapsing Soviet system – ideally, food distribution.

Conditions changed fundamentally for the better with the accession to power of Boris Yeltsin, who immediately declared his intention to liberalise the Russian economy and brought in committed expert reformers as ministers and advisers to help him do so. The following January, price controls were removed, internal trade was freed, the rouble was floated and measures were taken to slash the huge budget deficit. But the consequences for the Russian people of this necessary programme were severe. Once the first enthusiasm for change passed it was inevitable that

---

* A proposal contained, for example, in my speech to the Supreme Soviet of the USSR in Moscow on 28 May 1991.

political pressures on the President and his team would mount. The communist-dominated parliament became the centre of resistance.

This was the point at which the West should have been generous. But it was not. Western politicians and bankers seriously misread the situation, imagining that the small print of an economic programme was more important than the political reality. By the summer of 1992 President Yeltsin had felt compelled to drop the reformist Prime Minister, Yegor Gaidar, and instal the representative of the industrial cartels, Viktor Chernomyrdin, in his place. At the same time the former chief of the Soviet Central Bank was appointed to the post of chairman of the Russian Central Bank, where he immediately set the printing presses rolling. The IMF only now agreed its first big loan to Russia – seven months after the reform programme was launched, and after the true reformers had been ousted.

For a variety of reasons, that missed opportunity never recurred. Even during the periods when economic progress seemed to be made, the underlying conditions were actually deteriorating. Politics was largely at the root of this. The struggle between the President and the parliament was waged with increasing ferocity, largely over economic policy, with Mr Yeltsin's opponents (who had control over the Central Bank) trying to secure as strong a dose of inflationary socialism as possible. Western hopes rose, after the defeat of the parliamentary rebellion in October 1993, that the President would now be able to impose a full-blooded reform programme. To some extent, this was what happened. But the success of the communists and nationalist extremists in the parliamentary elections of December demonstrated how deep was popular disillusionment with the course proposed by the IMF. During 1994 the Chernomyrdin government pursued a policy which pushed up spending, borrowing and inflation, resulting in a collapse of the rouble in October.

Both the IMF and the Russian government now made greater efforts to agree a detailed programme of economic reform sustained by IMF financial support. The largest loan yet given to Russia – $6.8 billion – was announced on 11 April 1995. This was more than a matter of economics: it represented an investment in President Yeltsin, who faced an election in April 1996.

Mr Yeltsin won, but at what turned out to be a huge cost to himself, to Russia and to the West. First of all, he destroyed his health and could never recover his former energy and authority. Second, in order to win he made a large number of promises for extra spending which could not be afforded. Third, he had to rely on the support of Russian plutocrats whose interests lay rather in securing control over cartels in a corporatist economy than in creating a properly functioning free-market system.

For these reasons, Mr Yeltsin's second term was a serious economic disappointment. The appointment of Anatoly Chubais and Boris Nemtsov as First Deputy Prime Ministers seemed to signal an attack on the vested interests which stood in the way of change. But it was all too late. The rouble came under pressure as a result of fall-out from the East Asian financial crisis. In March 1998, in a move intended to signal a renewed drive for reform, Yeltsin appointed a new young Prime Minister, Sergei Kiriyenko, in place of Chernomyrdin. The concentration now was on measures to increase dwindling tax revenues and defend the rouble. The international market pressure on Russia continued to intensify and the IMF together with the World Bank and Japan provided $17.1 billion of new loans.

But the market would not be bucked. In August, after $4.8 billion of the loan had disappeared across the exchanges, the rouble was devalued and then floated. It lost over half its value against the dollar in just two weeks. The Russian stock market fell by 80 per cent. Some experts estimated the rate of capital flight as at least $17 billion per year.* Money poured out of Russia, doubtless much of it ours. Russians lost, perhaps permanently, faith in their own currency.

The political consequences were not slow in coming. Mr Yeltsin's authority was fatally weakened. Prime Minister Kiriyenko was dismissed and, after a delay in which Chernomyrdin's reappointment was rejected by the parliament, Yevgeny Primakov, backed by the Communists, took his place. He was joined by other throwbacks to the Soviet era.

The Primakov period, which lasted until his surprise dismissal

---

* *Washington Post*, 30 September 1998.

in favour of Sergei Stepashin in May 1999 – and then Vladimir Putin in August – was a time of stagnation. Economic reform in any meaningful sense was suspended. In Russia it was a time for political manoeuvring. In the West it was time for recrimination.*

WHY ECONOMIC REFORM HAS FAILED SO FAR

What is clear from this sketch of the tangled events of the period between the proclamation of reform at the start of Yeltsin's presidency and its effective abandonment some time before the end is that the IMF lacked the knowledge and the means to effect the major changes required to bring free-market capitalism to Russia. All they could be expected to do – and what they should have tried to do – was to support positive moves from within Russia and refrain from supporting negative ones. Having lost the only real opportunity to achieve transformation of the Russian economy by those who believed in the project, Westerners consistently overrated the prospects of half-baked reform at the hands of half-hearted reformers. The idea that a government run by Viktor Chernomyrdin, let alone by Yevgeny Primakov, could be relied upon to pursue the same objectives as Western economic liberals was laughable. Yet the rhetoric was always the same: 'reform' could only be achieved by more Western money and still greater Western forbearance.

The errors of wishful thinking were compounded by a failure to understand that the Russian economy depended upon Russian power structures. If the power structures remained inimical to reform, reform would simply not occur.

Without a proper rule of law, honest administration, sound banks and secure private property, it is not possible to create a free-market economy. President Yeltsin is often criticised for giving in to political pressures and slowing down or sidestepping the necessary appointments and measures. Perhaps someone with a less mercurial personality would indeed have made a difference.

---

* At the time of writing, Russia owes the West some $150 billion of debt, about $50 billion of this borrowed since the end of the Soviet Union.

But politicians have to find backing if they are to make changes. If Yeltsin could not gain the support he needed among an increasingly disillusioned electorate he had to find it from the powerful figures that have come to be known as the 'oligarchs'. With no previous experience of patience being rewarded, the Russian people became increasingly unwilling to go on making sacrifices.

The conditions in which most Russians live are hard indeed. They deserve better. But some of the statistics bandied about are somewhat misleading. When we hear (as we sometimes do) that the country's economic output is about half the level of a decade ago or that real incomes have fallen sharply, it is worth recalling that economic statistics under the Soviet Union were hardly more reliable than any other official statements. Moreover, a country that produces what no one wants to buy, and whose workers receive wages that they cannot use to buy goods they want, is hardly in the best of economic health. Comparisons between living standards in the last years of the Soviet system and living standards now suggest that measured by the most important criterion – what people are actually able to spend – there has been some improvement.*

Yet it has been very uneven, and there have been terrible moments. The harshest pressures, as public expenditure controls were imposed, were upon people dependent on the state for their living. There were large arrears in payments of wages and pensions and sharp falls in their value, as inflation soared. Probably the worst blow has been against savings. Nothing does more to undermine a society than when savers are impoverished, as the history of Germany's Weimar Republic shows.

But perhaps the most telling indices of misery are not economic but social – for Russia is sick, and at present it is really no exaggeration to say that it is dying. As one expert has remarked: 'No industrialised country has ever before suffered such a severe and prolonged deterioration [of public health] during peacetime.'†

---

* This point is made by Leon Aron (biographer of Boris Yeltsin) in *The Weekly Standard*, 4 October 1999, 'Is Russia Really "Lost"?'.

† Nicholas Eberstadt, 'Russia: Too Sick to Matter?', *Policy Review*, 95, June–July 1999, p.3.

Death rates in Russia are nearly 30 per cent higher than at the end of the Soviet Union – and public health was already bad in Soviet times. Deaths are now exceeding births by well over half, some seven hundred thousand a year. Life expectancy for Russian men today is about sixty-one – worse than Egypt, Indonesia or Paraguay. The main causes are extraordinarily high rates of heart disease and injuries, in which the common factor is apparently alcohol abuse. Life is simply so bad that the bottle offers the only refuge.

What makes so many ordinary Russians this depressed is, one suspects, not just frustration at their own prospects, but also anger at the way in which a minority flaunts huge wealth acquired from successful speculations, insider trading, cartels and gangsterism. The root of the trouble was that in Russia in the early 1990s, when reform was under way, there was no middle class in the European sense. Tsarist Russia never developed a substantial middle class anyway, but what there was fled or were impoverished or killed by the Bolsheviks.

Under communism no such class could emerge and 'bourgeois' values were, naturally, deplored. There were 'managers' of course. But these were just political bureaucrats, not entrepreneurs and owners. Consequently, those who found themselves with the knowledge, means and position to flourish in the early years of reform were the class of apparatchiks.

The prospering of this elite renders in the eyes of many Russians the mere notion of 'reform' suspect and its proponents odious. And though they are wrong, who can blame them?

Beneath the formalities of memoranda, declarations of intent, statistical projections and neatly typed balance sheets, a series of struggles for power have been conducted. Among the most important players have been: the bureaucracy; the armed forces, whose frustration at their penury has on occasion threatened the security of the state; the magnates, in control (directly or indirectly) of Russia's vast natural resources, particularly oil, which they bought cheaply and then obtained licences to sell at much higher international prices; and banks, which performed none of the functions of normal Western banks, but rather bought up in rigged auctions the shares of privatised companies.

In fact, a kind of economic theatre of the absurd was functioning well before the 1998 crash. Industries, which because of their inefficiency were incapable of making a profit, were kept afloat because their bosses used influence and connections to escape paying taxes to the government, gave worthless promissory notes to their creditors and often remunerated their workers in barter. The absurdities of the Soviet system were being recreated. As the joke ran in those times (referring to the fact that both industrial products and industrial wages were effectively worthless): 'We pretend to work – they pretend to pay us.' But now, as often as not, no one was paid. Such are the circumstances in which – in spite of the fact that 70 per cent of industry is notionally in private hands, that consumer prices have been deregulated and that a return to socialism is probably impossible – we have to conclude that economic reform has so far largely failed.

One of the most crushing verdicts on what has occurred is that of the economist and current adviser to President Putin, Andrei Ilarionov:

> ... [S]ince the summer of 1992, with few exceptions, the political struggle has not been over whether the government should implement more liberal or more interventionist economic policy. The real struggle has been over a different issue: who or whose team (group, gang, family) would control the state institutions and instruments that control the distribution and redistribution of economic resources ... The only distinction among the groups participating in the Russian transformation was their ability to camouflage their deeds to make them suitable for public consumption in Russia and abroad.*

The West cannot behave as if this were not the case. We have to learn from our mistakes. We have to face up to their consequences. And we have to do better.

---

* Andrei Ilarionov, 'Russia's Potemkin Capitalism', in *Global Fortune: The Stumble and Rise of World Capitalism*, ed. Ian Vásquez (Cato, 2000), pp.206–7. Such an honest appraisal from such a source offers some encouragement for Western observers of Russia's current attempts to escape her difficulties.

Developments since the crash of 1998 have provided Russia and the West with a breathing space. As one would expect after a dramatic fall in the currency, Russian goods are now cheaper and exports have soared. The economy has been growing again (by 5.4 per cent in 1999 and 8.3 per cent in 2000). The trebling of oil prices has also benefited Russia, one of the world's major oil producers, and the government is now raising US$5.5 billion annually from the energy sector.

These favourable conditions offer a new opportunity to tackle the fundamental obstacles to prosperity. As a basis for future action to shift Russia back on course towards becoming a 'normal country' I suggest the following:

- There must be no more self-deception. If the people and policies dominant in Russia at any time are opposed to real reform there should be no financial cushion provided by the West or the IMF. Such aid is worse than useless – it's doubly damaging, because it associates the cause of reform with failure
- We must keep the long-term goal in view, which is to create a real free-enterprise economy based on sound money, low taxes, limited government and above all a rule of law. Barely a start has been made on achieving these things. And while the foundations are rotten, so will be the economic edifice
- While connections, corruption, crime and cartels form the basis of the Russian system there can be no true freedom and no genuine democracy. The West must speak the truth about this openly to the Russian people
- We have to stop regarding the only people who matter as being the political and bureaucratic elite in Moscow. Russia is naturally extremely rich – with major deposits of coal, oil, gas, timber and strategic minerals. But its greatest potential wealth lies in the millions of young would-be Russian entrepreneurs. They must be helped to understand what capitalism is about – and what it is not about. Above all, perhaps, we have to be patient. Today's Russians face the Herculean task of undoing the harm done, not just by seventy years of Soviet communism but by previous centuries of autocracy. And ultimately only the Russians themselves can perform that task.

RUSSIA AS A MILITARY POWER

If almost a decade down the track from the end of Soviet communism we were now dealing in Russia with a 'normal country', that is a stable democracy with a functioning market economy, the West could afford to take a relaxed view of Russian military power, strategic interests and political intentions. Of course, even in those happy circumstances, the operation of the balance of power in Europe and possibly Asia would mean rivalries and tensions between Russia and the United States and its allies. But such problems would be more manageable and the reactions of Russia more predictable.

The worst error, as always in dealing with Russia, is naïveté. The Clinton administration initially sought to treat Russia as a 'strategic partner'. But, however important Russia remained in its own backyard, the Russians had neither the will nor the means to enter into any global partnership with the United States. Moreover, Russian Cold War rhetoric between 1995 and 1997, when it tried and failed to block NATO's expansion to take in Poland, Hungary and the Czech Republic, revealed the emptiness of any such project. This, it will be recalled, was when President Yeltsin warned: 'NATO will get as good as it gives. We have sufficient deterrent forces, including nuclear forces.'*

For as long as they could afford to do so, the Russians also frustrated Western aims in the countries of the former Yugoslavia. If Russia was supposed to be the West's partner there no one seems to have told the Kremlin. As a result of NATO's Kosovo air campaign against the Serbs in March–June 1999 Russia suspended all military contacts with NATO. But most revealing of the emotional temperature among Russia's military and political elite was the threatening language they again used. The chief of the General Staff pointed out that he supported 'the use of nuclear weapons to protect Russia's territorial integrity'. The chairman of the Defence Committee of the Duma helpfully suggested that the state's strategic concept should be amended to include the option

---

* Television interview, 17 March 1997.

'to deliver pre-emptive nuclear strikes'. Another retired general demanded Russia's withdrawal from the Intermediate Range Nuclear Forces (INF) Treaty.

The fact that the Russians acquiesced in Kosovo and eventually seem to have helped bring President Slobodan Milošević to the negotiating table reflected their weakness rather than their good will. Above all, it reflected their economic weakness, for the IMF was about to release a further tranche of $4.5 billion over eighteen months when the campaign began. Even then, the Russian generals (with or without the knowledge of President Yeltsin) sent Russian troops to seize Priština airport, for the sake of swagger, so risking with no apparent concern a major international confrontation.

Russia has for centuries grown used to compensating for its economic underdevelopment by means of its military strength. For the Soviet Union, particularly in the last decades of its existence, such an approach was the only means of remaining a superpower. Today's Russian leaders appear to have inherited something of that outlook.

But only something – for although it has over a million military personnel, and its defence spending still probably runs at over 5 per cent of GDP, the state of Russia's armed forces as a whole is pitiful.* Non-payment of wages or payment in kind has left soldiers and sailors in some areas forced to grow cabbages or to engage in black-marketeering to avoid starvation. Morale and discipline are generally bad.

This has made some Russian generals and politicians keen to maximise the effectiveness of their most sophisticated weaponry. Both President Yeltsin and President Putin have emphasised the central importance of Russia's nuclear defence. In November 1993 Russia's new military doctrine both ended the previous Soviet pledge of 'no first use' of nuclear weapons and outlined more flexible options for their use. In April 1999 President Yeltsin responded to the opening of NATO's bombing campaign against Serbia by holding a special meeting of his Security Council on the subject which he opened by stating that 'nuclear forces were and

---

* The estimated real size of Russia's defence budget is that from the IISS *Military Balance* 1999.

remain the key element in the national security strategy and Russia's military might'. Mr Putin chose to make one of his first visits as President to a centre for nuclear weapons research at which he told his audience: 'We will retain and strengthen Russia's nuclear weapons and its nuclear complex.' The symbolism and the message were clear.

Russia has been concentrating on the development of a new generation of missiles and warheads, while seeking to extend the life of existing weapons systems. The most important new programme is that of the SS-27 Topol-M Inter-Continental Ballistic Missile (ICBM). Russia's problem is that the cost of maintaining any kind of nuclear parity with the United States is likely to be prohibitive, given the rate at which Russia's existing arsenal is becoming obsolete.

President Putin was widely praised in the West for having secured the Russian Duma's endorsement of the START II treaty. He has more recently called for further substantial reductions to America's and Russia's nuclear arsenals. The driving force for these proposals is penury rather than mere goodwill. But they may well make sense all the same. For as long as Russia continues to hold a nuclear arsenal which it cannot afford properly to maintain, the rest of the world will be at risk of such weapons falling into the wrong hands or of an accidental launch. Furthermore, Russian scientists and advanced technology must if at all possible be kept in Russia to be productively redirected, not put up for sale to the highest international bidder.

Another potential worry for the West is posed by the former Soviet Union's chemical and biological weapons capability. Such weapons are notoriously difficult to detect by ordinary verification techniques. They can be easily hidden, as we know from Saddam Hussein's activities in Iraq. They can also be developed alongside or under cover of ordinary commercial, civilian processes. Three Russian officials have been reported as saying that Russia has twenty-four poison gas factories, six of which it plans to destroy and eighteen of which it has either converted or will convert to non-military uses.* Unfortunately for us, the Soviet Union's

---

* 'Undoing Chemical Arms', *International Herald Tribune*, 1 December 1999.

biological weapons programme was very closely integrated into ostensibly civil programmes of research. There are worries about how far the necessary disentanglement has gone. Above all, however, it is the possibility of such weapons developed covertly in a Russian laboratory falling into the hands of rogue states or terrorists that is the main worry.

In the end, it is probably upon the massed if uneven ranks of the Russian army that any credible projection of Russian power depends. At present Russia's armed forces are demoralised and their resources depleted. But it would not be wise to assume that this will always be so. The Russians are traditionally a martial nation. While it is most unlikely that Russia will ever again be a global superpower, it will remain a great power – too big to rest content within its own borders, too weak to impose itself far beyond them. All of which makes for troubling instability.

But the West has to cope. How?

- We must never forget that Russia has a huge arsenal of weapons of mass destruction. So some of the most important Western aid programmes are those, like the Nunn–Lugar programme aimed at ensuring proper oversight of Russia's nuclear weapons, which satisfy our own security needs. Indeed, in all our dealings with Russia, the right approach is to put our security interests always and everywhere first
- We must try to persuade Russia that its willingness to sell military technology to rogue states may well rebound against Russians – both for reasons of basic geography and in view of Russia's problems in its relations with much of the Muslim world
- Finally, we dare not take Russia for granted: the seeds of danger are often planted in the soil of disorder, as the world has learned to its cost before.

NATIONALITY PROBLEMS AND THE
'NEAR ABROAD'

Russia is a huge country that covers eleven time zones. Its border – thirteen thousand miles of it – is the longest in the world, running from Europe to Eastern Asia. This gives Russia a unique opportunity to interfere in other countries' affairs – particularly because so many of its neighbours were for so long subject to Moscow's domination.

The fact that Russia's nation-building and its territorial expansion were in tsarist times so closely interlinked means that Russia has traditionally regarded its frontiers as fluid not fixed. The Cold War stasis lent an appearance of permanence to the Soviet Union's external perimeter. But with the disintegration of the USSR into Russia and fourteen other independent states that situation ended.

Russia itself felt vulnerable, and this vulnerability explains some – though not all – of the subsequent aggressive rhetoric and man-oeuvring. Some twenty-five million ethnic Russians remained living outside the frontiers of the new Russian Federation after the winding up of the Soviet Union. For Russians this diaspora's existence is both a reason and an excuse to claim the potential right to intervene in other former Soviet republics. On the other hand, the population of the Russian Federation is far from homogeneous: almost 20 per cent of the Federation's inhabitants are non-Russian. The loyalties and aspirations of these non-Russian nationalities are among Russia's least soluble problems.

In facing up to such problems, today's Russian Federation and its neighbours find themselves once more living in the sinister shadow of the old Soviet Union. Stalin's policy towards the peoples of the USSR was a mixture of calculation and spite. Altogether he uprooted some two million non-Russians, about a third of whom died directly or indirectly as a result, and deported them to Central Asia and Siberia. There was also a planned movement of Russians in the other direction, out of the Russian heartlands, to take up industrial and other jobs in far-flung but important parts of the Soviet Union. These Russian minorities enjoyed a (relatively) privileged existence. Indeed, a policy of promoting

Russian interests against those of other nationalities, while trying to avoid any upsurge of 'bourgeois' Russian nationalism, was an important part of Moscow's policy towards the Soviet Empire.

Of course, it failed, and long before the end anyone outside the Kremlin knew it. Surely one of the most memorably stupid pronouncements of any Soviet leader was Leonid Brezhnev's of 1972 on the fiftieth anniversary of the formation of the USSR: 'The national question, as it came down to us from the past,' affirmed Brezhnev, 'has been settled completely, finally, and for good.'* Within twenty years nationalism would have helped abolish the Soviet Union 'completely, finally, and for good'. It remains to be seen whether it will do the same for the Russian Federation.

Against such a background, it is not surprising that ethnic and national suspicions are easily generated. In the years after the end of the Soviet Union a series of crises erupted in the territories of the Russian Federation and its neighbours. The common factors were threefold: Russia's concern for the Russian minorities in what it called, in a phrase with alarming overtones, the 'Near Abroad'; Russia's attempts to use the Commonwealth of Independent States (CIS) as a means of re-integrating the former Soviet republics into a Russian-led confederation; and Russia's struggle to control its own nationalities and their subordinate republics and regions.

Each region has had its own distinctive features. In some areas stability has returned. In others the outlook is uncertain. And in some of the latter the implications for the West are important.

Western countries have naturally been most concerned with events on Europe's – and now NATO's – eastern flank. The fate of the Baltic states was immediately bound up with that of the Soviet Union. One of the most reassuring acts of the new regime of Boris Yeltsin was his statesmanlike acceptance that Estonia, Latvia and Lithuania – which had only been snatched by the Soviet Union by force and fraud under the Molotov–Ribbentrop Pact in 1940 – had the right to be independent sovereign states. The

---

* Quoted by Hugh Seton-Watson – another much lamented source of wise instruction for me and others – in his essay 'Russian Nationalism in Historical Perspective', in *The Last Empire*, ed. Robert Conquest (Hoover Institution, 1986), p.25.

difficulties which subsequently arose about the Russian minorities – particularly in Estonia and Latvia where they represented about 30 per cent of the populations – were a direct result of the previous Soviet policy of swamping the local population with Russians. Naturally, the Estonians and Latvians were determined to restore control of their countries and their culture, which left Russians disadvantaged. Tensions are real and could still become extremely dangerous.

Left to themselves, the Baltic states will increasingly gravitate away from Moscow and towards their Scandinavian neighbours. These highly advanced, extremely talented and profoundly European peoples see themselves as part of the West and want closer integration with it. Russia has no right to stand in their way. Post-imperial hangovers affect all former great powers and are also a headache for their neighbours. It is perfectly understandable that Russia is concerned to secure decent treatment for its Russian minorities in the Baltic states. But it cannot expect to determine their potential orientation.

For our part, Western countries have to make this clear to Moscow, so as to reduce any Russian temptation to bully. The best way to do this will be to take the Baltic states into NATO. The timing, though, is important. We should always aim to inform the Russians of our intentions well in advance and try to reassure them that our actions pose no threat to Moscow's interests. President George W. Bush was, therefore, right to signal very clearly before he went to Slovenia for his first meeting with President Putin that he believed that the Baltics must indeed be brought within NATO.* It will be necessary to reiterate this at some point, so that Moscow is not misled into thinking that its cooperation in the war against terrorism has won for it a veto on NATO's expansion. But when we do take the final step, bringing the Baltics or indeed any other state within the Alliance, we should know what we mean and mean what we say – for, let us never forget, NATO membership is not merely symbolic. It implies that we would fight to preserve the territorial integrity of each and every member state.

---

* Speech to Warsaw University, 15 June 2001.

Equally important from the viewpoint of Western interests is the future of Ukraine. There was rather more excuse for the Russians to begrudge Ukraine its independence than the Baltics. Kiev was, after all, from the ninth to the twelfth centuries the centre of Kievan Rus, the predecessor of the Russian state. Large numbers of Russians still regard Ukraine as part of Russia. Mainly Orthodox Eastern Ukraine feels closer to Russia than does the fiercely independent west, which is predominantly Uniate. Potentially serious disputes between the new Ukrainian state and Russia existed as regards the fate of the Black Sea fleet and the future of Crimea. The fact that in the first years after independence Ukraine made even less progress along the path of economic reform than its Russian neighbour also raised questions about the country's prospects and indeed viability.

The government of President Kuchma, whatever its other shortcomings, in fact managed to resolve most of Ukraine's outstanding problems with Russia. A Ukraine is emerging which recognises its historic ties with its eastern neighbour, but which also looks to the West. Ukraine is large enough – with fifty-one million people – and potentially wealthy enough – its soil is rich, though its economy is in terrible shape – to be a pivotal country in Eastern Europe. It is thus also important to us in the West. Ukraine is not to be treated as falling within a Russian 'sphere of influence'. Rather, a strong Ukraine will act as a buffer between Russia and NATO. That would also probably be good for both parties.

In order to plot a path of independence, while seeking to resolve disputes as amicably as possible, Ukraine has vigorously resisted Russian attempts to turn the CIS into a pale imitation of the Soviet Union.* At the other extreme, Belarus's President Lukashenko has consistently sought to reunite his autocratically ruled state with Russia in a new political, military and economic union.

Most of the other former Soviet republics have pursued a path somewhere between the two, often altering course according to the requirements of the moment. The five Central Asian Republics

---

* The CIS was established between eleven former Soviet republics on 21 December 1991.

were all initially keen to join the CIS. None of them had been used to controlling their own affairs, which had been planned from Moscow, and their economies were still heavily dependent on links with Russia. But as the years have passed, other developments have affected their orientation – developments which are of some importance to the West.

First, the ethnic identity of the peoples of Central Asia has assumed greater significance. Four of the five states' populations – the majorities in Kazakhstan, Kyrgyzstan, Turkmenistan and Uzbekistan – share a common ethnic origin with the Turks. Although Turkey does not share a border with these states, it is active in the region and its influence as a prosperous, powerful, Westernised state is likely to grow.

Second, in the aftermath of the collapse of communism Islam has assumed much greater importance. It provides a rallying cry against corruption and abuses of power in Central Asia as elsewhere.

Third, partly in response to these perceived challenges – ethnic tension affecting local Russian populations, the influence of outside powers, above all the growth of Islamic militancy – Russia has reacted forcefully. There were thousands of Russian troops deployed in the Central Asian Republics long before the region became strategically crucial to America's campaign against the Taliban. Moscow provided strong support to the Tajik government in its war with Islamic forces. It stations seventeen thousand Russian troops on the border. Russia also backed Kyrgyzstan with military aid in 1999, and has 2500 troops there. Fifteen thousand more are based in Turkmenistan.

In June 2001 the Moscow-led reaction to Islamic insurgency took what now appears a significant step further. Russia, China and the four Central Asian states of Kazakhstan, Kyrgyzstan, Tajikistan and Uzbekistan agreed a security cooperation treaty in Shanghai. It was explicitly aimed at resisting Taliban-sponsored terrorism across frontiers.*

Three months later, in the wake of the attacks on New York and

---

* It also reflected both Russian regional ambitions and Russia's desire to achieve a new strategic relationship with China. On Sino–Russian relations, see p.26.

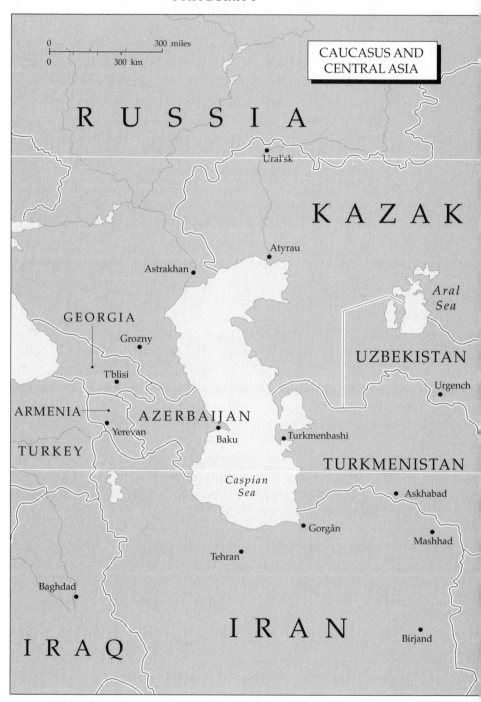

CAUCASUS AND
CENTRAL ASIA

0   300 miles
0   300 km

RUSSIA

Ural'sk

KAZAK

Atyrau

Astrakhan

Aral
Sea

GEORGIA

Grozny

UZBEKISTAN

T'blisi

Urgench

ARMENIA

AZERBAIJAN

Yerevan

Baku

Turkmenbashi

TURKEY

TURKMENISTAN

Caspian
Sea

Askhabad

Gorgân

Mashhad

Tehran

Baghdad

IRAN

Birjand

IRAQ

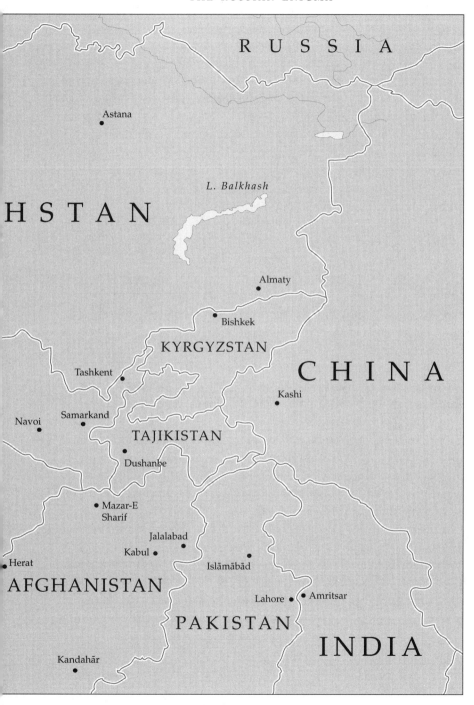

Washington, the Central Asia region acquired a sharply increased significance. In order to launch campaigns against al-Qaeda and the Taliban, while seeking to minimise potentially destabilising operations from Pakistan, the US sought the cooperation of the states bordering Afghanistan to the north. The governments of Uzbekistan and Tajikistan agreed, the former with particular enthusiasm, to welcome US bases. Kazakhstan also allowed the US to use its air space. The Uzbeks and Tajiks had their own special reasons to cooperate against the Taliban. But, as the dominant power in the region, it was Russia's support for US aims that was crucial in overcoming local fears and hesitations. (I shall examine later the implications of this for US–Russian relations in the longer term.)

Central Asia is also of strategic importance for economic reasons. It possesses great reserves of oil, natural gas, gold, silver, uranium and other valuable natural resources. Oil and gas, though, are the most important. It has been estimated that Kazakhstan and Turkmenistan together with Azerbaijan have oil reserves larger than those of Iran and Iraq. The known gas reserves of Turkmenistan alone are twice as large as those of the North Sea. Kazakhstan's Tengiz oilfield is one of the world's biggest. And by some accounts its Kashagan field, discovered in early 2001, is bigger still.

Oil and gas are equally crucial to the affairs of that ethnic tinderbox, the Caucasus – not just because of Azerbaijan's reserves but because of the need for pipelines to exploit the fabulous energy wealth of the whole Caspian region. Russia is determined to maintain control over this oil and has engaged in this new 'Great Game' as vigorously as it did the old. It has sought to ensure that Azerbaijan and the Central Asian Republics use Russian oil- and gas-pipelines from the Caspian to its Black Sea port of Novorossiysk.* Russia has shown in recent years that it can cause a great deal of trouble in pursuit of its perceived interests. In a region where convoluted conspiracies and counter-intuitive theories

---

* Alternative – as yet undeveloped – routes are: (a) an east–west route from Baku via Georgia to Ceyhan (Turkey), favoured by the US; (b) a route to Iran; (c) a route to China.

thrive one should be careful about ascribing particular actions to particular actors. But it seems clear that Russia backed the overthrow of the first post-Soviet President of Georgia, Zviad Gamsakhurdia, in January 1992; and that it then supported a separatist revolt in Abkhazia in order to drive Georgia into the CIS, where it could keep it under firmer control. Similarly, in Azerbaijan in 1993 the upright, pro-Western democrat President Abulfaz Elchibey, who wanted to agree with a Western consortium a contract for the exploitation of Azeri oil – thus excluding the Russians – was immediately put under huge Russian pressure. Russia cut off Azerbaijan's oil exports and used Armenia to increase the long-standing difficulties over Nagorno-Karabakh. Finally, when all else failed, Mr Elchibey was dislodged in a coup and the former Soviet Politburo member Haidar Aliev was installed in his place. And when Mr Aliev proved more recalcitrant than the Russians expected they backed two attempted coups against him.

The past results of Russian policy are easy to see, and they have been wholly destructive. Georgia, Azerbaijan and Armenia remain in a state of disorder, corruption and political decay. And the vast wealth of the Caspian is still not being properly used. The West has to try to ensure that law-based, stable states are developed in the region; that customers for oil and gas are not deprived of a vital alternative source to those of the Middle East; and that there is a sensible accommodation with Russian interests. For its part, Russia will need to accept that although both Central Asia and the Caucasus fall within its traditional sphere of interest, that sphere cannot be exclusive if these regions are to prosper. And it is in Russia's own interest that they should.

Coping with tensions in the Northern Caucasus is a still more difficult matter, for of course the region actually lies within the frontiers of the Russian Federation. The non-Russian peoples there have endured a miserable history, and they can hardly be expected to thank Russia for it. That is especially true of Chechnya.

In Stalin's deportation of 1944 some two hundred thousand Chechens lost their lives. When the USSR collapsed and the 'sovereign' republics of the Southern Caucasus escaped, the Chechens like the other non-Russian peoples who found themselves in the new Russian Federation were denied their freedom. They rebelled and declared independence.

In 1994 the Russians moved to repress the revolt. The Kremlin and the Russian armed forces were determined to demonstrate to other ethnic groups tempted to break away that their action would not be tolerated. The Russian campaign was also motivated by the desire to keep control of the vital oil pipeline which ran through Chechnya. As is well-known, this first campaign led to disaster from which only the charisma and negotiating skills of General Alexandr Lebed extracted the humiliated Russian forces.

Russia's second campaign against Chechnya in 1999 had similar motives. But it was far better prepared, the number of Russian troops involved was much larger, and – measured against the objective of crushing Chechnya – it was quickly successful. It was clearly intended as a showcase for Russia's military might. Even the well-documented brutality against civilians was intended to teach Russia's enemies a lesson. The message was that in spite of the West's edging Russia aside in Eastern Europe, in the Middle East and in the Balkans, Moscow was in charge of its own backyard.

The second Chechen campaign was waged with the enthusiastic support of the Russian people – and this is highly significant.* Of course, it is possible to argue that Russians were given a one-sided view of the conflict by their media. And it is certainly true that the Chechens played into Russian hands when its Islamic fanatics broke into neighbouring Russian Dagestan. But what aroused Russian nationalism was desire for revenge after a series of bombs in the late summer of 1999 left over three hundred Muscovites dead.

To this day no convincing evidence of Chechen involvement has been produced. But the Chechen campaign turned an almost unknown Prime Minister Putin into an overwhelmingly popular President Putin in the space of eight months. It also left a city desolate, thousands of civilians dead and a tide of pitiful homeless, hopeless refugees.

Russia's treatment of Chechnya has been inexcusable. But it is

---

* Opinion polls conducted during the later conflict recorded between 55 and 69 per cent support, compared with just 20 per cent during the earlier one.

not inexplicable, especially given the fact that – whoever planted the bombs in 1999 – the Chechens have, over the last three years, become increasingly involved in terrorism. Ominous developments have been hijackings, suicide bombings, attacks on civilian installations and growing ties with Islamic terrorists, including Osama bin Laden. None of this, though, provides a justification for Russia's refusal to respect the wishes and interests of the Chechen population. Most Chechens are far from being Islamic fanatics: it is national, not religious, grievances that matter most to them. Before 11 September the Russian people had started again to be weary of the brutal campaigns aimed at crushing Chechen resistance. Prosecution of the wider war against terrorism must not now become an excuse for the Russian authorities to renew their attempts to wipe out the Chechen nation. Otherwise Moscow will become the terrorists' main recruiting sergeant in the Caucasus.

- We have to speak the truth clearly about Russia's behaviour: in Chechnya it has been unacceptable
- We must make it clear that, while respecting the interests of a great power, we reject any right for Moscow to destabilise other countries of the former Soviet Union
- The Baltic states should be brought into NATO, as they desire, at the right time
- The West has important interests at stake in Ukraine (which borders NATO) and in the Central Asian and South Caucasian republics (which contain huge reserves of oil and gas which both we and Russia need to have developed); all these states should receive our attention and support – political, technical and economic
- We must continue to cooperate with Russia in resisting Islamist extremism in Central Asia.

DOING BUSINESS WITH MR PUTIN?

President Putin's personality and background have been the subject of a large amount of speculation and debate ever since it appeared certain that he would be master of the Kremlin. We know the basic facts; the difficulty is to be sure of what to make of them. Vladimir Putin fulfilled his childhood dream of joining the KGB, the Soviet secret police, in 1975 at the age of twenty-two. He spent the late 1980s working alongside the East German secret police, the Stasi, among other things spying on NATO (as he disclosed in a book-length interview in March 2000). In the early 1990s he returned to his native St Petersburg, first to work at the university and then joining the administration of the late Anatoly Sobchak, the reformist but allegedly corrupt mayor of St Petersburg. In 1996 Mr Putin was brought to Moscow to be Deputy Chief Administrator in the Kremlin. In 1998 he was appointed head of the Federal Security Bureau (FSB), the KGB's successor. He then moved from Secretary of the President's Security Council to become Prime Minister in August 1999, succeeding Mr Yeltsin the following March.

All of which tells us practically nothing; indeed, given Mr Putin's background in a profession where deceit and disinformation are all it may be less than nothing. It is always important in matters of high politics to know what you do not know. Those who think they know, but are mistaken, and act upon their mistakes, are the most dangerous people to have in charge.

Britain's current Prime Minister certainly felt no inhibitions about pronouncing judgement on Mr Putin. He enthusiastically described the then Acting President as a 'moderniser' and offered to allow him to benefit from the expertise of the Downing Street Policy Unit. Mr Blair stated as well that Mr Putin 'believes in a Russia which is ordered and strong but also democratic and liberal'.

A good deal of this was wishful thinking. Western leaders looked forward to dealing with a Russian leader who was healthy, sober, predictable and presentable. And they therefore hoped against hope that they were also dealing with a reforming democrat. It was, indeed, possible that such a person might have emerged from the stable of the KGB. But it was equally possible, and perhaps more probable, that Vladimir Putin was closer to the model of that other ex-KGB chief who became President, Yuri Andropov – hailed by the West at the time as a pro-Western liberal because he liked jazz and drank Scotch, ignoring the fact that he had also been a central figure in the brutal suppression of Hungarian freedom in 1956. Shortly before his election, Mr Putin solemnly unveiled a plaque to Andropov in the KGB's old Lubyanka headquarters. That was not, all things considered, a reassuring sign.

Since then a clearer, though far from unambiguous, picture of Mr Putin's presidency has been emerging. Its central approach is to create a strong state so as to restore order. For all its ominous overtones, that is what Mr Putin means by his oft-repeated phrase a 'dictatorship of law'. His view, like that of probably most Russians, is that the Gorbachev and Yeltsin years saw authority drained away from central institutions to the benefit of different selfish interests, such as financial oligarchs, the mafia and regional bosses. In the chaos and corruption that have followed, the Russian people have lost out and Russia itself has been humiliated. Thus populism and patriotism have provided the main themes of Mr Putin's campaigns. And he has been remarkably successful, winning a mandate of 53 per cent of the electorate and continuing – as of now – to enjoy widespread support.

In some respects, that is a programme with much to recommend it. Freedom without order is, indeed, mere anarchy. While Russia's society, economy and politics are heavily criminalised there is no prospect for lasting recovery. Government everywhere does need to be strong in carrying out its essential tasks, and particularly so when the obstacles are as formidable as in Russia.

But government in a free society must also be limited in size and scope; it must not intrude into those aspects of life which are by rights private; and, above all, it must uphold and abide by, not undermine or override, the law. The call for 'strong' measures and 'strong' men is often an all too well-known preliminary to some kind of dictatorship.

How does Mr Putin's programme measure up to this? Perhaps the most obvious feature of his analysis is its realism. He does seem to understand that Russia is in dire straits and that more of the same – whether the 'same' is communism or mafia-controlled quasi-capitalism – is not a viable option. In his State of the Nation Address to the Russian Federal Assembly in July 2000 he spoke in sombre tones about the country's parlous state – its demographic decline which (he said) 'threatened the nation's survival', the fact that the recent spurt of economic growth was unsustainable while structures were unreformed, and that 'a considerable segment' of that economy was in the hands of the criminal underworld. Mr Putin set out a programme of free-market reforms in language which sounds convincing – calling for lower taxes, less government interference and more competition. And some of this programme has since been implemented. The President has surrounded himself with at least some people who genuinely understand and believe in that programme.* Above all, he appears to have grasped that reform programmes are not simply a means of extorting fresh loans from gullible Westerners. He sees policies for economic revival as vital to prevent Russia being for ever under the thumb of non-Russians. This too makes sense. National pride has to be mobilised behind tough economic measures if they are to be given time to work – as we showed in Britain in the early eighties.

I sympathise too with the Russian President's desire to create efficient administrative and security structures. Russia is a huge country which is not easy to rule. It is probably necessary to reinforce central control in some areas in order to stamp out corruption. My Russian friends talk of the need to 'nationalise' the Kremlin once more after years during which it was 'privatised' to the benefit of various powerful interests. And it is only natural that when embarking upon such a programme one should want to rely on 'new men' chosen from among one's own friends and confidants. That is how politics works – particularly in the political jungle.

But, with all that said, I can also understand the worries of those – at present, it seems, a small minority – in Russia who are genuinely worried by some of Mr Putin's decisions – such as, to clip the wings of elected regional governors, to appoint his own associates with FSB backgrounds to key positions, and to clamp down on critical independent media. Are we seeing the restoration of authority or the beginnings of authoritarianism? The jury is still out.

---

* For example, his chief economic adviser, Mr Ilarionov, whom I quoted earlier: see p.87.

What matters most to non-Russians, however, is President Putin's approach to foreign relations. And again the signs are mixed. In some respects, Russia's attitudes have suggested continuity with those of the old Soviet Union.

Russia has shown itself determined to counter American global pre-eminence. To this end, it has sought to use the issue of ballistic missile defence and adherence to the ABM treaty to split Europe from America – with, it should be added, a good deal of help from the French and German governments. Russia has also been trying to build a broad 'strategic partnership' with China against the West.

In truth, these features of Russian foreign policy have never made any long-term sense, even for Russia. Mr Putin and his advisers must know that neither Moscow nor Beijing – nor even a combination of the two – can hope to compete in great-power politics with America. He must know that he will continue to need America's help, or at least forbearance, as he tries to restore his country's economy. He might also reflect that Russia could have to call upon the United States to use its planned ballistic missile defence system to bring down a missile aimed by an Islamic terrorist group or a rogue state at a Russian city.

Russia's plans to create a strategic partnership with China to combat American influence are also flawed. Some 300,000 Chinese now live in the Russian Far East (if migration continues at the current rate, that population could reach ten million in fifty years' time). Seven and a half million Russians face three hundred million Chinese across the border. Someone will eventually develop and exploit the natural riches of Russia's Far East: but will it be the Russians, or the Chinese? It would be more sensible to settle, once and for all, Russia's old territorial disputes with Japan, and then welcome in Japanese capital. That is certainly a more prudent course than accepting the region's economic dependency on China.*

There is, however, another side to Mr Putin's policies – one

---

* Since the Second World War Japan and the Soviet Union/Russia have been in dispute over possession of the four southernmost Kurile Islands lying between the Kamchatka Peninsula and Hokkaido.

which has dominated Western perceptions of Russia in the wake of the terrorist attacks of 11 September. The Russian President's reaction to these events was at once humane and shrewd. There is no reason to believe that his expressions of sympathy and his close *rapport* with President Bush in America's time of trial were anything other than sincere. But it is equally important to note that Russia has its own strong reasons for wanting the United States to adopt as its dominant goal over the next few years prosecution of the war against terrorism. Russian influence in Central Asia and the Caucasus and its hold on Chechnya will all be boosted by what has occurred. To be able to portray its opponents as Islamist extremists and terrorists is a propaganda weapon which Russia will be keen to seize.

Russia will also hope to gain other advantages. It may hope to extract larger concessions for eventually acquiescing in US missile defence plans. It will almost certainly expect more economic aid. It may demand early entry into the WTO.

Yet perhaps the thorniest issue will turn out to be Russia's relationship with NATO. As a clear-sighted pragmatist, Mr Putin will have noted that NATO is now as near a world policeman as exists, and that no other candidate can replace it. Hitherto, in large part as a result of lingering Cold War attitudes, Russia has sought whenever possible to prevent NATO's expansion, particularly since that expansion brings it ever closer to Russia's own borders. But from remarks he himself has made and from other signs emanating from Moscow, it seems increasingly likely that President Putin would like to see Russia itself as a NATO member.

It is easy to see why this might at first sight appear attractive to the West as well. What better way to seal the victory of freedom in the Cold War than to welcome our old adversary within our ranks? And in view of the dangers from Islamic extremism, and perhaps in the longer term from China, might it not make sense to turn Russia away from the East, bring it into Europe, and add to NATO another major power on whose resources we could draw?

The fact that such a prospect is even imaginable demonstrates how profoundly the world has changed since the Cold War. But what is imaginable is not necessarily desirable. It is, of course, true that Russia is not our enemy. It is not engaged in an ideological struggle with us. It is not in a position to embark upon a global struggle of any kind. So there is no reason in principle why Russia should not join. In practice, though, there are several reasons.

First, although Russia is not communist, nor likely to become so, it is certainly not yet a 'normal country'. Its internal problems are unresolved, and it is possible to imagine any one of these leading to dangerous instability, possibly involving other neighbouring states. It is easy to see how this could present the rest of NATO with irresolvable dilemmas.

Second, although Russia may over a number of years eventually become a stable, prosperous, liberal democracy, it is not going to change its identity. And that identity will always be Asian as well as European, Eastern as well as Western. These are immutable facts of geography, ethnicity, culture, religion and ultimately national interest. If NATO is to have any underlying coherence it must, in at least its core, be 'Western'. Russia can never be simply that.

Third, NATO today is already a sprawling alliance, comprising nineteen members. But it is effective because America leads. Anything which undermines that leadership weakens NATO. That is why, for example, the idea of a European army contains so many risks.* But bringing Russia within NATO would be even more dangerous. Russia will never willingly accept American dominance. Within NATO it would be in a position to obstruct, and it would quickly seek and doubtless find European collaborators in its objectives. Acknowledgement of these objections probably explains why President Putin has talked about NATO becoming a 'political' (as opposed to a primarily military) organisation. But NATO is first and last an alliance. And it must remain so if it is to be effective.

Yet, whatever one thinks of Russia's longer-term aims and ambitions, it is hard not to be impressed with the qualities which Mr Putin has shown. He is providing his country with strong, vigorous leadership after years of disorder and disarray. He is also clearly able to assess international events and to respond to them

---

* See pp.354–8.

boldly, shrewdly and effectively. It is not necessary to ascribe to him a tender conscience, nor the liberal instincts of a democrat, in order to appreciate his worth as a leader with whom the West can deal.

CHAPTER 4

Asian Values

PART I: WHY ASIA MATTERS

Asia is the largest continent, comprising a third of all dry land, and containing more than half the world's population. Its importance is growing and will, I am sure, continue to grow. And that conviction has been reinforced by every one of the thirty-three visits I have made to thirteen Asian countries since leaving office.

Westerners have a habit of getting it wrong about Asia. Its distance, size and what I can only call 'otherness' intrigue, mystify and sometimes frighten us. We are inclined to exaggerate. Thus in the late 1980s and early 1990s there was much fevered talk about the twenty-first century being the 'Asian' or the 'Asia Pacific' century – an era in which the focus of world events and the centre of world power would radically shift from West to East. For example, the distinguished historian Paul Kennedy wrote in 1988 that 'the task facing American statesmen over the next decade . . . is a need to manage affairs so that the relative erosion of the United States' position takes place slowly and smoothly'.* At the same time, in response to Asian economic advance, Western protectionism found new and extremely sophisticated advocates – such as the late Sir James Goldsmith.† In the United States the call to resist the inroads of Asian economic power was taken up

---

* Paul Kennedy, *The Rise and Fall of the Great Powers* (London: Fontana Press, 1988), p.690.
† James Goldsmith, *The Trap* (London: Macmillan, 1994).

by former presidential candidate Patrick Buchanan and others. In Europe a new impulse was given to federalism by those who envisaged a world of competing trade- and power-blocs, one or perhaps two of which would be Asian.

The subsequent crisis which affected most of the Far East's 'tiger' economies and the continuing problems affecting the mighty economy of Japan put paid to some of that hyperbole and hysteria. Indeed, alongside alarm at the global economic implication of this contagious bout of Asian economic 'flu there could be detected a certain *Schadenfreude*: many Westerners felt that Asia's problems vindicated their own system and outlook.

But simply because the rhetoric about an Asian century was exaggerated does not mean that Asia's advance has been halted. Indeed, the underlying realities all confirm that Asia matters – and it matters to the West. To see that this is so we need only consider the following.

First, Asia's population (as a whole) is growing while the West's (as a whole) is stagnating. By the year 2050, it is projected that Asia's population will increase to 5.2 billion out of a total global population of 8.9 billion.* Asian countries have pursued policies to try to limit population growth with varying success and with varying degrees of coercion, and will doubtless continue to do so. But in a global economy with mobile capital and technology, and given the right framework of laws and regulation, large populations mean large workforces and growing markets. Expanding Asian nations will be increasingly important for us, both as customers and as competitors.

Second, Asia contains three – and possibly four – emerging powers on whose fortunes and intentions much depends. China, a major regional power with vast economic potential and uncertain ambitions, represents an increasingly important global player in the greatest game. Japan, still the world's second largest economy, is deciding how in the long term it intends to protect and project its strategic interests. India, like China a vast country of more than a billion people, is the world's largest democracy and now

---

* *World Population 1998*, United Nations Department of Economic and Social Affairs, Population Division.

an established nuclear power. Indonesia, for all its continuing traumas, is the world's largest Muslim state: its direction will have a significant impact on Islam as a political force.

Third, although generalisation inevitably means oversimplification, Asian – particularly East Asian – values, habits and attitudes will have a continuing and increasing impact on us in various ways. Asian immigration to the West is the most obvious of these. But, most important, Asian cultural distinctness will be crucial in shaping the economic and political development of the Asian states with which we have to deal.

'Asian values' are, needless to say, a thorny subject. Westerners have over the years created images and stereotypes that caricatured

and offended Asians. One Asian commentator has, for example, recently argued that 'the most painful thing that happened to Asia was not the physical but the mental colonisation', adding that 'this mental colonisation has not been completely eradicated in Asia, and many Asian societies are still struggling to break free of it'.*

But the recent proponents of the notion that Asians are different – and that this explains why their economies and societies are more successful – have themselves been Asians. For example, Lee Kuan Yew, the former Prime Minister of Singapore, has stated: 'We [Asians] have different social values. These different values have made for fast growth.'† Again, according to Dr Mahathir Mohamad, Prime Minister of Malaysia, 'Asian values are actually universal values and Western people used to practise the same values.'‡

We ought to ignore the element of special pleading in all this. 'Asian values' do not provide an excuse for abuses of human rights. One would hope that the unacceptable treatment of the Burmese opposition leader, Aung San Suu Kyi, has silenced all but the most shameless proponents of Asian autocracy as a legitimate alternative. But the importance of culture as a component of economic success and as an influence on social and political institutions *is* a reality nonetheless.

Well-known characteristic features of Asian – particularly East Asian – societies that are important here are the strength of family ties, a sense of responsibility and the disposition to save and to act with prudence. As Francis Fukuyama has pointed out:

Many modern Asian societies have followed a completely different evolutionary path from Europe and North America. Beginning approximately in the mid-1960s, virtually every country in the industrialised West experienced a rapid increase in crime rates and a breakdown in the nuclear family. The only two countries in

---

* Kishore Mahbubani, 'Can Asians Think?', *The National Interest*, Summer 1998.
† *Time Asia*, 16 March 1998.
‡ *New Straits Times*, 4 September 1997.

the Organization for Economic Cooperation and Development not experiencing this disruption were the Asian ones, Japan and Korea ... similarly with the countries of South-East Asia.*

A number of Asian countries have drawn on these social characteristics to create successful economies, keeping the size and cost of government down by limiting welfare spending and excessive regulation. These policies, which minimise welfare dependency, should in turn reinforce the social and cultural values which have helped Asian economies to flourish.

I believe that this will remain particularly true of countries that have a majority or a significant minority of Chinese. Wherever they go, even when they are living under the ramshackle quasi-socialism of mainland China, they show the same qualities of enterprise and self-reliance.† And given the right economic framework, nothing is beyond them. Just consider Singapore.

PART II: THE TIGERS

SINGAPORE – A MAN-MADE MIRACLE

It is often the case that large truths are best elicited through miniatures. And in the case of South-East Asia that immediately leads us to focus on the remarkable reality of tiny Singapore.

Singapore is one of the world's smallest states, less than 250 square miles, consisting of one island and fifty-nine islets. It has naturally poor soil, lacks significant mineral resources, and it even has to bring in its water. Yet today it is one of the most commercially vibrant places on earth. It is the world's busiest port. Although it has to import all its raw materials, it is a major manufacturing centre – chemicals, pharmaceuticals, electronics, clothing, plastics, refined petroleum and petroleum products. Between 1966 and 1990 its economy grew by an average of 8.5 per cent. In short, Singapore is the hub of South-East Asia, itself one of the

---

* Francis Fukuyama, 'Asian Values and the Asian Crisis', *Commentary*, February 1998.
† I discuss China itself in the next chapter.

world's most dynamic economic regions. And Singapore's population of four million now enjoys an income per head higher than that of the United Kingdom, Germany or France.

Singapore, as we see it today, can be said to have had two founders. The first was the British colonial administrator Sir Thomas Raffles, who established the city in 1819 as a trading centre, uniquely placed at the passage between the South China Sea and the Indian Ocean. The British East India Company subsequently developed and exploited the port. Under British rule, the present population of immigrants of Chinese, Malay and Indian extraction grew up, with the Chinese in an increasing majority. The British did not exactly enhance their reputation in Singapore during the Second World War. But by the time we left, we had provided the inhabitants with the precious legacy of a rule of law, honest administration and a spirit of ethnic tolerance.

The second founder of Singapore was Lee Kuan Yew. To call him such is no exaggeration. Mr Lee almost single-handedly built up Singapore into one of the most astonishing economic success stories of our times, and he did so in the face of constant threats to his tiny state's security and indeed existence.* He was faced from the start with communist subversion and obstruction. Then in 1965, when Singapore was effectively forced out of Malaysia amid much acrimony, it seemed to many that its prospects were bleak. But in truth they were just about to shine. Lee Kuan Yew did not just pilot Singapore to prosperity, he became the most trenchant, convincing and courageous opponent of left-wing Third World nonsense in the Commonwealth. During the years when his and my terms as Prime Ministers coincided I saw time and again at first hand how much influence the leader of a tiny state may wield, if he has the wit and wisdom to do so.

Mr Lee and I do not agree about everything. He is nowadays more inclined to think well of communist China than I am. I also suspect that I might draw my own preferred line between freedom and order a little closer to the former than would he. But he is undoubtedly one of the twentieth century's most accomplished practitioners of statecraft.

Singapore's success, though, teaches lessons that go beyond politics or even economics. In a certain sense, this little city-state now has everything precisely because it began with next to nothing. Only the skill, creativity and enterprise of men could make it what it has become. It is when talented people – and no group is more talented than the Chinese who make up 80 per cent of Singaporeans – find themselves having to rely on their brains rather than their muscles, that societies progress. And it is when they are given the right framework for enterprise that such progress becomes an ever-accelerating advance.

---

* See the detailed account in Lee Kuan Yew's excellent and absorbing memoirs, *The Singapore Story* (Singapore: Simon and Schuster, 1998), and *From Third World to First* (New York: HarperCollins, 2000).

De Tocqueville expressed this thought in a passage which I particularly like:

> Do you want to test whether a people is given to industry and commerce? Do not sound its ports, or examine the wood from its forests, or the produce of its soil. The spirit of trade will get all these things, and without it, they are useless. Examine whether this people's law gives men the courage to seek prosperity, freedom to follow it up, the sense and habits to find it, and the assurance of reaping the benefit.*

So this insight is not new; it was merely for a while forgotten. Singapore's example should prevent that ever happening again, at least in Asia.

Singapore's success shows us that:

- **A country's wealth need not depend on natural resources, it may even ultimately benefit from their absence**
- **The greatest resource of all is Man**
- **What government has to do is to set the framework for human talent to flourish.**

ECONOMIC CRISES AND PROSPECTS

Singapore weathered the economic storm of the late nineties quite well. Its banks were solvent and well-regulated, its businesses were genuinely profitable, and its administration was honest – none of which was the case in the Asian countries which suffered most.

---

* Alexis de Tocqueville, *Journeys to England and Ireland* (London: Faber and Faber, 1958).

ASIAN FINANCIAL CRISIS, 1997–98
Chronology of Key Events *

1997

- 2 July: After intense currency speculation, Thailand's currency (the baht) is floated, dropping 20 per cent in value
- 24 July: The Indonesian rupiah, the Malaysian ringgit, the Thai baht and the Philippine peso slump
- 5 August: The IMF and Asian nations launch $17.2 billion loan package to rescue the Thai economy
- 14 August: The rupiah plunges in value after government controls removed
- 20 September: The ringgit falls to twenty-six-year low
- 19–23 October: The Hong Kong Hang Seng stock index loses nearly a quarter of its value, its greatest ever loss
- 31 October: IMF announces $40 billion aid package for Indonesia
- 24 November: Yamaichi Securities Co. collapses in Japan, the single biggest business failure in the country since 1945
- 3 December: IMF agrees to $57 billion bailout package for South Korea, the biggest in history

1998

- 15 January: Indonesia accepts IMF reform programme
- 14–15 May: Widespread riots rock the centre of Jakarta, resulting in over a thousand deaths
- 21 May: Indonesian President Suharto resigns
- 12 June: Japan announces that it has fallen into recession for the first time in twenty-three years
- 12 July: Japanese Prime Minister Ryutaro Hashimoto resigns; Malaysia announces that its economy is sinking into recession
- 1 September: Malaysian Prime Minister Mahathir imposes stringent currency controls
- 24 September: Tokyo's Nikkei index hits twelve-year low

---

* Sources: *Washington Times*, 22 December 1998; *Agence France Presse*, 28 June 1998; *The Economist*, 15 November 1997 and 7 March 1998.

- 23 October: Japanese government begins implementing $505 billion plan to rescue her economy and failing banks
- 10 November: IMF and World Bank pronounce that the global financial crisis has eased, with a recovery in sight for Thailand and South Korea. Asian stock markets begin to show signs of a revival

Experts will continue to debate the causes of the Asian economic crisis. Later in this book I shall suggest what can and what can't be learned from it when it comes to global economic management.* Here I would simply note three elements. The first is admittedly a truism. In economics, as elsewhere, what goes up must (at least sometimes and temporarily) go down. Economic advances are never regular, and economic advance at the pace of that which occurred in the Asia Pacific region since the Second World War was bound to lead to upheavals along the way. The solid recovery since confirmed that interpretation. What went down went up again.

Second, there was (and to some extent still is) a systemic problem in East Asian economies – with the notable exceptions of Singapore, Hong Kong and Taiwan. This is the pervasiveness of cronyism in the relationships between governments, businesses and banks; of inadequate financial regulation; and of an ethos of what can only, if undiplomatically, be described as corruption.

Third, there was an acute short-term problem in financial markets. The precise circumstances differed country by country. But the crisis which spread by a kind of contagion from one Asian currency to the next ended in a regional collapse, and at one time looked like precipitating a global one.

The economic typhoon first struck in Thailand. The Thais had made huge economic strides in the 1980s and early 1990s. But their immediate undoing was a combination of large current account deficits and a currency pegged to the US dollar. Something had to give, and on 2 July 1997 it was the Thai baht which, when floated, fell promptly by 20 per cent against the dollar.

The cyclone then moved on through the Philippines, Malaysia

---

* See pp.462–5.

and Indonesia, all of which had similarly been running large current account deficits and pegging their exchange rates to the dollar. Their currencies accordingly also now collapsed.

Indonesia, Thailand and the Philippines called in the IMF. In the Philippines, the process of adjustment ran reasonably smoothly. In Indonesia, however, the economic turmoil continued. By the end of January 1998 the Indonesian rupiah had lost 80 per cent of its value against the dollar. Malaysia, true to Dr Mahathir's instincts of economic nationalism and despite the advice of his then deputy Mr Anwar Ibrahim, sought to resist the logic of the global economy and imposed exchange controls. But by the end of 1997 that country's economy too had contracted by 7 per cent (compared with an 8 per cent annual growth over the previous decade); the Malaysian stock market had lost 45 per cent of its value; and the Malaysian currency, the ringgit, had fallen by 40 per cent against the US dollar.

South Korea's currency, the won, was the final victim. In fact, Korea's underlying situation was substantially different from that of the other tigers. Korea, like Japan though even more so, has evolved a very corporatist style of capitalism, based on the so-called *chaebol* system of mighty industrial conglomerates. All corporatism – even when practised in societies where hard work, enterprise and cooperation are as highly valued as in Korea – encourages inflexibility, discourages individual accountability, and risks magnifying errors by concealing them. Furthermore, precisely because the Koreans had been so successful in generating a vibrant economy which transformed living standards in a single generation, they were reluctant now to recognise the need for fundamental change. Korea's business and financial institutions had incurred excessive short-term foreign debts, which there were now far too little foreign exchange reserves to repay. This in turn created a crisis which prompted resort to the IMF for emergency assistance.

East Asian economies recovered strongly in 1999 and 2000. South Korea, Thailand and Malaysia enjoyed rates of growth equal to or exceeding those of 1996. Even unsettled Indonesia's economy started growing again. Moreover, because of (albeit incomplete) structural reforms, this progress was more soundly based. It seems unlikely that Asian governments will fall again into either of the twin traps of pegging their currencies to unrealistic US dollar rates, or of incurring short-term foreign debts to finance projects that will only yield long-term profits.

So what are the prospects now? East Asian economies – notably Singapore, Taiwan, Malaysia and South Korea – are again having to cope with recession. This time, however, the problem is not home-grown, but rather the effect of the sharp economic downturn in the US. The fortunes of open economies everywhere are always heavily dependent on what happens to their export markets. What policy-makers have to ensure is that the domestic economy of a country is structurally sound, so that it can both cope with bad times and take full advantage of recovery when it comes. These things are much better understood in Asia now than they were in the late 1990s.

Looking further ahead, the tigers will probably not race away in the future as they did in the days of their youthful exuberance: a brisk but steady pace is more likely. It is, after all, generally true, and indeed to be expected, that in their early stages of development economies grow at faster rates than do economies in their full maturity. This is because in the early stages of economic lift-off there are fewer social and regulatory obstacles and there is no legacy of outdated industries to act as a drain on productive enterprise. These advantages do not last. At a certain point, outlooks and institutions change, people's expectations increase, regulations are imposed, taxes rise, industries move upmarket, workforces increase their bargaining power. But even slower growth in a now large and sophisticated economy brings great and accumulating advance. Above all, given that the other conditions for Asian economic success – small government and a culture that values both enterprise and discipline – are still operating, there is every reason why Asian countries should continue to prosper mightily in the century ahead.

I conclude that:

- There was nothing mysterious about the causes of the 1997–98 Asian economic crisis, even though few predicted it
- Equally, the underlying conditions for long-term Asian economic

success are still present and will show through once the current downturn is over.

POLITICAL CRISES AND PROSPECTS

But what of the wider effects of the Asian economic meltdown? Some of the states which endured it turned out to be as politically fragile as they had been economically successful, and once economic failure set in the political strains became intolerable. At the time this development was widely welcomed, as what were seen, particularly in the West, as undemocratic and illiberal governments collapsed amid recriminations and unrest. The movement was even compared on occasion to that which brought down the Berlin Wall and liberated Eastern Europe from communism in 1989.

But this actually shows that some people understood even less about communism than they did about Asia. Communism really *is* different in kind to the other undemocratic alternatives. Whereas those generally leave the legal and social structures untouched, while limiting political activity and expression, communism seeks total control – which is the classic distinction between authoritarianism and totalitarianism.* Apart from China, Burma and to a degree Vietnam, Asian populations did not live under regimes which were totalitarian before the 1997–98 economic crash. The predominantly military government in Thailand, the quasi-authoritarian government of Kim Young Sam in South Korea, and the personal government of President Suharto in Indonesia – the governments which did fall as a result of the crash – were not in the full sense democratic. But neither were they responsible for evils on the scale of communist China. Moreover, China and the other oppressive socialist states of Asia actually withstood the economic crisis quite well – prisons offer, after all, their own kind of security to the inmates. And Malaysia, which one would previously have regarded as at least partly free, far from becoming more politically liberal, has become less so. It is thus difficult to

---

* The fundamental difference between authoritarian and totalitarian regimes was brilliantly explored in Ambassador Jeane Kirkpatrick's seminal article, 'Dictatorships and Double Standards', *Commentary*, November 1979.

see how it is possible to speak of a new wave of democracy surging through South-East Asia.

Nor should we expect one. As I have explained above, I do not believe that liberty and democracy are somehow alien to Asia – one only has to look at the enthusiasm with which the Hong Kong Chinese welcomed the changes briefly introduced between 1992 and 1997 to grasp that. But nor do I believe that it is possible in any country – Asian or non-Asian – which lacks an understanding and experience of what is involved, to introduce democracy at a stroke without risking trouble. That is particularly so when there is a background of violence. Indonesia is a case in point.

INDONESIA – A MAN-MADE MESS

Before the 1997 economic crisis, one could have listed Indonesia alongside its tiny neighbour Singapore as a man-made miracle. And, politically incorrect as it may now be to say so, the main architect of all this was undoubtedly ex-President Suharto. It was Suharto who in 1967, at the head of the army and with considerable popular support, put an end to the economic chaos which the anti-capitalist and anti-Western policies of the then President Sukarno had generated. President Suharto's policies of opening up the country to Western investment and promoting modernisation and private enterprise turned Indonesia from a sloth into a tiger, with growth running at 7 per cent a year between 1985 and 1995. Mr Suharto succeeded in bringing about a marked improvement in the country's general living standards, cutting the proportion of the population living in poverty from 60 per cent to just 11 per cent.*

It is true that there was bloodshed and repression. But it is also true that the country faced a communist revolution – and, whether victorious or defeated, communist revolutions generally entail the shedding of blood in abundance. Moreover, although it is sometimes forgotten, the circumstances of Indonesia's annexation of Portugal's former colony of East Timor in 1975 were not dissimilar – a vicious civil war was underway and a communist-backed faction seemed about to take over.

I feel no need to justify all the actions of the Suharto govern-

---

* *The World Bank and Indonesia*, The World Bank Group, 2000.

ment. I also think that President Suharto would have been wise to step down some years earlier than he did. But there is still something rather nauseating about watching Western countries, which were anxious to back him when he was useful, now parrot the slogans of human rights activists, without acknowledging the immense practical benefits which his government brought to the country and indeed to us in the West.

I talked with President Suharto on a number of occasions before and after leaving office. The last time was in 1992, when he took me to visit his stockbreeding farm at Tapos – like many Indonesians he was almost obsessively interested in agriculture, and wanted to ensure that the rural way of life benefited from scientific and technological advance to check the destabilising flow of population to the cities. I am perfectly prepared to believe that Mr Suharto and his family exploited their position financially, as is not unusual among autocrats. But I am equally convinced that he wanted the best for Indonesia, and on any objective criteria his rule must be judged a success.

These reflections on the Suharto regime are of some practical relevance now. Although the threat of communist subversion in South-East Asia as elsewhere has been lifted, the other threat with which Suharto had to cope has not – that is, the threat of disintegration of the Indonesian state. In their anxiety to dislodge him, the IMF used the economic crisis that struck Indonesia in 1997 to set terms which they must have known he could not meet and survive. The IMF rescue became, in short, a political rather than a financial operation. In particular, the Fund insisted on huge increases in fuel and food prices at a time when ordinary Indonesians had already seen their living standards plunge as a result of devaluation.

These changes, some of which were doubtless in themselves desirable, were when imposed in these circumstances enormously disruptive, and they destabilised not just the government but the country as a whole. I am reminded of Ambassador Kirkpatrick's observations regarding:

> ... [The] idea ... that it is possible to democratise governments, anytime, anywhere, under any circumstances ...

[In traditional autocracies] the fabric of authority unravels quickly when the power and status of the man at the top are undermined or eliminated. The longer the autocrat has held power, and the more pervasive his personal influence, the more dependent a nation's institutions will be on him. Without him, the organized life of the society will collapse, like an arch from which the keystone has been removed.*

And this is what happened in Indonesia, despite the best efforts of President Suharto's ally and successor, B.J. Habibie. The chaos then worsened sharply under Abdurrahman Wahid until his removal, and it remains to be seen how the new President, Megawati Sukarnoputri, will cope with it.

I am not a believer in the West intervening to prevent the break-up of states, where the constituent peoples demand it and where sensible options are available. But neither should the West promote such political dissolution by contriving to create a breakdown in central authority – particularly when that puts the West's own interests at risk.

Indonesia is a huge country – a state of over two hundred million people speaking 250 languages and inhabiting six thousand islands stretching across a third of the earth's circumference. Throughout its existence as an independent country, the authorities' overriding concern has been to bolster national unity. That, for example, is the purpose of the five principles of '*Pancasilla*' incorporated in the constitution to provide Indonesia's governing philosophy – one of religious inclusiveness and mutual respect. And the importance of such concepts has been shown by the massacres that have been taking place of Christians in the Moluccas and of the Madurese in Kalimantan (Indonesian Borneo) since President Suharto disappeared from the scene.

It remains to be seen whether Indonesia in its present form will survive. It was right that East Timor should have been allowed its independence – though whether the inhabitants of that poverty-stricken little community will eventually think their struggle against Jakarta worthwhile remains to be seen. But it is clear that

---

* Kirkpatrick, 'Dictatorships and Double Standards'.

substantial minorities – perhaps even majorities – in other parts of Indonesia are now tempted to follow suit. Strongly Islamic Aceh, source of 40 per cent of the liquefied natural gas that is one of Indonesia's most important exports, is demanding autonomy and may try to secede. There are similar, though weaker, movements in Papua, Riau and East Kalimantan – all of which are also rich in natural resources. Fierce resentment of the small but rich and powerful Chinese community of Jakarta, which has led to murderous riots, also threatens the basis of the Indonesian state.*

It is in the West's interests that Indonesia should remain broadly intact and that it should become an orderly, prosperous power once again. We should remember that two-fifths of the world's shipping passes through this far-flung archipelago. Nor must it be overlooked that, as the world's largest Muslim state, Indonesia has a still wider significance in the extraordinarily delicate and important matter of managing the West's global relations with Islam. If Indonesia can evolve into a successful democratic Muslim country, that will provide a welcome example to the rest of the Muslim world.

So it seems to me that:

- Western attitudes towards Indonesia have been ill-advised and short-sighted
- We should resist the temptation to try to sweep away unsatisfactory regimes like Suharto's without thought for the consequences
- In so far as it lies within our power, we should now try to see that Indonesia survives and flourishes.

PART III: JAPAN

THE JAPANESE PHENOMENON

'Asian values' are, for the West at least, most strikingly and memorably exemplified by the extraordinary phenomenon of modern Japan. Japan's economy is, as I have noted, the world's second

---

* It is widely said that the ethnic Chinese, who constitute just 3 per cent of the Indonesian population, control 70 per cent of the country's economy.

largest. By the usual measurement, it is still over four times bigger than China's. Thanks to twenty years of current account surpluses, Japan is also the world's largest creditor nation, holding some $1.2 trillion of overseas assets. It is worth recalling all this, because so much of what has been written about Japan in recent years has centred upon the country's problems and weaknesses. The real story of modern Japan remains one of astonishing success.

During my years in office, I spent many hours in the company of Japanese leaders. Their personalities varied a good deal more than the caricatures suggest. For example, Prime Minister Yasuhiro Nakasone (1982–87) was outgoing and Westernised in manner, which doubtless helped him strike up a warm relationship with Ronald Reagan; Prime Minister Noboru Takeshita (1987–89), by contrast, was a far more 'typical' figure, a party boss who though very successful in his own culture would probably never have risen to the top in a Western country's political system; and, finally, Prime Minister Toshiki Kaifu (1989–91), who was a breath of fresh air in Japanese politics, seems rather to have fallen between both stools.

Unfortunately, the 1980s were not the most promising years during which to gain deeper insights into the real Japan. This was because Western contacts with the Japanese in those days always seemed to be dominated by arguments about their trade surpluses. With the benefit of hindsight, we can see that these were crucial years for the world economy. Had President Reagan given way to anti-Japanese protectionist pressures at home, the West would not only have badly damaged relations with our main partner in the Far East; we would also have derailed progress towards the lowering of global tariffs that underlies the prosperity we enjoy. The fact remains, however, that most of my conversations with Japanese Prime Ministers seemed to end in my asking for restrictions on British imports to be removed – and my opposite number politely explaining why the Japanese distribution/taxation/value system was 'different'.

Actually, there was a good deal of truth in this. Japan is, indeed, different. And the 'difference' goes beyond retailing and consumption patterns; it is a reflection of the Japanese phenomenon itself. But it was really only after leaving office that I was able to study and experience more of that for myself.

There is, in any case, another problem which confronts serving politicians who have dealings with Japan. This is that by tradition Japan's brightest and best have often not gone into politics at all, preferring a life in business or the civil service. Over the last few years I have paid seven visits to Japan. Although I have kept up some political contacts, it is through coming to know Japanese people in business and other walks of life that I feel my understanding has grown.

It is not a novel insight but it is true nonetheless that Japan is a unique and often perplexing mixture of Western and Asian. In some respects, Japan's attitude to the West over the centuries has not been dissimilar to China's. Both for many years deliberately closed their societies against the West. Both were then forced in deeply humiliating circumstances to accept Western commerce, representation and influence – in the case of the Japanese by the unwelcome arrival of the American Commodore Matthew Perry and his squadron in Nagasaki in 1853. But it was at precisely this point that the fundamental difference between the Chinese and Japanese mentalities became manifest. Whereas the Chinese, with just a few voices to the contrary, concentrated upon a fierce and futile resistance to the West, the Japanese embraced it.

The fall of the Tokugawa shogunate and the restoration of the power of the Japanese Emperor – the 'Meiji Restoration' of 1868 – marked the beginning of the creation of modern Japan. The capital was transferred to Tokyo. The army and navy were reorganised. Universal education began: by the early twentieth century literacy levels reached almost 100 per cent. Industrialisation was strongly promoted. And the whole programme was based upon the intelligent use of Western knowledge and expertise by Japanese for the strengthening of Japan. It is well-known where all this later led – not just to modernisation but to expansionism, to war and finally to disaster. But the important lesson we should absorb now is that the Japanese have shown throughout their history as a modern state – and not just in very recent times – a unique ability to seek out and apply other people's discoveries for their own purposes.

It is possible, of course, to be dismissive of this tendency and to see in it a lack of originality: some have done so. But such an ability seems to me a kind of genius. There are, after all, good reasons why most other societies have been unwilling to follow the Japanese in borrowing, and then ruthlessly applying, other people's ideas. Doing so requires a rare amount of humility: it is unpleasant for ancient civilisations to admit that despite their cultural achievements they lack the technique to cope with the modern world. But it also requires at another level an equally rare self-confidence: for is it not always true that when we open up and adapt to the world we risk the loss of our own roots and identity? Unusually, the Japanese have a consuming desire to learn all that they can from and about foreigners, while retaining an unshakeable consciousness of being 'different' and being determined to remain so. This may not make them universally popular. But it does make them extraordinarily effective.

One can speculate about why Japan has been able to square this circle – one that lies at the heart of all the current debate about the effects of globalisation upon culture. Perhaps it has something to do with Japanese religion – notably, the importance of Shintoism, which ascribes such a significant role to the spirits of one's ancestors and thus to the legacy of the past. It is probably also related to the quasi-mystical attitude towards the Japanese landscape that echoes through Japanese poetry. Both influences have given the Japanese a powerful sense of 'place'. I also suspect that Japan's deep sense of identity stems from the historical fact that, at least until the end of the Second World War, the country had never been invaded. It had absorbed outside influences – literary from China, religious from Korea – and then reshaped them, while remaining secure and separate as only island races can. The results were the ethnic homogeneity and national distinctness which any visitor to Japan notices. These in turn have provided Japan with sure foundations upon which to build new structures derived from Western models.

Modern Japan cannot, though, be understood without reference to the Second World War. The Japanese are generally reluctant to discuss these events, and understandably so. Japanese forces inflicted appalling suffering on those who opposed them. Many Chinese and Koreans may never forgive Japan for what happened in their countries. The visits of Japanese leaders to foreign, particularly Asian, states are still plagued by arguments about what is or is not a sufficient apology for the actions of those years.

But there is no excuse for failing to understand how the Japanese feel. Not all that Japan did in Asia was unwelcome to Asians. And the suffering of Japan itself by the end of the war was intense – 1.7 million military personnel and 380,000 Japanese civilians died during the course of the Second World War. Japan is the only country that has felt the force of nuclear weapons. Moreover, the application of collective guilt, running from one generation to another, is a dangerous doctrine which would leave few modern nations unscathed.

Perhaps it is the end, not the start or the course, of the war in the Pacific which is most significant in understanding Japan today. On 14 August 1945, for the first time ever, the people of Japan heard their Emperor's voice, announcing over the wireless the nation's surrender. His final words were:

> Let the entire nation continue as one family from generation to generation, ever firm in its faith of the imperishableness of its divine land, and mindful of its heavy burden of responsibilities, and the long road before it. Unite your total strength to be devoted to the construction for the future. Cultivate the ways of rectitude, nobility of spirit, and work with resolution so that you may enhance the innate glory of the Imperial State and keep pace with the progress of the world.

It seems to me that this is, more or less, what the Japanese have since done – devoted their 'total strength to the construction of the future' and 'kept pace with the progress of the world'.

The new Japanese constitution outlawed war and indeed in theory the armed forces. But in any case, Japan's trauma was such that the vast majority of Japanese had – and have – no wish to pursue again the path of military aggrandisement. They decided instead, by some collective inner resolution which could remain unspoken because it was so strong, to pursue an alternative path of economic greatness. Economic recovery was, of course, in any case vital, because the country was in ruins. But it was also undoubtedly a matter of pride. The Japanese, who were to make out of their country an economic superpower, were working not just for themselves and their families, as we Westerners generally do, but directly for Japan – or 'Japan Incorporated', as the phrase has it. I think that this helps explain some of the differences between Japanese and Western capitalism.

JAPANESE CAPITALISM

Japanese-style capitalism has certainly worked for Japan. Japan's growth rates during the 1950s, sixties and seventies were at least twice those of its main competitors. When the Allied occupation of Japan ended in 1952, Japanese GNP stood at just over a third of Britain's. By the late 1970s, it was as large as Britain's and France's combined, and more than half the size of America's. Between 1950 and 1990 real incomes rose in Japan by 7.7 per cent a year – compared with 1.7 per cent a year in the United States – from $1,230 (at 1990 prices) to $23,970.*

This success was – initially at least – almost entirely based on manufacturing. Within a generation, Japan's share of world manufacturing output rose from 2–3 per cent to about 10 per cent. By the 1970s Japan was producing as much steel as America. It was a world leader in electronic goods and seized almost a quarter of the world car market. Nor did the Japanese fail to adapt as other lower-cost competitors emerged: they moved upmarket into higher technology products such as robotics and computers, and also invested in new plants outside Japan.

By the time that I became Britain's Prime Minister it was widely accepted that Japan would rise and rise, and that this had por-tentous implications for the rest of us. Professor Ezra Vogel, for example, wrote a well-known book called *Japan as Number One: Lessons for America*, whose contents may be judged from its title.[†] The same expert some seven years later still argued that 'there are many reasons to believe that Japan will extend its lead as the world's dominant economic power', and speculated as to whether

---

[*] Kennedy, *The Rise and Fall of the Great Powers*, p.539; *The Economist*, 6 March 1993.

[†] Ezra F. Vogel, *Japan as Number One: Lessons for America* (Cambridge, Massachusetts: Harvard University Press, 1979).

Japan would 'use its economic dominance in world affairs to become a military superpower'.*

A fierce debate, much influenced by specifically Western political considerations, also raged about just why the Japanese had been so spectacularly successful. Was it because they had perfected a special kind of industrial policy? In such discussions the Japanese Ministry for Trade and Industry (MITI) was sometimes credited with well-nigh superhuman abilities. Its far-sighted interventions and strategic purpose were thought to be the driving force of the Japanese juggernaut.

On closer examination, this does not seem to have been true. Doubtless, MITI had within its ranks some extremely able people. Moreover, according government so much economic influence was certainly less damaging than it would have been in Britain, where our trade unions would have made it disastrous. But even in Japan the system had drawbacks.

First, government interventions often contrived to limit competition, which, as always, resulted in inefficiencies. One recent study of different sectors of Japanese industry, which sought to understand why some succeeded and others did not, concluded that 'the single biggest lesson from Japan's failures is that the government should abandon its anti-competitive policies'.†

Second, the traditional Japanese preference for investing resources for long-term strategic purposes established by government rather than with a view to profit and dividends for shareholders was bound in the end to lead to problems. In some cases, particularly when an industry is in its infancy, such an approach may work. It may also result – as in Japan – in a greater level of investment in research and development, which can bring benefits. But once profit ceases to be the driving force, companies become dependent not upon satisfying the customer but rather upon satisfying the government and the banks. And both governments and banks can, and do, get it wrong.

---

* Ezra F. Vogel, 'East Asia: Pax Nipponica?', *Foreign Affairs*, spring 1986. To be fair, Professor Vogel concluded that it probably would not.

† Michael E. Porter and Hirotaka Takeuchi, 'Fixing What Really Ails Japan', *Foreign Affairs*, May/June 1999.

This leads on to the third difficulty of the Japanese model, particularly as it was extolled by Western admirers. Japanese companies were far more reliant than their Western equivalents upon cheap finance from the banks, both public and private. They did not, therefore, have to raise most of their funds for investment by share issues, which would have opened up their affairs to private shareholder scrutiny.

Such interlocking of banks and industrial companies fitted in with a tradition that had been established in pre-war times, when the financial-industrial conglomerates, called *zaibatsu*, controlled most of the economy. The partial break-up of these conglomerates after the war did not change the mentality which underpinned them, which can best be described as corporatist.

Corporatism has consequences. In this case, lack of competition combined with cheap money and a dearth of profitable opportunities for its investment led to an enormous inflation of land prices. These overpriced assets in turn encouraged the banks to finance further expansion into unsustainable projects. In the late 1980s and early 1990s the bubble burst.

Although these are serious criticisms, they should not be allowed to detract from the real and abiding strengths of Japan's industrial system. A revealing report from McKinsey & Company into the problems of the Japanese economy suggests that neither the hype nor the gloom adequately reflects the reality of what has been happening. It shows that the world-beating Japanese industries – cars, steel, machine tools and electronics – are still highly efficient and successful. But in much of the rest of the economy – such as retailing, healthcare, construction and food processing – productivity is now and has always been quite poor. These inefficiencies are the result of stifled competition, and if such impediments are removed (it is suggested) both productivity and incomes will rise.*

The possibilities for renewed growth and progress exist because, of course, the underlying causes of Japan's phenomenal progress still apply. Some of these factors have been mentioned earlier,

---

* 'Why the Japanese Economy is not Growing: Micro Barriers to Productivity Growth', *McKinsey Global Institute*, July 2000.

because they are Asian rather than Japanese. But the Japanese, as ever, have applied them in their own way.

The Japanese workforce, at least in the successful sectors, is by and large extremely well-educated. The roots of this certainly lie in Japanese society and the expectations which Japanese families have of their children. They also, I am convinced, are buried in the national psyche which emerged from the war.

But even workers who have been schooled and skilled need to be motivated, and here again the Japanese have proved remarkably successful. It has long been argued that the corporate ethos which Japanese companies so carefully develop depends upon the practice of lifetime employment. If that is so, Japan will have problems, because no economy can offer that assurance in an age when flexibility and adaptability are required in order to succeed. But in any case, such lifetime employment was largely the result of the labour laws introduced at the behest of left-wing Westerners after the war: it is not necessarily cast in concrete as a permanent part of Japanese industrial practice.*

Some features of that practice definitely grate with Westerners: they would, I am sure, with me. Many of us are uneasy about company songs and lapel badges. Earnest collective discussion of common problems is inclined to strike us as artificial. And it is not the habit in Britain at least to allow so much of our recreational time to be taken up with company activities. Business and pleasure, public and private, collective and individual – we Westerners generally like to live our lives relegating these things into more or less separate compartments.

But Japanese management practices have in other respects proved eminently transferable. Japanese managers may in the early days have found British – indeed, Western – workers exasperating, but over time the Japanese approach had a highly beneficial effect – and not just upon Japanese-owned companies but upon other businesses with which they came into contact. The approach that

---

* This point is made by Akio Morita – founder of Sony – who ought to know, in his fascinating autobiography: Akio Morita with Edwin M. Rheingold and Mitsuko Shimonura, *Made in Japan: Akio Morita and Sony* (London: Harper-Collins, 1994), pp.139, 145. See also below, pp.137–9.

consists of trying to win over the consent and gain the understanding of all members of the workforce for the objectives of the company must make psychological sense. It is the antidote to the old counterproductive confrontation between 'two sides' of industry which had become so much a feature of Britain's industrial relations by the 1970s that people spoke of the 'British disease'. The fact that Britain is now cured of that ailment owes more than a little to our absorption of the lessons that the Japanese have taught.*

In one respect, I believe that Japan's future is rosier than even many Japanese would dare to hope. This is because the new is about to come to the aid of the old. In the past, the values and structures of Japanese society, profoundly reflected in Japanese education, discouraged free-wheeling individualism. Yet epoch-determining advances, above all in pure science, are generally made by people whose minds and personalities strike their contemporaries as eccentric – and Japan traditionally has had no room for eccentrics. The younger generation of Japanese now being educated or working in America and elsewhere in the West will have a more cosmopolitan, individualistic outlook when they return to Japan. This may lead initially to some challenges to traditional lifestyles. But it will also provide an element of inspired initiative which has often been lacking in Japan's economy. Once Japan masters this vital requirement for success in the age of the information revolution, it may again astonish the world.

- So we should be wary of oversimplifications: Japan was never quite as successful, nor is it now as unsuccessful, as we are often led to believe
- Japan's economic success owed more to capitalism without adjectives ('Japanese', 'Asian', etc.) and less to government than many pundits suggested

---

* Up-to-date evidence of the beneficial effects of Japanese industrial practice on Britain is provided by the fact that according to the World Market Research Centre the two most efficient car plants in Europe in 2000 were Nissan's at Sunderland and Toyota's at Burnaston. *Financial Times*, 28 June 2001.

- But Japanese management techniques *have* been exported to good effect and should continue to be so
- Japan's underlying strengths are unchanged and will help ensure that its mighty economy rises again
- And as the younger generation of Japanese brings in new thinking to leaven old ways the economic results may again astound us.

AKIO MORITA

Over the years, I have met many leading Japanese industrialists. Some of them are extremely well-educated and well-informed about international matters. But what consistently impresses me most is how many of them are first-class technicians, frequently engineers, in their own right. Although I realise that it is impossible for the man (or woman) at the top to be an expert in every skill and function required of an organisation – all leaders have to some extent to be generalists – I am always suspicious when I find that the head of a large corporation lacks detailed knowledge of its products. This deficiency is something that is very rare in Japan. And that fact, I am convinced, is largely responsible for the admirable reputation that leading Japanese companies have acquired for quality and reliability.

The outstanding Japanese businessman of modern times is undoubtedly the late Akio Morita, co-founder of Sony. I developed great admiration for him during my time as Prime Minister and we continued to meet on my visits to Japan. I was delighted to be present in Tokyo when he was invested with an honorary KBE in October 1992 – an award that gave this great anglophile tremendous joy.

Akio Morita was so much a cosmopolitan figure – friend of Western politicians and tycoons, opera buff, golfer, linguist, witty raconteur – that it was easy to imagine that he had lost something of his Japanese identity. But this would have been an error – just as it is an error to imagine that when the Japanese nation strives to master Western ways it is abandoning itself. Akio Morita was lively, individualistic, direct and much more outspoken than the great mass of his fellow countrymen. He himself was conscious of this, he worked at it, and he was even keen to set an example in these respects to a Japanese corporate community whose besetting weakness, as many Japanese will admit in private, is conformism. On the other hand, he developed and practised these qualities within a very Japanese context. And he was deeply patriotic and very proud of his own national culture and achievement.

The story of Sony, the electronics company which he and his great friend and collaborator, the engineering genius Masaru Ibuka, founded in the ruins of post-war Tokyo, is in microcosm the story of Japan's resurrection from the ashes of defeat. But it is more than that. It is a demonstration to all of us of the human qualities required for business success.

Akio Morita always had a clear view of what Sony had to achieve. He sometimes made mistakes, as he admitted, and mistakes were inevitable for someone who was pioneering new products and leading Japan's breakthrough into Western markets. But he never lost faith in his vision. His philosophy consisted first in devising and perfecting a product; then in promoting it in carefully judged markets; and all the while creating within his company a positive, enthusiastic, collaborative ethos. Sony's success with televisions, video players, sound systems and camcorders bore eloquent tribute to the value of this business philosophy, at least when applied by two geniuses. But, as Morita himself recognised, it is probably the Walkman, Sony's hugely popular portable stereo player, that best exemplifies the approach.

Whenever I see young children listening to their favourite music, and leaving the adults in peace, I reflect on the process by which this brilliantly simple product was created. Akio Morita records how Ibuka came into his office, complaining that he could not listen to his music without disturbing those around him unless he carried around a portable tape-recorder with standard-sized headphones. Without any market research and against the scepticism of his engineers, Morita ordered the adaptation of one of Sony's small cassette tape-recorders by stripping out the recording circuit and speaker and replacing them with a stereo amplifier. Morita dictated the specifications and even set the selling price – low enough to suit young people's pockets. We know the result.

Akio Morita was also, as I have noted, an internationalist. He was both an ambassador for Japanese business and a sometimes controversial spokesman for change within Japan. Tragically, he was struck down by a debilitating stroke in 1993 and died six years later.

Japan today is struggling to cope with a crisis of confidence in its system and its future. As it does so, Akio Morita's insights are sorely missed. And whatever resolutions are found, Japan desperately needs more like him.

OUT OF THE DOLDRUMS?

In recent years Japan's economy has ceased for many Japanese to be a source of pride, becoming rather a cause of bewilderment verging on despair. For the reasons I have already given, that seems exaggerated: underlying Japanese strengths are undiluted. But it is easy to understand how *Angst* has taken hold. Since 1990–91 when the economic bubble burst, Japan has endured its deepest and longest recession of modern times. The economic downturn in the US, sharply worsened by the crisis of confidence occasioned by 11 September, has brought more bad news. Unemployment, which was virtually unknown, has become a problem – all the more traumatic for being a novel experience. Living standards have stagnated and after decades of rapidly catching up Japan has fallen further behind America. Moreover, the problem of bad debts in the financial sector remains largely unresolved.

The origins of the crisis are not really mysterious, though one can debate the relative importance of the different elements: unsound banking practices, an unsustainable property boom, lack of competition, inflexibility.* But as generations of mariners have learned, sailing out of the doldrums is much more difficult than sailing into them.

Japan's recovery was, of course, made much more difficult because of the broader Asian crash in 1997–98. But its own problems preceded that and themselves made Asian recovery slower. Japan's economic problems have to be tackled in two ways.

---

* Manipulation of international exchange rates at the West's instigation also contributed. The 1987 Louvre Accord, involving the printing of massive amounts of Japanese yen and buying of US dollars, helped create the 'bubble' of 1989–90, which later burst.

First, it is necessary to press ahead with all the structural changes required. During my time as Prime Minister, I tried repeatedly to persuade the Japanese that opening up their markets made sense for them as well as for us. But at the time this was met with polite scepticism. More recently, however, Japan has somewhat reluctantly undertaken reforms along similar lines to those which Britain undertook in the 1980s.

In 1998 Japan introduced its equivalent of Britain's 1986 'big bang' financial reforms to liberalise its highly regulated financial markets. They included the lifting of controls on foreign exchange transactions and on international ownership of Japanese banks. Japan's market deregulation brought about a substantial rise in investor confidence – the Tokyo stock market nearly doubled in value between October 1998 and March 2000. There is also major restructuring underway in Japanese industry, even in the once heavily protected construction industry, where scores of inefficient businesses are being forced to close by market forces.

Structural changes of this sort do not yield immediate results. But over time they can transform the whole economy – as they did Britain's. As these reforms take effect in Japan, and as long as they are seen through, we can expect to see much more than a one-off gain in efficiency. The prospect of such progress occurring appears to have brightened with the appointment in April 2001 as Japan's Prime Minister of Junichiro Koizumi. Encouragingly, Mr Koizumi has talked of the need to concentrate on far-reaching supply side reforms. If that radical approach is pursued, there is no reason why continuing improvements in productivity should not drive the mighty Japanese economy ahead with new momentum.

The second focus for economic policy changes – domestic demand – is more tricky. The well-known observation of the eighteenth-century writer Bernard Mandeville to the effect that 'private vices [produce] public benefits' – i.e. (in modern terms) greed fuels growth – has been stood on its head by the Japanese.* Japan is in one of those rare predicaments where the propensity to save is

---

* Bernard Mandeville, *The Fable of the Bees and Other Writings* (Indianapolis: Hackett Publishing, 1997).

so strong that it is undercutting all attempts to increase domestic demand. Of course, saving is generally good. It is how people ensure that they and their families do not become a burden on their neighbours or the state. Moreover, saving is the basis of investment, and so of future profits and progress. In Japan, however, personal saving is occurring at the expense of private spending, and that is why the government has launched successive public spending packages to boost total demand.

It is, though, generally better to boost demand, when necessary, by monetary rather than fiscal means. That is why in the – at the time very controversial – 1981 budget in Britain we decided to cut public borrowing and lower interest rates when the country was in the depths of recession. Contrary to the prevailing Keynesian orthodoxy, this approach resulted in renewed and sustainable economic growth.

Japan's problem, however, is that its interest rates are already very low, only just above zero. So instead the authorities have turned to what are known as 'open market operations', printing yen and buying Japanese government bonds. The expectation is that eventually the flood of yen will stop the current deflation and begin to reflate the economy. The technicalities are, of course, important. But they are not essential to choosing the overall strategy – which should be to increase the money supply.

I am much more sceptical about the fiscal measures that have been taken, especially the public spending packages. While it is true that these helped produce a resumption of growth, I am not at all sure that they will make it sustainable – quite the opposite, in fact.

As a result of these fiscal packages, Japan's budget deficit has widened to more than 8 per cent of its national income (GDP). Its gross public debt has increased from 70 per cent of GDP in 1990 to 130 per cent at the end of 1999. The IMF forecasts that Japanese debt will rise to 150 per cent by 2004. Moreover, these figures substantially understate the true position. They do not take account of the workings of the Fiscal Investment and Loan Programme by which money from Japan's post office savings and state pension funds is channelled into construction and other projects. Nor do they take account of unfunded pension liabilities as a result of Japan's ageing population. Enlarge the estimate to cover all these elements and the debt total increases to over two and a half times Japan's GDP.*

It is a very good rule in politics, including economic policy, to assume that people by and large behave rationally. Of course, they do not always do so. Irrational optimism and the occasional panic are not unknown. But if the general public are not behaving as we want or expect, policy-makers are better advised to reflect than to complain.

The Japanese are behaving quite rationally when they prefer to save than to spend. This is because that is what their circumstances demand. Japan's population is ageing faster than that of any other country. As one expert has strikingly put it: 'Twenty years ago, Japan was the youngest society in the developed world. By 2005 it will be the oldest.'† By 2015 one in four Japanese will be sixty-five or over. These people have to save for their future – one in which there will also be fewer people of working age to support them.

A second reason, however, is that many Japanese are understandably worried about the security of their savings. In the past the availability of such large sums earning low rates of return provided a huge boost to Japanese industry. But in many cases this money has also been 'invested' in white-elephant projects which benefit only Japan's politically powerful construction industry.

A third reason is provided by those same huge fiscal boosts which are leading to mounting public sector debt. Of course, if the economy grows fast enough, the burden it imposes will diminish. But if not . . . ? Higher taxation would then be inevitable – which, of course, demands more saving to pay it.

In prescribing cures for Japan's economic ailments one has to take account of the reality of Japanese psychology and the society which generates it. The same deeply conservative instincts which frustrate the wheezes of economic policy-makers will allow Japan to withstand severe strains, though only once there is a consensus

---

* These figures come from *The Economist*, 22 January 2000.

† Peter G. Peterson, *Gray Dawn: How the Coming Age Wave will Transform America – and the World* (New York: Random House, 1999), p.72.

that these are the price for national progress to be made. Japan's families are immensely strong. The work ethic is deeply ingrained. There is also a sense of responsibility for elderly members of the family which shames us Westerners. Japan's is a society that can cope, as it has proved time and time again.

These considerations suggest to me – admittedly an outsider with the temerity to advise insiders – that the path of no-nonsense supply side reforms accompanied by a sufficiently loose monetary policy is more likely to lead to recovery than will public borrowing sprees. This is particularly so since so much of the emphasis has hitherto been on capital spending rather than tax cuts. Although Japan's tax revenues are comparatively low, its marginal tax rates are too high.* Any – limited – fiscal change should concentrate on cutting these rates.

Japan's leaders also need to convince the population that they and the major financial institutions are not playing fast and loose with Japanese savings. This requires giving real substance to promises of greater transparency and absolute honesty. In turn, that may well require changes in the political culture. Japan rightly prides itself on its democratic achievement. But true democracy requires open debate of the issues, discussion of alternatives, and, above all, the willingness to exercise leadership. I am not one of those who believe that such things are impossible in Japan. And nor did Akio Morita.

- Japanese financial and industrial restructuring must continue, if Japan is to move ahead
- The West has done Japan no service by pressing it to make ever bigger fiscal boosts: the main effect has been to pile up debt
- Within the financial leeway available, it is better to concentrate on tax cuts to boost incentives rather than construction projects which may turn out to be white elephants
- Japan's policy-makers will only succeed in boosting demand if they persuade ordinary Japanese that their savings and their futures are safe

---

* Alan Reynolds, 'Toward Meaningful Tax Reform in Japan', Cato Institute Center for Trade Policy Studies, 1998.

JAPAN AS A WORLD POWER

Japan's economic difficulties suspended but did not by any means end a debate which had been conducted for several years about the country's strategic role. Japan's post-war constitution was, of course, drawn up in such a way as to preclude any such thing. It renounced not only war and the 'threat or use of force as a means of settling international disputes', but also stated that in order to accomplish that aim 'land, sea and air forces, as well as other war potential, will never be maintained'. A country which has no capability of exerting force can have no security role, except as a battleground or a launchpad. Clearly, that was bound to be unacceptable to a sovereign Japan and hardly less so to the United States, which would have been left to defend Japan's territory and waters alone. Rightly, these clauses were therefore reinterpreted over time and may indeed soon be subject to formal revision by a constitutional amendment. This approach is supported by a majority of Japanese MPs and now also by Japan's new Prime Minister, Mr Koizumi.

In fact, Japan is now a major military power. It has the world's second largest defence budget. It has 1160 main battle tanks, fifteen submarines, sixty-two warships of various kinds and over two hundred fighter aircraft. Japanese military technology is well-advanced. These forces have, however, strictly defensive tasks and no combat experience. In a crisis it is Japan's ally, the United States, which would have sole responsibility for strategic, offensive and counter-offensive missions. To this end, America keeps over forty thousand military personnel stationed in Japan.

This broad approach is still valid. For well-known historical reasons, it is important that the Japanese are seen by their neighbours to avoid anything which smacks of militarism. That will not, of course, stop the communist Chinese from polemical accusations, largely aimed at trying to increase Japanese financial aid to China. But Japan knows that it is the rest of Asia that it has to satisfy.

On the other hand, it is at the same time important that Japan continues to update and strengthen its conventional forces. There are three reasons for this.

The first is that within the East Asia region only Japan can counterbalance China. China is an ambitious power, whose ambitions could yet lead to general instability in the area. The Chinese are always ready with anti-Japanese vitriol when Japan gets in their way, but they know perfectly well that Japan's interests must be respected and can indeed be defended. This – maintaining the Asian balance of power – is the fundamental reason why Japan must be stronger.*

The second reason for the Japanese to continue a steady improvement in their military capabilities is because this will cement the vital relationship with the United States. America must continue to lead in the Asia Pacific as elsewhere, but leadership does not exclude an element of partnership. And it is important both psychologically and practically – and both in America and Japan – that this is seen to be the case.

During the Cold War Japan was, of course, America's key ally in the Asia Pacific. But with the end of that conflict there was a re-evaluation by both parties. In the United States, trade issues came to dominate considerations of security in relations with Japan. In Japan, influential commentators urged concentration upon links with the rest of Asia rather than with America. And both these trends were mutually reinforcing. The Gulf War, if anything, increased the difficulties. Many Westerners were critical of Japan's failure to do more in a conflict which because of Japan's total dependence on imported oil threatened Japanese interests even more than America's. For their part, the Japanese were rightly offended that the large financial burden they assumed for the costs of the campaign – amounting to $9 billion – went largely unrecognised.

It was the renewal of external threats which gave both Japan and the United States a revived sense of their common interests. One source was China. For years, Japan had been a major investor there. Japan has always taken a close and usually a sympathetic interest in developments in Beijing. But as China stepped up its militarisation the Japanese became increasingly worried. Beijing's nuclear tests in 1995 provoked Japan into cutting its development

---

* For China's armed forces, see pp.178–83.

assistance programme to China. In 1996 Chinese ballistic missiles used to intimidate the Taiwanese landed near Japanese shipping lanes. In the same year, disputes sharpened over the Senkaku/Diaoyutai Islands in the East China Sea. And as Japan has reacted to the perceived threat from China by drawing closer to America, the Chinese rhetoric against Japan has grown ever fiercer – thus further confirming Japanese concerns.

The other and still less predictable source of danger has been North Korea. In 1992 the North Koreans were discovered to have been kidnapping Japanese citizens to be trained as spies. In 1993 Japan was not alone in being alarmed by North Korea's tests of its Nodong-1 missile, with a range of over six hundred miles. In 1994 Japan felt extremely vulnerable during the crisis arising over North Korea's secret nuclear weapons programme. And within a few years that sense of vulnerability was amply justified: in August 1998 North Korea launched a new and more advanced Taepodong missile that flew over northern Japan.*

Under these pressures, Tokyo and Washington have taken steps to shore up their alliance. The Japanese – with a little assistance from their own economic difficulties – are no longer, it seems, beguiled by the illusory goal of an East Asian 'sphere of influence' of which Japan would be the hub. And the Americans – with the same assistance – have recognised that it is never worth jeopardising security because of trade. In April 1996 President Clinton and Prime Minister Ryutaro Hashimoto publicly reaffirmed their commitment to the Japan–US security relationship. This was followed by revision of the guidelines for bilateral defence co-operation. President Clinton's ill-judged decision to visit China but not Japan in 1998, talking of a US–Chinese 'strategic partnership', and even lecturing the Japanese on their economic policy when in Beijing, set back US–Japanese relations. But Japan proved mature enough to overlook the snub and US–Japanese cooperation has continued.

That cooperation should, though, be further strengthened. Both sides need it. For America, Japan is strategically vital as its main Asian ally. Equally, Japan needs to come to terms with the fact

---

* See p.214.

that it cannot opt out of the confrontation between Washington and Beijing. Naturally, the Japanese want to keep on reasonably good terms with their unpredictable neighbour. But Japan's security needs require that it cannot allow itself to remain unprotected against threats, and only US cooperation can provide such protection. So I believe that the US–Japanese joint research programme to create an effective Theatre Missile Defence system should press ahead and lead to early deployment. I am equally convinced that as America's closest ally in the region it would send precisely the wrong signals to potential aggressors if Japan failed to support America's decision to press ahead with global missile defence.

The third reason why Japan should be equipped with the most up-to-date conventional weapons – supported by a ballistic missile defence shield – is so that it never has to become a nuclear power. The Japanese do not themselves want to become a nuclear state. Japan's Asian neighbours certainly do not want it to become one either. But a great power with far-reaching interests, if it is to be secure, has to be strong in other respects that compensate for lack of the ultimate deterrent.

Japan will not be a global military power in the ordinary sense of the expression. All-too-vivid memories of past events will never permit this. But Japan does have a world role in other respects. Once present difficulties are resolved, it will return to being one of the strongest pillars of the international economic system. It also needs to be able to play a more active role in peacekeeping missions – probably outside Asia. The Japanese constitution may have to be amended in order to allow this to take place.

Although Japan, with the support of Britain and the United States, has been pressing to become a Permanent Member of the UN Security Council, I believe that this would be a mistake. Security Council membership is not a kind of passport of international respectability: if it were, the present Chinese regime would hardly deserve a place. The historical and strategic reason why the present Five are permanently represented and can thus exercise a veto on UN decisions is because each of these states possesses the nuclear weapon and so the ability to defend its interests by the ultimate means. The Security Council is what brings the loquacious internationalism of the General Assembly down to earth: to bring in non-nuclear states as Permanent Security Council Members would add a new and potentially dangerous element of uncertainty to great-power politics. Being a major nuclear power should be a necessary, though not sufficient, condition for membership: thus, for example, I would under the right circumstances be prepared to consider India's claim, but never, of course, that of any of the 'rogue states'.* Those who have been encouraging Japan to pursue this goal do so in the misguided belief that somehow the modern world is organised according to merit not power. They are mistaken.

- We should welcome Japan's strengthening of its armed forces, which should continue
- Japan has a vital role in counterbalancing China
- Japan will remain America's principal strategic partner in Asia and should be treated accordingly
- Japan must know that she is able to rely not just on the American nuclear umbrella, but also on the shield of ballistic missile defence
- The Japanese could undoubtedly fulfil more international roles, and this should be encouraged
- But it is neither in their nor our interests that Japan should become a Permanent Member of the United Nations Security Council.

THE KOBE EXPERIENCE

I understand that the name of Kobe, Japan's largest port, perched on a narrow strip of land sandwiched between high mountains and the Bay of Osaka, means 'God's Door'. The 'door' was presumably envisaged as leading inland to the ancient Japanese capital of Kyoto. But when I arrived in Kobe on Monday, 17 October 1994 to launch a giant Taiwanese container ship built in the Mitsubishi Heavy Industries shipyard, all eyes were focused on the bay. Chang Yung-fa, Chairman of the Taiwanese Evergreen shipping company, named the ship. I administered a vigorous chop to the supporting rope with the axe provided. The traditional bottle of

---

* For India, see pp.194–206.

champagne smashed against the bow. And to loud applause from the crowd the giant vessel duly roared down its slipway into Kobe harbour. As a symbol of Japanese industrial prowess, the scenes at the launch of *Ever Result* would surely be hard to beat.

Three months later, at 5.46 a.m. on Tuesday, 17 January 1995, Kobe suffered the worst earthquake endured by Japan in half a century. Four thousand five hundred people died. Some fourteen thousand were injured. Almost seventy-five thousand buildings were destroyed. Worst affected were the smaller, traditionally constructed wooden houses, home to the city's poorer families. Tens of thousands of these simply collapsed, trapping the occupants. Fires then raged, consuming much of what the shock of the earthquake had left. The Okura hotel, where I had stayed, along with many newer buildings was undamaged. But the Mitsubishi shipyard where I had launched the ship was devastated. By some miracle, *Ever Result* herself had escaped out of 'God's Door' on her maiden voyage just hours before the earthquake struck.

It was, though, the camera shots – immediately flashed around the world – of the overturned expressway pillars which for many came to symbolise the disaster. Not all the science of Japan could predict the earthquake. Not all the technology of Japan could create structures to withstand it. Not all the resources of Japan could mobilise effectively to cope with its immediate aftermath. Along with the Sarin gas attack on the Tokyo underground of the same year, the numerous political and financial scandals and the stagnant economy, the Kobe disaster provoked soul-searching by the Japanese and foreboding in the outside world.

I revisited Kobe in 1996 as the guest of Kawasaki Heavy Industries for their centenary celebrations. The scars were still evident and the continued human suffering real. But the rubble of destroyed houses had been cleared away. Now that the initial confusion had passed, the city was rising again. Those expressways were already rebuilt, and we sped along them as in 1994. It was not so much reconstruction as the continuing travails of the Japanese economy which were causing most problems for Kobe.

Kobe is, therefore, a more complex – and for that reason more satisfactory – symbol of Japan than either the ship launch of 1994 or the earthquake of 1995 might suggest. The truth is that Japan finds it difficult to react quickly and flexibly. It can therefore be caught off-balance by sudden crises. But Japan endures and the Japanese never lose their nerve. They reflect, consult, and then move forward with heroic effort to attain the goal that has been set. That is why the Japanese succeed, and will continue to do so.

CHAPTER 5

Asian Giants

PART I: CHINA

HARD POUNDING IN BEIJING

On Tuesday, 10 September 1991 I arrived in Beijing as the guest of the Chinese government. It was a time of great international tension. Three weeks earlier, hardline communists in Moscow had tried, and in due course failed, to seize power. President Gorbachev had been released, but it was Boris Yeltsin who was the hero of the hour. Far from holding the Soviet Union together, the coup had brought about its dissolution. The Soviet Communist Party was utterly discredited (later, of course, it would partially recover). I had myself been involved on the fringes of these great events.* *En route* to Beijing, the aircraft in which I was travelling stopped at midnight to refuel at Alma Ata in Kazakhstan, where President Sultan Nazarbayev drove out to the airport to see me and for several hours we discussed all that was happening. He is a shrewd tactician and appeared now to be mediating in the troubled relations between Mr Gorbachev and Mr Yeltsin. Consequently, by the time I arrived in China the following evening I was preoccupied with one question above all: what did events in the Soviet Union mean for the future of communism and of China?

I knew that the Chinese leadership were similarly preoccupied, though clearly from a very different perspective: the British Prime Minister and Foreign Secretary, John Major and Douglas (now

---

* See: *The Path to Power*, pp.512–14.

Lord) Hurd, had visited Beijing just a little while before and Mr Hurd sent me a note about what had transpired. For decades the Chinese had, of course, rejoiced at everything that weakened their old Soviet rivals. But now they were deeply worried about the implications for their own regime. They had suppressed liberty in 1989 when the tanks had done their job with brutal effectiveness in Tiananmen Square. It was alarming for them to see similar repression fail so spectacularly in Moscow – where a tank served merely as Boris Yeltsin's podium for democracy.

In Beijing I was to be accommodated at the Diaoyutai state guesthouse, a very heavily guarded compound in which Mao's wife Chian Ch'ing had plotted with her radical leftist friends and finally been arrested. The house – or 'villa' – in which we stayed had a cavernous sitting room, furnished in the grand and gloomy style much favoured by communist decorators everywhere. It contained an astonishing array of bottles of spirits. The Chinese, however, understand enough of the price mechanism to limit consumption of these by ensuring that their guests pay for what they drink.

It was past eleven o'clock at night by the time we arrived, but I was anxious for a full briefing from British officials: the following day's schedule would be hard and I wanted the latest information. Consequently, I asked my interpreter to tell the woman in charge of the villa to stand down the staff so that they could get to bed, and that we would look after ourselves. The interpreter was an expert, but it took him four efforts to make her understand: she was clearly incredulous. Anyone who thinks that communism is about equality should perhaps have a word with that lady about it.

Alongside the more orthodox briefing which I now received was some further information which I put to good use. I was told the substance of the conversation between Henry Kissinger, in Beijing just before me, and the Chinese Prime Minister Li Peng. What interested me were the replies which Li Peng made to Dr Kissinger's observations. It is always good to know how the other side thinks. But with the Chinese it is particularly useful, since you can be sure that after your first meeting they will know exactly what *you* think, for each of your hosts diligently briefs the next.

My first meeting the following day was with the Chinese Foreign Minister, Qian Qichen. Mr Qian is a tough, intelligent professional diplomat in something of the Gromyko mould. His expertise is as a Russian specialist, but he also speaks excellent English. He won his Politburo spurs by his unflinching defence of the Party line when head of the Information Department of the Chinese Ministry of Foreign Affairs. Nor did he shift an inch from his brief on this occasion.

China, he told me, was keen that the Soviet Union should be preserved and had a strong interest in its stability. The twin problems at present, he added, were the Soviet economy and 'Russian chauvinism'. I replied, deliberately shifting the focus, that I was optimistic about the Soviet Union's future – wrongly, as it turned out – because the response by the people to the coup had been so decisive. In a none-too-subtle reference to the events in Tiananmen Square in 1989, I said: 'In the contemporary world tanks and guns cannot overpower people's aspirations.'

Mr Qian began to look ill at ease. Nor did he become any more relaxed when I talked about the need for China to observe its public commitments to human rights. At the end of the meeting I suggested that a new world had been brought into being by the advances in communication: it required new thinking and new measures. The people's wishes could not be ignored by their leaders. That was the significance of what had happened in Eastern Europe and now in the Soviet Union. (I hoped that the unspoken message was clear.)

My next engagement was with an unusual gentleman called Rong Yren. Mr Rong was officially termed Deputy Chairman of the People's Congress, but this conveys nothing of his significance. He was, in fact, Beijing's own (very) tame capitalist. Before the Revolution Mr Rong had been hugely wealthy. But unlike most of the Chinese tycoons who fled and finished up in Hong Kong or further afield, he had made his peace with the communists. The authorities thought – most of the time – that it was important to persuade influential Westerners that the rich could still flourish in China with the Party's blessing. Mr Rong provided the proof. He had suffered, as he told me, under the Cultural Revolution, but he was then rehabilitated, and he was now living in some style.

Mr Rong has a Hu Tong courtyard house. These are now rare and much sought-after, but they were the traditional houses of Beijing, which indeed at one time largely consisted of such court-yards – grey with red roofs, and often enclosing beautiful gardens.

Mr Rong's drawing room into which I was now shown was almost bulging with Late Ching furniture and ornaments. Each item was enormously expensive. A huge piece of calligraphy by a well-known artist hung on a wall, on a corner of which Deng Xiao Ping had scribbled a note expressing his appreciation. The effect was somewhat marred by Mr Rong's dog – stuffed and in a glass case. I did not know quite how to react.

Formal conversations with Chinese dignitaries are always uncomfortable. This is because the chairs are arranged next to each other, so that you have to turn at an angle in order to speak. You can, therefore, never look one another straight in the eye, which perhaps is the intention. This conversation, however, was more stilted than most. Mr Rong and I discussed the Cultural Revolution, but found that we drew quite different lessons from it. He had concluded that the great need was for stability. I countered that the only way to achieve that was through democracy. He tried to argue that democracy had failed in the West, because it had not sufficiently advanced the role of women. I looked hard at him and he moved nervously onto other ground.

My relief at the announcement that we were now to go in to lunch was short-lived. We sat down at an enormous table which almost filled a smallish room, to be served with course upon course of what I was assured were delicacies from Mr Rong's home province, but which might have been selected for the torture of Western guests. First there were huge boiled grey prawns. They were still in their shells, their big black eyes staring hopelessly through an oily sauce that gave off an unappetising odour. It became clear that the way to eat this dish was to chomp steadily through the prawn while allowing the macerated shell to extrude and then fall from the side of the mouth. After the plates were cleared away, there appeared a vast tureen. It was entirely filled with something round and white. This turned out to be a huge ham, covered in thick white fat. Gobbets were broken off and served. And so the ordeal continued.

Then it was briefly back to the Diaoyutai guesthouse. The journey was a slow one and the afternoon was now hot. The Chinese had provided me with a long, old-fashioned 'Red Flag' limousine, a copy of the original Zil designed for Stalin. Whenever we stopped, Chinese bicyclists would gather to peer at me in the back of the car. I struggled to look cheerful and, above all, to stay awake.

It was certainly necessary to regain some composure, for my next meeting was the most important of the day. At three o'clock I was due to see Li Peng.

The Chinese Prime Minister, like all the senior Chinese figures, lives and works in Zhong Nanhai. This is the exact communist equivalent of the Imperial Forbidden City, which indeed it adjoins. It is a walled and heavily guarded compound containing apartments, offices, pools and pavilions.

Within the rarefied atmosphere of this quarter of Beijing a political power-struggle was at this time underway in which Li Peng was pitted against Jiang Zemin to succeed Deng Xiao Ping as China's supreme leader. This struggle was mainly personal. But there were elements of doctrine involved too. Li Peng was known to have personally ordered in the tanks to crush the protests in Tiananmen Square. That had tainted him in the eyes of foreigners and of many Chinese. He was seen as representing those who put stability above reform, even economic reform. Jiang Zemin, a former Mayor of prosperous Shanghai, had the advantage of not being Li Peng. He was hardly a liberal, of course – indeed, his personal views remain to this day indefinable – but he carried less ideological baggage.

The car swept me into a side entrance of Zhong Nanhai up to an ornate Ching pavilion. Inside, on being ushered into a large hall, I was surprised to find a great semi-circle of chairs. Li Peng greeted me and we sat side by side at the top. All the chairs next to him were occupied by senior Chinese figures and behind them were more chairs for their officials. By my side sat only my interpreter, with all the other places empty. At first sight it was an unequal contest. But as the proceedings developed it became increasingly clear that those beside and behind Li Peng were less supporters than spectators. They wanted to know how he would perform.

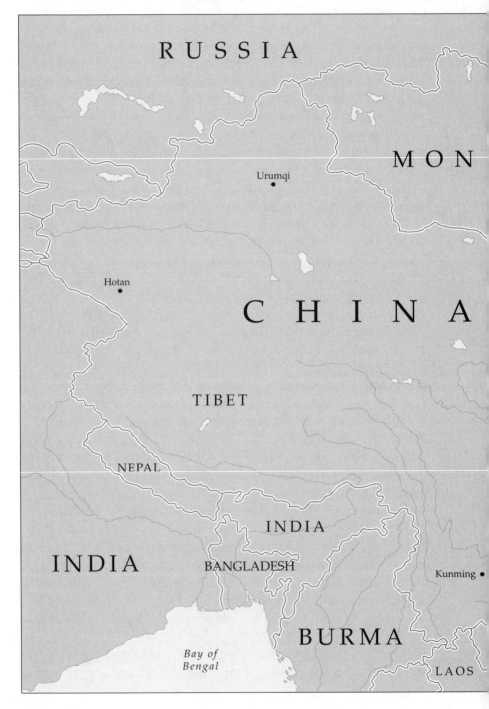

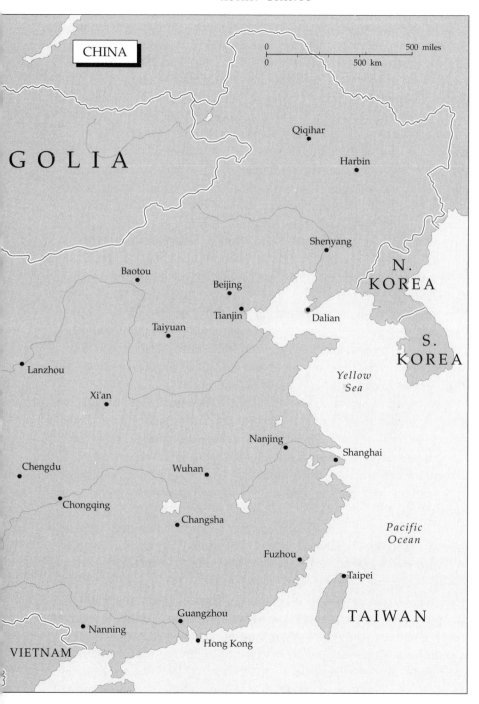

CHINA

0 _____ 500 miles
0 _____ 500 km

Qiqihar

Harbin

G O L I A

Shenyang

N.
KOREA

Baotou

Beijing

Tianjin

Dalian

S.
KOREA

Taiyuan

Lanzhou

Yellow
Sea

Xi'an

Nanjing

Shanghai

Chengdu

Wuhan

Chongqing

Changsha

Pacific
Ocean

Fuzhou

Taipei

Guangzhou

TAIWAN

Nanning

Hong Kong

VIETNAM

Our initial discussion concerned Zhao Ziyang, the disgraced former Prime Minister whom I had got to know during the negotiations about Hong Kong in 1982 and who had been dismissed because of his opposition to the use of force in Tiananmen Square seven years later. I had asked to see him while in Beijing. But Li Peng now explained that this was not possible because he was still 'under investigation' by the Communist Party. I asked when this process might be completed, because I felt loyalty to all my old friends – as I did to Mr Gorbachev (who had also effectively been imprisoned by hardline communists). Li Peng dismissed the comparison. But he undertook to pass on my best wishes. He said that Mr Zhao was living comfortably in his old residence. Indeed, his salary had increased, added the Prime Minister with a mirthless laugh.

We then discussed events in the Soviet Union. Li Peng said that the USSR needed a 'restoration of order and discipline'. The recent changes had had, he admitted, an undesirable impact in China, but not a very great one. I took issue with this analysis. The 'disorder', I argued, had been the result of a refusal to decentralise, notably the refusal to let go of the Baltic states. And the worst disorder of all, of course, was the coup.

I went on to say that while I could understand how the background to the recent coup by hardliners in the Soviet Union had arisen, I could not have believed that China would have pursued a similar path. Its experiences during the Cultural Revolution should have removed any temptation to return to the past. Yet the Chinese government had set the army on their own people. How could they do that?

Li Peng now became very angry. The cliché about Chinese inscrutability was on this occasion very wide of the mark. He grew red and his whole face coarsened. He launched into the classic Chinese defence against every criticism from foreigners, which is to retail all the horrors inflicted by outsiders upon the Chinese people over the centuries – particularly dwelling upon those of the Japanese. I replied by reminding him that in fact the Chinese Communist Party had killed many more Chinese than foreigners ever had – indeed, just remember the Cultural Revolution. Li Peng then repeated another standard line – namely that the Communist

Party had subsequently addressed those mistakes. Mao had acknowledged that there were excesses. I said that Mao ought to know: after all, he was himself the archpriest of the Cultural Revolution. This, I knew, was something that even today's Chinese communists are not prepared to admit. Li Peng at this became altogether incoherent.

The meeting – which had overrun by half an hour at the expense of another with the Vietnamese Foreign Minister – now drew to an end. As I prepared to leave, Li Peng left his colleagues and asked somewhat sheepishly if I would brief the press that the meeting had been conducted in an 'amicable atmosphere'. I reflected and then said that I would not brief the press at all. And I did not.

This, of course, is the exact opposite of what some Western visitors do. They adopt a relaxed demeanour in private discussion with the Chinese leadership, making no more than a few mild admonitions about Chinese abuses. Then they tell the outside world that they behaved like lions. This cuts no ice at all. The Chinese need to know that we mean what we say, and that we are genuine in our convictions and our criticisms. They will take more notice still if, after that, we show them that we are prepared to behave professionally.

My final appointment of the day was a meeting followed by dinner with the then Communist Party General Secretary (and today President), Jiang Zemin. Our discussions flowed over very much the same territory as those with Qian Qichen and Li Peng. But the mood was very different. Mr Jiang specialises in amiability. When he argues, he does so without really touching on the heart of the matter, and this keeps him out of trouble. Probably what he had heard of Li Peng's earlier experience confirmed him on this occasion in that astute approach. He concluded the meeting by making what appeared to be a prepared statement directed at the Chinese officials present, reiterating China's determination to continue along the road of socialism with Chinese characteristics, as well as to maintain the 'open door' and reform policies. In other words, he was restating his adherence to Deng Xiao Ping's approach.

Dinner turned out to be a jolly affair. Mr Jiang, who has

considerable talents as a linguist, demonstrated his knowledge of Shakespeare. He also regaled us with a Romanian folksong – doubtless learned in the good old days of the Ceausescus.

Many Western analysts cannot understand how Jiang Zemin could get to the top of Chinese politics, let alone stay there. But it is not really that surprising. Two presumed successors to Deng Xiao Ping – Hu Yaobang and Zhao Ziyang – had already fallen into disgrace, before the emergence of Mr Jiang. It is said that Hu Yaobang, whom I rather liked when I met him in London, had signed his own dismissal notice when he was foolish enough to agree with one of Deng's many declarations that it was high time he handed over power to a younger man. Zhao Ziyang had been destroyed because he opposed the repression in Tiananmen Square. For his part, Jiang Zemin understood, as do so many who flourish at imperial courts, that it pays to conform and that no one fears an entertainer. Jiang's experience as Mayor of Shanghai also gave him a basic understanding of how China could prosper. Crucially, he was lucky enough to join the leadership after Tiananmen Square: thus Li Peng was left to take the responsibility for what even Chinese communists now regard as an error which will eventually be disowned. Whether those attributes sufficiently qualify President Jiang to manage China's fortunes at this defining phase in her history is still being tested.

THE PAST AND THE PRESENT

Two countries have radically benefited in terms of global power and importance from the end of the Cold War. One, naturally enough, is the United States. The other, more surprisingly perhaps, is China. This should leave us with mixed feelings. China's apparently unstoppable rise reminds us that, whatever other benefits victory in the Cold War brought, an end to communism has not so far been among them.

China was, after all, the second most important communist-controlled state after the Soviet Union. Its quarrels with the Soviets were largely about tactics, frontiers and status, not about ultimate objectives. (Mao retained a great admiration for Stalin, whose personality cult he emulated to the end of his days.) China's warmer relations with America and the West after President

Nixon's diplomatic breakthrough in 1971–72 were the fruit of the Chairman's resentment of Moscow and his opportunism, not of any liberal inclinations.

The system developed by Mao and his colleagues was, in fact, one of the most villainous tyrannies that the world has known. The madness of China's 'Great Leap Forward' programme of 'modernisation' by methods which were as brutal as they were futile resulted between 1959 and 1961 in the greatest man-made famine in history, when anything between twenty and forty-three million Chinese perished. Mao's 'Cultural Revolution' led to hundreds of thousands – perhaps millions – more deaths between 1966 and 1976.* While it is true that much has changed for the better since Deng Xiao Ping took over after the Great Helmsman's death, today's China is still essentially the state that Mao built on the twin foundations of Leninist doctrine and applied terror. How to assess, predict and influence this new would-be superpower of bloody lineage and uncertain intentions is one of the greatest challenges faced by statesmanship now.

The proper starting point for such analysis has to be in the pre-communist, indeed the pre-modern, era. This may seem paradoxical. The history of China in the twentieth century is, after all, that of a series of attempts to break with the past. Out went the ancient Confucian-based system of government (1905), then the Imperial dynasty itself (1912), then the Republican Nationalism of the Kuomintang (1949), then more recently what have become seen as the bureaucratic excesses of traditional socialism (1978 –).

But change is often more apparent than real. The modernisers in power always seem to be repeating, more or less consciously, episodes of the past. Mao's doctor records, for example, how the Chairman always seemed to have some work of ancient imperial history in his hands and relished lecturing his audience on lessons to be drawn from it.† The Chinese military has long regarded the

---

* Jean-Louis Margolin, 'China: A Long March into Night', in *The Black Book of Communism* (Harvard University Press, 1999), pp.495, 513.

† Li Zhisui, *The Private Life of Chairman Mao* (London: Chatto and Windus, 1994), pp.122–5. Harry Wu tells me that this absorbing book is still one of the few banned in China.

ancient manual known as *The Art of War* as a key text of military doctrine. (It contains such insights as: 'O divine art of subtlety and secrecy! Through you we learn to be invisible, through you inaudible; and hence we can hold the enemy's fate in our hands.' It may therefore also interest US counter-intelligence services.)

Of course, the history of China is far too long and convoluted to summarise here. But what even the non-specialist like me can see, particularly if he or she has gained a certain insight into how the Chinese actually behave today, is that there is a distinctive mentality among China's rulers that is inextricably connected with specific past events.

The first feature of that mentality is a sense of innate superiority. It should at once be added that for much of China's history that sense was eminently justified. After all, the Chinese have had a written language for more than three thousand years. They achieved levels of scientific, technical, artistic, cultural and institutional development which were for most of that period greatly superior to ours in the West. The self-confidence which this generated in the later centuries, notably under the Ming dynasty (1368–1644), increasingly resembled self-absorption. Fatefully for China, this was also the period that saw the rise of modern Europe, with which in the late eighteenth and nineteenth centuries the Chinese made ever closer and more disturbing contact. When in August 1793 a British delegation to China showed their hosts a terrestrial globe, it turned into a diplomatic incident, for the Chinese were furious to see that their empire covered so little of it.* For centuries the Chinese had thought of themselves as 'The Middle Kingdom', that is the centre of the civilised world.† To see otherwise was a shock.

This leads on to the second feature of the Chinese mentality – a sense of vulnerability. Looking at China today, it is difficult for Westerners to give credence to the endless Chinese talk of military plans and projects being hatched against them. And certainly we

---

* The incident is related in Alain Peyrefitte, *The Collision of Two Civilisations: The British Expedition to China in 1792–4* (London: Harvill, 1993), p.147.

† I understand that the name which the Chinese still use for their country today, *Zhonghua*, means 'central land'.

are right to take this with a large pinch of salt. Paranoia makes no more sense even if it is entirely unfeigned, and it may actually increase by being humoured. The fact remains, though, that China's rulers *have* traditionally felt vulnerable to the inroads of less civilised but more powerful neighbours. Both the Mongols who established the Yuan dynasty (1279–1368) and the Manchus who ruled as the Ching (1644–1911) fell into that category. And, above all, so did we Westerners.

The outcome of contact with the West was the humiliations of the Opium War (1839–42) – when Britain forced China to open five treaty ports and relinquish Hong Kong – and of the so-called 'unequal treaties', which almost all Chinese still regard as a grave affront to their nation's dignity. I came face to face with this attitude myself in 1982 in the course of my discussions with Deng Xiao Ping about the future of Hong Kong. I had hoped that the Chinese would draw a distinction between those territories which were held by Britain on the basis of a lease, and Hong Kong island, which we held in sovereignty.* But Deng made it clear he was having none of it. The Chinese were determined to avenge the humiliations they had suffered, and though they preferred to have Hong Kong back in an orderly, prosperous condition, they would have seized it by force if necessary – and damn the consequences.

These elements – superiority, vulnerability, humiliation – explain much of what motivates the Chinese government today. They are, moreover, important because they will influence, albeit less crudely, any non-communist successor regime. They also help explain what the Chinese now want from the West. They are seeking to use Western expertise, technology, investment and market access in order to mobilise their own vast resources so as to make themselves once again our equals – if at all possible, our superiors.

Paradoxically, such atavistic outlooks are particularly evident in today's modernising China. Whatever hold communism once had over the masses has been dissipated, and so the Chinese Communist Party finds it convenient to whip up patriotic fervour in

---

* In fact, over 90 per cent of the total territory of Hong Kong was held on a lease which expired in 1997.

order to maintain its grip. That, of course, is much of what lies behind their obsession with Taiwan.* It's an old communist tactic, in fact, practised by cynical despots from Stalin in the Soviet Union, to Zhivkov in Bulgaria, to Ceausescu in Romania.† But in China, for the historical reasons I have set out at some length above, it is particularly potent. This combination of a communist ruling class with an increasingly nationalistic populace is a powerful mixture which could explode against the West, given the occasion.

I believe that in dealings with China

- We should be fully aware of the historical legacy which distorts China's attitude towards us
- But we should never take all its indignant rhetoric at face value.

CHINA TODAY: THE ECONOMY

China's complex psychological make-up matters to us today because of Chinese present and prospective power. And the basis of that power is most obviously economic.

The Chinese are one of the world's most enterprising peoples. But their systems of government in both imperial and communist times have conspired to frustrate those entrepreneurial instincts. Thus in the past it was left to foreigners to build up the great city of Shanghai. And even now the lack of an indigenous Chinese middle class, whose beginnings were crushed by Mao, means that great reliance is placed on foreign capital and expertise. Moreover, although it is considered bad form to say so, a large part of China's current business success is based on pirated intellectual property and breach of Western copyright.

---

* This cynicism is not new. Mao's doctor records the Chairman's view: 'Some of our comrades don't understand the situation. They want us to cross the sea and take over Taiwan. I don't agree. Let's leave Taiwan alone. Taiwan keeps the pressure on us. *It helps maintain our internal unity*' (emphasis added). *The Private Life of Chairman Mao*, p.262.

† Todor Zhivkov (1911–98), President of Bulgaria, 1971–89, and First Secretary of the ruling Bulgarian Communist Party Central Committee, 1954–89. Zhivkov was the longest-serving leader in the former communist Eastern Bloc countries. Nicolae Ceausescu (1918–89), President of Romania, 1967–89.

The fact remains that China's economic record over recent decades has been phenomenal. Growth has averaged nearly 8 per cent a year since 1979. In 1978 international trade totalled roughly 10 per cent of China's GDP; by the late 1990s it accounted for 36 per cent. China has thus become both wealthier and much more integrated into the international economy. Its membership of the World Trade Organisation (WTO) will accelerate that.

Yet it is also necessary to keep a sense of proportion. One can read the (notoriously unreliable) statistics about China's economy in more than one way. Measured by purchasing power parity, China is reckoned as having the second largest economy in the world – ahead of Japan's. Viewed in terms of current exchange rates, however, it is the world's seventh largest. And when it comes to GDP per head it falls to 150th in global ranking, below Indonesia.

That 'health warning' is even more appropriate if we are calculating the West's direct economic interest in China. In 1998 British exports to China accounted for less than 1 per cent of Britain's total exports abroad; US exports to China constituted just 2 per cent of America's world exports in the same year. And China's share of world trade (visible and invisible exports) is less than that of the Netherlands or Belgium and Luxembourg.*

We Westerners also have to be careful about our own impressions when we visit China. Beijing now has the feel of a great modern city. That is still truer of Shanghai and indeed of the whole coastal strip, especially Guangdong (Canton) Province. But the interior of China is a different country, with poor communications, underdevelopment and, particularly in rural areas, poverty. As usual, China is other than it appears.

Both China's economic progress and the qualifications which must be made about it can be traced back to what happened in the late 1970s. By December 1978 Deng Xiao Ping was sufficiently

---

Ceausescu was executed with his wife Elena after the downfall of his brutal regime in December 1989.

---

* CIA World Factbook 2000; Heritage Foundation, US and Asia Statistical Handbook, 1999–2000; The Economist World in Figures, 2001.

in control to have the Communist Party adopt the so-called 'Four Modernisations' which underpinned his programme of reform.

The first steps in a new political direction are always perilous. But in economic terms this was the easy part. It was as if a naturally robust and otherwise healthy patient had stopped taking daily doses of poison disguised as medicine. Marxist economic prescriptions were now discarded – by encouraging private farming (though not yet ownership) of land, by reducing central planning of industry, and by ending the freeze on foreign inward investment. The results were swift and exceeded all optimistic expectations.

Deng himself was a pragmatist – hence his oft-quoted remark: 'I don't care if it's a white cat or a black cat, it's a good cat so long as it catches mice.' Market reforms were to be welcomed simply because they strengthened and enriched China. For a shrewd old communist like Deng, the abandonment of Marxist economics must have seemed a small price to pay if it helped keep the Communist Party – and him with it – in power.

This explains why Deng saw no contradiction between his suppression of opposition in Tiananmen Square in 1989 and his continued determination to press ahead with economic reform. In his eyes, the purpose of China's prosperity was to avoid democracy, not promote it.

In 1992, at the age of eighty-eight, Deng visited the Shenzhen and Zhuhai Special Economic Zones in order to defend his policies against Party critics. It was at this time that he also brought in Zhu Rongji as an economic adviser, one of Deng's most crucial decisions.

The Chinese economy had by now moved well beyond the early days of heady if chaotic expansion unleashed by the first wave of reforms. Problems as well as benefits had appeared. The changes had, in truth, gone far enough to generate growth, but not to create the framework to sustain it. The quasi-private sector was thriving. But inefficient state-owned industries had been afforded more and more credit, just to allow them to continue functioning. The result was overheating and inflation. And then when the inflation was quelled by an austerity programme, there was still that huge state sector, sicker and greedier than ever, threatening either to collapse amid social upheaval, or to drain off all the benefits that enterprise was bringing.

Despite these problems, the Chinese economy has continued to grow, albeit more slowly. It sailed through the turbulence of the Asian economic crisis of 1997 – partly because it was still, for all the changes, a relatively closed economy.

So China's resilience has been impressive. But the most important cause for optimism is that it now has a properly thought-out programme of economic reform, as well as an extremely able Prime Minister in Zhu Rongji to give it effect. I had the opportunity to discuss the situation with him in London in April 1998, just a fortnight after he succeeded to the premiership.

Mr Zhu is sometimes referred to as 'China's Gorbachev', and he does not like it one bit. I imagine that the comparison is somewhat unhealthy in Beijing. In any case, Mikhail Gorbachev, for all his achievements, never understood much about economics, of which Zhu Rongji has a formidable grasp.

Zhu Rongji first came to international attention when he was Mayor of Shanghai, the showcase of Chinese progress. He moved to the centre of affairs in 1991 and was put in charge of industry, energy and transport matters. He was promoted to the Politburo in 1992. In the spring of 1993, when Li Peng was temporarily disabled by a heart attack, Mr Zhu's importance sharply increased and he began to be referred to as Executive Vice-Premier. It was then that he was put in charge of all economic management, and between 1992 and 1995 he was also Governor of China's Central Bank.

I found him in person to be lively, direct, confident and possessed of a certain *esprit* which the blinkered plodders from Party stables lack. He seemed genuinely open to suggestions and was interested to compare notes with how we in Britain in the 1980s had set about restructuring industry. It was clear to me that he was fully aware of the scale of the undertaking.

Mr Zhu told me that his plans to cut back the size of the state sector would mean reducing the number of central and local government employees by half. State-owned enterprises too were greatly overmanned. On top of that, there was a need to create jobs for those migrating from the countryside to the cities. And at the same time, China would be moving rapidly into the new technological age.

But he also thought that China would cope. What gave him confidence was the way in which China's agricultural performance had been improved by market reforms. Even if the worst happened, China could now feed its people.

His judgement may well be right: I hope so.

China today faces much the same kind of problems that we had to tackle in Britain after 1979. The common cause is, in a word, socialism; and the whole paraphernalia of socialism – its structures, institutions and attitudes – has to be demolished if progress is to be made. Without that, China will remain a Third World country with the unfulfilled potential of an economic superpower.

And China's problems are far worse than Britain's ever were. According to Chinese government statistics, about half of the state-owned industries are loss-making; they absorb more than 75 per cent of domestic bank credit; and about 20 per cent of these loans are non-performing (Western estimates for all these figures are much higher). Viewed in cold economic terms, those are huge obstacles.

But there is also more than economics to consider, for China is already, even before the required changes, undergoing enormous social disruption. Because of the marked increase in agricultural productivity, and because of the age-old lure of city life for country people, there is a large floating population of perhaps eighty to a hundred million. These people need work and housing, and they need to put down new roots. Moreover, their numbers are bound to swell – not least because of extreme and growing differences in living conditions. These income imbalances contrast urban with rural, and coastal with interior China; some Chinese economists estimate that they may be of the order of twelve to one. Although China is a vast country with poor communications, people no longer live entirely marooned in local communities. They know about the inequalities, and in a socialist state, whose basic rationale is to oppose them, they spell deep trouble.

So can the political system take the strain? In order to provide an answer, it is first necessary to describe what that system actually is.

But before doing so, I should sum up my view of China's economic prospects:

- China is undoubtedly on course to become an economic superpower
- But it is not there yet, by any means
- And it can only achieve its potential by undertaking fundamental economic reforms on a scale that no one anywhere has successfully attempted
- All of which must leave the country's social and political future in doubt.

CHINA TODAY: POLITICS

Many Western analysts are nowadays reluctant to attach the epithet 'communist' to China. This in some cases is just squeamishness. But it also reflects a real dilemma about how to sum up the contrasting realities of China today.

Clearly, the Chinese are no longer living under the same conditions as obtained under Mao. Their living standards have been transformed. Incomes have risen, even in poorer areas. Many Chinese now buy luxury consumer goods, some take foreign holidays, and an increasing number listen to satellite broadcasts and communicate via the Internet – despite government controls.

The political system too is somewhat kinder and gentler. When political leaders fall into disgrace, they nowadays go into private obscurity rather than a torture chamber. There are also the beginnings of a rule of law, required in the first instance to provide stability for business, but with longer-term implications of huge importance for ordinary citizens and their rights. And although we should never confuse the rule of law with the rule of lawyers, it is significant that the number of legal practitioners in China has increased from three thousand in 1980 to over sixty thousand now.*

There are also some glimmers of local democracy. There have been more or less democratic elections of local committees at village level, albeit under Communist Party scrutiny. As we saw

---

* Henry Rowen, 'The Short March: China's Road to Democracy', *The National Interest*, autumn 1996.

in the last years of the Soviet Union, such quasi-democracy has a habit of prompting demands for the real thing.

These are all positive developments which could yet lead to a fundamental change in the regime. But neither should we fall into the trap of supposing that such a change has already occurred.

In these matters we should pay as much heed to the words of Chinese dissidents as to the views of the Western pundits. Both Harry Wu and Wei Jingsheng have separately warned me against believing all that the regime has to say about itself, and I find their analyses persuasive.

I first met Mr Wu shortly after his arrest, show trial, release and subsequent deportation from China. His offence in the eyes of the Chinese authorities was to have exposed the penal regime of 're-education' through forced labour, known as *laogai*. He told me of his own experience of and researches into this inhuman system, which in its combination of doctrinaire socialism with cynical materialism is not untypical of modern China.

Of course, the Chinese do have a huge problem with crime – real crime of the grossly material kind we in the West know so well. But their crime wave is worse, as sudden prosperity works on a society already heavily based upon connections, behind-the-scenes influence and graft. That said, there is, of course, absolutely no excuse for the abuses of the penal system which Mr Wu and others have exposed.

A few days after my meeting with Harry Wu, I flew to Beijing where I was scheduled to make a speech at a conference organised by the *International Herald Tribune* in collaboration with the Chinese authorities. The Chinese were showing their vindictive side at the time: although Mr Wu had been freed after US pressure, the pro-democracy dissidents Wei Jingsheng and Wang Dan had been sentenced respectively to fourteen and eleven years' imprisonment.*

---

* Wei Jingsheng (b.1950), imprisoned by Chinese authorities from 1979 to 1993, and 1995 to 1997. Wei was released early on medical grounds following the 1997 Sino–US summit, and he now lives in exile in the United States. Wang Dan (b.1969), leading figure in the Tiananmen Square demonstrations of 1989. Served four years in jail before release on parole in 1993. Given eleven-year sentence in 1996, accused of plotting to overthrow the Chinese government. Freed in 1998 on medical parole and lives in the United States.

There are two temptations for a public speaker on such occasions. The first is to adopt the line of least resistance. This may be justified by reasoning which ranges – in reverse order of merit – from the reflection that 'What they do to their own people isn't my/our affair,' to 'It's rude to insult your hosts,' to 'I'd rather just take my fee and leave quietly.' But there is another temptation. That is to create an international scene – and the Chinese are great ones for scenes – which is not just disruptive, but may actually be counter-productive. I chose a middle way.

In my speech I praised the reforms which were taking place, while suggesting areas for more progress – the rule of law, upholding contracts, reforms of banking, privatisation, wider Internet access, and protection of property rights. I then trod onto more sensitive territory by arguing that these economic changes were 'bound to lead in time to change in the way in which China is governed'. I had considered inserting a specific mention of the *laogai* but was persuaded to drop it – otherwise the Chinese would all walk out. But I did say:

> I do not want to paint an overly rosy picture. There are still aspects of life in China which are deeply worrying to those of us fortunate enough to live in democracies and under a full rule of law. And I have to say the recent harsh sentences on Mr Wei and Mr Wang have caused dismay in the wider world.

The Chinese never mince words in their own public statements, but they expect everyone else to do so. On this occasion, there was no walk-out; but Wu Jie, the senior official of the Economic Ministry who spoke after me, tersely observed: 'Britain has plenty of its own problems, and next time we meet for a conference perhaps we can debate those instead.'

A fair point, of course. We too have blemishes. But we do not imprison people because they demand the right to vote.

We have to speak publicly about the abuses in China now for the same reason that it was right to do so when the perpetrator was the Soviet Union. We must do business with the Chinese, as we did with the Soviets, but we do not have to kowtow to them. The Ming and Ching Emperors disliked Westerners for this quirky refusal of obeisance in previous centuries, and China's communist rulers are equally resentful now. But if we do not tell the truth, who will? For two years running, Britain and the rest of the European Union have refused to co-sponsor a United States resolution at the UN Commission on Human Rights condemning China's record. This attitude is not just shameful: it is also foolish. Any plaudits from the Chinese authorities for such actions are short-lived, nor are they needed: after all, in almost every field, the Chinese need the West more than we need China.

China's treatment of those whom the regime considers hostile or merely dispensable remains grim, indeed recently it has appeared to be worsening. The persecution of dissidents has increased: by the end of 1999, almost all the leaders of the China Democracy Party, set up to challenge the Communist Party's monopoly on power, had been sentenced to long prison terms.

There are three further groups whose claims are anathema to China's present leadership. The first are Chinese women and their babies. One can debate whether China's concern for population growth is well-judged. On the one hand, over-population in some rural areas is a real problem. On the other, there is evidence that China may yet finish up with its own version of the demographic crisis that afflicts many Western countries and Japan – namely an increasing elderly population with too few people of working age to support it.* What is truly abhorrent, however, is the brutal fashion in which the 'one child' policy is still carried out in parts of China, involving forced abortions and infanticide.†

The second group which suffers harshly from Chinese communist rule are the non-Chinese minorities. Unlike the Soviet Union, and indeed unlike today's Russian Federation, China is remarkably homogeneous. Ninety-three per cent are Han (ethnic) Chinese, but the 7 per cent minority population occupies 60 per cent of China's territory, which means it is of disproportionate strategic significance.

---

* Nicholas Eberstadt, 'China's Population Prospects: Problems Ahead', *Problems of Post-Communism*, January/February 2000.
† See US Department of State, *1999 Country Report on Human Rights Practices*, and *Sunday Times*, 27 August 2000.

That is especially the case with Tibet. The Chinese claim to Tibet is dubious on historical grounds. In the late seventeenth and eighteenth centuries Tibet became a Chinese protectorate. However, in the nineteenth century Beijing's control weakened until it was virtually symbolic. Between the overthrow of the Empire in 1912 and the Chinese communist invasion of 1950–51, Tibet functioned as an independent state.

Yet the fact remains that no modern Chinese government is going to allow Tibet full independence, and the present Chinese leadership is unwilling even to negotiate with the Tibetans' spiritual and temporal leader, the Dalai Lama, on any real autonomy. It is not just that the Chinese have convinced themselves that Tibet is part of historic China. Equally important is the fact that it is one of the principal locations of their nuclear weapons and missile arsenal. The Chinese now appear to have resolved upon a programme of 'modernisation' that involves shifting the ethnic balance in favour of Han Chinese and away from Tibetans, as a final solution to the continuing resistance. I hope that they do not succeed. Some 2700 Tibetan monasteries have already been destroyed since the communists marched in fifty years ago. The systematic extinction of a nation and its culture is unpardonable. But, the fact is that the West has no fundamental security interests in Tibet. This limits what we can do – though not, of course, what we should say in every international forum.

The third group which is discriminated against, and on occasion persecuted, by the Chinese authorities are the members of 'unauthorised' religions. Since 1978 freedom of religion has been officially permitted, and in any case the main traditional religious and philosophical systems in China – Buddhism, Taoism and Confucianism – pose no real threat to communist control. It is a different story when it comes to Islam and Christianity, both of whose proponents have the awkward habit of placing God's law above the Party's interests, or on occasion their own.

Even here, the authorities are prepared to be tolerant as long as they feel that they are in ultimate control. They make an exception, however, for the Muslim inhabitants of the Xinjiang Uighur Autonomous Region which borders Kazakhstan and Kyrgyzstan, who are subject to harassment and arrests because of their suspected revolutionary separatism.*

The Chinese government has also adopted an attitude of unremitting hostility towards those Christians who are not prepared to sever their links and loyalties to authorities lying outside Beijing's control. When the communists took over they initiated in China, as previously in the Soviet Union, a brutal persecution of Christianity. But later, adopting a well-honed communist technique, they sought to establish 'front' organisations through which the Party could exercise control, while permitting an appearance of free activity. This is the basis of the so-called 'Patriotic Churches' with which all places of worship are supposed to register. Many Christians are content to go along with these arrangements, because they at least allow some churches to stay open. But Protestants and Roman Catholics who refuse to collaborate in this way are subject to sporadic but often severe persecution.

Catholics have traditionally found it particularly difficult to reconcile their loyalty to Rome with membership of the 'Chinese Catholic Patriotic Association', because this state-run body explicitly rejects the Pope's authority, including that to appoint bishops. Numerous priests, several bishops and many of the faithful are even now interned for attending unauthorised Masses.

More recently, the Chinese authorities' paranoia in religious matters has become apparent in the persecution of the Falun Gong spiritual movement. It was banned in July 1999 and thousands of its members have since been arrested.

As with Tibet, there is not a great deal in practical terms that we can do to prevent these grave abuses. But we should not remain silent about them. Nor can we allow the victims to feel that they are friendless and forgotten.

On 12 March 2000 Cardinal Kung-Pin Mei died in Stamford, Connecticut, at the age of ninety-eight. He had first been arrested by the communists in 1955 in Shanghai and taken to a stadium to make public confession of his crimes. To the consternation of the authorities he instead stepped forward and shouted: 'Long

---

* The Chinese will undoubtedly try to justify their repression as an aspect of the war against terrorism. We should not fall for this ploy.

live Christ the King! Long live the Pope!', evoking embarrassing applause from the crowd. For over thirty years he was then held in prison, usually in solitary confinement, only being released to go to the United States on health grounds in 1988. He then set up a foundation to assist and keep track of those imprisoned in China for their faith.

Do the communists really imagine that they can ultimately prevail against men like that?

These unpleasant features of the Chinese regime are not just incidentals. They are fundamental to it – because they are fundamental to communism. So while the leading role of the Chinese Communist Party is still unchallenged there, I shall continue to speak of *communist* China.

In assessing the nature and motivation of China's leaders we have to remember that:

- They enjoy their present position through the Communist Party's monopoly of power, which they are, therefore, highly unlikely to abandon willingly
- Although there have been large improvements in living standards, and the system is much less harsh than in the past, China is far from being a free country
- The Chinese leaders will only improve human rights if we embarrass them into doing so: we must therefore be prepared to speak out.

PROSPECTS FOR REFORM

But how much longer will it be necessary to make such a gloomy assessment? Not long, if you accept the views of some commentators. The basis of their optimism is the much discussed link between economic progress and democracy. As countries become wealthier, their populations become more insistent upon respect for their political rights. To judge by comparisons with what happened in Taiwan and South Korea, where authoritarian governments gave way to democracy once a certain income per head was reached, China ought to become democratic in about 2015.*

---

* Rowen, 'The Short March'.

On the other hand, if one looks at the potential strains and stresses in China and at the strength of the forces arrayed against change, one has one's doubts. The Chinese leadership have every reason to try to prevent economic change leading to political freedom. They know that most of them could never maintain their position if there was open competition between different political parties and candidates. In any case, they have seen what happened in the Soviet Union once political reform began. They certainly do not want China to go in that direction.

I am not myself prepared to predict when communism will end in China. Historical background, culture, the capacity of individuals to shape the future by inspiration, leadership, or plain miscalculation – these things are at least as important in determining events in such cases as are economics. Moreover, in the case of China, unlike Taiwan and South Korea, we are dealing not just with an authoritarian but rather a totalitarian regime – albeit one whose power is nowadays less than total. Communists, even when under pressure, enjoy one advantage over authoritarians in their efforts to cling to power: in communist states there is no true law and no civil society, and so fewer opportunities for democratic opposition.

On the other hand, I do believe that China will in due course become, if not necessarily a Western-style democracy, at least a country whose population enjoy most of the benefits of freedom. Rising living standards are one reason for such modest optimism. But there are others, which are even more important.

Hitherto many of the benefits of enterprise have been lining the pockets of Party apparatchiks, and this has reinforced rather than weakened their hold on power. These people have no interest in seeing a genuine free market, because the exploitation of public power to secure private economic advantage is their passport to prosperity. And they certainly do not want to see the leadership of the Communist Party weakened by political pluralism.

But this situation cannot last indefinitely. As the years go by, and barring major upheavals, these people will begin to be edged aside by a real middle class – 'real' in the sense that one is talking about the class referred to by Marxists as 'bourgeois', with values and goals that are different from the class of quasi-capitalists that has emerged from the Communist Party apparatus. Moreover, just as it was the lack of a strong middle class which in the past caused country after country to fall into dictatorship, so it is the rise of a middle class which can now pave the way for liberty.

Such a middle class always demands property rights secured by an equitable and effectively administered rule of law. That is why I would be more inclined to emphasise the progress made in these respects than I would in local democracy in predicting when fundamental change will occur. Once there are a substantial number of people who own savings, shares, houses, businesses and plots of land, there is created an effective buffer against state power. And although this buffer may at first sight appear to safeguard only the better off, in fact the rights and interests of all are protected. This is not just reflected in incomes, which rise as wealth is spread. It is still more importantly reflected in institutions. A true rule of law cannot be administered in a state where the Communist Party appoints the judges and is thus able to determine verdicts. And the point at which China will change fundamentally will be that at which it is law that governs, rather than the Party.

China's membership of the WTO will encourage such developments. The power of the Communist Party to control, and so benefit from, China's growing prosperity will be shaken if the changes envisaged by the WTO are put into effect. More opportunities for Chinese exports will encourage the growth of private business. As China cuts its tariffs and removes restrictions on investment, inefficient state-owned industries will be opened up to foreign competition. Allowing full access to foreign banks will make it impossible to maintain the present system of allocating credit on political rather than market principles. And of huge importance in the political sphere will be the removal of restrictions on foreign ownership of Internet service providers and the linked development of China's telecommunications. In these circumstances, the government will find it all but impossible to check an explosion of information into the homes of millions of Chinese.*

---

* These arguments are developed in an excellent survey by Mark A. Groombridge in 'China's Long March to a Market Economy', Cato Institute: Centre for Trade Policy Studies, *Trade Policy Analysis*, No. 10, 24 April 2000.

So:

- In due course communism *will* fail in China, as it has elsewhere
- We can then reassess our approach to China as a great power
- But until that happens – and it is probably not about to happen soon – we should be on our guard.

THE CHINESE THREAT

The fact that China has so much unsettling historical baggage, and is still communist, means that it is fundamentally hostile to the West. One has only to scratch the surface to see that this is so. The attacks by thousands of demonstrators on the US Embassy in Beijing in the wake of the accidental bombing of the Chinese Embassy in Belgrade in May 1999 were politically staged; but they were also politically significant.*

Anti-Western propaganda drips in its poison steadily, and so when necessary the appropriate outbursts are easy to engineer. Moreover, the most viscerally anti-Western institution in China is precisely that from which serious trouble is most likely to come – the People's Liberation Army (PLA). A recent detailed study of the attitudes of the PLA leadership concluded: 'Their nationalism is fierce, sometimes bordering on xenophobia. Many senior PLA officers evince a deep suspicion of the United States and Japan in particular.'†

The threat from China is real. But we must not lose sight of its true nature. We do not now face, and we are most unlikely in the future to face, a challenge from China of the kind posed by the Soviet Union during most of the Cold War. This is partly because China is not a military superpower and – for reasons I shall explain – is not likely to become one. But it is also because China has no internationally contagious doctrine which it can use in order to advance its power and undermine ours. The days when mindless

---

* On 7 May 1999 a NATO warplane dropped precision-guided bombs on the Chinese Embassy in the course of a bombing raid on Belgrade as part of the Kosovo operation. Several Chinese were killed. The accident was the result of faulty intelligence data.
† David Shambaugh, 'China's Military Views the World', *International Security*, 24/3, winter 1999/2000.

students could be found waving Little Red Books and chanting Mao's banalities have long gone. China today exports televisions not ideas. And when it imports our secrets it does so courtesy of Westerners' venality not their misguided idealism.

Moreover, although from its seat on the UN Security Council China can cause innumerable irritations, its main diplomatic objectives nowadays are defensive. It opposes – sometimes rightly, sometimes wrongly – all attempts to intervene in states' internal affairs, believing that these could become precedents for intervention in its own. Its basic posture is thus in favour of the *status quo*.

These considerations limit the international threat which China poses. But they do not negate it. In fact, since it is the West which is now most forceful in promoting international interventions, China's very stolidity is a further source of tension – as during the intervention in Kosovo.

In one respect, moreover, China is still a major force for international instability – through its proliferation of weapons of mass destruction and missile technology. Here one should distinguish between Russia and China. The Russians supply advanced weaponry to dangerous regimes mainly because Russia is undergoing economic collapse and is desperate for money. But the Chinese proliferate *as a matter of policy*. As one expert has noted: 'The Chinese seem to have perfected the art of proliferation of clandestine nuclear and missile transfers as a tool of Chinese national security policy.'*

Proliferation is for the Chinese a way of bringing pressure on America, by emphasising their capacity to cause trouble, without going as far as provoking a damaging conflict. At the same time, China poses as an honest broker – offering its services in order to defuse the crisis between the two nuclear powers India and Pakistan, and to exert restraint over North Korea. This subtle game is intended to help make China the dominant power in Asia. China proliferates and then it offers to curb proliferation. And the West says thank you.

---

* Mohan Malik, 'China Plays "the Proliferation Card" ', *Jane's Intelligence Review*, 1 July 2000.

Ultimately, of course, it is China's own military strength, or lack of it, which will be decisive in any confrontation. And here there are three important and complementary points to grasp.

First, China is making great efforts to enhance its military capabilities. Since 1989, it has increased real defence spending each year, and the official figures greatly understate the reality.* China has been fundamentally restructuring its armed forces, turning them from a mass 'people's army' into a smaller (though still some two million strong), more professional and better trained force. The concentration is on acquiring new equipment and up-to-date technology. Most of the equipment is coming from the Russians. But for the technology the Chinese have benefited substantially from penetrating the West's military secrets.

Although the experts continue to debate the extent of the damage that has been done, the situation revealed by the Cox Report to the US House of Representatives in 1999 is alarming. The report suggests that China has stolen information on 'seven US thermonuclear warheads, including every currently deployed thermonuclear warhead in the US ballistic missile arsenal'.† Other information has been acquired by the Chinese both as a result of insufficiently rigorous monitoring of commercial contracts and as a result of the extraordinary – and potentially self-destructive – openness with which we in the West publicise scientific and technological advances. Just what use the Chinese will be able to make of this information, which they are doubtless continuing to obtain, is speculative. But we should not underrate their ingenuity or determination.

My second point, though, substantially qualifies the first. Although it is true that the Chinese are striving to increase their military strength, they still have a long way to go. So rapid are current advances in US military technology that the Chinese have

---

* The IISS *Military Balance* estimates the real level of Chinese defence spending as three times the official figure.

† *Report by the United States House of Representatives Select Committee on US National Security and Military/Commercial Concerns with the People's Republic of China*, chaired by Representative Christopher Cox.

to run in order to stand still. Much of China's existing arsenal is old and becoming obsolete. Russia, its main supplier, does not have the resources to develop the next generation of weapons that China will need. The Chinese defence budget in 1999 was less than a twentieth of America's and less than a third of Japan's.* And in terms of the ultimate deterrent – inter-continental ballistic missiles capable of delivering a nuclear warhead – while China has perhaps eighteen ICBMs with single warheads which it could use on the United States, America has some six thousand warheads able to hit China.† This means, of course, that if America's leaders should be foolish enough to leave the United States vulnerable to missile attack by failing to develop BMD, the West could be blackmailed by the Chinese; but it still could not be beaten. The Chinese must know this, and the knowledge will make them cautious. For the foreseeable future, therefore, China will be in no position to challenge America as a global superpower.

But superpower status on a parity with America is no more than a delicious fantasy for Beijing – and the Chinese are not in the last resort given to fantasy when it comes to foreign relations. The Chinese are aiming, in truth, at something much more attainable – to become the dominant regional power; and that is the third point we in the West have to grasp.

The starting point for considering China's regional ambitions is, naturally enough, the East Asia region itself. China is physically at its centre and is by far the most populous state. Although its armed forces received an embarrassing and unexpected bloody nose from Vietnam in 1979, on land it is probably now dominant. Yet that in itself is not enough to secure its supremacy, for many of the most important states do not abut its territory at all, being islands or archipelagos. As one analyst has put it: 'Geography limits the ability of China to be militarily preeminent in all of Asia because the PLA is woefully unbalanced in terms of military capability. Its ability to project militarily decisive

---

* *The Military Balance*, 1999–2000.
† David M. Lampton and Gregory C. May, *Managing US–China Relations in the Twenty-First Century*, The Nixon Center, 1999.

force beyond China's immediate neighbours is almost non-existent.'*

China is determined to overcome this by modernising its navy, and is making great efforts to do so. But its main focus has been on strengthening its arsenal of ballistic missiles, while investing heavily in guidance systems and satellites to improve missile accuracy. Above all, in recent years it has concentrated upon assembling a force of hundreds of surface-to-surface missiles in order to intimidate and if necessary attack Taiwan. (These missiles can be equipped with nuclear warheads.) The build-up continues.

It can be argued – and rightly – that Taiwan is not just another regional issue: after all, the Chinese regard it as part of China. But Taiwan is *also* a regional issue for three reasons. First, the overthrow or even the neutering of democracy in Taiwan, which is what Beijing effectively demands, would be a major setback for democracy in the region as a whole. Second, if the Chinese were able to get their way by force in Taiwan, they would undoubtedly be tempted to do the same in other disputes. And third, there is no lack of such disputes to provoke a quarrel. Not the least of these are competing claims in the South China Sea – an area of 648,000 square miles dotted with hundreds of islands, reefs, shoals and rocks. The goal is exploitation of what are believed to be huge reserves of oil and natural gas. The Chinese have become ever more preoccupied with such matters since they became net importers of oil in 1993. Competing with China, and with one another, are Vietnam, the Philippines, Thailand, Malaysia, Brunei and indeed Taiwan. The Spratly Islands, in particular, have been the focus of acrimonious disputes. But China is dominant. The Chinese are determined by hook or by crook to assert control over the hydrocarbon resources of the region, and it currently looks as if they will.

The Chinese traditionally view international relations in terms of the balance of power: this requires that the West should adopt the same approach to the East Asia region, if China is to be

---

* Michael McDevitt, 'Geographical Ruminations', in Larry M. Wortzel (ed.), *The Chinese Armed Forces in the Twenty-First Century* (US Army War College: Strategic Studies Institute, December 1999).

managed effectively. China should not be regarded as a monster, but as a somewhat unpredictable giant whose phobias should be anticipated and whose ambitions must be restrained. This, though, will not be easy and it will require strong nerves. China showed by its behaviour in the wake of the collision between a US reconnaissance aircraft and a Chinese fighter jet in April 2001 that it will test Western patience to the limit – and perhaps beyond.

From all this I conclude that:

- We should be in no doubt that China regards itself as being in military competition with us and that its main aim in strengthening its forces is to challenge US power in the region
- But, equally, it faces great difficulties in doing so, and has no present prospect of becoming a global military superpower
- China, therefore, must be watched, and when necessary constrained, so that it behaves peacefully towards its neighbours.

TAIWAN – TROUBLE SPOT

Maintaining a balance of power always involves a willingness to counterbalance accumulations of power – such as China's now against Taiwan. China's build-up of missiles in the Taiwan Straits is a threat not just to Taiwan itself but to the stability of the whole region, and thus to America's interests as a global superpower. What is to be done?

The starting point is to take what both the People's Republic of China (PRC) and the Republic of China (Taiwan) say seriously. Beijing is not prepared to see Taiwan establish itself as a sovereign state. The communists are quite determined about that. On the other hand, the Taiwanese, now that they have both prosperity and democracy, are not prepared to accept a variation on the theme of 'One Country, Two Systems', which is the best that Beijing is prepared to offer. However much finessing of language or tact is expended in managing the admission of the two Chinas into international bodies like the WTO, the two sides are fundamentally irreconcilable.

It is debatable whether mainland China could bring Taiwan to heel by military means. It could intimidate and gravely wound it by means of its missiles. In the longer run it might even be able to blockade Taiwan into submission. But in either case what is envisaged would be a major war, not a bloodless takeover.*

Is the West prepared to see this happen? If not, there is only one course open to us. It is to ensure that Taiwan is equipped to defend itself and then to demonstrate to China that if it chooses to assert its claims by force we will ensure that it fails.

Unfortunately, in recent years the PRC has been receiving mixed messages on the subject. Since 1979, when America formalised its relations with China and officially broke off diplomatic ties with Taiwan, US–Taiwanese relations have been governed by the Taiwan Relations Act, which states:

> The United States' decision to establish diplomatic relations with the People's Republic of China rests upon the expectation that the future of Taiwan will be determined by peaceful means;
>
> ... any effort to determine the future of Taiwan by other than peaceful means, including boycotts or embargoes, [is] a threat to the peace and security of the Western Pacific area and of grave concern to the United States.

The United States government has honoured the Taiwan Relations Act by supplying Taiwan with up-to-date weaponry. In 1996 the Clinton administration rightly dispatched two aircraft carriers to the area when China fired missiles in order to try to intimidate Taiwan during the latter's presidential elections. But two years later President Clinton unfortunately appeared to weaken US support for Taiwan by declaring on a visit to Beijing America's opposition to Taiwan's independence or to its membership of any organisation for which statehood was a requirement. The Chinese must, therefore, have been left in some uncertainty about the seriousness of America's commitment.

The greatest dangers when dealing with regimes like China's

---

* Differing estimates of the PRC's capabilities *vis-à-vis* Taiwan are given by Bates Gill and Michael O'Hanlon, 'China's Hollow Military', *The National Interest*, No. 56, Summer 1999, and by James Lilley and Carl Ford, 'China's Military: A Second Opinion', *The National Interest*, No. 57, Fall 1999. I would prefer to work on the more pessimistic estimate of the danger.

usually arise from confusion and perceived weakness that lead them to miscalculate. President George W. Bush has since ended this doubt, observing that the use of American military force was 'certainly an option' if China invaded Taiwan.* America is also supplying destroyers, aircraft and submarines to the Taiwanese. Naturally, the Chinese do not like it one bit. But the President was right to speak and act firmly.

I hope that the United States will go further in this direction by supplying Taiwan with an effective Theatre Missile Defence system. This would largely nullify China's efforts to use missiles as the means of coercing Taiwan to accept communist rule. Consequently, Beijing has protested furiously against the plan. That itself strongly suggests that Theatre Missile Defence should be made available to Taiwan soon. After all, if China had no designs on its small neighbour, why would it be objecting?

- Taiwan, therefore, is not, and can never be regarded as, a merely 'internal' Chinese matter, and Beijing must understand that
- It is vital to the stability of the region and to US interests that Taiwan should be effectively defended.

TAIWAN – MODEL

Taiwan is, therefore, certainly a potential trouble spot. But in the long run it is also a source of hope.

Taiwan's connections with mainland China have been loose or non-existent for many years. In 1895 it was seized by Japan and then remained Japanese until 1945. It was then briefly returned to rule from Beijing. Four years later the defeated Kuomintang (Nationalist) forces under General Chiang Kai-Shek sought refuge on the island and effectively, though not formally, created a separate state.

The one thing on which both Chiang and Mao agreed was that Taiwan was part of China. It was simply that each side saw the other as in rebellion against the legitimate government. Each of the 'Two Chinas' took a different path. Taiwan, protected by the United States and under the authoritarian rule of Chiang Kai-Shek

---

* Reported in *The Times*, 26 April 2001.

and then his eldest son Chiang Ching-Kuo, pursued the path of capitalism; Mao sought to create in China a socialist economy and society. In the ensuing competition between capitalism and communism, the former won hands down.

As a result, Taiwan has become one of the world's most successful economies. Economic growth has averaged about 8.5 per cent over the last three decades. Taiwan has become a leading global exporter in areas such as advanced electronics. Much of this economic success has been generated by Taiwan's entrepreneurial small-business culture, with one company per every eighteen Taiwanese.*

Taiwan's path of economic progress has also led to political reform, for which President Lee Teng-Hui deserves most of the credit. The 1989 general election which saw him become President was the first at which opposition parties were able to take part. The fact that he was the first native of Taiwan to assume the presidency also signalled a new era.† The 1996 elections which saw President Lee returned to power were not only the first ever direct elections for President in Taiwan. Their significance is all the greater when one considers that this was the first time in five thousand years of Chinese history that a Chinese leader had been chosen by the populace. And let us remember that this democratic transformation was achieved during a period of national emergency – precisely the circumstances in which governments usually choose to remove liberties, not broaden them.

The most recent elections of March 2000, which saw Chen Shui-bian become President, marked the final stage of transition, as the Kuomintang handed over power with good grace to the candidate of another party. The transformation of Taiwan into a modern democratic state was complete.

---

* *Barclays Bank Country Report*, 21 September 2000; *The Economist*, 7 November 1998.

† From the end of the seventeenth century, Taiwan was firmly part of the Chinese Empire, and there followed large-scale Chinese immigration. The 'Taiwanese' who consist of over 80 per cent of the population are mainly the descendants of those Chinese who emigrated then and later. The 'Chinese' (some 14 per cent) are those who came to the island with Chiang Kai-Shek, and their descendants.

Even before Deng Xiao Ping began his reforms, Taiwan's economic performance demonstrated that given the right conditions to flourish, the entrepreneurial spirit of the Chinese was second to none. And the way in which the Kuomintang was first prepared to create democracy and then to hand over power to the opposition shows that it is possible for Chinese leaders to make the transition to political freedom with wisdom and maturity. If the same should prove impossible in the People's Republic of China, the world will know for certain whom to blame – not the Chinese people, but the Chinese Communist Party.

- So Taiwan should not just be viewed as a problem: it is also an example – which is why China fears its continued success
- And that is also precisely why Taiwan must be permitted to flourish.

REFLECTIONS ON A LOTUS BOWL

In the afternoon of Sunday, 30 August 1992 I arrived in Taipei, the capital of Taiwan. It was my first visit: for serving Prime Ministers even to set foot on that island would be to incur Chinese wrath, and while Britain was locked in the negotiations about Hong Kong's future it had been out of the question.

Taiwan was only just starting to emerge from the status of political pariah to which much of the world had consigned it since the 1970s. But the island's economic miracle had forced even those who would have preferred to ignore it to sit up and take notice. By the time of my visit, Taiwan was the thirteenth largest trading nation, with the largest gold and foreign currency reserves in the world. I was therefore not at all surprised to find myself surrounded by economic dynamism and burgeoning prosperity.

I also came to understand in the course of my stay that Taiwan's impressive economic progress was complemented by a sense of order and tradition. This went far beyond the symbols of the Kuomintang – which was, of course, really quite modern in terms of Chinese history. What Taiwan has preserved is, rather, a degree of cultural continuity with the old China that communism on the mainland has spent decades trying to eliminate.

My final day in Taiwan convinced me of this. I had passed a

rather disturbed night. I had been relaxing in the enormous whirl-pool bath in my hotel suite when I looked up and noticed that the room was swaying. The earthquake – for such it was – continued, and with each tremor quantities of soapy water slopped over the sides of the bath. It seemed best to stay where I was until the quake stopped altogether, and later someone came in bringing a dressing gown. Neither I, nor the hotel, nor, as far as I know, the rest of Taipei was the worse for it. But it was an odd, unsettling experience.

The following morning I was taken by my hosts to the National Palace Museum. This extraordinary structure is built into a hillside on the outskirts of Taipei. It is on eight levels, with only the first above ground. Thirty-five galleries function as the sites of permanent and special exhibitions open to the public.

The museum contains more than six hundred thousand pieces and is without doubt the finest collection of Chinese art in the world. It represents the core of the Imperial collection, artefacts made by the Imperial workshop or given by foreign dignitaries and tributaries, through the Sung, Yuan, Ming and Ching dynasties – some eight centuries.

There is also no doubt that had these treasures not made their way to Taiwan they would have been damaged, dispersed or destroyed during the bouts of chaotic vandalism under Mao. Indeed, the detailed story of how the collection was rescued and transported is almost as absorbing as its contents. When the last Ching Emperor was finally expelled from the Forbidden City in 1924, the Imperial Treasures were fully catalogued and organised. In the face of the Japanese invasion the great collection was then moved south, first to Shanghai and later to Nanking. Finally, as the communists closed in, the finest pieces were selected for transport to Taiwan in 1949.

On the morning of my visit I was first taken around the public exhibitions, containing ceramics, jades, lacquer, enamel, ivory miniatures, paintings, embroideries, books and ancient documents. The learned commentary was occasionally interrupted by fourteen camera crews bumping into display cases of priceless exhibits. After lunch with the Taiwanese Prime Minister, General Hau Pei-tsun, an old soldier of the Kuomintang, I was accorded the special privilege of being taken down into the depths of the museum to see some of the treasures which were kept there.

The pieces are stored in ordinary-looking tin trunks, rather like the ones I used to pack for my children when they went back to school. These trunks are placed along two sets of wooden shelves stretching the length of both wings of the museum. The passageways are fully lit and spotlessly clean, and the temperature and humidity are carefully controlled. Beside the lift shaft on one of the subterranean floors was placed a green baize table. Having donned special gloves, I was allowed to inspect some of the most delicate artefacts in the museum – exquisite tiny tea bowls, rings, boxes and figurines.

What intrigued and delighted me most was the porcelain. I have been a collector of porcelain since soon after I was married. But, fine as it can be, English and European porcelain cannot compete for delicacy and refinement with the best Chinese. The Sung dynasty (960–1279), with their taste for elegance, encouraged its manufacture and it was then that some of the very finest pieces were made. The glazes vary from ivory, to pale blue, to reddish brown, or even black. But the most beautiful are, to my mind, the pale green celadon porcelains from the kilns of Ju-chou. The museum contains one of these which is justly regarded as a gem. It is a warming bowl in the shape of a ten-petalled lotus flower, an ancient symbol of purity.

It is, of course, possible for a civilisation to produce works of art of the highest quality and yet to be marred by social evils. But artefacts like the Ju-ware lotus bowl speak of a history that cannot be denied or obliterated if China is to find herself again. As we have seen in Eastern Europe, it is only by recapturing their past and drawing upon the legacies of collective memory that nations heal the wounds which totalitarianism leaves behind. The lotus bowl offers a clue, and provides a signpost, to China's destiny.

HONG KONG POSTSCRIPT

All my dealings with China, both as Prime Minister and since leaving office, were to a greater or lesser extent overshadowed by Hong Kong. Having placed my signature on the Joint Agreement for the return of Hong Kong to Chinese rule, I felt (and feel) a strong moral obligation to do my best for the former colony.

Moreover, this was more than optimistic aspiration. The Chinese attach much greater importance to former Prime Ministers and ex-Presidents than do Western countries. This is partly because they assume that, as in their own system, real power is as likely as not wielded from behind the scenes by those without prominent official positions. It is partly also because they have a deeply ingrained respect for the wisdom that – it is assumed – comes from age. The Chinese had no particular reason to be pleasant to me personally: they knew what I thought of communism and its methods, particularly after my bruising visit in 1991; they also understood that I had negotiated hard to preserve as much as possible of Hong Kong's capitalist system. But they like to deal with people who keep their word and who are strong enough to deliver on the promises they make.

I was aware that my successors had no easy task. John Major and Chris Patten, who became Hong Kong's Governor in 1992, had to manage the period up to the handover (on 1 July 1997) in such a way as to entrench economic and political freedom as deeply as possible. But this had to be done in strict compliance with the terms of the Joint Agreement and without overly offending the Chinese, who, of course, had the power if they wished to ruin Hong Kong at any moment.

The way in which Governor Patten went about his duties provoked a good deal of controversy. Some of the criticisms were reasonable; but many of them were not. The democratic reforms to the Hong Kong Legislative Council which Mr Patten introduced were extremely modest: they were also in full conformity with the Joint Agreement and the Basic Law (which sets out Hong Kong's constitutional arrangements). They were less than Hong Kong itself would have liked. But they proved excessively strong meat for Beijing and they have since been rescinded.

I gave full public and private support to Mr Patten. Nor do I regret doing so. The Chinese could have accepted the changes he proposed without any loss of face or damage to their essential interests.

By the time of my visit to China in March 1995 relations

between the Chinese government and the Governor had sharply deteriorated. There were only two years to go before the handover and several important issues for the future of Hong Kong were still outstanding. The Foreign Office and Mr Patten encouraged me to try to break the logjam. The main outstanding questions were the establishment of the Court of Final Appeal, and the financing of the new Hong Kong airport. The Chinese were also, I was told, suspicious that Britain intended to carry off Hong Kong's financial reserves before China took control. I could hardly treat this last point seriously – until I recalled my discussions with Deng Xiao Ping in 1982. Deng's understanding of the basis of Hong Kong's wealth had been limited then as well. He had imagined that at any time I could stop the outflow of money from Hong Kong, simply by issuing an instruction.* (I also later reflected that looting the reserves is exactly what the Chinese themselves would have done in our position before the handover.)

On arriving in Beijing I was greatly struck by the change since my previous visit. The whole scene was more lively, the clothes were of better quality and brighter, the traffic jams were almost as bad as London's, and everywhere you looked vast construction projects were underway.

That afternoon I went to Zhong Nanhai for a meeting with Li Peng. The cameras had been assembled to photograph us on the verandah. I took the opportunity of telling the press that I wished to speak about progress on Hong Kong. This intrusion of substance into ceremony seemed initially to disconcert my host, but after a few minutes of private discussion inside he became more relaxed. In fact, I found him more urbane and at ease than he had been four years earlier: perhaps losing the power struggle with Jiang Zemin, who was now President and China's real ruler, had taken off the pressure. I began by emphasising that Britain wanted to transfer Hong Kong to China in a strong financial position, which meant, naturally, that the reserves would be intact. I found Mr Li amenable about the other points of substance. In discussion of the Court of Final Appeal, I urged speed, while Li Peng was more interested in insisting that no decisions be taken without

---

* See *The Downing Street Years*, p.262.

China's agreement – an obvious echo of the polemics directed against Chris Patten. Indeed, it became all too clear that he was extremely hostile to the Governor and to his reforms, which he described as 'violating' the Joint Agreement. I denied this and argued that the changes were the least that the Governor could have made in the light of popular demands. But on this matter no headway was possible.

Li Peng then made a prepared statement about the situation in China. His emphasis was very much upon continuity. Deng Xiao Ping (who had handed over the Chairmanship of the Central Military Commission – his last formal post – to Jiang Zemin in 1989) was, said Li Peng, in good condition for someone of ninety-one. The new leadership would, in any case, continue on the course which Deng had set. But Li Peng gave a characteristic slant to this message by adding that China was not very familiar with the market economy and that state-owned industries would continue to be the mainstay of the economy. At the end of our talk I gave him a copy of a Chinese-language edition of my memoirs, which he handled with some caution. I somehow doubt whether it is to be found on the bookshelves of his study.

I had once again on this visit asked to meet Zhao Ziyang. But I was told that this was still not possible. It is good to ensure, though, that he is not forgotten. On this occasion, I sent him a note with a present of a tie that I had bought in London. I know that he likes ties.

Two other memories remain with me of that visit. The first is of the shops and shoppers. As I went around a state-run 'friendship store', full of excellent-quality produce, I was deluged with people demanding autographs and wanting to be photographed with me. This was doubtless proof of celebrity status rather than indicative of political sympathy. But the fact that it could happen at all, and that no one intervened to stop it, suggested that there were now practical limits to the power of the government.

The other recollection is of the final event of my stay – an *al fresco* reception given by our excellent Ambassador, Sir Leonard Appleyard and his wife for Chinese students who had studied in Britain. It was a beautiful spring day. Around about us in the garden hundreds of pot plants were being removed from their long winter hibernation – spent in huge pits covered with thick matting – and placed out in the daylight. It was a cheerful background to my discussion with the students, who turned out to be bright, self-confident and full of praise for Britain. One young man told me that he had been reading Police Studies at Exeter University. I said that I hoped our techniques would soon be introduced into China. But for this, I fear, we will have to wait.

Since the handover of Hong Kong the Chinese have generally honoured their commitments. They have upheld the provisions of the Joint Declaration and the Basic Law. Freedom of assembly and association is practised. Provisions allowing the banning of demonstrations on security grounds have not been invoked. The four thousand Chinese troops on the island mainly keep out of sight and are not involved in policing. This is not to say that everything is as the British left it. The Chinese exert a good deal of covert influence. There is also much concern in Hong Kong about the precedent set by what amounts to the overturning of a ruling by the Court of Final Appeal on immigration.* It is, though, too early to know whether this was a blunder by the authorities or a more worrying indicator for the future. The Chinese certainly appear to have no intention of tolerating any progress towards real democracy, of which they remain deeply afraid.

While the political signs are therefore mixed, the economic prognosis is good – even better than many expected. The integrity of Hong Kong's financial system has been upheld. Indeed, the authorities showed considerable skill in weathering the Asian economic crisis. The long-term future of Hong Kong, politically and economically, will inevitably depend heavily upon the future of China itself.

---

* In January 1999 the Hong Kong Court of Final Appeal affirmed that under the provisions of the Basic Law seventeen Chinese from the mainland had a right to live in Hong Kong. The Hong Kong government, however, then referred the interpretation of the Basic Law to the Standing Committee of the National People's Congress – communist China's 'parliament'. The latter disagreed with the court's ruling and gave a more restrictive interpretation of the relevant Basic Law provisions. The court in December duly reversed its earlier decision. This was widely seen as demonstrating that the central government could and would overrule Hong Kong's Court of Final Appeal.

Hong Kong's experience also, however, provides some clues to that future. The Chinese authorities have not changed their basic position. They want to enjoy all the benefits of capitalism without running the risks of democracy. But, in Deng's expression 'seeking truth from the facts', they have gradually come to recognise some connections between the two. They know that they cannot benefit from Hong Kong as a gateway for investment and expertise if they shatter its confidence or drive away its talent by coercive political measures. They probably also grasp that a rule of law, which is essential to successful finance and commerce, also has to guarantee some non-economic rights. But the present Communist Party elite will never take the final logical step of recognising the interdependence of political and economic liberty. It cannot afford to. Yet change will come. And when it does the lessons learned by the Chinese in Hong Kong should make it less traumatic, and perhaps less violent.

PART II: INDIA

There is something slightly artificial in considering India as merely 'Asian'. It is a vast country in its own right. It is distinct by reason of civilisation, of religion, and of historical experience from East Asia. And its preoccupations since independence have principally been with disputes involving Pakistan, Kashmir and, on occasion, Sri Lanka. Yet, looking ahead further into this twenty-first century, India has, I believe, the potential to be a mighty force, both regionally in Asia and indeed globally. In particular, it will increasingly provide a counterweight to China – whose own vast population India's will exceed within fifty years.*

THE BRITISH LEGACY
I have always been fascinated by India. Back in Grantham, I remember as a young girl following closely the events leading up to independence. Already I was something of a romantic imperial-

---

* *World Population 1998*, United Nations Department of Economic and Social Affairs Population Division.

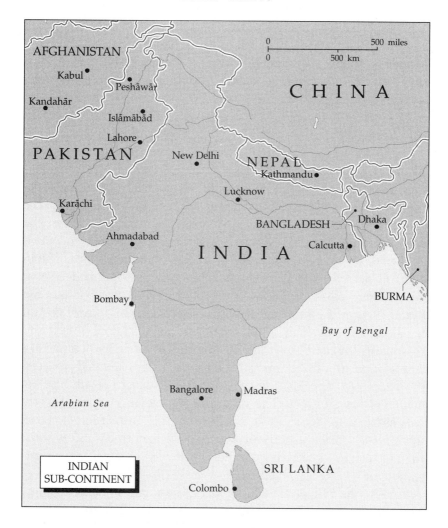

INDIAN
SUB-CONTINENT

ist. In 1935 when I was ten years old I had been asked at a family gathering, as children are, what I wanted to be when I grew up. I replied that I intended to join the ranks of the Indian Civil Service – that less-than-a-thousand-strong elite which brought good governance to the sub-continent. My father, more perceptive than many, wryly commented that by the time I was an adult there might not be an Indian Civil Service to enter. He turned out to be right. I had to settle for British politics instead.

Jawaharlal Nehru, India's first Prime Minister, once remarked:

'The English are a sensitive people, and yet when they go to foreign countries there is a strange lack of awareness about them.'* Many foreigners today would agree with at least the second part of that statement. But, for all the misunderstandings and even abuses, the legacy of the British in India was overwhelmingly positive – in the words of Churchill, 'a monument worthy of the respect of nations'.†

First, out of the Raj flowed a secure, mature democracy. The British bequeathed Indians not just the institutions of parliamentary government but an understanding of what attitudes make them work – something that is far more difficult to instil. The result is that in spite of successive crises the fundamentals of the constitution have been respected; no elections have been prevented or their results ignored; and the army has remained under civilian control. Second, the British left behind them a codified rule of law, largely eliminating the most barbaric excesses of the old India, such as the burning of widows (*suttee*), child sacrifice and female infanticide. Third, India inherited a tradition of honest and reasonably efficient government. The Indian Civil Service which I had aspired to join became steadily more evenly divided between the races, so that on the eve of independence about half its members were Indian. The much larger Provincial Civil Service was entirely so. As a result, by the time the British left in 1947 there was in place a body of experienced local men and women to take on the tasks of running the newly independent megastate.

Finally, the British gave India a common and official language. This was essential for a country covering more than a million square miles and whose population spoke twelve main languages and 220 dialects. Nowadays Hindi – spoken by about 30 per cent of the population – is the official language, but English is an associate language for many official purposes. Moreover, the fact that English is now also the dominant global language of business

---

* Quoted by Geoffrey Moorhouse in his excellent *India Britannica* (London: Harvill Press, 1983).

† Quoted by Lawrence James in *Raj: The Making and Unmaking of British India* (London: Little, Brown and Company, 1997), p.640.

means that India possesses a marked potential advantage in this respect over most of its Asian competitors.

LOST OPPORTUNITIES

Unfortunately, however, 'potential' is a word that comes all too frequently to mind when one considers India's record since 1947. After the horrors of violent mass population shifts that accompanied partition with Pakistan, Indian political life settled into an undistinguished if democratic rut. Its inherited problems – terrible poverty, grotesque inequalities, including the caste system, ethnic and religious strife – were not effectively tackled. India made, in fact, most of the wrong choices. Its governments adopted socialist theories, applied interventionist and protectionist policies, and mouthed militant Third World rhetoric. India's rulers were more interested in their quarrels with Pakistan than in benefiting from Western expertise and investment. Just below the surface, most of India's politicians were eaten up with post-colonial resentments. And it showed. During the Cold War, India was officially 'non-aligned', but in the event of a crisis like that when the Soviets invaded Afghanistan in 1979 the alignment was clear enough – towards the USSR, and away from America.

The results were really not at all surprising. Under a system of controls and tariffs, India's economic potential went unfulfilled. Between the 1950s and the late 1980s its share of world trade actually fell.

As Britain's Prime Minister towards the end of that period I had much to do with India and its rulers. In particular, I got to know Indira Gandhi well.* I found her charming, intelligent and cultured – though she was also a cunning and sometimes ruthless politician. I could not help liking her and I also admired her determination, if not her methods. But it was her prejudices which were the problem, and these, like those of her father Jawaharlal Nehru, were those of socialism. Her son Rajiv† I also knew and liked, even though he was one of my most vocal critics in the Commonwealth in the days when no summit was complete

---

* Indira Gandhi (1917–84), Indian Prime Minister 1966–77 and 1980–84.
† Rajiv Gandhi (1944–91), Indian Prime Minister 1984–89.

without tantrums from someone about South Africa. Unlike his mother, Rajiv had begun to understand that India could never prosper unless it embraced free-market reforms. I suspect that he probably also grasped that India's old left-leaning international posture was outdated as the Cold War came to an end. Tragically, as with his mother, it was India's problems of inter-communal strife rather than those of geopolitics or economics which sealed his fate: he was assassinated by a Tamil extremist when campaigning in the elections of May 1991.

THE PATH OF REFORM

By then I was out of office. But I still followed events in the sub-continent closely. India's economic problems remained unsolved. Indeed, the country was on the edge of defaulting on its external debt obligations. Only in June 1991 was there a significant change of course when the new government of Prime Minister P.V. Narasimha Rao embarked on a radical opening up of India's economy. His Finance Minister, Manmohan Singh, was the real architect of the new policies. Indeed, Mr Singh deserves to be numbered with Leszek Balcerowicz in Poland, Vaclav Klaus in the Czech Republic and most recently Zhu Rongji in China in the international roll-call of outstanding economic leaders.

In 1994 and again in 1995 I went to India to see for myself what was being done. On each occasion I had the opportunity to speak with Prime Minister Rao, Finance Minister Singh and – equally important – a large number of bankers and entrepreneurs who could tell me what was actually happening in the real economy. The more I heard, the more I was struck by the boldness of what was being attempted.

It is one thing to cut back regulation, lower import tariffs, relax foreign exchange controls, open up the market to foreign companies and privatise state-owned industries where there is a strong safety-net of benefits and little serious poverty. But in a society like India where much of the population, particularly in rural areas, lead lives of great deprivation it is a still more formidable challenge. In a poor Third World country free-market policies are no less necessary or beneficial than in well-developed states –

and, because there are fewer inherited obstacles, growth, once it starts, can be faster. But the special problem economic reformers face in the Third World is that they have to show positive results sooner. The initial impact of sound, free-market policies on any country that has grown used to inflation, high public spending, overmanning and protection is bound to be painful. But a poor country has fewer resources on which to draw during the lean years.

The truth is that there are two Indias, which do not as yet converge. One of these is uneducated, often illiterate, disproportionately subject to health hazards, no longer starving – there has been a beneficial revolution in Indian agriculture since the 1970s – but still lacking most of what Westerners would consider the basic amenities. This is the image of India which still impresses and appals us – and it constitutes a part of the reality.

But the other India, equally real – the India of the future – is one that excels in science and engineering, is home to first-rate universities and is a leader in information technology and knowledge-based industries. This second India is rapidly producing that vital social component of economic progress, a business-oriented middle class. Although there are still too many factors holding this second India back – too much bureaucracy, too little electric power, too few educated workers – the Indian economy has astonished those who once spoke glibly of an innate cultural (Hindu) hostility to enterprise. The Indian economy has been growing steadily at 6 per cent a year; a sustainable rate of 8 per cent is believed by many economists to be within reach; and India proved almost entirely immune to the bout of Asian economic 'flu that floored so many others.

Despite fears expressed at the time in some quarters, the Bharatiya Janata Party (BJP – Hindu Nationalist)-led government has since 1999 broadly pursued the free-market policies begun by its predecessor. I am convinced that within the next few years, and as long as the path of market reform is pursued, we will see fulfilment of India's potential and its transformation into one of the world's major economic powers.

I would like to see:

- India accorded the importance she deserves in Western geopolitical thinking
- A much wider appreciation of her political achievements and economic potential.

CONFLICT RESOLUTION

India is also on the threshold of great-power status in military terms. And that too is something new.

Since the Second World War – when very large numbers of Indians were decorated for valour – India's armed forces have not been greatly tested. Against China in 1962 its army performed poorly. If it has drawn or won its wars with Pakistan, that has been due to overwhelming numerical superiority, rather than military expertise. These events, however, are unreliable pointers to the future.

India still has a huge number of men under arms – at some 980,000 it has one of the world's largest armies. It is also now applying technology, both locally developed and imported, to achieve radical modernisation. Like China, India has, for example, been concentrating on the military uses of the information technology which Indian business has become so successful at developing – notably high-performance computers and sophisticated software. The BJP government is sharply increasing military spending and is developing a navy which will project power into the South China Sea. India, like China is a major purchaser of weapons from Russia.* Also like China, India has, of course, become a fully-fledged nuclear power.

I have explained elsewhere why this last seems to me to have been inevitable.† But in any case, no matter what promises are extracted from the Indians now, the process is irreversible. The Indian Defence Minister, George Fernandes, responded to US criticism of India's nuclear tests by asking: 'Why is it that you feel yourself so close to China that you can trust China with nuclear weapons . . . but you cannot trust India?' He has a point.

---

* Victor M. Gobarev, 'India as a World Power: Changing Washington's Myopic Policy', *Cato Institute Policy Analysis*, No. 381, 11 September 2000.
† See pp.52–3.

Above all, I would like to see India emerge as a powerful counterweight to China. It has the size and population; it has much of the same economic potential; and it is a well-established democracy. Some will reply that this democracy is flawed. And that is true. I have no illusions that Indian society is a model of tolerance and harmony – it isn't, as almost daily killings, riots and persecutions of minorities show. But, equally, I have no doubt that an Asia which adopts the political path of India rather than that so far taken by China is likely to be easier company for the West.

What principally disturbs Western observers at this moment, however, is not India's relations with China but rather with Pakistan, which has also demonstrated its nuclear capability. India can only emerge as a major power outside its own region of South Asia if it is able to stabilise that relationship. But is this possible?

At the moment, perhaps not. The basis for this somewhat gloomy assessment lies, however, in Islamabad, not in Delhi. Even before the events of 11 September and the start of US operations against the Taliban, Pakistan was, in its way, almost as important to the West in strategic terms as India. In the wake of the Soviet invasion of Afghanistan in December 1979, Pakistan became home to several million refugees. Pakistan was a major source of support to the Afghan resistance, and, conversely, it was itself much affected by the rise among Afghans of Islamic militancy. Under President Zia the state of Pakistan was increasingly Islamicised and the Sharia became the law of the land. During the Cold War, when the West was struggling to ensure the defeat of the Soviets, the rise of militant Islam in the region was not a significant source of concern. Perhaps in retrospect it should have been. But in geopolitics, as in life, we can only tackle one major threat at a time. Soviet communism was such a threat. And both devout Muslims and secular Westerners shared a common goal in resisting it.

Pakistan's involvement in Afghanistan did not end with the end of the Cold War. Pakistan's rulers remained anxious to combat Russian and Iranian influences over its northern neighbour. Ethnic links – between fellow Pathans – and religious links – between fellow Sunnis – were also important factors. And in any case Pakistan remained host to a large community of Afghans. For all these reasons, the Pakistan government needed to find an apparently amenable faction to support, which could take power in Afghanistan. From the early 1990s it settled on the Taliban, which from 1996 formed a more or less fragile government in Kabul. Although Pakistan itself remained a broadly moderate Muslim state, the Taliban, who were to a large extent Pakistan's creation, quickly revealed themselves to be extreme and intolerant Islamic fanatics. This posed increasing problems for the pro-Western government of Pakistan – problems which came to a crisis with al-Qaeda's attacks on America and the Taliban's refusal to hand over the culprits.

But in considering how to manage relations with Pakistan now we also need to consider its longer-term difficulties and weaknesses as a state. Never since independence has it experienced any prolonged period of successful democracy. It has been plagued by corruption and misgovernment. Much of its population accordingly remains locked into abject poverty, with little hope of escape.

Another continuing source of instability has been rivalry with India. Historical reasons – and particularly the issue of Kashmir – lie behind this. But it is the more destabilising because Pakistan is clearly the weaker of the rivals. Its awkward shape, and the fact that it is so much smaller (with a population of 138 million) than India, cause Pakistan with good reason to fear its giant neighbour.

The armed forces in Pakistan are the one great national institution which commands respect. Even before the coup in which General (now President) Pervais Musharraf took power in 1998, the army was responsible for overseeing or even running major civil enterprises, such as the Water and Power Development Agency. This was why the population of Pakistan gave the coup such an enthusiastic welcome: the army was seen as the only force in public life that could clean out the corruption and restore sound administration.

But Pakistan's pride – and the army's pride – is also offended by the situation in Kashmir. It is worth briefly recalling the basic facts. The partition of British India into two new states – predominantly Hindu India and predominantly Muslim Pakistan – involved not just the allocation of the two-thirds of the subcontinent that were directly administered by the British, but also the third which consisted of states ruled by Indian princes. Kashmir was one of these states. It had had a Muslim majority for many years, but it was ruled by a Hindu. This prince, Maharajah Hari Singh, faced with an inrush of Pathan tribesmen, probably organised by Pakistan, signed an Instrument of Accession transferring the princedom to India. This was accepted – indeed welcomed – by Lord Mountbatten, the last British Viceroy, but only on condition that (in his words) 'as soon as law and order have been restored and its soil cleared of the invader, the question of the State's accession should be settled by a reference to the people'. This proposal was endorsed by United Nations Resolutions in 1948 and 1949.*

Contrary to its initial undertakings, India has never allowed this plebiscite to be held – for the very good reason that the Muslim majority would almost certainly vote to take Kashmir out of India. In the meantime, violence and abuses on both sides have certainly not contributed to making most Kashmiris any fonder of Indian rule.

This does not necessarily mean that India has no case. In fact, it has at one level a very strong one – the case of its own national security and strategic interests. If a great power like India decides that its fundamental interests apply in an area which, like Kashmir, does not directly affect the fundamental interests of the West, I am not in favour of pointless interference. That remains my view despite the renewed pressure to 'solve' Kashmir – just as there is pressure to 'solve' the Middle East – in order to enable effective pursuit of the wider war against terrorism. Patched-up diplomatic solutions designed to answer the needs of the moment rarely last, and as they unravel they can actually make things worse.

Looking ahead, it is impossible to imagine the state of Pakistan, and Kashmiris of varying degrees of militancy, ever placidly accepting India's hold here. And for as long as the conflict goes on, India, for its part, will remain distracted from its manifest destiny of acting as an Asian regional superpower. A full-scale

---

* A useful summary of the complex historical background is provided by Alexander Rose, 'Paradise Lost: The Ordeal of Kashmir', *The National Interest*, Winter 1999/2000.

war with Pakistan on the issue could never be in India's interests, involving as it would the risk of a nuclear exchange. But even a low-level struggle exacts a toll.

The way to a long-term solution is probably not through international peace conferences. Progress will only occur if and when both Pakistan and India conclude that they have more important matters to consider than Kashmir, and so become willing to compromise. In the meantime, the only course is to continue to urge restraint on both sides, pointing out the dangers if low-level clashes were allowed to escalate into war.

In Pakistan, the military regime, whatever one thought about the circumstances in which it arose, offered a new start. It had an opportunity to do something of what General Pinochet did for Chile – namely radically to reform the economy by making decisions that no democratic government at that time was prepared to envisage. Pakistan above all needed a breathing space, time to set its affairs in order, and to build a national consensus in favour of honest and in due course truly democratic government. The West should have helped President Musharraf to begin rebuilding the state and the economy. Instead, we just cajoled and threatened.

In the wake of 11 September this attitude has changed. The sanctions imposed on Pakistan (and India) after the nuclear tests in 1998 have been lifted. Aid to Pakistan has resumed. Across-the-board assistance should be continued and increased. The West's help for Pakistan is not mere philanthropy. Nor is it simply a reward for President Musharraf's cooperation – though it is that. The most important consideration is that the West has very significant security interests at stake. We must do everything we can to prevent Pakistan falling into the hands of Islamic extremists. These people want to gain control of Pakistan's nuclear weapon so as to wage *jihad* against Hindus, Sikhs, Christians and Jews alike. If the Musharraf government were to fall as a result of his closeness to the West, that could be as dangerous to us as when the Shah of Iran was overthrown for similar reasons in 1979. A new wave of Islamic fanaticism would be unleashed; our sworn enemies would take new heart; and they would have at the core of their *jihad* a state with a nuclear weapon. Such a prospect is unthinkable.

These considerations also bear upon the timetable for a return to democracy in Pakistan. Ultimately military rule cannot give Pakistan the long-term stability it needs. But 'ultimately' can wait. On 14 August 2001 President Musharraf promised to hold elections late in 2002. In other circumstances, it would have been right to hold him to that timetable. But if in his judgement the return to full democracy has to be postponed because of the backlash from events in Afghanistan, we should support him. Better a friendly state with some liberty than a hostile state with none – particularly if that state has a nuclear weapon.

In the longer term, India's future is of still greater importance to us than that of Pakistan. Thankfully, India is in far better shape than its neighbour and generally well able to sort out its own internal problems. But she too deserves more patience, understanding and respect from the West. India should be acknowledged for what she is – already a great power, and soon to become a regional superpower.

This raises the question of whether India should become a Permanent Member of the UN Security Council. My present feeling is that the Council's membership should not be expanded at all. I cannot see how any change is going to be acceptable to those excluded, and if too many powers try to sit at the top table there will be paralysis. But I do believe that if such expansion were indeed pursued India would have a very strong claim – and stronger than many others mentioned as possible candidates.

It is in the West's interests to advance India's great-power status. The emergence of this huge democracy as a major player on the global stage can bring many benefits. Not least of these is the opportunity it will afford for Western statecraft to achieve a regional counterbalance to China, just as thirty years ago President Nixon made his opening to China in order to counterbalance the Soviet Union.

The West, therefore, has to:

- **Accept that India is a great power and accord it the status that implies – perhaps including, in due course, permanent membership of the UN Security Council**

- Stop pointless protests about India's or Pakistan's nuclear capabilities
- Stop trying to 'solve' the presently unsolvable problem of Kashmir, but continue urging restraint on both sides
- Concentrate on helping Pakistan come to grips with its huge difficulties and ensure that our proven friends remain in charge there
- Welcome the development of India's role as a regional superpower to balance China.

CHAPTER 6

Rogues, Religions
and Terrorism

WHAT IS A ROGUE?

Rogue states, religious extremism and international terrorism – since 11 September 2001 these three scourges have become inextricably linked in the public imagination. Each in its own right threatens civil peace and international stability. But when each feeds off the other, the sum of evil is even greater than that of the individual parts.* The death toll in New York and Washington allows no doubt of this.

The concept of the rogue state is relatively new. It achieved official status as an element of American foreign policy through a speech made by President Clinton's National Security Advisor, Anthony Lake, in September 1993. Mr Lake put forward a vision of post-Cold War foreign policy of which the centrepiece was a 'strategy of enlargement of the world's free community of market democracies'. Part of this strategy was to 'seek to isolate' rogue

---

* The symbiotic connection between terrorist organisations and sponsor states has long been internationally recognised and condemned. As Prime Minister, I was one of the heads of government at the 1986 Tokyo G7 summit who pressed most strongly for the declaration: '[we] strongly reaffirm our condemnation of international terrorism in all its forms, of its accomplices and of *those, including governments, who sponsor or support it*. Terrorism has no justification' (emphasis added).

states 'diplomatically, militarily, economically and technologically'.* This thinking was not altogether original. President George
Bush's concept of a 'New World Order', expounded in September
1990 in his speech to the United States Congress, contained the seeds
of the approach.† At its heart was the idea that with the end of the
Cold War and the approach of the 'end of history' (in Fukuyama's
sense of the phrase) there would exist a global community of
orderly, cooperative, open and, above all, democratic states. Outside this ever increasing circle a small number of miscreants or
'rogues' might continue to cause problems. But by mobilising the
resources of the enlightened majority against them, mainly through
decisions of the United Nations Security Council, they could be
thwarted, contained, quarantined and ultimately extinguished.

Like many such concepts – the 'New World Order' itself is an
example – that of the 'rogue state' contains an important element
of truth. I have used the phrase myself in speeches, because it is,
after all, a useful shorthand description of relatively small powers
which have the motives and means to cause disproportionate
trouble. Beyond that, however, the weakness of the concept is that
it suffers from imprecision.

It makes, in fact, two tacit assumptions. The first assumption
is that all the non-'rogue' powers have such strong interests in
common that cooperation between them is assured. The second
is that one 'rogue' is very much like another. But both assumptions
are actually wrong. Rogue states never turn out to be quite the
pariahs they are deemed. They are only able to cause, or at least
threaten to cause, mayhem because they enjoy the covert support
– usually by means of technology transfers – of one or more major
powers within the charmed circle of global 'good guys'. Moreover,
the individual states that the world thinks of as 'rogues' often have
different priorities and capabilities.

All of which might suggest that I would therefore have been
pleased to learn that the American State Department, in deference
it seems to the feelings of Stalinist North Korea, no longer wished

---

* Report of a speech at the School of Advanced International Studies, Johns
Hopkins University: *New York Times*, 22 September 1993.
† For the 'New World Order' see pp.28–9.

to speak of rogue states at all, but rather of 'states of concern'.* But quite apart from the awful English, this expression hardly got us any further. It merely substituted the vacuous for the simplistic. And it should certainly 'concern' all of us if that sort of approach ever gained favour among the policy-makers of the greatest power on earth. Thankfully, under the present administration this silly exercise in semantics has, it seems, come to an end.

The usual candidates for rogue state status are held to be North Korea, Iraq, Syria, Libya, Iran and (possibly in a lesser category) Sudan.† I would not quarrel with that list. The regimes of these states are all in various ways and in varying degrees unsavoury and dangerous. None is democratic. None is governed by what we would understand as a rule of law. All persecute dissident individuals and opposition groups. All are in the grip of ideologies which make them fundamentally hostile to the West and its allies. All are at various stages of acquiring weapons of mass destruction (WMD). These commonalities are indeed important. But a closer analysis is required before we can hope to construct policies to cope with the threats they pose.

NORTH KOREA

North Korea is a classic rogue state – a doctrinaire dictatorship controlling a closed society, at once oppressive and aggressive, armed to the teeth with conventional weapons, anxious to develop and export WMD. But it is also unusual, because it is one of the last redoubts of the hardest of hardline communism.

Television shots of the North Korean Stalinist dictator Kim Jong Il and thousands of his subjects cheerfully greeting South Korean President Kim Dae Jung and later US Secretary of State Madeleine Albright hardly do justice to the reality of life north of the 38th

---

* Report of remarks by the then Secretary of State Madeleine Albright: *New York Times*, 20 June 2000.

† Afghanistan under the Taliban might also be classified as a rogue state. But its circumstances and significance are so distinctive that I deal with it separately. See pp.37–9.

Parallel. North Korea is still one of the most secretive and sinister places on earth. After Mrs Albright arrived back in the United States she admitted that North Korea's human rights record was 'not good at all'.* From the patchy information that has leaked out about how North Koreans live – and die – that appears something of an understatement. But we will probably have to wait for the regime to collapse before the full horrors can be assessed.

From 1945, when the north of the Korean peninsula passed under Soviet control, the area was characterised by political violence. From 1948, when the People's Democratic [sic] Republic of Korea was created, the regime headed by Kim Il Sung planned the violent attempt to conquer South Korea that led to the Korean War two years later. Frustrated in that endeavour, and only narrowly surviving the consequences, Kim Il Sung turned his country into a giant political prison. Like the rulers of Albania and Cambodia, he sought to keep insiders in and outsiders out – with the exception of forays to kidnap people whose skills or influence he thought might prove useful. The Communist Party was subject to recurrent purges, one of the most brutal being that of opponents of Kim's designating his son as successor. The whole nation was subject to relentless indoctrination reinforced by systematised terror in support of the bizarre ideology of *Juche* (basically, totalitarian socialist self-sufficiency). North Korea vigorously supported terrorism. It murdered part of the South Korean cabinet in Burma and provided a haven for Japanese terrorists who blew up an airliner in 1987. The death of Kim Il Sung in 1994 did not mark any improvement in the regime's conduct. Kim Jong Il appointed new men to some key positions, but there was no let-up in repression or aggression.

It has been estimated on the basis of the limited data available that since 1948, one hundred thousand people have died in party purges, and 1.5 million in concentration camps. To those must be added the more than 1.3 million deaths in the Korean War, which was a war of aggression launched by Pyongyang with Moscow's agreement. And perhaps half a million may have died more recently of famine – brought about immediately by natural disas-

---

* *Washington Times*, 3 November 2000.

ters but fundamentally by the grotesque incompetence of the political system and those who control it. That amounts to over three million in a country of twenty-three million.*

Kim Jong Il has spelt out his priorities, if anyone has the patience to search for them amid his rants and ramblings. He is convinced, probably rightly, that his power rests on the army. He knows that he has to keep his commanders happy. He has complained, for example: 'We cannot win a war with the enemy if we have no food for the military. It is unjustifiable that we cannot supply food to our army ... Food for the military should be unconditionally guaranteed.'† The main reason he is prepared to modify application of *Juche* and accept, even solicit, foreign food aid is to feed his soldiers, not his people.

The recent changes which have occurred in North Korea have been the result of external not internal developments. The collapse of the Soviet Union cut off one source of aid, trade, support and protection. China's reorientation towards the West and a market economy has meant that it too is less inclined to shore up a basically unviable regime. North Korea has therefore settled on a strategy of establishing relations with the rest of the world on a new basis.

One aspect of this has already been mentioned – exploitation of the West's compassion. Here we are in a real dilemma. We do not know enough about the scale and nature of the famine – which is undoubtedly real – to make a judgement as to what is the best way to help. The regime blames natural disasters for it. The same excuse was offered by the Soviet Union and socialist states in Africa. But it is hollow. Efficient economies have the resources to cope with whatever nature throws at them, if not immediately, at least over time. By contrast, a country like North Korea in which private ownership of land is outlawed is ultimately condemned to starve. Nor does providing food aid offer a long-term answer;

---

* Some estimates of the effects of famine are much higher. These figures come from Pierre Rigoulot, 'Crimes, Terror and Secrecy in North Korea', in *The Black Book of Communism*, pp.547–64.

† Address on the Fiftieth Anniversary of Kim Il Sung University, 7 December 1996.

indeed, many economists see this kind of 'aid' as positively harmful because it undermines local agriculture. It may sound harsh, but the most effective and perhaps even the quickest way to save North Korea from starvation is to precipitate a change of government.*

The second aspect of North Korea's approach – the one which marks it out fairly and squarely as a 'rogue' – is what one expert has nicely termed 'a carefully managed stratagem of military extortion'.† This stratagem was successfully established by Pyongyang in 1994, when it faced down Western threats after North Korea was discovered to be on the verge of becoming a nuclear power. North Korea then agreed to freeze this programme, and in exchange the US promised to send an annual half-million tons of free oil and to pay for the construction of two light-water nuclear reactors at a total cost of $4 billion. This was a major diplomatic defeat for the West and a notable success for a bankrupt basket-case. As a result, North Korea is now probably the largest recipient of American aid in Asia.

Even more astonishing, North Korea did not as part of this arrangement halt, or even slow down, its development and sale of advanced missile technology. Seen from its point of view, why should it? North Korea desperately needed the foreign currency which this lethal trade could bring; its role as chief 'rogue' reinforced its prestige among anti-Western states, near and far; and it could also hope at the right moment to extort new instalments of Danegeld from America and her allies.‡

North Korea is deeply engaged in programmes to develop, test and export shorter-range 'Scud' surface-to-surface missiles, longer-range Nodong intermediate missiles, and Taepodong intercontinental ballistic missiles (ICBMs). It probably earns $100 million a year in selling these weapons and associated technologies. Scuds have gone to Egypt, Syria and Vietnam. The Nodong and

---

* There is evidence that in any case the worst of the famine is over and that food production has again risen. *South China Morning Post*, 22 May 2000.
† Nicholas Eberstadt, 'The Old North', *The World and I*, 1 June 2000.
‡ Danegeld, as my British (and doubtless Danish?) readers will know, was the tribute paid by the Anglo-Saxons in the ninth century to the Danes in order to induce them not to invade and pillage.

related technology have been sold to Iran, Libya and Pakistan.* North Korea's missile programmes are indeed the main driving force for proliferation in the world today, constituting a truly global threat.

But that threat is also directed specifically against us in the West. The regime is rooted in hostility to us. It is quite possibly mad enough to risk an attack with an ICBM armed with a nuclear, chemical or biological warhead. We would be extremely foolish to assume that this risk has gone away or even been reduced as a result of recent goodwill gestures. Although the most likely victim of such an attack would probably be Japan, North Korea almost certainly has or will soon have the means to strike both America and Europe – Alaska and Norway and Finland. Nor should my fellow countrymen be complacent. As one expert analysis puts it: 'The North Korean long-range missile programme is arguably a greater threat to Western Europe's security than to that of the USA.'† That thought should – but probably won't – induce the Europeans to modify their strident and unthinking campaign against US ballistic missile defence plans.

North Korea's attitude to these possibilities is brutally simple. In 1998 its official media announced that it would 'continue developing, testing and deploying missiles' as a matter of principle, but added that if America really wanted to prevent this it should 'make compensation for the losses'. In early 1999 North Korean officials suggested that a starting point for that compensation would be $1 billion a year.‡ Blackmail by any other name has already begun.

Of course, that is not how the spokesmen of some of the great powers want to portray it. During the visit he made to Pyongyang in the summer of 2000, Russia's President Putin pretended to take seriously an offer from Kim Jong Il to cease development of ballis-

---

* *Jane's Defence Weekly*, 26 January 2000.
† Ben Sheppard, 'Ballistic Missile Proliferation: A Flight of Fantasy or Fear?', *Jane's Intelligence Review*, 1 October 1999.
‡ Nicholas Eberstadt, 'The Most Dangerous Country', *The National Interest*, autumn 1999. North Korea specialises in such things. The regime also demands $10 billion 'compensation' from Japan, against which it keeps up a ferocious propaganda campaign, for wartime atrocities.

tic missiles as long as North Korea was given access to other countries' space launch vehicles to enable it to continue its satellite programme. As a former KGB operative, Mr Putin must have known that this was mere flummery. North Korea is not interested in using space for any other means than warfare. Indeed, this was a re-run of what may be a unique Stalinist joke: in 1998 North Korea claimed that the rocket it fired over Japan was actually intended to launch into space a satellite broadcasting 'immortal revolutionary hymns' as well as '*Juche Korea*' in Morse code. Needless to say, no such satellite has since been traced.*

Both Russia and China, which has also been trying to make North Korea improve its image, have very good reasons to act as honest brokers between Pyongyang and the West. The Russians and Chinese are desperate to prevent America going ahead with an effective global ballistic missile defence, because they fear this would weaken the credibility of their nuclear deterrent. They also know that North Korea is regarded in Washington as the main source of the threat of ballistic missile attack. If they can stop North Korea making waves, they can employ the resultant calm to suggest – with the help of the usual suspects in the Western media – that BMD is irresponsible, provocative, unnecessary, unproven, unworkable, etc., etc.

More difficult to understand was the willingness of the US State Department and the Clinton administration to fall into North Korea's propaganda trap. When Mrs Albright visited North Korea in October 2000, Kim Jong Il apparently 'quipped' (to use the then US Secretary of State's expression) that a vast array of placards depicting a Taepodong long-range missile was 'the first and last satellite launch'. The Americans responded that they took this 'offer' seriously – though Kim Jong Il was later reported as having told some visiting South Koreans that the offer was a 'joke'. Whether a quip or a joke, the offer is basically meaningless. North Korea already has the missile technology it needs to threaten us. It will continue to test missiles, and undoubtedly to sell them. All we can expect to be on offer are gestures aimed at gaining concessions and money from the West.

---

* *Jane's Missiles and Rockets*, 1 October 1998.

This leads naturally on to the third and most recent element of North Korea's engagement with the West – the opening with the South. It seems likely that it was Chinese pressure – as well as the pressure of economic hardship – that caused Kim Jong Il to change his attitude. His counterpart in the South, President Kim Dae Jung, had since his election in 1997 been seeking reconciliation with North Korea through what he called a 'sunshine policy' of engagement. But this had hitherto made little progress, until the dramatic meeting between the two leaders amid politically staged celebrations in the Northern capital in June 2000.

Sentiment in South Korea understandably ran high. Families were desperate to be reunited after fifty years of strictly enforced separation. Koreans long for reunification. And it now looks, with the evident collapse of North Korea's economy and frustration of its aggressive ambitions, as if unity will come on the South's terms. Korea's own 'Wall' will look ever shakier as (still limited) human contacts on either side of it multiply. When reunification in conditions of freedom occurs it will bring final vindication for all those who fought and died in the Korean War to prevent the whole of Korea falling to communist tyranny. It will also vindicate the enormous effort that the United States still makes, stationing thirty-seven thousand troops along the border.

The trouble is that the opening up of contacts between the two Koreas does not of itself remove the threat which North Korea still poses to the West's – and indeed to the South's – security. We do not know when the communist regime in Pyongyang will collapse. And we do not know whether collapse will come peacefully or with the violence that has been such a feature of Korea's modern history.

There is a temptation to believe that we are about to see a repetition of the events of 1989, when East and West Germany were reunited as ordinary people voted with their feet against communism and in favour of healing the divisions it had imposed. North Koreans, I am sure – despite the years of relentless propaganda – would dearly love to act as the East Germans did then. But they are unlikely to be given the chance. The frontier along the 38th Parallel is heavily mined and tightly guarded by huge numbers of communist forces. Hardly anyone has escaped across it. This is no porous Berlin Wall: it is an impregnable barrier of steel. Nor, I fear, are Kim Jong Il and his colleagues going to pursue a path of peaceful reform. They repeatedly express their contempt for the way in which the Soviet Union under Mikhail Gorbachev undermined – as they see it – its own capacity to resist.

- Of course, almost anything is possible when dealing with a bizarre regime like North Korea's. But we should assume that when Pyongyang is making apparent concessions it is really buying time and seeking aid – while trying to drive a wedge between America and South Korea and continuing to plot the latter's destruction. I do not believe that North Korea will succeed in that. But I do believe that it would be the height of folly at any stage to give it the benefit of the doubt. I am reassured that the present US administration clearly shares this caution.

  We should maximise pressure on North Korea not just to suspend but to give up entirely its missile development and sales, and we should require full inspection of all its facilities to ensure that it has no weapons of mass destruction
- Without that there should be no more aid, with the exception of very limited emergency food aid when necessary
- The United States would be wise always to ensure that in its contacts with the North, its South Korean allies recognise that security issues are every bit as important as humanitarian ones
- There should be no tiptoeing around the issue of North Korea's appalling record of brutality towards its own people
- And we should reckon that the collapse of the North Korean regime, though ultimately inevitable, may yet be a slow, dangerous and violent affair.

CHALLENGES OF ISLAM

Communism was a pseudo-religion. Islam is most certainly a real one. Marxist-Leninist ideology was developed as a kind of substitute for faith. It provided its adherents with an inner commitment to a set of material objectives. But, as we have seen in so much of the Muslim world since the end of the Cold War, secular ideology, unless reinforced by coercion, shrivels in the face of religious belief. In country after Middle Eastern and North African country, the main opposition to existing regimes is nowadays no longer communist but rather Islamist. What are we in the West to make of this?

It would, of course, appear to be polite and even prudent to make nothing of it at all. According to the liberal Western ideas which nearly all of us embrace without really thinking about them, personal convictions are almost by definition not the business of the state. America, the leader of the West in this as other ways, has taken that view to arguably excessive lengths, barring any intermingling of Church and state.* But that is not how Muslims view the matter. Islam does not distinguish as clearly as does Christianity – at least its Western variants – between the 'things that belong to Caesar' and the 'things that belong to God'. To the contrary, Islam emphasises unity of life. It is not for nothing that 'Islam' means 'submission'.

As a conservative, and indeed as a Christian, I can appreciate much of what I come across when I visit Muslim countries and read of the opinions of sophisticated Muslim writers. I admire the strong family ties, the stigma attached to anti-social behaviour, the (generally) low levels of violent crime and the sense of obligation to the poor.

One Muslim scholar, explaining his faith to others, has written of the Prophet Muhammad in terms that convey his enduring appeal:

> [The Prophet's] respect for learning, tolerance of others, generosity of spirit, concern for the weak, gentle piety and desire for a better, cleaner, world would constitute the main elements of the Muslim ideal. For Muslims the life of the Prophet is the triumph of hope over despair, light over darkness.†

There is, though, another side to Muslim society, exemplified

---

* For example, by the banning of prayers in public schools.

† Akbar S. Ahmed, *Discovering Islam: Making Sense of Muslim History and Society* (London: Routledge, 1988).

WORLD RELIGIONS

Arctic Ocean

GREENLAND

SWEDEN
NORWAY
ICELAND   GERMANY

CANADA

IRELAND
UNITED KINGDOM
FRANCE

PORTUGAL
USA   SPAIN
                                      MOROCCO

Atlantic
Ocean

ITALY

LIBYA
ALGERIA

WESTERN
SAHARA
CUBA   MAURITANIA
MEXICO   DOMINICAN   MALI   NIGER
                REPUBLIC
                                      SENEGAL
        BELIZE   NIGERIA
GUATEMALA   HONDURAS   GUINEA
EL SALVADOR NICARAGUA   SIERRA LEONE
                     VENEZUELA   LIBERIA
COSTA RICA   GUYANA   IVORY COAST   GHANA
PANAMA   SURINAM   CAMEROON
COLOMBIA   FRENCH   GABON
                     GUIANA   CONGO
ECUADOR

PERU
                BRAZIL   Atlantic
                              Ocean   ANGOLA
Pacific
Ocean   NAMIBIA
        BOLIVIA

                     PARAGUAY
CHILE

                ARGENTINA URUGUAY

MAJORITY
RELIGIOUS GROUPS

	Chinese religions
	Protestant Christianity
	Catholic Christianity
	Orthodox Christianity

	Shi'a Islam
	Sunni Islam
	Hinduism

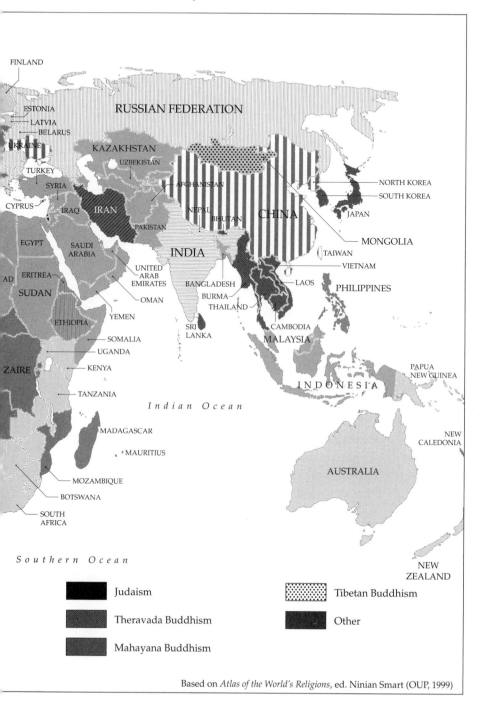

▮	Judaism	▦	Tibetan Buddhism
▨	Theravada Buddhism	▮	Other
▩	Mahayana Buddhism		

Based on *Atlas of the World's Religions*, ed. Ninian Smart (OUP, 1999)

in the corruption and hypocrisy of some of those in powerful positions, the sometimes oppressive treatment of women, the cruelty of some traditional practices and especially punishments, and a seediness and backwardness which afflict so many cities of the Middle East.

Today, however, it is the connection between Islam and violence that is so disturbing. Apart from North Korea, all of the states classed as 'rogues' – Iraq, Syria, Libya, Iran and Sudan – are mainly, and in some cases militantly, Muslim. This is also true of those countries listed by the US State Department as 'state sponsors of terrorism'. Apart again from North Korea, and this time Cuba, all the others – Iraq, Syria, Libya, Iran and Sudan – are Muslim states. Fifteen out of twenty-eight of the organisations designated as terrorist by the State Department can (in the broad sense) also be regarded as Muslim. Islamic scholars and Western experts will continue to argue about what the Koran says and means on the subject. But in the world today there appears to many to be a close connection between Islamic extremism and terrorist violence. Osama bin Laden's obscene punctuation of his threats against the West with invocations of the Divinity reinforces that impression.

But an important point of qualification needs to be made. Although the phrase is in practice inescapable, and so I too use it as required, 'Islamic terrorism' is something of a misnomer. Terrorism should not just be analysed and it cannot ultimately be combated by concentrating on its 'causes', religious or secular, political or economic, social or ethnic. There are many definitions of terrorism.* But it is the means adopted rather than the reasons – or excuses – given for violence that make terrorists so feared and detested. The terrorist seeks to achieve his goals not just through violence but through the fear of violence. He wishes to intimidate just as much as to kill and maim. His targets are, therefore, always indirectly, and often directly, the civilian population.

---

* Walter Lacqueur observes that more than a hundred possible definitions have been offered: *The New Terrorism: Fanaticism and the Arms of Mass Destruction* (London: Phoenix Press, 2001), p.5. Disputes focus on, for example, whether the violence must be politically motivated and whether it has to be performed by a non-state organisation.

His violence is in this sense always indiscriminate. Terrorism has no inherent limits, for it recognises neither domestic laws, nor international conventions, nor the standards of morality. Osama bin Laden's terrorism – violence which targets thousands of innocent people – can thus be seen as the ultimate terrorism: but it is only a final – or perhaps not yet final – step along a path which every terrorist down the ages has trodden.

Religion has, indeed, often played a role in providing a twisted justification for terrorism. From the Assassins of the twelfth century through to their successors, the suicide bombers of Hamas, Hizbollah and Islamic Jihad in the twenty-first century, professed Muslims have certainly been involved. But the Tamil extremists, who used a suicide bomber to kill Rajiv Gandhi, claim to be Hindus. ETA, the bloodstained Basque terrorist organisation, and the murderous Shining Path guerrillas in Peru are both Marxist. Even where religion appears to be at the core of violence, appearances can deceive. Most Irish Republican terrorists long ago stopped considering themselves – and stopped being treated by the Church – as Catholics. They, like their counterparts, the 'Loyalist' paramilitaries in Ulster, have now largely turned their attention to protection rackets, money laundering and drug trafficking. Even the mullahs of the Taliban, for all their oppressive piety, are delighted to finance their regime and buy their weaponry by exporting heroin. As a motive for terror, religion has more often than not required a good deal of lubrication by lucre.

It would, however, be wrong to leave the matter there. Osama bin Laden's view of Islam is shared by few. His actions have been widely condemned by devout Muslims – though by no means universally. What is troubling, however, is that the conditions under which he and his organisation could operate have been created over the years by many who are now appalled by the results. Muslim religious leaders who regularly denounce Israel and who call for struggle against America should not be surprised that some members of their flocks act upon what they think they are hearing. And when, as so often, subsequent condemnations of terrorism come allied with equivocations suggesting that the West must share the blame because of the policies it pursues, the force of those condemnations is lost. The Islamic world is not responsible for what bin Laden did. But in the past too many influential Muslims have failed to speak out openly against what he and his kind represent.

There is also a different and broader problem which has to be faced in assessing how best to deal with the challenges posed by Islam. This is the inability, so far at least, of predominantly Muslim states to evolve liberal political institutions. Only Turkey and Indonesia can, with qualifications, be said to have made much progress in doing so. And the resultant political problems which Muslim nations have faced have also led in most cases to economic underdevelopment.

It is too much, and certainly too early, to state finally that Islam is incompatible with democracy. But it does seem probable that the values of Islamic society will always strongly affect the form any emergent democracy takes. These values place less emphasis on the individual and more on the community – above all the community of believers (the *ummah*) – than in non-Muslim societies. There is traditionally a greater respect for authority at all levels. The role of Islamic law, the *sharia*, is also distinctive. It is recorded how towards the end of the eighteenth century a Muslim visitor to England was taken to see the House of Commons at work. He later wrote of his astonishment at finding that the British Parliament actually made laws and fixed punishments for their infraction – because unlike Muslims the English had not accepted a divine law revealed from heaven and therefore had to resort to such unsatisfactory expedients.* Muslims still understand the expression 'the rule of law' very differently than do most Westerners.

It is perhaps also significant that those governments of Muslim states with which Westerners are generally happiest to deal and which seem least threatening are not at all like Western-style liberal democracies. Morocco, for example, is a country in which Christians are welcome and in which Western – particularly French – elements have been incorporated into a rich national tradition.

---

* The incident is reported in Professor Bernard Lewis's superb *The Middle East: 2000 Years of History from the Rise of Christianity to the Present Day* (London: Weidenfeld and Nicolson, 1995), p.223.

But under the late King Hassan I, one of the Arab world's shrewdest and bravest rulers, Morocco was certainly not a democracy, as those who challenged his rule found out.

Or again, most of the Gulf states enjoy a large measure of stability and welcome Westerners who stick to the rules and respect the local customs. In time, there will probably be a gradual move towards more direct popular participation. But particularly in smaller, more traditional states which are not so oil-rich that they attract unwanted outside attention from greedy powers like Iraq or Iran, the ancient systems of government work remarkably well. Western liberals who complain about the absence of parliamentary democracy often underrate the importance of the direct personal links between the ruler and his people. Regular audiences are held to which anyone can come and present his request or complaint amid little formality or even security. These audiences can keep the Emir and his Ministers more closely in touch with popular moods and expectations than are many elected Presidents.

Moreover, we should not shy away from the blunt facts of national self-interest. Saudi Arabia and the Gulf states are the West's most important allies in a region which is itself the principal source of the world's oil. Any power or influence which seeks the overthrow of our allies there poses a direct threat to us. To ignore – or even worse to appease – such a challenge would be foolish in the extreme.

Turkey is another major ally which deserves the West's total support. It is, in fact, as much a European as it is a Middle Eastern power, and I shall consider policy towards its aspirations later. But in view of all of the criticisms levelled against the Turkish political system we should not lose sight of the main point – namely that it works.

Turkey is perhaps the only example of an ancient nation and great power which has been successfully *re*-created. Through the ruthless genius of Kemal Ataturk, Turkey was turned into a functioning Western-style secular republic. But it was and is also a state in which the armed forces are accorded a much larger role than would be acceptable in modern Western liberal democracies. Islamist parties are banned, and words or actions deemed to smack of Islamic extremism are severely punished. The concern for the

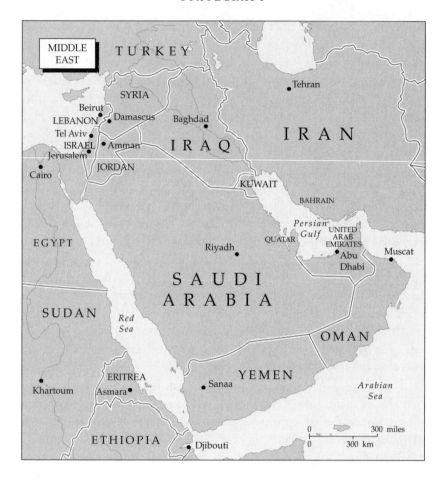

unity and security of the state has also led to fierce action to suppress Kurdish separatism. It is tempting to say that despite all this Turkey is the most pro-Western, broadly tolerant and nearly democratic Muslim state. But instead of 'despite' we would be better to say 'because'. I have no doubt that the determination of the Turkish state – supported by the Turkish armed forces – to contain those posing a threat to the state is amply justified. It is, in any case, always questionable whether people and parties espousing anti-democratic ideologies have a right to enjoy the same privileges as those that accept democracy. In a state like Turkey, which though powerful is also fragile, a democracy with limits and freedom with restrictions are certainly better than totalitarianism or chaos. And they are also better than the kind of 'democracy' which can be summarised as 'one man, one vote, once'.

So it is right, then, to continue to ask questions about the long-term impact of Islam on politics. Over time, the Muslim world itself may even provide clear answers. But meanwhile Westerners should avoid the temptation to try to tell Muslim countries how to balance the competing requirements of security and human rights: rulers and local political elites are likely to understand all this better than we do. If they are friendly towards us, look like being able to stay in power, and also behave decently towards their own people, such governments should be strongly supported – particularly now.

IRAQ

And then again, there is Iraq. I have already discussed the lessons to be drawn from the West's dealings with Iraq during and since the Gulf War.* But Saddam Hussein's relations with the rest of the Muslim world are also illuminating. During the Gulf War Saddam suddenly developed a very public commitment to Islam. He was photographed praying in mosques and his rhetoric developed along lines more associated with Iranian mullahs. This, though, was a total sham, whose transparent purpose was to project his aggression against Kuwait as a kind of *jihad*.

In truth, the politics of the Iraqi regime were rooted in an entirely different tradition – that of Baathism. The ruling Baath parties of Iraq and Syria represent secular Arab nationalism, with a strong admixture of ideas stemming from both socialism and fascism. The government of Iraq is a corrupt, violent, brutal dictatorship. Saddam and the clique around him are motivated simply by the desire to hold on to and exploit power. While the Iraqi people are still living with the consequences of international sanctions, Saddam has recently opened a large resort on the shore of Lake Tharthar eighty-five miles west of Baghdad at which he and his friends can cavort in luxury. It houses one of his many palaces. A massive bronze statue of the dictator in uniform reminds anyone

---

* See pp.28–30, 49–50.

tempted to forget it just who is boss. There is a casino and a safari park. Two buildings accommodate his female playmates.*

The regime is hardly, therefore, an advertisement for Islamic asceticism. Indeed, its secular nature is reinforced by the fact that a majority of the Iraqi population is Shiite, while those in charge are Sunni† (Saddam's Deputy Prime Minister, Tariq Aziz, is a Christian). If religious issues ever became decisive, Saddam's own position would be seriously threatened. To ensure that it is not, he continues ruthlessly to suppress Shia dissent, sends tanks against their towns, deprives them of food and medicine, and in March 1999 he ordered the assassination of the most senior Shia religious leader in Iraq.

Saddam is also, of course, hostile to the Iraqi Shias because he is fearful of Iran. In fact, during the eight-year Iraq–Iran War, when one million died and Saddam used chemical weapons against his own (Kurdish) population, he adopted the guise of pro-Western container of Islamic fundamentalism. But the war was actually all about power and money – in this case control of Iran's oil-rich province of Khuzestan and the strategically vital Shatt al'-Arab waterway. Moreover, it was futile. Iraq had to concede all its claims in search of a quick peace when it decided to attack Kuwait in 1990.

Had Saddam's invasion of Kuwait that summer been allowed to stand he would have gained control of a quarter of the Gulf's oil reserves. If he had been permitted to go further and advance right down the Gulf he would have gained control of over 60 per cent of the world's oil reserves. There was no high-minded or complex motive behind the attack on Kuwait, any more than there was behind that on Iran. Saddam's Iraq is not just a rogue but a robber – and his victims almost always turn out to be other Muslims. Understanding that, Muslim states refused to support him in 1990: only the Palestinians and Jordanians did so openly, and suffered for it greatly as a result of the expulsion of Palestinian and Jordanian guest-workers from the Gulf states.

---

* *The Times*, 6 November 2000.

† The Sunni and Shiite traditions form the two main wings of Islam. Shiites make up roughly 10 per cent of the Muslim world, while the Sunnis constitute the remaining 90 per cent.

Anyone who has doubts about the wickedness of Saddam – and there is not much excuse for doubters in the light of all that has surfaced about life in Iraq – might wish to visit Kuwait. I myself did so in November 1991, and then again in February 1998.

From the point of view of my hosts my visit in 1991 was an occasion to say 'thank you' for the role Britain had played in my last months as Prime Minister in ensuring a swift and overwhelming response to Saddam's aggression. The Amir and his family's words and the cheering crowds were something of a tonic for me at a difficult time when I was still coming to terms with life outside Downing Street. One memorable slogan painted by the side of the road read aptly enough – whether by accident or design – 'Tank U Thatcher'.

I flew out by helicopter into the desert to the Baghdad road and saw everywhere the remains of Iraqi tanks, lorries and cars – all burnt out as a result of the devastating Allied attack on Iraqi columns. The Iraqis had paid a terrible price for Saddam's folly. But looking at the devastation they left behind, my sympathy was limited.

I visited the sites of burnt-out structures and equipment around the oil wells that the Iraqi forces had set alight (the last fire was only extinguished the day I arrived). The desert around about was covered in a thick coating of rotting black oil. I was not well-dressed to walk over it and destroyed a new pair of shoes doing so.

My hosts also showed me a half-ruined building where a number of Kuwaitis had resisted and met their deaths, hopelessly outnumbered and outgunned by the invader. I went inside and imagined their last moments. The ruin has been preserved and is known as the Martyrs' House. I also spoke for some time with the wives – perhaps widows? – of some six hundred Kuwaitis who had been seized by the retreating Iraqis and whose whereabouts were still not known. The families were desperate for news and feared the worst. I promised to do what I could to ensure their voices were heard by people who might – just might – be able to force Saddam to at least disgorge this information.

By the time of my return visit in 1998 a huge amount of reconstruction had taken place. But when I again talked to the womenfolk of those abducted I was distressed to learn that little progress had been made. The desert was blooming in places, green and covered in exquisite flowers thanks to an unusually wet winter. But there were still filthy black areas of oil-drenched sand, reminders of the ecological vandalism that Saddam had deliberately perpetrated. The main concern was, as ever, security. Saddam Hussein had not been finally defeated. In 1994 he had even massed forces on Kuwait's border. The Amir and I discussed the situation at some length. He told me that anyone else but Saddam would have learned the lesson of the Gulf War. That seemed – and seems – a gloomily realistic analysis.

It is, therefore, essential to enforce strictly the international sanctions which were imposed at the end of the Gulf War. If Iraqis are malnourished or deprived of medicine, that is Saddam's fault, not ours. The UN Sanctions Committee has approved almost all the so-called 'oil for food' contracts submitted by Iraq and there is no obstacle to the import of medicines. But Saddam is determined to break free of all these constraints in order to rebuild his military machine, and he uses every propaganda opportunity in order to do so. That is why we have to scrutinise minutely any proposal that the Iraqis make, even though we open ourselves up to accusations of callousness. A regime which puts palaces before people cannot enjoy the benefit of the doubt.

And there can surely be no doubt either, in view of the regime's rejoicing at the terrorist attacks against America, that Iraq will enthusiastically assist any individual or movement planning to harm its great enemy. Whether Saddam Hussein was indeed involved in bin Laden's wickedness is – at the time of writing – unclear. But if he was, he must be made to pay the price.

- **We cannot emphasise too strongly in our dealings with the Muslim world that Saddam Hussein is no Islamic martyr but rather someone who cynically and ruthlessly exploits religion and his fellow Arabs**
- **Sanctions must stay**
- **There will be no peace and security in the region until Saddam is toppled.**

SYRIA

Viewed from the perspective of the Gulf War, Syria might appear to be a friend of the West. The late President Hafez al-Assad was one of the strongest Arab supporters of the Allied Desert Storm operation, for which he was well-rewarded with some $2 billion of aid. But this is misleading. President Assad was primarily motivated by rivalry with and hatred of Saddam Hussein. The roots of this competition and envy were to be found, paradoxically, in the two regimes' similarities. Like Iraq, Syria has in recent decades been ruled as a dictatorship in which the dominant ideology is provided by the Baath Party. Like Iraq, Syria's formal status as a republic has not prevented its evolution into something approaching a hereditary monarchy, or (perhaps better) tyranny. Just as Saddam is grooming his son to take over, so Assad did the same. Current Syrian President Bashar al-Hassad's main training for the job appears to have been acquired as an ophthalmologist, which might in most states be considered somewhat inadequate. Just as Saddam and his friends and relatives from the area of Tikrit represent a tiny group whose power can only be maintained over the majority by force, so the Assad family and its connections come from the Alawite religious minority that constitutes just 11 per cent of Syria's (mainly Sunni Muslim) population. The Alawites thus cannot afford to allow Islamic radicalism to prosper. Accordingly, Islamic parties and groups are ruthlessly suppressed. In 1982 Hafez al-Assad put down a rebellion by the Muslim Brotherhood in Hamah with such ferocity that the city was reduced to rubble, and an estimated twenty thousand people died.

Syria, therefore, has a very unpleasant regime, even if that unpleasantness is directed more against Muslims than against Westerners. But neither has Syria been above promoting terrorism outside its borders, and, of course, it continues to cause a great deal of trouble to Israel, whose interests so closely involve America's. Within the Lebanon, which it effectively controls with thirty-five thousand troops and where it has acquired large financial interests, Syria has consistently supported terrorist groups determined to destabilise Israel and block peace with the Palestinians. Moreover, despite Israel's risky pull-out of its troops from

Southern Lebanon, Syria continues to be thoroughly obstructive in the Middle East Peace Process.

The Israelis agreed to hand back to Syria the Golan Heights, occupied in 1967 during the Six Day War. But the late Syrian President wanted more, namely Israel's withdrawal to the demarcation line that existed before that conflict. This would mean Syria's regaining control of the north-east shores of the Sea of Galilee. At this Israel balked. Hafez al-Assad had himself been Syrian Defence Minister at the time of the 1967 conflict, and it was always thought that for this reason he could not bring himself to sign any agreement that failed to restore every inch of lost territory. His son presumably has no such sentimental block. On the other hand, to judge from the threats and abuse which Bashar al-Hassad has levelled at Israel, the new President has no intention yet of moderating Syria's obdurate policy.*

Most serious for the West, however, is the way in which Syria's hostility to Israel – and to some extent to Israel's ally and the Arabs' traditional *bête noire*, Turkey – appears to be leading Damascus along the path of acquiring weapons of mass destruction. US and Israeli officials are reported to have confirmed that Syria is continuing to build chemical weapons and ballistic missiles. This programme was begun by the late President in order to counter Israel's superiority in conventional weapons, which has greatly increased in recent years. Syria began producing a Sarin-gas-based warhead in the mid-1980s, and it has since been pressing ahead with acquiring and building ever-longer-range Scud missiles to carry them. It is apparently now developing with North Korean assistance a Scud with a seven-hundred-kilometre range, which could hit Israel from a point much deeper in Syrian territory, making the launchers more difficult to locate and hit. Such a weapon could also reach Ankara.† By acting in this fashion, Syria is sharply upgrading the threat it poses to our own broader security

---

* The Syrian President has, for example, described Israel as 'more racist than the Nazis'. He added: 'History is on our side. Every Israeli knows that he does not own this land. This is Arab land.' *Washington Times*, 28 March 2001.

† Andrew Koch, 'USA, Israel Say Syria Continues with WMD', *Jane's Defence Weekly*, 11 October 2000.

With Ronald Reagan in front of a section of the Berlin Wall at the Reagan Library, California, in February 1991.

Coffee with Ronald Reagan at his Los Angeles office in February 1995.

Receiving the Presidential Medal of Freedom from George Bush at the White House in March 1991.

Greeting Mikhail Gorbachev at Prague Castle in November 1999, during celebrations to mark the tenth anniversary of the Czech 'Velvet Revolution'.

Dwarfed by a B-2 bomber at Air Force Plant 42, Palmdale, California, March 1991.

Meeting students as Chancellor of the College of William and Mary, Virginia, in February 2001.

With Vaclav Klaus at the unveiling of Churchill's statue in Wenceslas Square, Prague, in November 1999.

Receiving an honorary doctorate at Brigham Young University, Utah, in March 1996.

Walkabout with Boris Nemtsov through the centre of Nizhny Novgorod in July 1993.

Meeting with Lee Kuan Yew at the Senior Minister's office in Singapore in September 1993.

At the launch of *Ever Result* at the Mitsubishi shipyard in Kobe, October 1994.

With Jiang Zemin in Beijing, September 1991.

Being met by Li Peng on a visit to Beijing in September 1991.

Meeting Lee Teng Hui during a visit to Taipei in September 1992.

Graffiti in Kuwait City from the aftermath of its liberation from Iraqi occupation, November 1991.

Talks with Yitzhak Rabin during a visit to Israel in November 1992.

Visiting Vukovar hospital in September 1998, from where hundreds of Croatian civilians were led away to be killed by Serb paramilitaries in 1991.

Paying respects to British war dead at San Carlos Water in the Falklands, June 1992.

Visiting General Pinochet and his wife Lucia at the Wentworth Estate, Surrey, in March 1999.

Talking with Silvio Berlusconi in London in February 2001.

interests, and it must be made to understand that this cannot and will not be allowed to continue.

Such behaviour reminds one again of Iraq. But there are also three important differences between Syria and its Iraqi rival – each of which is relevant to deciding our approach. First, as the above discussion suggests, Syria's interests are inextricably tied up with the Israeli–Palestinian problem, whereas Iraq merely wishes to use it for propaganda. Second, Syria is a poor, underdeveloped, primarily agricultural state, whereas Iraq is oil-rich. Third, Syria is a real, historically rooted, Arab nation-state, whereas Iraq is in truth an artificial construct put together from three Ottoman provinces at the end of the First World War.

These considerations suggest that although firm action must be taken to ensure that Syrian programmes for developing weapons of mass destruction are halted, Syria is potentially a state with which at some future time we may be able to 'do business'. The impulse towards much of its misbehaviour comes from the unresolved Israeli–Palestinian dispute: any progress we can make in solving this should make Syria less obstructive. Because it is not a major oil producer and so cannot simply rely on 'black gold' revenues to survive, Syria has no long-term alternative but to develop a properly functioning market economy. For that it needs Western expertise, technology and investment. This may also make it in the long run more cooperative. Finally, despite the fragile position of the present regime based on a religious minority, an anti-Western ideology and a powerful army, Syria does have the makings of a broadly stable country. Unlike Iraq, it is not perpetually threatened with dissolution. That basic long-term stability should eventually help Syria to become a normal country.

- Syria fulfils all the criteria of a 'rogue' and deserves no favours at present
- Our top priority should be to apply all possible pressure to halt the WMD programmes that threaten our allies Israel and Turkey and indirectly threaten us
- In the longer term, and subject to alleviation of tensions between Israel and the Palestinians, Syria could become a more positive force in the region.

LIBYA

The regime in Libya, like the regimes in Iraq and Syria, is the result of a military coup. In this case, in September 1969 a group of officers overthrew the monarch, King Idris, and established a republic of which Colonel Muammar al-Qaddafi (or Gadaffi) was the dominant figure. Gadaffi soon turned the country into a brutal totalitarian dictatorship ruled officially according to the bizarre doctrines contained in the so-called 'Green Book' of his thoughts. Some of these were turned into a pop song, which unsurprisingly soared in the Libyan charts. Among the lyrics:

> The universal theory has seen the light,
> Bringing to mankind peace and delight,
> The tree of justice, people's rule and socialism,
> Completely different from laissez faire and capitalism.*

(At least the last line is correct.)

Libya's new ideology was perfectly conducive to extremism, violence, terrorism and revolution, all of which Gadaffi practised with gusto during the 1970s and 1980s. Libya was a leader of the Arab countries which rejected President Anwar Sadat of Egypt's attempts at reconciliation with Israel. It supported a number of Palestinian terrorist groups. It was a generous provider of arms, explosives (semtex) and money for Irish Republican terrorists. It sponsored a series of terrorist actions against America and its allies – until, with my strong support, President Reagan taught Gadaffi a lesson in the US raid of 1986.

Libya was clearly behind the bombing in 1988 of a Pan American aircraft over Lockerbie in Scotland that killed 270 people. In January 2001 a Scottish court sitting in the Netherlands found guilty one of the two Libyans accused of the outrage, while acquitting the other.† The man was a Libyan intelligence agent, and it exceeds the bounds of credibility to imagine that he was not doing

---

* *Sunday Times*, 12 September 1999.

† On 31 January 2001 Abdul Baset Ali al-Megrahi was sentenced to life imprisonment. His appeal, at the time of writing, is still to be heard.

the Libyan leader's bidding. The facts that Colonel Gadaffi accorded the other suspect a hero's welcome on his return to Libya, that he publicly denounced the verdict, and that he contemptuously refused compensation for the victims' families, all show that he remains unrepentant and a menace. In this context, it is also interesting to note that a French court in March 2000 sentenced *in absentia* six Libyans – secret police and diplomats – to life imprisonment for the bombing of a French airliner over Niger in 1989 which killed 170 people. Such terrible crimes ultimately demand not just sentences passed against those who directly carried them out, nor financial reparations – though both are necessary. They also demand the removal from power of the Libyan dictator himself – though that is something probably best left to his own people.

America finds it hard to bear a grudge for long. This is an admirable quality in itself. But it can sometimes lead the United States to assume that its enemies also prefer to forgive and forget. In the case of Colonel Gadaffi, it is clear that the optimists are half right; but it is the wrong half. While Gadaffi wants to forget his own past crimes, he has no intention at all of forgiving those who humbled him. Thus in a recent interview Gadaffi arrogantly refused to deny his involvement in terrorist incidents in the 1980s, observing: 'These incidents that you mention belong to the past.' (This reflection, it may be thought, is unlikely to appeal to the family of WPC Yvonne Fletcher, murdered by gunfire from the Libyan People's Bureau in London in 1984, or to countless families mourning loved ones murdered by the Provisional IRA with weapons and explosives the Colonel provided.) On the other hand, in the same interview, Gadaffi delivered the following thoughts about the United States: 'We feel that America is much like Hitler. We have no explanation for this, except that it is a religious, fanatical, racist position [*sic*] . . . Libya is a victim of American terrorism.'*

To the question, 'Is Colonel Gadaffi mad?', I would have to reply, 'I don't know, but it doesn't matter.' Whether posing as the

---

* Milton Viorst, 'The Colonel in his Labyrinth', *Foreign Affairs*, Vol. 78, No. 2, March–April 1999.

unifier of the Arab world, the promoter of World Revolution, or the future President of a United States of Africa, Gadaffi presents a consistently ludicrous spectacle. But then so did Idi Amin. Ex-President Numeiri of Sudan is said to have remarked of Gadaffi that he was 'a man with a split personality – both of them evil'. That is really all one needs to know about the Libyan leader's motivation and intentions.

But what of his current capabilities? Here the picture is less clear. It appears that in recent years Gadaffi may have suspended his support for terrorism and his programmes for the development of weapons of mass destruction.* This is, of course, part of his attempt to win his way back to international acceptability and is all of a piece with the handover of the two Libyans suspected of the Lockerbie bombing. Gadaffi received his reward when Britain and the European Union re-established diplomatic relations with Libya, though the US did not. In the post-Cold War world, and at a time when not even Libya's great oil wealth can any longer cope with the economic consequences of thirty years of socialist waste and incompetence, Gadaffi has a strong incentive to moderate his actions somewhat. He needs our money and our markets.

But chemical weapons programmes are not difficult to reactivate or to conceal. Moreover, Libya is continuing to press ahead with its ballistic missile programme. Recent seizures of Scud engine components in London and Switzerland on their way to Libya from North Korea confirm this. I would certainly not rule out Libya's attempting to buy or develop a long-range ballistic missile which it could arm with a nuclear or chemical warhead to threaten or use against the West or our allies. An oil-rich state controlled by an unstable dictator with a visceral hatred of America can never be regarded as anything other than a danger. And I am afraid that it would be the height of naïveté to pay heed to Gadaffi's opportunistic expressions of regret at the attacks on America on 11 September. The old saying that 'My enemy's enemy is my

---

* Andrew Koch, 'USA Rethinks Libya's Status', *Jane's Defence Weekly*, 19 July 2000.

friend' holds good on many occasions – but not when, in his heart, he remains my enemy. Gadaffi is an enemy.

- A Libya ruled by Colonel Gadaffi can never be 'safe'
- Although limited incentives and rewards for good behaviour may be useful elements of a strategy to limit the harm Gadaffi does, the only way of containing his ambitions is through the credible threat of force.

IRAN

Iraq, Syria and Libya are all secular socialist dictatorships which rule Muslim countries. When Saddam or Gadaffi parade their Islamic credentials it is with a political, not a religious, purpose. But the case of Iran is different. There brutal power-struggles are pursued, corruption is rife, and the mullahs seem rather well-versed in how to take maximum advantage of Iran's enormous oil wealth. But the difference is that Iran, since 1979, has been in the grip of religious revolution that it has sought to export around the Middle East.

Although Iran has a President, and although the re-election of Mohammad Khatami to that office in June 2001 has been widely (and probably accurately) viewed as a further move away from extremism, the Iranian state is essentially a theocracy not a democracy. The highest authority in the state lies with the 'Supreme Leader', the Ayatollah Ali Khameni. The leadership of the country is in the hands of clerics whose own political views are profoundly illiberal and anti-Western and who are resolved not to let other opinions be heard. Moreover, the extreme elements have a pivotal role through the Islamic Revolutionary Guard, which is believed to be in charge of Iran's chemical, biological and nuclear weapons programmes and its missile forces.

In any case, like the other 'rogues', Iran has its own specific characteristics and objectives. The first of these stems from the religious doctrine that underpins the state. This is revolutionary Shia Islam. The Shia are traditionally the outcasts of the Muslim world, associated with protests rather than power. Only in Persia/ Iran did Shiism become the creed of the rulers as well as the ruled. From the early sixteenth century, political rivalries between Shiites (centred on Persia) and Sunnis (represented by the Ottoman

Empire) continued to fester. If Islamic revolution was to occur in Iran, as it did under the Shah, it was therefore bound to be Shiite. And because of the extraordinary power and respect enjoyed by the Shiite clergy, who have no parallel in Sunni Islam, such revolution was likely to generate a clerical-political elite that would exercise all power. The Ayatollah Khomeini's enormous prestige and charisma then turned Iran into a fully-fledged Islamic revolutionary state.

Khomeini and those around him wanted to export revolution throughout the Muslim world. Their own brand of Islam had (and has), however, only limited appeal. Although Muslims in many countries warmed to the Ayatollah's denunciations of the 'Great Satan' (America), they did not (and do not) necessarily want to live like Iranians. And, crucially, the overwhelming majority of Muslims are anyway Sunni and fear or despise Shiism.

There is also a powerful movement of Islamic revolution among Sunnis. This includes most notably: the Muslim Brotherhood and its offshoots, which have been responsible for numerous acts of terrorism and violence, including the murder of President Sadat of Egypt; the regime in Sudan, which both shelters terrorists and carries on a bloody campaign against Christians and Animists in the south of the country; and, of course, the Taliban. But none of these forces is disposed to enter into coordinated Islamic action with Shiite Iran – indeed the Iranians and the Taliban are at daggers drawn. One authority on the matter has summed up the matter as follows:

> Although there is a great wave of Islamic revivalism in Muslim societies, the Iranian revolution is to a large extent tied to the Shia view of history and society. It is for this reason that a similar revolution based on the Iranian model is not possible in Egypt and Pakistan, where Sunnis form the majority of the population.*

Even among the Shias, the Iranian call to arms has been less successful than might have been expected. Iran sought to mobilise

---

* Akbar S. Ahmed, *Islam Today: A Short Introduction to the Muslim World* (London and New York: I.B. Tauris, 1999), p.47.

Shiites in Iraq against Saddam Hussein during the Iran–Iraq War, but without significant success. It has also consistently tried to foment trouble in the Gulf states and Saudi Arabia which have significant Shiite minorities. In Bahrain, which is majority Shiite, you can hear during the night (as I have) a series of explosions as the Shiite youth express their disgruntlement by heating gas canisters over fires until they explode, so as to disrupt the dreams of the rulers. There have also been riots. But so far that is the limit of the radicalism. Where Iranian destabilisation has, by contrast, proved effective, it depends principally upon the provision of arms and other material support, as with the terrorists of Hizbollah, Hamas and Palestinian Islamic Jihad in the Middle East.

This leads on to the second feature of Iran's regime, a feature which has become increasingly important since the death of the Ayatollah Khomeini in June 1989. Iran is not, and never has been at any stage since the overthrow of the Shah, *only* a force for Islamic revolution: it is a major power, which will be very strong as soon as it stops dissipating its strength. Persia/Iran is an ancient civilisation whose rulers have for centuries been accustomed to regard themselves as the dominant force in the region. It now has a young, fast-growing population of over sixty million, from which it will be able to continue to recruit a large army. It demonstrated its willingness to assert its interests by force when in 1992 it unilaterally seized from the United Arab Emirates the islands of Abu Musa and the Tumbs, which are vital to control of the Straits of Hormuz. And, of course, like the Shah, today's rulers of Iran have at their disposal enormous oil and gas resources – Iran's oilfields and natural gas reserves are among the richest in the world.

The election of President Khatami, who is less interested in *jihad* and more in *Realpolitik*, has shifted the balance back towards foreign and security policies based upon the more traditional criteria of national interest. This tendency and the easing up – though by no means the end – of persecution of opponents within Iran led Western leaders at the end of the 1990s openly to consider a *rapprochement* with the regime. In the case of the United States, this represented a major departure from the previous strategy of 'dual containment' of *both* Iraq and Iran. In the case of the European Union states, it was a reversion to earlier policy. The present

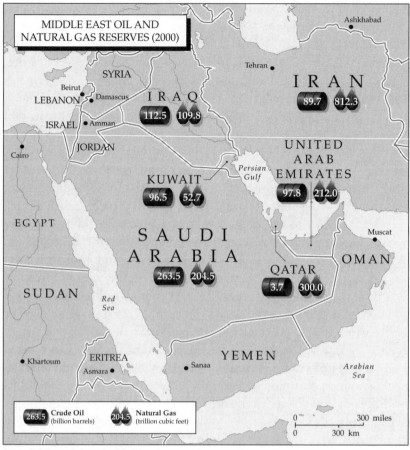

MIDDLE EAST OIL AND
NATURAL GAS RESERVES (2000)

SYRIA

Beirut
LEBANON
Damascus

ISRAEL
Amman

JORDAN

Cairo

Ashkhabad

Tehran

I R A N
89.7   812.3

I R A Q
112.5   109.8

UNITED
ARAB
EMIRATES
97.8   212.0

Persian
Gulf

KUWAIT
96.5   52.7

EGYPT

Muscat

S A U D I
A R A B I A
263.5   204.5

QATAR
3.7   300.0

OMAN

SUDAN
Red
Sea

Khartoum

ERITREA
Asmara

Sanaa

YEMEN

Arabian
Sea

263.5 Crude Oil
(billion barrels)

204.5 Natural Gas
(trillion cubic feet)

0 — 300 miles
0 — 300 km

Source: U.S. Energy Information Administration

US administration seems keener to keep up the pressure on Iran. It deserves European support in doing so.

In truth, though, neither model of 'containment' or 'engagement' altogether fits the bill. There will always be arguments for and against individual measures taken to signal our disapproval of dangerous regimes like that of Iran. Sometimes sticks, sometimes carrots, have to be applied. What is really important, however, is the basic judgement about whether a state is rootedly hostile or whether it can be persuaded to pursue common goals. Viewed objectively, Iran remains in the first – hostile – category. Indeed, in significant respects the threat which it poses is growing.

We should always recall that all the main players in the political game in Iran are deeply opposed to America. For the zealots this is a matter of dogma. For the pragmatists, like President Khatami, it is a matter national interest. These Iranian nationalists are anxious to achieve a diminution of American power and presence in the Gulf so that Iran can extend its influence over the emirates and Saudi Arabia which are themselves hopeful of reaching their own accommodation with Tehran. As Mr Khatami has said: 'The security of the area will only be preserved through the evacuation of the alien forces in the region.' Mr Khatami has also attacked the Israeli–Turkish alliance, which he sees as opposed to Iranian great-power aspirations. True, Iran still fears Saddam Hussein. But this does not make it any better disposed towards the United States, which has struggled without much success to keep Saddam in check. The Iranians believe that in case of war with Iraq they will probably have to deal with Saddam themselves.*

After its near defeat in the Iran–Iraq War, the regime in Tehran decided to strengthen its military forces as far and as fast as possible. The most cost-effective way of doing this was deemed to be acceleration of existing programmes to acquire and deploy weapons of mass destruction. As one expert has put it: 'Nuclear weapons may ... be the only way for Iran to become a military power without destroying its economy. While a nuclear-weapons programme could cost billions, rebuilding its conventional military would cost tens of billions of dollars.'†

The evidence that Iran may indeed be poised to become a nuclear power comes from three sources, which together seem irrefutable. First, there are strong suspicions that Iran's attempts to acquire fissile material in Russia and other former Soviet republics, and to press ahead with a nuclear-research programme and the building of uranium-producing reactors, indicate military purposes. Second, there are now numerous statements on the record

---

* Ray Takeyh, 'Pragmatic Theocracy: A Contradiction in Terms?', *The National Interest*, spring 2000.

† Michael Eisenstadt, 'Living with a Nuclear Iran?', *Survival* (published by the International Institute of Strategic Studies), Vol. 41, No. 3, autumn 1999. This study is a mine of information and analysis on which I have drawn.

by Iranian high officials about the need for the country to have a nuclear capability. Third, there is the significance to be attached to the Iranian missile programme. While it is relatively easy to conceal programmes for the development of chemical, biological or even nuclear weapons, missile programmes are much more obvious. But this has not deterred Iran. Using North Korean technology, it has produced and successfully tested a Shehab-3 missile (range eight hundred miles), is developing a Shehab-4 (probable range 1200 miles) and is planning a Shehab-5 (range perhaps six thousand miles). It is difficult to understand why Iran would be making such efforts to develop ever-longer-range, and highly expensive, missiles only to place upon them conventional warheads.

Iran may, of course, be embarking upon the path of acquiring advanced weapons of mass destruction in order to deter rather than launch attacks. But that is beside the point. If it acquired nuclear weapons, the consequences could be very dangerous indeed. On the one hand, secure behind such a deterrent, the Iranians might well be tempted to embark upon renewed campaigns of international terrorism, which could themselves provoke (and demand) retaliation. On the other hand, and even given American assistance in creating an effective ballistic missile defence, Israel may not be prepared to risk its sworn enemy becoming a nuclear weapons power. The possibility of Israel's launching a pre-emptive strike – as against Iraq in 1981 – cannot be ruled out. Such an eventuality could provoke a regional and perhaps global crisis. Against this background, Western politicians need to exert maximum pressure upon Iran to draw back from the brink.

Nothing that has happened since 11 September causes me to modify that assessment. Iran, having backed a Shiite faction in Afghanistan and being deeply engaged in opposition to Pakistani influence in that country, naturally enough was willing to condemn al-Qaeda's attack on America. But that does not mean that the Iranian regime intends to stop backing terrorists who kill the citizens of America's ally Israel. And as the British Foreign Secretary's ill-conceived visit to Tehran made abundantly evident, the Iranian authorities are not even prepared to support punitive action against their old enemies the Taliban – so deep is their hatred of the West. President Bush said in his stirring address to Congress: 'Any nation that continues to harbour or support terrorism will be regarded by the United States as a hostile regime.' Iran is such a nation.

- Far from relaxing our guard against Iran, we should regard it as posing a growing threat to the security of the West and its allies
- It is nowadays not so much Islamic revolution, whose potential was always overrated, but rather Islamic weaponry that should command our attention
- The West should send unambiguous signals to the regime in Tehran that while we are prepared to respect Iran's regional interests, we are not prepared to envisage its becoming a nuclear weapons state – a development which could have the gravest consequences for Iran itself.

THE HOLY LAND

Time and again, relationships between Arab states and the West are thrown off-balance by events in what for centuries has been called the Holy Land. For Islamic zealots, American support for Israel confirms the existence of a vast conspiracy against the Muslim world. For cynics, the Israeli–Palestinian conflict provides a fail-safe opportunity to rally young Arabs everywhere to dubious causes. That is why no wider strategy to isolate rogue states and support legitimate governments can ignore this narrow strip of land on which so many tears and so much blood have been shed.

The political life of Israel seems to generate outstanding characters. This is probably because since its inception in 1948 the state of Israel has either been threatened by war or fighting it. Political leaders are thus frequently military leaders, and even if not they very quickly have to be military strategists. All Israelis know that their Arab foes can go on losing wars and survive to fight again. For Israel defeat means destruction.

In their different ways all the Israeli Prime Ministers with whom I had dealings have been impressive. Shimon Peres is certainly the wisest. Benjamin Netanyahu is probably the cleverest. But the late Yitzhak Rabin was undoubtedly the most charismatic – a truly inspiring figure. He was also the man for the hour – a credible advocate of peace precisely because he had proved himself in battle.

As I write these lines, Rabin's efforts to secure a lasting settlement with the Palestinians are to all appearances in tatters. Yet the message that he delivered at the time of his historic meeting at the White House with the PLO Chairman Yasser Arafat on Monday, 13 September 1993, is true and remains timeless. I was in the United States myself on a speaking tour at that moment, and perhaps the immediacy helped create the extraordinary impact for me. Prime Minister Rabin said:

> Let me say to you, the Palestinians, we are destined to live together on the same soil in the same land . . . We who have fought against you, the Palestinians, we say to you today in a loud and clear voice: Enough of blood and tears. Enough!
>
> We have no desire for revenge . . . We, like you, are people – people who want to build a home, to plant a tree, to love, live side by side with you in dignity, in affinity, as human beings, as free men . . . The time for peace has come.

I read subsequently a wonderful commentary by Britain's Chief Rabbi, Jonathan Sacks, on the biblical allusions which were interlaced throughout Rabin's remarks and which I then understood had lent them such mystical and prophetic force. As Dr Sacks has written, it was a 'religious moment', and although 'religion can fuel conflict . . . it can sometimes move us beyond it'.[*]

On 4 November 1995 Yitzhak Rabin was assassinated at the end of a rally in Tel Aviv. There was a spontaneous outpouring of grief at the loss of yet another martyr for peace.

Three years later, I visited Israel to attend the celebrations of the country's fiftieth anniversary. The joy, as so often in the Middle East, was marred by violence. Even while I was discussing the situation with Prime Minister Netanyahu, news came through to him of a pipe nail-bomb attack in Tel Aviv which had injured over twenty people.

---

[*] Jonathan Sacks, *Faith in the Future* (London: Darton, Longman and Todd, 1995), pp.97–8.

Jerusalem is the city of pilgrims, and next morning I decided to make my own personal pilgrimage. Yitzhak Rabin's tomb lies on a plinth in the National Cemetery on Mount Herzl. Golda Meir's stands nearby. One half of the Rabin grave was of white alabaster, ready for Leah Rabin, who has herself since died. The other, in which the former Prime Minister lay, was of black marble. It was quite plain, with no fuss, bearing just his name in Hebrew. As is the Jewish custom, I placed a pebble that I had brought from England, gathered on a Cornish beach, upon the grave.

There are very few international questions in which compromise is more necessary or more difficult than in the conflict between Jews and Arabs in Israel/Palestine. Throughout my political life I have usually sought to avoid compromise, because it more often than not turns out to involve an abdication of principle. In international affairs, it is often also symptomatic of muddle and weakness. But over the years I have been forced to conclude that the Arab–Israeli conflict is an exception. Here a historic compromise is, indeed, necessary. This is because both sides have unimpeachable moral cases, because neither side can fully prevail without loss to the other, and because shared interests in security are ultimately greater than those which divide the parties. A very brief and necessarily oversimplified account of relevant events demonstrates, I hope, the validity of all three assertions.

The moral claims of both Jews and Arabs to the land which used to be known as Palestine are based upon solid foundations. Leaving aside the ancient 'biblical' claims of Jews – not because they are unimportant, but because many non-Jews find them insufficiently compelling – it is to the Balfour Declaration of 1917, made in response to the leaders of Zionism, that the origins of Israel can be traced. This noted that the British government would 'view with favour the establishment in Palestine of a national home for the Jewish people and will use the best endeavours to facilitate the achievement of this object, it being clearly understood that nothing shall be done which may prejudice the civil and religious rights of existing non-Jewish communities in Palestine, or the rights and political status enjoyed by Jews in any other country'.

Whether and to what extent this undertaking violated others given to the Arabs is disputable. But the approach laid down in the Declaration was that which was the basis of the League of Nations Mandate for Palestine of 1922 and of subsequent international declarations.

What was increasingly at issue was the area to be allotted to the Jewish homeland. This became of crucial importance with the increase of Jewish immigration from the mid-1930s precipitated by the Nazi persecution that culminated in the Holocaust. After the end of the war, Britain, which was by now facing a terrorist campaign by Jews demanding an end to restrictions on immigration and the establishment of a Jewish state, decided to withdraw entirely. A United Nations plan of partition, similar to that previously proposed by the British, was adopted in 1947. This envisaged the Jewish state receiving 56 per cent of the territory of Palestine. That carve-up, however, outraged the Arabs and attacks began on Jewish settlements.

In advance of the final British withdrawal, the state of Israel was proclaimed by Jewish leaders. It was the signal for the first Arab–Israeli War, in which against enormous odds and by dint of extraordinary determination Israel was triumphant. As a result of subsequent armistice agreements, Israel retained 75 per cent of Palestine. There ensued a huge exodus of Arabs – estimated by the UN at over seven hundred thousand – from the lands which they had held and which were now under Israeli control.

As is well-known, the Six Day War of 1967 very much repeated this pattern of first Arab hostility, then Israeli victory, and then Israeli territorial expansion – in this case involving Israeli control of Gaza and Sinai, East Jerusalem and the West Bank, and the Golan Heights. Although more Palestinians went into exile, the most important demographic change was that 1.5 million Arabs were now living within these Israeli-occupied areas (this is, of course, over and above the million or so Arabs living within the old frontiers of Israel).

It took a further defeat for the Arab nations in the Yom Kippur War of 1973 – which also, however, involved heavy Israeli losses – to bring about the conditions for the first real progress towards a settlement. It was clear to rational Arabs that Israel was not going to be destroyed. And it was equally clear to rational Jews that some kind of lasting accommodation with Israel's Arab neighbours was desperately urgent. This was the background to Egyptian President Anwar Sadat's peace mission to Israel of 1977 and to the subsequent Camp David agreement between the two countries, negotiated by the US, in 1979. In alternating circumstances of peace, tension, terrorism, and assertions of Israeli strength (as in Lebanon in 1982), these remained the basic political conditions – until the late 1980s and early 1990s.

Two events at that point altered the way in which both Israelis and Palestinians looked at one another and at the world about them. The first was the so-called *intifada* – an uprising of Palestinians living within the occupied territories – which disrupted life and induced insecurity for six years. Although Israel was well capable of dealing with direct threats, indirect threats proved more intractable. It became increasingly clear to Israelis that it was not enough to try to ensure peaceful relations with the surrounding Arab states: it was also necessary to resolve the Palestinian problem, if Israel itself was to enjoy peace. The demographic facts also supported this conclusion. If the occupied territories were to remain part of Israel, then Israel itself risked ceasing to be predominantly Jewish. Alongside 4.7 million Jews were living another four million Arabs, and Arab birth rates are substantially higher than Jewish birth rates.

The other turning point was the Gulf War, which had a profound psychological effect on all the parties – Israelis, Palestinians and the Arab states alike. First, Israel's vulnerability to Saddam Hussein's missile attacks brought home the changed strategic situation. Although defensible borders were clearly going to remain important for Israel, they were no longer in themselves sufficient to ensure its security. Consequently, the idea of exchanging 'land for peace' (as the phrase has it) began to have renewed attractions. Second, the Palestinians picked the wrong side. By supporting Saddam Hussein against Kuwait they lost the favour of the Saudis and other Gulf rulers who had for years provided them with political clout, aid and jobs. It thus became much more important to find an accommodation with Israel. Third, the Arab states – like other states situated in traditional trouble-spots – saw in the Gulf War irrefutable proof of American military and political dominance. They now knew for sure that they would have to pursue policies acceptable to Washington, and they also knew that Washington would never allow the vital security interests of Israel to be jeopardised.

All of which brings us back to Yitzhak Rabin's words on the White House lawn. But it also, of course, brings us still closer to the present – for at the time of writing Israel and the Palestinians are again involved in what can only be termed a low-intensity war. I am not so foolish as to imagine that I could – or should – offer a 'solution' to the present crisis. That heavy responsibility must rest upon the Israeli and Palestinian leaders. But in the light of experience it does seem right to urge upon those involved attention to some basic principles.

- The United States – not the United Nations or the Europeans – is the only credible outside peacemaker
- But not even the US can impose peace: it has to be genuinely acceptable to the parties involved
- It is understandable that America should be impatient with what it often sees as Israel's stubbornness, as the US seeks maximum international support for its war against terrorism; but the State Department should recall that Israel had been living with terrorism at the hands of Islamic suicide bombers long before 11 September
- So Israel must never be expected to jeopardise her security: if she was ever foolish enough to do so, and then suffered for it, the backlash against both honest brokers and the Palestinians would be immense – 'land for peace' must also bring peace
- But neither should mediators or Israelis forget that the Palestinian leaders need to show results – and that means progress towards real autonomy and ultimately statehood – if they are to survive: otherwise more radical and more dangerous figures already lurking in the wings will predominate
- For their part, the Palestinian authorities will never secure Israel's trust unless they arrest and punish those who foment and practise terror; so far, Yasser Arafat has not sufficiently demonstrated the will to do this
- Moreover, Palestinians have to come to terms with the fact that even when they obtain a Palestinian state, it will be small, vulner-

able and (initially at least) very poor. It will require strong support from Jordan; but it will also remain economically dependent upon Israel – and so the Palestinians have a long-term interest in ensuring that such a state is established with maximum Israeli good will

- Whatever the future holds, the patience of Job will be required: after all, this is the 'Holy Land', the most fought-over land in history, where the three great faiths meet and compete, and where all sides can claim to have right on their side. Not for nothing did the Psalmist urge, 'Pray for the peace of Jerusalem.'* He was right. We should.

---

* Psalm 122.

CHAPTER 7

Human Rights and Wrongs

RIGHTS AND THE RIGHT

It is nowadays a brave politician who openly questions the value of putting human rights issues at the heart of foreign policy. Just a few years ago, I would never have thought that I might find myself in that position.

Like others of my generation whose attitudes were shaped by events during the Second World War and the early years of the Cold War, I went into politics with a strong, indeed passionate, commitment to upholding the rights of individuals in the face of the state Leviathan. A principled and consistent opposition to the manifold intrusions of government on individual liberties was the distinctive mark of our approach in the 1980s. Anyone young enough or forgetful enough to doubt the truth of this need only leaf through the newspapers of the time. Indeed, 'extreme' individualism at the expense of society or community was the left's principal charge against me. Actually, on that score I plead not guilty: for me duties precede rights, and though charity begins, it does not end at home. But the important point here is that few of our critics thought that we paid too little attention to individual liberty.

This fundamental division between conservatives and socialists, with the former much concerned about liberty and the latter more keen on equality, applied to domestic policy. But it applied to international affairs as well. Listening to the New Left preen itself on its pluralism and inclusiveness, you might be forgiven for thinking that it was they (in former political incarnations) who expended their energies in pressing conservative governments to respect human rights. But that, of course, is nonsense. It was, rather, the capitalist West which compelled the socialist East to treat its subjects as human beings, rather than as pawns or chattels.

This, for example, was what 'Basket Three' of the Helsinki Accords was all about in the mid-1970s, during the somewhat misleadingly termed period of *détente*. As part of the Soviet Union's strategy of disarming the West while maintaining its own military superiority, Moscow was prepared to make some concessions in order to appease Western critics of its systematic abuse of human rights. The Soviets were eventually persuaded to concede the principle that how a state treats its citizens is of legitimate concern to others outside its borders. But they only gave way because they thought that they could as easily break their promises in this as in other matters.* And that is, indeed, precisely what they did – until relentless pressure from the West forced them on the defensive.

President Reagan must take the lion's share of the credit for this. The 'Reagan Doctrine', which he first formulated in a speech to both Houses of Parliament in London in June 1982, stressed that 'freedom is not the sole prerogative of a lucky few, but the inalienable and universal right of all human beings'. It also provided an answer to the so-called Brezhnev Doctrine which asserted that once a state had become part of the socialist bloc, there it stayed. Moreover, unlike benevolent but ineffectual Western leaders before him, President Reagan gave his doctrine of liberty teeth through military strength and political will.

This short survey should be sufficient to demonstrate that conservatives have excellent credentials to speak about human rights. By our efforts, and with precious little help from self-styled liberals, we were largely responsible for securing liberty for a substantial share of the world's population and defending it for most of the rest. So why, then, does the current obsession with human rights make me so uneasy? The answer is that rights no longer

---

* For my own – very different – reservations about the Helsinki process see *The Path to Power*, pp.349–53.

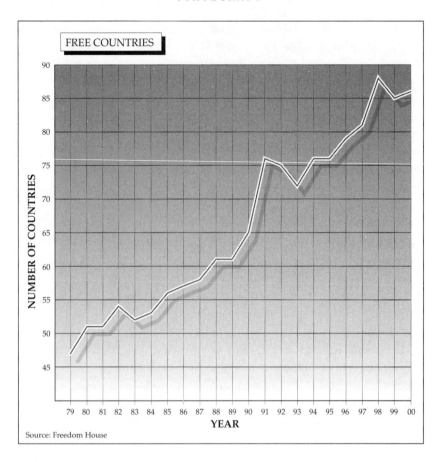

FREE COUNTRIES

Source: Freedom House

seem to mean what they used to do, and are being used to diminish not expand liberty.

WHAT HUMAN RIGHTS MEANT – AND DID NOT MEAN

We have to recall how the concept of human rights emerged. The idea that an individual human being has a moral value in his or her own right does not really need to be given a special historical pedigree. I suspect that it is present in some measure in all the great religions. As soon as the concept of a unique and eternal human 'soul' is accepted we are well on our way to recognising someone as a 'person', and such a person must be accorded dignity and so rights. Christianity – though not by any means every action undertaken in its name – has also emphasised the role of the individual who is called to a personal encounter with God. But today even more important than any principles of theology or philosophy are the *assumptions* which we make. We assume that we *should* treat others as we ourselves would wish to be treated – the so-called 'Golden Rule' – even when we fall short of that ideal in our behaviour.

Within the English (and then British) tradition the emphasis has been very much upon pragmatism and practicality rather than lofty declarations. I hope that I will not be misunderstood if I say that the British mind has a tendency to the concrete. This is manifest in the constitutional documents to which we most often refer. Anyone, for example, who reads Magna Carta is likely to be struck by the very specific (and, of course, necessarily anachronistic) obligations into which the King enters. The Charter speaks of wards, bailiffs, assizes, lay-fees, castles and escheats – for the good reason that the barons who were twisting the King's arm cared very much about these things at that time. Only two clauses of the Charter still ring out in modern ears with majestic authority:

> No freeman shall be taken, or imprisoned, or be disseised of his freehold, or liberties, or free customs, or be outlawed, or exiled, or any otherwise ruined; nor will we go or send against him, except by the lawful judgement of his peers or by the law of the land. (Chapter 39)
>
> To no-one will we sell, to no-one will we deny or delay right or justice. (Chapter 40)*

Similarly, anyone who reads the (English) Bill of Rights of 1689 – which placed further limits upon the royal prerogative, reinforced the powers of Parliament, and placed a seal upon the previous year's 'Glorious Revolution' – will encounter a very matter-of-fact document.† There are no new principles established. Indeed, the

---

* For further discussion of Magna Carta, see also pp.467–71.
† In the Glorious (or Bloodless) Revolution of 1688 James II was deposed as King to be replaced by his daughter Mary and her husband William of Orange, who ruled with her as William III.

'Lords and Commons Assembled' were anxious to deny any such intention. They claimed rather to be stating '*known* laws and statutes, rights and liberties'. What makes Magna Carta and the Bill of Rights so significant – and they are significant – is the tradition which they embodied and themselves developed, one which strengthened and broadened down the centuries.

In this process, the rights of Parliament and of the subject grew organically. Not, of course, uninterruptedly, or at a consistent pace, but with a momentum that increased precisely because it was surrounded by a certain mystery and legitimised by the passage of time. The two pillars upon which the limitation of government and the strengthening of individual liberties were built were the common law and the rights of Parliament (in practice, the rights of the House of Commons). Sometimes the former was the more important; sometimes the latter. Particularly during the seventeenth century, the crucial period for the development of English liberty, the pronouncements of judges and political events marched together. Indeed, the same mentality was evident in both, not least because many of the greatest judges were inspirational political thinkers. For example, the famous Lord Chief Justice Sir Edward Coke, whose judgements repeatedly challenged the royal prerogative, was one of the main parliamentary draftsmen of the Petition of Right in 1628. When a man like Coke declared, 'Magna Carta . . . will have no Sovereign,' he spoke with an authority which not even the chief Ministers – not even the King – could match. So by the eighteenth century, Britain had achieved the undisputed status of the freest country on earth. But, as history would show, it was still not free enough for the American colonists.

Read by the side of the statutes and judgements that mark out Britain's long path towards parliamentary democracy and the undisputed rule of law, their American counterparts – the Declaration of Independence (1776), the Constitution of the United States (1787) and the Bill of Rights (1789) – seem much more radical and ambitious. The Declaration of Independence, in particular, with its arresting opening statement, 'We hold these truths to be self-evident, that all men are created equal, that they are endowed by their Creator with certain unalienable Rights . . .', has an idealistic, even utopian tone.

There are some who would take these statements at face value and apply them out of context, overlooking the fact, for example, that for many years they were seen as compatible with the existence of slavery. In truth, even Thomas Jefferson's bold assertions must be understood, like their more prosaic English equivalents, against a specific set of historical circumstances. The great documents setting out the political and legal framework of the United States were part of a tradition – and that tradition was English and British before it was American. The attitude of the rebelling colonists was of sorrow and anger, but even in the Declaration of Independence they still spoke of 'our British brethren' who had 'been deaf to the voice of justice and of consanguinity'. Still more obviously, the terms of the American Bill of Rights, with its clear and practical qualifications to the US Constitution, ensuring due process and checking the power of the federal institutions, breathe the spirit of British justice and the instincts that nurtured it.

What can therefore accurately be termed, as Winston Churchill called it, the English-speaking peoples' conception of human rights is one that has an institutional context and is the fruit of a living tradition.* It did not evolve in a vacuum, and no one until very recently would have imagined that it could be applied in one.

The tendency to generalise about natural or human rights which predate and are not contingent upon specific laws – a tendency that was never unchecked in America until the modern age of political correctness – carried all before it in Revolutionary Europe. Paradoxically, the more ambitious and far-reaching natural rights are taken to be, the more likely it is that in the end liberties are going to be lost.

This can be perceived in the French Declaration of the Rights of Man and of the Citizen of 1789 and in its practical consequences. That document begins with the astonishing, and unhistorical, claim that 'ignorance, forgetfulness or scorn for the Rights of Man are the only causes of public ills and the corruption of governments'. It states that 'liberty consists in being able to do everything which does not hurt another. So the exercise of the

---

* For Churchill's words see p.20.

natural rights of each man has only those limits which assure to other members of society the enjoyment of those same rights. These limits can only be determined by law.' And what is law? The document answers that 'law is the expression of the general will'. Probably some at least of the draftsmen of this famous Declaration knew what they meant. But on any straightforward reading the arguments are circular and the reasoning impossibly woolly. As Revolutionary France lapsed into bloody tyranny justified by this doctrine of effectively unconstrained central power it became increasingly clear – not least on the English side of the Channel – that the guarantees offered to individuals by habit, accumulated tradition and the common law were a great deal sounder than 'democratic' principles applied by demagogues. This led Edmund Burke, the father of conservatism, to say of natural rights that 'their abstract perfection is their practical defect'.* And as usual, he was right.

The American and French declarations influenced other states' constitutions, as did the British model of parliamentary democracy and common law influence our former colonies. It is, though, only in the mid-twentieth century that international conventions relating to human rights began to appear.

The preamble to the UN Charter (1945) rousingly declared: 'We the peoples of the United Nations [are] determined . . . to reaffirm faith in fundamental human rights, in the dignity and worth of the human person, in the equal rights of men and women and of nations large and small . . .'. But the key clauses of the Charter in actual fact describe a system which assumes that sovereign states, not any international body, exercise power within their borders; in which the legitimate scope for interventions is extremely limited; and in which real control is exercised by a few great powers. Indeed, this combination of far-reaching statements of principle with very limited means of giving effect to them is characteristic of international human rights discourse over most of the intervening period.

---

* Edmund Burke, *Reflections on the Revolution in France, Select Works of Edmund Burke* (Indianapolis: Liberty Fund, 1999), p.151. Edmund Burke (1729–97), political philosopher, Member of Parliament 1765–94.

Contemporaneous with the Convention on Genocide (about which more shortly), the fundamental document is the Universal Declaration of Human Rights (1948). This lists a series of admirable goals, some general and some specific, but as the text continues it quickly becomes clear that liberty is becoming confused with other things – good, bad and indifferent – which may actually be opposed to it. For example, the Convention proclaims such 'rights' as 'social security' (Article 22), 'the right to work . . . and to protection against unemployment' (Article 23), 'the right to rest and leisure' (Article 24), 'the right to a standard of living adequate for the health and well-being of [oneself] and [one's] family' and to 'education' which among other things should 'further the activities of the United Nations for the maintenance of peace' (Article 25). Finally, 'everyone is entitled to a social and international order in which the rights and freedoms set forth in this Declaration can be fully realised' (Article 28).

The document thus displays a kind of catch-all approach, in which numerous – usually – worthy aims are declared 'rights', without recognition that their fulfilment depends upon circumstances and, above all, upon the willingness of one group of people to accept burdens on behalf of another. Moreover, the awkward ambiguities of expression betray the difficulties which the draftsmen encountered in trying to generalise about their objectives. Despite these flaws, I agree with Professor Mary Ann Glendon, who has concluded that 'the Universal Declaration has played a modest but not a trivial role in keeping the spirit of liberty alive. For that, it should get two cheers.'*

Much the same could be said of the other UN conventions on human rights which have followed in the wake of the Declaration. These have addressed, respectively, the Political Rights of Women (1952); Racial Discrimination (1965); Economic, Social and Cultural Rights (1966); Civil and Political Rights (1966); Discrimination against Women (1979); Torture (1984); and the Rights of the Child (1989). It would require a book much longer than this

---

* These words come from the text of an unpublished lecture given by Professor Glendon in July 2000 at the Institute of United States Studies, University of London.

one to examine just what the draftsmen and signatories sought to achieve in these documents. Doubtless, motives were mixed. But it is clear that, by and large, those who ratified these agreements on behalf of their states did not imagine that they were detracting from national sovereignty. At best, they regarded the conventions more as aspirations than as prescriptions – otherwise they would never have allowed so many ambiguities and contradictions to survive. Governments which conclude treaties relating to matters that they think are going to have a significant practical impact upon their own behaviour within their own countries do not accept the sort of vague terminology contained in these documents. To repeat, this does not mean that the twentieth-century international preoccupation with human rights has been a waste of time: it is simply that these documents came out of, and were assumed to apply within, an international order based upon sovereign states, whose own governments had the ultimate responsibility to give them effect. And that assumption was surely wise. From all that I have written here, I hope that it is clear that limits upon the powers of government, checks on abuses, legal rights and safeguards can never be effective if they are not grounded upon and in conformity with national circumstances, institutions and habits. Constitutions have to be written on hearts, not just paper.

GENOCIDE AND NUREMBERG

At first sight, the obvious exception to this is the Convention on the Prevention and Punishment of the Crime of Genocide (1948). This was the UN's first legal response to the mass-murder of the Jews by the Third Reich. Its focus was more narrowly defined than might in other circumstances have been expected – namely the attempted destruction in whole or in part of groups identifiable on the basis of *nationality, ethnicity, race or religion*. So, for example, Pol Pot's extermination of two million – that is about a quarter – of his fellow countrymen in Cambodia between 1975 and 1979 would not be covered by the Convention. This was because, when it came to the framing of the document, the Soviets ensured that *politically* defined groups did not count: for Stalin, with the blood of twenty million Soviet citizens on his hands, that would have been much too near the mark. This Convention unusually overrode any claims of sovereign or other immunity by specifying that those responsible would be punished 'whether they are constitutionally responsible rulers, public officials or private individuals' (Article IV).

This, again, was plain commonsense. Precisely because genocide is a crime that is only likely to be committed by or with the collaboration of those in power, it is very unlikely that the ordinary procedures of a national court will be sufficient to secure its punishment. Only in instances like that of Rwanda today, where the previous genocidal regime was overthrown, are such cases likely to come to trial.

It is thus the activity of the Nuremberg Tribunal which is the most important reference point for discussion of the advantages and disadvantages of international criminal courts erected to dispense justice to those accused of this most heinous of crimes. Unfortunately, what happened at Nuremberg has often been 'misremembered' – to adopt the expression of Professor Jeremy Rabkin – and, as a result, some of the wrong lessons have been learned.[*]

The prosecuting authorities at the Nuremberg Tribunal were, of course, heavily influenced by knowledge of the Holocaust. But they were more interested in securing convictions of the Nazi leaders on the charge of planning and initiating a 'war of aggression' than for 'crimes against humanity'. In other words, it was the waging of war against sovereign countries, rather than other offences, which figured largest. This in turn reflected the fact that, as Professor Rabkin notes: 'It is questionable if the Nuremberg Trials should actually be considered an "international" venture at all.' The cases were thus brought by 'the United States of America, the French Republic, the United Kingdom of Great Britain and Northern Ireland and the Union of Soviet Socialist Republics', not as was originally suggested 'the peoples of the United Nations'.

---

[*] Jeremy Rabkin, 'Nuremberg Misremembered', *SAIS Review*, summer–autumn 1999, pp.223–39. I have drawn on his penetrating analysis in what follows.

The Nuremberg trials were attacked at the time as 'victor's justice'. And this is precisely what they were – and were intended to be. Far from being staged by uninvolved outsiders, they were organised by the powers which together had defeated and occupied Germany. It was these occupying powers which now exercised sovereignty there.

Why is all this so important? Because those now advocating ever greater intrusions of international justice into the affairs of sovereign nations repeatedly claim that in some sense they are building upon and fulfilling the aims of Nuremberg. And this is quite wrong. It was only because the Allies had already achieved the total defeat of the Third Reich, captured most of its key personnel, and acquired a large fund of irrefutable documentary evidence that the cases could be brought at all.

I have no doubt that the twelve Nazi leaders sentenced to death for their part in the Nazi crimes deserved their fate. The Holocaust was the greatest crime committed against any group, nation or race. The disadvantage of treating the means by which these terrible figures received their just deserts as a trial with all the panoply of judges and lawyers was that it set an ambiguous precedent. But it is a great deal less ambiguous than the campaigners for international tribunals in modern times are prepared to recognise.

THE YUGOSLAV AND RWANDA CRIMINAL TRIBUNALS

The 1948 Convention on Genocide envisaged the possibility of setting up an international tribunal, and in the same year the UN General Assembly invited the International Law Commission to study the 'desirability and possibility' of such a proposal. But, for very good and practical reasons, nothing came of this. Although from time to time the idea was revived, it was the genocide in the former Yugoslavia and in Rwanda which prompted loud calls for international tribunals to be established. I deal in detail with the conflict in the former Yugoslavia and the lessons to be drawn from it in the next chapter. But here it is worth pointing out that for the main powers, and particularly for the West, there were strongly persuasive arguments for setting up tribunals to deal with these two crises, which did not necessarily apply more generally, and which were certainly not predicated upon conviction of the desirability of setting up an international criminal court.

The establishment of the tribunal for the former Yugoslavia (by UNSC Resolution 827 on 25 May 1993) and that of the tribunal for Rwanda (by UNSC Resolution 955 of 8 November 1994) were both admissions of defeat by the West and the wider international community. In the countries of the former Yugoslavia – Slovenia, Croatia and Bosnia – Slobodan Milošević and his agents had used the Yugoslav army and gangs of extremist Serb paramilitaries to wage war against non-Serbs. He had done this in a manner that was so barbarous and so shameless – and so close to the West – that it was impossible for Europe and America to overlook it. Yet for reasons which need to be examined more closely in a different context he had been allowed to get away with it. Indeed, at various stages he had been given what appeared in Belgrade to be a 'green light' to continue his efforts. Having made the wrong decisions when the conflict started in 1991, and having assiduously sought to place the blame equally on victim and aggressor, the greatest world power, America, had to find a way to respond to mounting horror around the world. The fact that the height of Serb butchery in Bosnia – where some two hundred thousand people have probably died – roughly coincided with a new US administration temperamentally more favourable to internationalism led the Americans to champion the idea of a special tribunal to punish those to blame.

I welcomed this decision. I would, it is true, have preferred a different policy right from the start. But given previous errors, and given the continuing weakness of international leadership, the tribunal was the best we could expect. It appeared to mark a new and welcome determination to stop the slaughter. The then US Ambassador to the United Nations, Madeleine Albright, greeted the decision to set up the tribunal in these words: 'The Nuremberg principles have been reaffirmed. The lesson that we are all accountable to international law may finally have taken hold in our collective memory.'

This rhetorical flourish was definitely excessive. I do not think that 'we are all accountable to international law', and I certainly do not believe that this is why we set up special tribunals to deal with those who plan and practise genocide.

The circumstances in which the tribunal on Rwanda was created were also ones in which the West and the international community had failed. But here I cannot claim to have had any better foresight than anyone else. There certainly were experts on tribalism in that part of Africa who must have known what was brewing. Hutus and Tutsis have been killing one another in large numbers from time to time over the last half-century or so.

The Tutsis are in a minority in both Rwanda and neighbouring Burundi. They remain in control of Burundi. They were also dominant in Rwanda when it was a Belgian colony. But in 1959 the Hutus slaughtered large numbers of Rwandan Tutsis in order to secure power on independence, when it came in 1962. In this they were successful, but the exodus of Tutsis provided the seeds of a rebel movement which almost three decades later invaded from Uganda.

After several years of fighting, a peace deal was then brokered and a power-sharing arrangement between the two tribes was agreed. But a large and powerful group of Hutu extremists were irreconcilable. When the Hutu President of Rwanda's aircraft was shot down, probably by these Hutu extremists, on 6 April 1994, a well-laid plan of genocide was put into action. Some eight hundred thousand Tutsis were killed in cruel and hideous fashion. Later that year the Hutu government was overthrown by Tutsi forces which quickly began to try those they held responsible for what had happened. Most of the Hutu extremists fled, however, and the whole struggle became increasingly part of the greater one that currently pits different African tribes and states against one another in shifting alliances in the Democratic Republic of the Congo (formerly Zaire).

Like those of the Balkans, the interrelations of the peoples of Central and Eastern Africa is a subject that is inclined to fox even the most assiduous student of international affairs. But – again just like the Balkans – certain constants do apply and certain basic lessons must be learned. Action by any outside powers has to be taken early, if it is to be effective. And if the outside force which has greatest influence in the region backs no one side – as in the Balkans – or the wrong side – as in Rwanda – the results can be disastrous.

In Rwanda it was France which was best placed to head off trouble. It had strong links with the francophone Hutu government. It armed and trained the Hutu army – according to some reports, until suspiciously late in the day. When the French did intervene in June 1994, though, the main effect was to allow the already defeated Hutu extremists to make off with their weapons to find safe haven in the Congo. It was in these circumstances, where the mistakes, misjudgements, lethargy and on occasion suspect motivations of the great powers had compounded disaster, that – as for the former Yugoslavia – a special tribunal was appointed as a kind of last resort.

It is no reflection on the judges and other personnel associated with these two – closely linked – tribunals to say that their performance was often disappointing. If one of the intentions of setting up a tribunal for the former Yugoslavia was that it would deter new atrocities, that was certainly not the effect. The notorious massacre of Muslims at Srebrenica in Bosnia in July 1995 took place some two years *after* the tribunal had begun to sit. It is only after the Serb forces were heavily defeated in 1995 and once the Western powers effectively took over running Bosnia that the net began to close on the war criminals. It is only because the Serbian forces were again defeated in Kosovo in 1999 that the Serbs turned against Milošević, threw him out of power, consigned him to prison, and finally despatched him to The Hague. And, at the time of writing, several of the worst villains are still at large. In other words, the court's effectiveness has throughout mainly been determined by events outside its control, notably the outcome of military conflict, and it has only been of value when its decisions were given practical effect by force – more often than not, force applied by British troops.

Nor can one say that the proceedings of the tribunal offer an ideal model for the administration of justice more widely. Again, this is no reflection on the integrity or professionalism of those involved. But as at Nuremberg, the tribunals for the former Yugoslavia and for Rwanda operate according to rules that would be out of place in an ordinary British or American court. Justice of this sort in wholly exceptional circumstances, like those of post-war Germany, Yugoslavia and Rwanda, is doubtless better than no justice at all. But these experiences do not suggest that international judicial systems are inherently better than national ones – far from it.

Like the tribunal on Yugoslavia, that on Rwanda got off to a slow start. Indeed, it was four years before it secured its first conviction. This delay, it appears, was due to a mixture of administrative shortcomings – Arusha in Tanzania is not the best place to organise an international tribunal – and obstruction. As with the Yugoslav tribunal, Rwanda's has since then handed down a growing number of convictions. But whereas over forty people have been detained and eight convicted by the tribunal, most of the trials for what happened are occurring in the local courts within Rwanda. There more than 120,000 have been detained, over two thousand convicted and three hundred sentenced to death. With the fighting between Tutsis and Hutus continuing in the Congo and elsewhere, these trials must be considered – to adapt Clausewitz – as the extension of war by other means.* But then, is international justice ever anything other than 'victor's justice'?

THE PROPOSED INTERNATIONAL
CRIMINAL COURT

Actually, the answer to that question can be 'yes' – but only if the United States and its allies are foolish enough to surrender power over their decisions and personnel to the proposed International Criminal Court at The Hague. For the victors of the Cold War to submit to an unelected, unaccountable, and almost certainly hostile body such as that envisaged would be the ultimate irony. Thankfully, with President George W. Bush in the White House, I am reasonably confident that this is not going to happen. I hope

---

* Karl von Clausewitz (1780–1831): Prussian military terrorist and soldier.

that the Bush administration will pursue the sort of approach advocated by one of the projected court's most acute critics – that of the 'Three Noes'. No financial support, directly or indirectly. No collaboration. No further negotiations with other governments to 'improve' the Statute.* And other states should be left in no doubt of the consequences for their relations with the US if they support court actions which prejudice America's interests or personnel.

All of which may seem perverse, even shocking, if one accepts the UN Secretary General's prospectus for the International Criminal Court. According to Kofi Annan:

> In the prospect of an international criminal court lies the promise of universal justice. That is the simple and soaring hope of this vision . . . Only then will the innocents of distant wars and conflicts know that they too may sleep under the cover of justice; that they too have rights, and that those who violate those rights will be punished.†

But Mr Annan's 'vision' is more likely to turn into a nightmare, for several very good reasons. The first is that the court is in practice most likely to be brought into action against the soldiers or statesmen of the generally law-abiding countries, rather than those of the rogue states which will simply ignore its jurisdiction. Indeed, it is easy to envisage politically motivated prosecutions of Westerners undertaken in order to provide 'balance'.

The second fatal defect of the proposed court is that a global judicial institution of the kind proposed would require a global police force and, at least in embryo, a global government in order to ensure that its decisions were actually carried out. That, of course, is why the project has such appeal among the advocates of what is termed nowadays 'global governance'. These enthusiasts also

---

* John Bolton, Statement before the House International Relations Committee on the International Criminal Court and the American Service-Members' Protection Act of 2000, 25 July 2000. Mr Bolton is now Under-Secretary of State for Arms Control and International Security.
† Speech to the International Bar Association, New York, 11 June 1997.

turn out – not at all surprisingly – to be distinctly unenthusiastic about the current US-dominated, unipolar, international system. They envisage the new court as a way of holding the American superpower and its allies to account for their actions at the 'bar' of international opinion. This visceral anti-American attitude is, indeed, quite undisguised. When the United States was outvoted in Rome on the draft statute of the Court by 120 votes to seven – and so found itself in the minority, along with Israel, China, Libya, Algeria, Yemen and Qatar – it is reported that the conference room burst into prolonged applause, with human rights activists and foreign diplomats demonstrating their joy at America's humiliation.*

Yet it is not at all clear that the proponents of the court will have the last laugh. Their fundamental problem remains that there exists no adequate means of coercion to overcome the opposition of sovereign states, let alone of a superpower, to such a court's decisions. This lack of available instruments is not, moreover, a hurdle which could be surmounted merely by another grand conference dominated by proponents of world governance, leading to the creation of more new international institutions. The absence of world police forces and world armies reflects the fact that there can be no democratic legitimacy for such structures. There *is* no world government, because there *is* no world 'nation', no world political identity, no world public opinion. Thus the only way to fulfil the UN Secretary General's (doubtless sincerely held) aspirations would, paradoxically, be to suppress democratic instincts, resist democratic pressures, and drain democracy of all real meaning.

The third reason why the International Criminal Court can only lead to trouble is because to whatever extent it *is* effective it will render the West's capacity to intervene less so. The Clinton administration seriously mishandled the discussions – on the one hand

---

* The humiliation of America at the hands of those who regard themselves as representing the 'international community' has since continued. In May 2001 the US was voted off the UN Human Rights Commission. But Pakistan (with a military government), Sudan (with an Islamist regime conducting a genocidal civil war) and Sierra Leone (the scene of terrible abuses) are all represented. So much for the UN's conception of human rights.

appearing to support the principle, but then opposing the practice. Thus, having extolled the merits of international justice, the US took fright – partly because of the well-judged warnings of Senator Jesse Helms – and tried to restrict the scope for the court's prosecution of American personnel. The US delegation thus sought the requirement of a referral by the UN Security Council before the court could investigate any particular conflict. This would have allowed America to exercise its veto – though, naturally, the moral pressure not to do so would still be considerable. But in any case the other delegations at Rome were not prepared to accept this provision. And so the Americans found themselves deserted.*

All this is enormously dangerous. Major international interventions are doomed unless the US is directly or indirectly involved. But if American politicians, officials and servicemen are to be put at risk of arrest and prosecution, the United States will be most reluctant to act in order to curb aggression or prevent genocide. So the effect of the court may well be to diminish, not increase, the numbers of (in the words of the UN Secretary General) 'innocents of distant wars and conflicts'.

What is truly astonishing, though, is the fact that Britain has been in the forefront of all this. Given the likely anti-American bias of the court and the fact that the United States is still feared by its enemies, it is very likely that, initially at least, they will move against a power they consider as a close American ally and proxy. One obvious possibility is Israel, as the Israelis fully recognised – hence their opposition to the court. But another is Britain. Britain's then Foreign Secretary, Robin Cook, pooh-poohed such talk. 'This,' he told BBC's *Newsnight*, 'is not a court set up to bring to book Prime Ministers of the United Kingdom or Presidents of the United States.'† And doubtless he would have added Foreign Secretaries to that list.

But Mr Cook may have been over-confident. For example, Article VIII lists among 'war crimes' over which the court would

---

* At the time of writing, thirty-six countries have ratified the Rome Statute of the International Criminal Court. Sixty ratifications are required in order for the court to begin functioning.

† Quoted by *The Times*, 26 September 2000.

have jurisdiction those of 'attacking civilians' and 'attacking civilian objects'. I would not be too sure, if I were Mr Clinton or Mr Blair or their advisers and subordinates, that *nothing* that had happened in the course of our military actions against Saddam Hussein, Slobodan Milošević or Osama bin Laden could open us up to accusations on that score. And since I consider the West's responses against all these villains completely justified, I view the potential for the court's mischief-making with alarm.*

The final reason why I oppose the International Criminal Court is because it is only the latest and most powerful expression of a trend towards the internationalisation of justice, through what is nowadays called 'customary international law', that will itself lead to injustice. Here it is necessary to reflect on what has been happening in recent years. Jeremy Rabkin notes:

> Freed from its traditional moorings, international law no longer needs to be demonstrated by actual practice ... International human rights law is not the product of court rulings, but of international conferences. Abstract pronouncements are enough. At that, they need not even be the authoritative pronouncements of supreme governmental authorities. Words spoken by diplomats at conferences are given much weight, and then the reconfiguring of those words by commentators is supposed to give more weight ... Soon there is a towering edifice of words, which is then treated as a secure marker of 'customary international law'.†

This is no way to make law – any law. It is a recipe for confusion, and it provides endless scope for interpretation and so opportunities for bias. That is what we can expect from the International Criminal Court, unless we stop it. And anyone who thinks

---

* The suggestion, which has been frequently heard since 11 September, that bin Laden's terrorism reinforces the case for an international criminal court is wide of the mark. The crimes committed were against (mainly) US citizens on US territory. If the cases are to be tried it should be by US courts. There is no reason, in any event, to imagine that the Taliban would have been willing to hand over bin Laden and his henchmen to an international court.

† Jeremy Rabkin, *Why Sovereignty Matters* (Washington DC: American Enterprise Institute, 1998), p.55.

that I am exaggerating should reflect upon the case of Senator Augusto Pinochet Ugarte, which took up so much of my time and energy during the more than five hundred days of his detention in Britain.

THE PINOCHET CASE

I only met General Pinochet after he had ceased to be President of Chile. But I had indirect contact with him much earlier, at the time of the Falklands War in 1982. At that time Chile provided vital assistance to us without which, I am convinced, many more of our servicemen would have lost their lives.

Most important was the provision of intelligence. The Chilean airforce regularly gave us early warning of Argentinian air attacks. I only learned later one poignant detail. Near the end of the conflict the Chilean long-range radar had to be switched off for twenty-four hours for overdue maintenance. The result was tragedy. On that same day – Tuesday, 8 June – the Argentinian airforce success-fully attacked and destroyed the *Sir Galahad* and *Sir Tristram* landing ships, with heavy casualties.

All the assistance which Britain received was secretly authorised by President Pinochet. Of course, the help that Chile gave was not simply the result of traditional Chilean sympathy for the British – real as that was and (despite everything) still is. Chile was itself under threat at that time from neighbouring and more powerful Argentina: so if Britain managed to defeat the Argentine *junta* Chile would also benefit. The fact remains that what President Pinochet did entailed considerable risks: we might, after all, have lost.

I felt grateful to the Chilean President and to Chile, and this influenced my later action when ex-President Pinochet found him-self in difficulties. But I was moved by more than sentiment. It is in a country's interests to keep faith with its allies. States in this sense are like people. If you have a reputation for exacting favours and not returning them, the favours dry up. A medium-sized power with global interests, like Britain, is particularly in need of favours from allies in every region. The continued uncertainty about

Argentina's intentions towards the Falklands Islands is just one important illustration of that fact.

It is also worth trying to put right another misconception about my attitude towards – as he now was – Senator Pinochet. It is sometimes suggested that I was unconcerned about the abuses of human rights of which he was accused, and that I was supporting him simply for what he had done for Britain during the Falklands War. I do not know how I would have felt if I had thought that he was guilty of great crimes. I would still have considered that his arrest was wrong – because of the way it was carried out, because of the consequences for Britain and for Chile, and because of the dangerous precedent it set. But I never had to wrestle with that problem because although I could not be sure about every detail of every accusation, I was and am convinced that General Pinochet by his actions turned Chile into the free and prosperous country we see today.

This is not the place to go into detail about what happened in Chile in the 1970s and 1980s. But I stand by the contents of the speech which I delivered to a packed meeting at the Conservative Party Conference in Blackpool on Wednesday, 6 October 1999. I summed up in a sentence the real charge against General Pinochet: 'What the left can't forgive is that Pinochet undoubtedly saved Chile and helped save South America.'

But I also tried to deal fairly with the evidence, in so far as it could be pieced together – and by the time I spoke I had myself been over many of the details. As General Pinochet himself freely admitted, there had been abuses in the wake of the military coup of September 1973. And some of these continued. The precise responsibility for what happened could only, however, be judged in Chile, not in Britain. Pinochet (with other members of the military *junta*) had, of course, been in political charge at the time. But there is an important difference between political and criminal responsibility, which is conveniently overlooked. A head of government – any head of government – must accept a large measure of political responsibility for whatever happens when he or she is in office. But that does not mean that he must accept *criminal* responsibility for everything that is done, whether he authorised it or not, whether he overlooked it or not, even whether he knew about it or not. On that basis, as I pointed out in Blackpool, the current British Prime Minister and Home Secretary should accept criminal responsibility for everything done in every prison or police station throughout the United Kingdom – and then, if necessary, be extradited to Spain to answer for it.

Actually, of course, though it had judicial trappings, the action taken against Senator Pinochet in Britain was political. As such it required, at least in part, a political response. So I reminded my audience of the Pinochet government's real and remarkable achievements – that Chile was turned from chaotic collectivism into the model economy of Latin America, that Chileans were decently housed, that medical care was improved, that infant mortality plummeted, that life expectancy rose, and that highly effective programmes against poverty were launched. Above all, to balance all the talk of Pinochet's 'dictatorship', I noted that it was he who established a constitution for the return of democracy; who held a referendum to decide whether or not he should remain in power; and who, having narrowly lost the vote, respected the result, and handed over to an elected successor.*

These arguments for a positive evaluation of President Pinochet's record still strike me as persuasive. And equally so are the arguments for a negative evaluation of the political and judicial treatment which he later received in Britain.

Among the most notable incidents in this extraordinary and shameful affair – incidents which are replete with ominous implications for the future – are the following:

1. Senator Pinochet came to Britain on a diplomatic passport as a special ambassador for his country.
2. At no point until his arrest in a London clinic at about midnight on Friday, 16 October 1998 was he warned that he was at risk – indeed the Chilean Embassy was deceived by the Foreign Office about the imminent arrest.

---

* President Pinochet gained 43 per cent in his referendum. This compares not unfavourably with the 44.4 per cent of the vote won by the Labour Party under Tony Blair in the May 1997 British general election, and their 40.7 per cent in 2001.

3. The warrant on which Senator Pinochet was arrested was unlawful, as was later confirmed by the court. He was held for six days illegally under this warrant.

4. The British Crown Prosecution Service in the meantime collaborated with the Spanish prosecuting magistrate who had issued the first warrant to draw up a new one.

5. That Spanish magistrate had originally levelled accusations at Senator Pinochet so ludicrous that they had quickly to be dropped – for example he was accused of 'genocide'.

6. The British Divisional Court unanimously ruled that the Senator, as a former head of state, enjoyed sovereign immunity. But on appeal a majority of the Law Lords voted that he had no immunity at all. One of those judges was then found to have failed to declare an interest in the case, and for the first time ever a judgement by the Lords had to be set aside. When they reheard the case the Law Lords came up with a completely different decision – namely that Senator Pinochet did enjoy immunity for crimes of torture, but only up to the time when in 1988 Britain adhered to the Torture Convention.

7. This judgement, which accorded the Convention a meaning never before accepted, namely that it overrode sovereign immunity, left only one of the alleged incidents held against Senator Pinochet by the British prosecuting authorities admissible – and this was not a case of torture (as the term would normally be understood) but one of police brutality.

8. Not to be deterred, the Spanish prosecuting magistrate almost immediately faxed through to Britain more cases which had been provided by 'human rights' organisations and which he had clearly had neither the time nor the inclination to examine in any depth.

9. At no stage in these proceedings was evidence considered on its merits by the British courts, nor was Senator Pinochet given the right to answer, because under the terms of the Extradition Act of 1989, which encapsulated in British law the European Convention on Extradition, the case could only be heard in Spain.

10. The likelihood of the Senator receiving a fair trial in Spain was minimal – not least because a number of those who could

testify on his behalf dared not set foot on Spanish soil because they too were threatened with arrest. After the Law Lords' ruling of 24 March 1999 none of the cases for which Senator Pinochet's extradition to Spain was sought involved a Spaniard. All related to incidents concerning alleged crimes committed by Chileans against Chileans in Chile. But the Spanish courts insisted on claiming 'universal jurisdiction' of such offences.

As is well-known, the strains of captivity caused Senator Pinochet's health to deteriorate. Just before his arrest he had come to tea with me in my house. I later visited him twice at the modest rented house on the Wentworth Estate just outside London where he was kept under close guard – in the early days not even allowed to walk on the lawn outside. I was therefore in a position to see the effect of the ordeal upon him.

I should also say, however, that I never saw him bitter. He blamed Britain's Labour government, but he always said that you cannot judge a nation by its politicians. His dignity throughout was complete.

Because he was medically determined unfit to stand trial, Senator Pinochet was finally allowed to return to Chile. While the Chilean aircraft was standing on the runway about to leave I had a silver Armada dish taken over to him. The Chileans understandably know more about the details of their own historic battles with Spain than about ours, so I enclosed with my gift a short note of explanation. It read:

> I hope that by the time you receive this letter you will be safely on your way back to Chile. Your detention in Britain was a great injustice which should never have taken place.
>
> With your return to Chile, Spain's attempt at judicial colonialism has been decisively – and I trust permanently – rebuffed. In order to celebrate this, I enclose with this letter a silver Armada dish. These dishes were first produced in England in order to celebrate another victory over the Spanish – that of our own navy against the Spanish Armada in 1588. I am sure that you will appreciate and enjoy the symbolism!

I was amused to learn that the Spanish, who still suffer from an inferiority complex about the Armada, were furious and the Spanish Foreign Minister apoplectic. I had clearly made my point.

Back in Chile, Senator Pinochet was still for a time subject to what seemed to me more political and judicial hounding – though I was not in a position to assess all the rights and wrongs of the matter. I hope that commonsense and compassion will now prevail. Whatever the darker side of those years, Chileans have an enormous amount for which to thank Senator Pinochet. I suspect that most of them know it.

The human rights activists and left-wing politicians are right on one score: the wider impact of the Pinochet case will continue to be felt. Indeed, the early results are already evident, as more and more attempts are made to use the mechanisms of international justice in order to threaten or embarrass present and former statesmen.*

We have, in fact, passed into a new era in which the whole basis upon which nation states have traditionally conducted their affairs is in the process of being overturned. The fact that the concept of sovereign immunity is now under sustained attack may evoke cheers from those who never expect to serve their country in high office or to do their country's bidding in crises. But the cheerleaders might care to remember that the rationale of sovereign immunity is not that it protects statesmen who have committed serious crimes, but rather that it protects those who authorise or carry out controversial acts from facing politically motivated charges in the courts of unfriendly foreign states. The effect of removing or attenuating such immunity will be to make leaders very reluctant to take tough decisions, particularly if these involve arousing the ire of the organised international left. The Torture Convention, whose provisions were adapted by prosecutors and judges to serve the purpose of trapping Senator Pinochet, could,

---

* Belgium with its claims of universal jurisdiction has effectively rendered itself a no-go area even for serving international statesmen against whom some allegation can be made. In July 2001 Israel's Prime Minister Ariel Sharon cancelled a visit to Brussels after a war crimes lawsuit was brought against him by a Palestinian group there. *Daily Telegraph*, 3 July 2001.

after all, be made to apply in many other cases. In 1999 Amnesty International claimed, for example, that torture or ill-treatment by security forces, police or other state authorities was carried out in 132 countries – including France, Spain and Belgium.*

Hardly less worrying, though, is what the Pinochet affair showed about the unscrupulousness of legal and political authorities when presented with the opportunities for advancing their doctrinaire objectives offered by international law. These people do not see themselves in this light, of course. They think that they are crusading for a better world. And that conviction is precisely what makes them so dangerous. Left-wing zealots have often been prepared to ride roughshod over due process and basic considerations of fairness when they think they can get away with it. For them the ends always seem to justify the means. That is precisely how their predecessors came to create the gulag.

We have to act urgently if we are to prevent a wholesale erosion of what we have traditionally understood by the rule of law. And we must be prepared to argue from first principles the case for national rather than international justice.

We in Britain should:

- Reform extradition law to ensure that what the American Constitution calls 'full faith and credit' is no longer automatically given to extradition requests by courts in countries (like Spain in the case of Senator Pinochet) where a fair trial cannot be guaranteed†
- Consider carefully what the law on sovereign immunity should be and legislate on it, rather than leave such matters to be determined by judges on the basis of the dubious science of customary international law
- In the light of judicial decisions about the effect of the Torture Convention, review which other international conventions may pose unacceptable risks to the orderly conduct of our affairs.

---

* *Amnesty International Annual Report 2000.*

† In terrorist cases, though, I would make it easier to extradite and deport, as I explain below. See pp.277–8.

And I would strongly urge the United States:

- To have nothing to do with the International Criminal Court and to exert maximum pressure on others to do likewise
- To use its full weight to oppose all further attempts to curtail sovereign immunity or to claim universal jurisdiction over matters which are properly left to democratic decisions and national courts.

EUROPE AND HUMAN RIGHTS

I suppose I should not be surprised that a substantial share of the difficulties in the Pinochet case are traceable to Europe, and more specifically to the European Convention on Extradition. I was Prime Minister when the Extradition Act of 1989 was passed. Its aim was to enable Britain to ratify the Convention by dispensing with the requirement that a state requesting extradition must establish a *prima facie* case, by providing sufficient evidence to warrant trial of the suspect if the alleged offence had been committed in the United Kingdom. There was a good deal of pressure to do this because other European states were said to be deterred by the technicalities of the *prima facie* rule from seeking extradition – and that in turn meant that we were less likely to have their cooperation when we sought some suspect's extradition to face justice in Britain. As I have outlined above, it is now clear that the assumption that the courts of all European countries in all circumstances could be relied upon to adopt our standards was wrong.

But that is not the only European aspect which has to be considered. The European Convention on Extradition (1957) was a Council of Europe rather than a European Union initiative. Thus in place of the Treaty of Rome's 'ever closer union' we find in the Convention's preamble the rather less ambitious objective of 'a greater unity between [the Council's] members'. However, nowadays the institutions of both the Council of Europe and the European Union work to much the same agenda – that is the advance of supra-nationalism at the expense of national sovereignty.

Consequently, it is right to link two recent 'European' initiatives which the present British government has taken.

The first is the incorporation of the European Convention on Human Rights (ECHR) into British law through the Human Rights Act. The ECHR (1950) itself was essentially intended to commit the countries of Continental Europe to the kind of respect for human rights which the United States and Britain had for centuries taken for granted. This point, which British politicians then and since have usually been too diplomatic to make, should always be kept in mind in discussion of the impact of the ECHR on British law. It was precisely because the written constitutions of Europe had proved so much less capable of guaranteeing individual liberties than the unwritten constitution of the United Kingdom that some new fundamental statement of rights was felt necessary. It is, therefore, deeply ironic, and suggestive of a degree of muddled thinking, that Britain has now incorporated the ECHR into our domestic law, thus giving us for the first time what amounts to a written constitution.

Whether it is in the United States or in mainland Europe, written constitutions have one great weakness. This is that they contain the potential to have judges take decisions which should properly be made by democratically elected politicians. At the very least, the process creates uncertainties about what the effect of legislation will be. At worst, it can lead to judges exercising what amounts to sovereignty. As this point approaches, the pressures for the politicisation of justice become all but unstoppable. In the end, as in the United States, the politicians will demand the right to confirm or reject the judges who wield such huge power. Indeed, once a certain degree of politicisation of justice has been reached political confirmation becomes necessary, for it places some power back in the hands of the people's representatives. Because I prefer the traditional British way of appointing judges – and welcome the traditional limits which they place upon their own exercises of judicial power – I believe that incorporation of the ECHR in our law will turn out to have been a bad mistake.

But we must also face up to the defects of the ECHR itself, not merely its incorporation into British law. It is not jingoism to complain that the very approach of the Continental Europeans to rights and laws is radically different to ours. The organic development of British freedom has involved the placing of clear limits upon government's powers to coerce: we can then do whatever is not explicitly forbidden by law. European understandings of rights, however, usually involve the granting of so-called 'positive' rights guaranteed by the state.

European judges are also much more likely to take a very broad view of statutes and thus to come up with conclusions that frustrate the intentions of legislators and those who elect them. On quite a large number of occasions in recent years – that is even prior to full incorporation – the European Court of Human Rights (which pronounces upon alleged violations of the ECHR) has thus come up with judgements that seem to many people in Britain incomprehensible or just plain wrong. For example, in 1995 the court ruled that British Special Forces had in 1988 (when I was Prime Minister) violated the rights of IRA terrorists whom they shot before those thugs could commit a planned outrage in Gibraltar. In 1996 the court ruled that the Home Secretary, to whom this power belonged by Act of Parliament, could not decide how long juvenile criminals detained 'at Her Majesty's Pleasure' should stay in jail. In 1999 the court ruled against the long-standing ban on homosexuals serving in the armed forces. And in May 2001 it ordered Britain to pay £10,000 each to the families of ten IRA terrorists killed by the security forces in Northern Ireland.

What incorporation of the ECHR in British law will mean is that this kind of wayward judicial activism will be encouraged in British courts as well. Although it is denied that the Human Rights Act will undermine parliamentary sovereignty, that will in practice be the effect. The courts will be able to issue 'declarations of incompatibility' if they find that legislation is contrary to the terms of the ECHR. In theory the law stays as before; but in fact it is envisaged that by a 'fast track' procedure, involving the government's amendment of primary legislation with no previous debate of the merits of doing so, the law would quickly be amended. It is difficult to envisage any government – let alone the present British government – failing to act to change the law in this way to bring it into line with the court's ruling.

Moreover, that is likely to occur in a wide range of areas. Police stop-and-search of suspects, rules regarding the granting of bail, procedures affecting life sentences, prison conditions, courts martial and military discipline are all obvious targets. But the destabilising effect of judges' trying to apply the new norms could go much further. For example, schools, hospitals and security companies are all in varying states of alarm at how they will be affected. Will such fears prove justified? Time will tell soon enough. But if we take into account the combination of a spirit of judicial activism, growing litigiousness, and the apparently irresistible lobbying by powerful non-governmental organisations (NGOs), the chances are that such worries will prove more than warranted.

The urgent review of national security which followed the terrorist attacks on America of 11 September has brought to light – or, more accurately perhaps, brought into sharper focus – other problems connected with the ECHR and the Human Rights Act. It has become enormously difficult in Britain to extradite or deport suspected terrorists, particularly to America. And the scandalous abuse of asylum procedures has at the same time made it all but impossible to exercise proper checks on those who come here. This can provide cover for dangerous figures to operate against our interests or those of our allies.*

Rightly, there has been much discussion about how to rectify this situation. But the various legislative options all, in varying degrees, run up against the courts, either British courts or the European Court of Human Rights. The basic principle has to be re-established that where national security is deemed to be at stake the government of the day should have the power to act swiftly to protect it. At the very minimum, the provisions of the Human Rights Act should be formally excluded from applying to deten-

---

* The scale of the abuse of asylum is reflected, for example, in two significant statistics. First, since the end of the Cold War, that is since most of the world was freed from the oppression of communism, the number seeking asylum in Britain has approximately trebled. Second, whereas 5 per cent of would-be refugees from Algeria are granted asylum if they make their application in France, no less than 80 per cent of such cases are successful if they apply in the UK.

tion, deportation and asylum cases where the national interest is involved.*

As if the uncertainties stemming from the ECHR and the Human Rights Act were not sufficient, a further – as yet shadowy – element has been introduced in the form of the European Union's so-called Charter of Fundamental Human Rights. Even a committed Euro-enthusiast must surely be tempted to question why the EU and the European Court of Justice (in Luxembourg) have to duplicate the work of the ECHR and the European Court of Human Rights (in Strasbourg).

The British government claims that the new Charter is purely declaratory. A British Minister even suggested that 'people will bring the document up in the European Court of Justice as if it were the *Beano* or the *Sun*'.† But this is no joke, particularly if the government is foolish enough, after the experience of all that has happened in Britain's relations with Europe over recent years, to think that any such initiative will not become an element in the drive towards creating a European superstate. It is not, after all, as if the proponents of the Charter, particularly the French, would have invested so much time and effort in the project if it was no more than high-minded rhetoric. Their intention, which may have to wait a few years before it is fully accomplished, is to turn the Charter into a Constitution for Europe.‡

Moreover – and this is particularly why it so interests our French friends – this Constitution is intended to ensure that under the cover of enforcement of 'social rights' the competitive advantage of

---

* In his illuminating study of these issues, *Tackling Terrorism: The Human Rights Convention and the Enemy Within* (London: Politeia, 2001), Martin Howe notes that Article 57 of the ECHR permits states to enter 'reservations' which have the effect of excluding specific laws from the application of the Convention. This would involve withdrawing and then re-adhering. But there are, in any case, good reasons for simply withdrawing – as I argue below.
† Keith Vaz, then Minister for Europe at the Foreign Office; Labour MP since 1987. The *Beano* is a popular British comic magazine. The *Sun* is Britain's top-selling tabloid newspaper.
‡ The French Prime Minister, Lionel Jospin, has publicly reaffirmed France's commitment to a 'European Constitution' of which the Charter would be 'at the heart'. Speech in Paris, 28 May 2001.

Britain's freer markets, looser state controls and lower government spending is lost. One has only to list some of these rights and to consider the interpretation which the expansionist and activist European Court might come to put on them to see how this could happen:

> Every worker has the right to working conditions which respect his or her health, safety and dignity. (Article 31)

But who is to say what working conditions are 'dignified'?

> Young people admitted to work must have working conditions appropriate to their age and be protected against economic exploitation and any work likely ... to interfere with their education. (Article 32)

But who defines 'exploitation'? And there is always, at any age, some trade-off between work and education.

> A high level of human health protection shall be ensured in the definition and implementation of all Union policies and activities. (Article 35)

But how high?

> Union policies shall ensure a high level of consumer protection. (Article 38)

Again, how high?

Of course, it is quite possible to read through the text of the European Charter of Fundamental Rights and give a hearty cheer after almost every article. But experience tells us that beneath these general expressions lie an agenda and a philosophy. The agenda consists of the subordination of sovereign states, democratic decision-making and national law to international institutions and pressure groups. And the philosophy, sheltering beneath the umbrella of 'human rights', is eminently recognisable as that of the Old Left operating in new conditions. This truth is so obvious that only very sophisticated people seem unable to grasp it. Of course, it is never enough to establish *parti pris* in order to disprove an assertion. On the other hand, we would equally be extremely naïve if we did not observe that nowadays the proponents and practitioners of human rights seem nearly all to be from a particular political camp.

Just consider the following. Soon after the left's hate figure, Augusto Pinochet, was arrested a Spanish court was also asked to issue an international warrant against the left's hero, Fidel Castro, for the alleged murder of fifty-one Europeans and Americans (including five Spaniards). The request was peremptorily dismissed. The killings for which Castro is responsible far outnumber those which the Chilean Truth and Reconciliation Commission found occurred under Pinochet – between fifteen thousand and seventeen thousand Cubans were executed by firing squads at Castro's orders and thousands more have died trying to escape his regime, whereas 2279 people (including members of the security forces) were killed under Pinochet's rule.* Moreover, although Castro might claim sovereign immunity *now*, he was not even President – just the Great Revolutionary Leader – when the worst atrocities occurred, which might give any fair-minded judge food for thought. But, then, was it not in retrospect inevitable that Pinochet – on the right – not Castro – on the left – would be in the dock? That, after all, is what 'human rights' are nowadays all about.

- **Conservatives everywhere must go on the counter-offensive against the New Left human rights brigade, and with as much intellectual vigour as we employed in struggles with the Old Left in days gone by.**

Specifically, we in Britain should:

- **Immediately legislate to limit the harmful effects of the Human Rights Act**

---

* Figures for Cuba from Pascal Fontaine, 'Communism in Latin America', *The Black Book of Communism*, p.664.

- Give six months' notice of our intention to denounce the Convention itself, so that the European Court of Human Rights is no longer able to play fast and loose with our laws and democratic decision-making
- Oppose any attempt to enforce the provisions of the European Charter of Fundamental Rights – though this must, as I describe later, be part of more far-reaching changes to Britain's position *vis-à-vis* the European Union.

CHAPTER 8

Balkan Wars

A SUITABLE CASE FOR INTERVENTION

Bismarck, it is alleged, once remarked: 'The Balkans are not worth the bones of a Pomeranian grenadier.' In this opinion, the Iron Chancellor has found many adherents.

Those of the 'Bismarckian' school believe that the United States and/or the countries of Europe have no significant interests at stake in the region and that the inhabitants had better be allowed to sort themselves out – or, more likely, not sort themselves out. For those who favour a non-interventionist approach because of lack of strategic interest usually also assume that the region is a political morass. Its history is thus viewed as baleful. Its leaders are understood to be irrational. Its peoples are regarded as frankly impossible. In such circumstances, it goes without saying that ordinary strategic and moral criteria do not apply. We may lament what happens, but 'twas always – and will be – thus. This is only a slightly over-simplified description of the sort of views that were widely expressed in the media in the early 1990s, as the Balkans began to hurtle into genocide.

There is, however, another view, almost equally widely held, particularly today when Balkan non-interventionism *tout court* is less respectable. This is the belief, which is particularly prevalent on the liberal-left, that the Balkans are a litmus test, and that events there offer lessons which apply far beyond the region. These people are convinced that the only way to stop nationalism creating wars and atrocities is – to put it bluntly – to banish nationhood itself. They think that it is only international bodies – political, military and judicial – that can be relied upon to maintain acceptable standards of conduct. And just as they seem to want to turn the Balkan region into a kind of quasi-protectorate involving NATO, the UN and the EU, so their ultimate ambition is to extend the multinational approaches developed there and apply them to more and more of the 'global village'.

I have already, I hope, explained why I believe that this second group's brand of utopian internationalism is unrealistic and indeed harmful.* Whether at home or abroad, the task of statesmen is to work with human nature, warts and all, and to draw on instincts and even prejudices that can be turned to good purpose. It is never to try to recreate Mankind in a new image. And, more practically in this case, attempting to build a perfectly just and permanently peaceful Balkans could lead the West into a disproportionate and unacceptable diversion of effort and resources.

The trouble is that the first, 'Bismarckian', approach to the region was a terrible failure when it was pursued in the early 1990s. Actually, there was never a policy of complete non-intervention. 'Pure' isolationism would probably have been less harmful than the policies that were in fact then adopted. The West, after all, *did* intervene to try to keep the old Yugoslavia together and put heavy and public pressure on those who had the temerity to want to leave it. Western nations, among others, imposed an arms embargo which gave the aggressor an overwhelming advantage and which thus encouraged aggression. Finally, the West brokered numerous ceasefires (which were not heeded) and issued numerous threats (which were ignored). So it would be better to describe the Western attitude at that time as ineffectual interference rather than true disengagement.

In any case, it is a very short-sighted view of national and strategic interest that fails to take account of the indirect alongside the direct impact of crises. Allowing flagrant aggression to succeed is always dangerous, even if the immediate consequences seem limited, because of the precedent it sets. That is doubly so when such aggression occurs in a region that is historically part

* See pp.34–5, 262–7.

BALKANS

ROMANIA

Galati

Brăila

Bucharest

Craiova

SLAVIA

BULGARIA

Sofia

Priština

KOSOVO

Skopje

MACEDONIA

Thessaloniki

GREECE

Aegean Sea

of Europe, that adjoins NATO, and that is itself deeply unstable.

It is nowadays sometimes forgotten just how many countries risked being dragged into Slobodan Milošević's wars. His suppression of ethnic Hungarians and others in Vojvodina risked conflict with neighbouring Hungary. His brutalities towards ethnic Albanians in Kosovo outraged neighbouring Albania and inflamed Macedonia's Albanian minority. Serbia's traditional ambitions to seize, or at least partition, Macedonia suggested that this new state also was lined up for destruction. And this in turn would undoubtedly have brought in Serbia's old ally, fellow Orthodox Greece, which regarded Macedonia with predatory hostility. Nor were the Greeks the only NATO members who could have been drawn into the maelstrom. Turkey, whose links with the Bosnian Muslims rest on history, culture, religion and indeed the presence of some two million ethnic Bosnians still living on Turkish soil, was rightly furious at the abandonment of Bosnia-Hercegovina. Clearly, any conflict which threatens to involve so many nations, some of them the West's closest allies, cannot fail to involve our own national interests too.

There is, though, another reason why a sensible strategy in the Balkans required diplomatic toughness, credible threats of force and, as matters worsened, effective military action: and this was the nature of the enemy himself. Any properly informed assessment of Slobodan Milošević, the goals which drove him, and the means he possessed to achieve them, would have shown that he had to be stopped – and, equally important, that he *could* be stopped.

The aims which he and his collaborators had set themselves were well enough known. The Serbs, though capable of great duplicity in negotiations, enjoy a certain amount of crude but frank bragging about their ambitions. In a manner that most of us would find astonishing, Milošević spoke like this even on the very eve of his mass ethnic cleansing of the Kosovars. General Klaus Naumann, former Chairman of NATO's Military Committee, gave the following account of one conversation:

He [Milošević] said to us, 'I will solve the Kosovo problem once and for all in spring 1999' . . .We asked him, 'How will you do it, Mr President?'

'We will do to them what we did to the Albanians in Drenica in 1945.' So we said to him, 'Mr President, we do not know what you did to the Albanians in 1945. Would you be so kind as to elaborate?'

'It is quite simple. We got them together and we shot them.' That was his answer.*

Yet the other side to the question is equally important. The Serbian war machine was never as strong as the Serbs made out, or as most international observers thought. A great deal of silliness was talked about how Tito and the Partisans had held down between twenty and thirty German divisions during the Second World War.† But this apparent parallel overlooked the enormously important consideration that Milošević's forces were up against numerous and highly motivated, if initially poorly armed, forces of Croats, Bosnians and Kosovars. It was the Serbs who were in this case the occupiers of other nations' territory and were thus in the equivalent position of the wartime German forces. Moreover, while it is true that by some measurements the Yugoslav army began the conflict as the fourth largest army in Europe, it was rapidly affected by desertions, poor morale and loss of weaponry which was either captured, destroyed or disabled. The Serb paramilitary organisations – known as Chetniks – upon which the regular forces increasingly relied were more highly motivated because of their visceral hatred of non-Serbs. But they too were generally more adept at raping and slaughtering civilians than at confronting well-disciplined military opponents.

I would, though, add a further reason why action was required to stop Milošević. In circumstances where great evils – and genocide is indeed such an evil – threaten, the West has a moral duty to prevent them if possible and to stop them if that is manageable. This assertion too could probably be justified on grounds of broad national interest. But the truth is that countries whose populations

---

* Fourteenth Report of the House of Commons Select Committee on Defence: *The Lessons of Kosovo*, 23 October 2000.
† Professor Norman Stone has comprehensively demolished this and other myths, writing in the *Sunday Times*, 16 August 1992.

and political leaders once stop being indignant about wickedness on such a scale cease to be fully human. In some cases – and one such case was, surely, Bosnia – we know in our conscience that the situation which thousands of innocent men, women and children face cannot be endured and must no longer be ignored.

Such considerations – both strategic and moral – do not mean that we should at any stage suspend our critical faculties. Soft hearts are no excuse for soft heads. We have always to assess, and if necessary reassess in the light of events, the acceptable cost to us and our forces of whatever kind of engagement is proposed. We should first try to find solutions which do not involve excessive risk to our people – while remembering that caution can on occasion be as dangerous as boldness. We must, in the case of military interventions in the Balkans as elsewhere, know how to get out as well as how to go in. Finally, no matter how shocked we are by what is wrong, we cannot assume that we will be able to put everything right. But we must also – I repeat – be prepared to act decisively and with whatever force is required to prevent, deter or reverse the triumph of great evil.

VUKOVAR

It is important for all of us, particularly perhaps for political leaders, to come up at least once in our lives against the physical reality of evil. We know – or at least we should know – that evil exists. But it is only when we can see, touch and smell it, as I did on a visit to Vukovar in Eastern Croatia in September 1998, that it adopts a presence that is so real that one can never forget it.

A series of tangled negotiations had preceded my Croatian visit that autumn. In 1993 I was awarded *in absentia* an honorary doctorate at the University of Zagreb in recognition of my support for the Croats in their struggle to break free of communist rule from Belgrade two years earlier. But I then cancelled my visit to collect the degree in protest at the attacks by Croat extremists on Muslims in Bosnia. One of the worst episodes, the massacre at Ahmići in April that year, convinced me that any such visit would have been taken by Croatia as a signal that the world would overlook such barbarity. The fighting between the two sides was brought to an end the following year. But somehow the occasion for a visit never seemed quite right, until 1998.

That year the territories of Croatia's Eastern Slavonia were finally – and peacefully – reintegrated within Croatia. I wanted to see for myself the true situation in the wake of the withdrawal of Serb occupying forces and of part of the Serb population. I also believed, as I had since the start of the conflict in the summer of 1991, that Croatia as a new democratic state needed whatever encouragement she could get, and that what she had received so far from the West was niggardly. So I now accepted President Franjo Tudjman's and the government's invitation to make my long-postponed visit.

Croatia is a profoundly European country – more so than

Britain in some ways. Its Dalmatian coast is by geography, history and culture part of Mediterranean Europe. The rest of Croatia is, in the same way, part of Central Europe. The Croats, like their neighbours the Slovenes, thus understandably resent being described as 'Balkan'. (If, on occasion, in what follows I lump together all the national components of the former Yugoslavia under that heading, it is only for convenience.)

Dubrovnik, which I would also visit that September, is certainly the most beautiful and venerable of the Dalmatian cities. That is why the Yugoslav army's barbaric attacks on it, whose effects I saw, were so shocking to the whole world. Bombarding Dubrovnik was surely the stupidest tactic employed by Belgrade in the course of its aggression. It forced international opinion to demand that Western leaders act with some firmness. It also accelerated international recognition of Croatian independence.

I am sure that it was little consolation to the inhabitants of Dubrovnik, as they sheltered in cellars without water or electricity, that they were 'news'. But those trapped within Vukovar did not have even that modest comfort.

If you look at the old photographs of Vukovar, before the Yugoslav army and Serb paramilitaries destroyed it, you will see a charming provincial city, its centre built in the traditional Central European baroque of the Habsburg era. A river runs through the place, and the local population in their leisure moments used to enjoy themselves fishing and boating.

The 1991 census records that the municipality of Vukovar contained some eighty-four thousand people, of whom 44 per cent were ethnic Croats, 37 per cent ethnic Serbs, and the rest a mixture of Ruthenians, Slovaks, Hungarians, Ukrainians and others. It was, in short, a mix of nationalities, used to living together and getting on with one another – in this respect again typically Central European.

The Vukovar which I discovered when I arrived by helicopter on the afternoon of Thursday, 17 September 1998 presented a frighteningly different reality. The destruction was all the more shocking because it was nearly – but not quite – total. Shattered skeletons of public buildings reminded you of a peaceful and dignified existence that had been irretrievably lost. The once stocky little private houses set out in orderly rows had now lost their roofs, their windows were blown out, their walls were pockmarked by shells, and their interiors were burnt black. Personal odds and ends were scattered among the piles of rubble and helped reinforce the sense of violation. Many of the structures were booby-trapped to catch the unwary who came too close, and the land around was heavily mined. The churches had all been systematically shelled. Daubed slogans in Cyrillic script showed where the Chetniks wanted to make their mark. Some of the houses, though, stood out as in reasonably good repair and clearly inhabited. These were where the Serbs lived, and indeed still do.

Don't let anyone tell you that real evil is passionate. Go to Vukovar. You will see that evil is ice-cold.

The agony of Vukovar's siege, which ended when the city fell on 19 November 1991, is not, however, to be fully understood amid the ruins. It is not even to be grasped in the cellars of the hospital (through which I now walked), where the wounded and dying had been treated in primitive conditions by doctors and nurses who as each day passed had ever more reason to fear for their own lives. It is, rather, the graves which explain what Vukovar's destruction and indeed what this war was all about.

The Croats have inherited from their Habsburg past a somewhat Germanic exactitude. Thus the statistics of death in Vukovar are as clinically precise as the detailed scientific tests, carried on under international supervision and aimed at identifying the dead before reburial, can make them. One thousand, eight hundred and fifty-one people are known to have been killed. Six hundred and seventy-nine more are 'missing' (who must be presumed dead). In and around Vukovar are several mass graves. On that dull autumn afternoon I visited the main ones.

Largest is the grave discovered adjoining the main cemetery. From parallel trenches dug across the reddish clay soil 938 corpses had been exhumed before reburial. The ages of the victims ranged from six months to 104 years of age. Of those identified, 484 were Croats, thirty-eight were Serbs, twenty-eight were Ruthenes, eleven were Ukrainians, sixteen were Hungarians. The broad ethnic mix is significant.

Hundreds of people, mainly women, had gathered at the scene. I lit a lamp and placed it beside the many others which recalled the death of a loved one. When I went to speak to the women, some of whom I had met previously in my office in London, they clutched at me, weeping. Many held out pictures of the missing, still vainly hoping that someone like me could secure their return alive and well.

This mass grave was dug and filled by the Serbs with the corpses scattered around the captured city. But in the middle of a maize field at nearby Ovčara is something still more sinister. This is where 260 patients from the Vukovar hospital were taken in trucks by the Serb paramilitaries, tortured, shot, thrown into a pit and covered with earth. The bodies have now been reburied elsewhere. But in the middle of the muddy field stands a cross. I lit another lamp beside it.

It is worth recalling the circumstances of the evacuation of the hospital, because it reminds us of the international community's weakness. The day after the defenders of Vukovar agreed to surrender, but before the International Red Cross and other representatives of the international community had arrived at the scene, the Yugoslav army entered the hospital complex. They began to move out the patients without waiting for international supervision, and when that evening the Red Cross did eventually arrive they were held back by contemptuous Serb officers. And all the while the patients – who had been assured that they were to be transferred to another hospital – were secretly being led away through the back of the building to their terrible fate at the hands of the Chetniks.

Finally, I was taken in the jeep to another site, still being excavated. This too is a field. The place is called Sotin, and I shall not forget the name. I do not know how many were buried there. Those conducting the exhumations had covered up the bodies before my arrival and I was glad of that. But at the far end of the field, where it slopes down through brambles and bushes to the river below, there were the partly exposed remains of two of the victims. Apparently, the Serb paramilitaries had told them to run and then shot them like dogs.

One reason for giving this detailed account of what I found at Vukovar is because the city needs to be rebuilt and repopulated, and it will not be if it is quietly forgotten by everyone else. Another reason is because the three officers of the Yugoslav army who have been indicted for these crimes are (as I write) still at large, and they should face justice.*

I am not saying that Vukovar was unique: by all accounts Srebrenica in Bosnia was, in terms of slaughter, still worse. I am certainly not saying that everywhere else the Croats were guiltless – some of them clearly were very guilty indeed in Bosnia in 1993. But in Vukovar – as in Sarajevo – we can see the reality of the war which Belgrade fought and sponsored. The victims were of different national groups and religious beliefs. The perpetrators were united in their fanatical commitment to a doctrine of ethnic purity to be achieved by terror and violence. In order to understand how that came to be, it is necessary to consider how the Balkan past does – and does not – affect the Balkan present.

CHRONOLOGY OF KEY EVENTS IN THE BALKANS, 1987–2001

1987
- April–December: Slobodan Milošević gains control of Serbian Communist Party

1989
- 27 February: Yugoslav troops sent to suppress unrest in Kosovo
- 8 May: Milošević becomes President of Serbia
- 28 June: Milošević addresses mass rally of Serbs at Kosovo Polje on the six hundredth anniversary of Battle of Kosovo

1991
- May: Beginning of Croatian-Serb rebellion
- 25 June: Slovenia and Croatia declare independence
- 27 June: Yugoslav army attacks Slovenia
- 25 September: UN imposes arms embargo on all of former Yugoslavia
- 19 November: Fall of Vukovar to Serb forces

---

* The three are Colonel (later General) Mile Mrkšić, Captain Miroslav Radić and Major Veselin Šljivančanin.

1992

- 2 January: UN mediator Cyrus Vance negotiates ceasefire for Croatia
- 15 January: EC recognises Croatia and Slovenia
- 21 February: UN sends fourteen thousand peacekeeping troops to Croatia
- 29 February: Bosnia-Hercegovina declares independence. Bosnian Serbs proclaim separate state
- 5 April: Bosnian Serbs begin siege of Sarajevo

1993

- 2 January: Cyrus Vance and David Owen unveil plan at Geneva peace talks to divide Bosnia into ten semi-autonomous provinces
- 22 February: UN sets up war crimes tribunal (ICTY) for former Yugoslavia
- 6 May: UN declares six 'safe areas' for Bosnian Muslims: Srebrenica, Žepa, Sarajevo, Bihać, Tuzla and Goražde
- 15–16 May: In a referendum Bosnian Serbs vote for an independent Bosnian Serb state

1994

- 5 February: Sixty killed and two hundred wounded in mortar attack on Sarajevo
- 18 March: Bosnian government and Bosnian Croats sign US-brokered accord
- 13 May: Five-nation Contact Group announces new plan and eventual partition of Bosnia
- 20 July: Bosnian Serbs reject peace plan
- 21 November: NATO launches major air strike on Serb airfield
- 25 November: Serbs detain fifty-five Canadian peacekeepers

1995

- 1 May: Ceasefire expires. Croatia launches offensive to retake Western Slavonia ('Operation Lightning')
- 26 May: Serbs take more UN peacekeepers hostage. Eventually 370 seized
- 28 May: Aircraft carrying Bosnian Foreign Minister Irfan Ljubi-

jankić shot down by Serbs over Bihać. US, Britain and France send thousands more troops to Bosnia

- 15 June: Serbs step up shelling of Sarajevo and other 'safe areas'
- 11 July: Serbs overrun Srebrenica 'safe area'
- 12–13 July: Thousands of Muslim men detained (later murdered), while twenty thousand Muslim women, children and elderly are expelled to Tuzla
- 25 July: Serbs take Žepa. War crimes tribunal indicts Bosnian Serb President Radovan Karadžić and Bosnian Serb General Ratko Mladić for genocide in Bosnia. Croatian Serb leader Milan Martić charged with war crimes for missile attack on Zagreb
- 4 August: Croatia launches assault on rebel Serbs in Knin (Serb 'Krajina'), recapturing most Serb-held territory in four days ('Operation Storm')
- 28 August: Bosnian Serb shell kills thirty-seven in Sarajevo market. UN secretly pulls peacekeepers out of Goražde
- 30 August: NATO launches major air strikes on Serb guns around Sarajevo. Serbs retaliate by shelling Sarajevo
- 1 November: Bosnian peace talks begin in Dayton, Ohio
- 21 November: Dayton Accords signed. Fifty-one per cent of Bosnian territory granted to Muslim–Croat federation, 49 per cent to Serbs
- 22 November: UN Security Council suspends sanctions against Serbia
- 23 November: Karadžić accepts peace plan
- 30 November: UN votes to end peacekeeping mission by 31 January 1997
- 1 December: NATO authorises deployment of sixty thousand troops to Bosnia
- 14 December: Serbs, Bosnians and Croats sign peace plan. Bosnian and Serb governments agree to formal diplomatic recognition
- 20 December: NATO takes over command of Bosnia peace mission

1997
- 15 June: Tudjman re-elected President of Croatia
- 15 July: Milošević becomes President of Yugoslavia

1998

- 31 March: UN Security Council condemns Yugoslavia's excessive use of force in Kosovo and imposes economic sanctions
- August: Serb forces attack Kosovo Albanian villages in Drenica region, forcing thousands to flee

1999

- January: Evidence comes to light of Serb massacre of Kosovars at Račak
- 6 February: Rambouillet peace talks begin in France. Milošević refuses to attend
- 18 March: Kosovo Albanian delegates finally sign autonomy plan at Rambouillet. Serbs refuse, and begin exercises in Kosovo the following day
- 24 March: Kosovo air war begins
- 27 May: ICTY announces indictment of Milošević
- 9 June: NATO and Yugoslav authorities agree terms for Serb withdrawal from Kosovo
- 10 June: NATO suspends bombing. UN Security Council adopts Resolution 1244, permitting deployment of international civil and military personnel in Kosovo
- 12 June: Russian troops take control of Priština airport. NATO forces move into Kosovo
- 14 June: Ethnic Albanians begin flooding back into Kosovo. Over six hundred thousand return within three weeks
- 20 June: Serb forces complete withdrawal from Kosovo

2000

- 24 September: Vojislav Koštunica defeats Milošević in Yugoslav presidential election
- 5 October: Koštunica declares himself President

2001

- 1 April: Milošević surrenders to Serb authorities
- 28 June: Milošević handed over to the ICTY in The Hague.

WAR AGAINST SLOVENIA AND CROATIA

When Slovenia and Croatia declared their independence from Yugoslavia on 25 June 1991, they could be said from one point of view to be taking a step that had been logical ever since the creation of the first Yugoslavia – more accurately the Kingdom of the Serbs, Croats and Slovenes – in 1918. Multinational states are always inherently unstable. They can only work in one of two ways. The first is if each of the constituent peoples respects the others, and the state then functions as some kind of confederation. The second is if there is an authoritarian central power able to enforce its will. In Yugoslavia it was the second option that was applied, originally under the royal dictatorship and then under communism. Indeed, since its foundation Yugoslavia was under authoritarian or totalitarian rule for nearly all of its existence. Once the central power was weakened, the country suffered the same fate as that other artificial unit knitted together by communism, the Soviet Union.

This analysis contains part – but only part – of the truth. Tito's death in 1980 and the creation of a 'revolving' federal presidency certainly did allow the inherent contradictions of Yugoslavia to become ever more obvious and the fissiparous tendencies to grow apace. But the drive of Slovenia, followed by Croatia, followed by Bosnia, for full independence can only really be understood if one grasps that these were responses to pressures originating from Serbia. Historians of the Balkans often trace the rise of an aggressive Serb nationalism aimed at the creation of a Greater Serbia, incorporating (as the phrase has it) 'all Serbs everywhere' in one single Serb state, to developments in the nineteenth century. But in modern times it was the resurfacing of this programme in the form of a notorious Memorandum by the Serbian Academy of Arts and Sciences in the mid-1980s which signalled the beginning of the madness that was to come. As communism lost its grip on the masses, hardline nationalism offered a substitute for those who wanted power. Yesterday's Marxists in much of Eastern Europe suddenly became born-again patriots. But no one performed this chameleon-like self-transformation with greater cunning or more deadly consequences than Slobodan Milošević in Yugoslavia.

Milošević remains in some ways a mystery. Was he always just an opportunist? Or did he from the start subscribe to the hate-filled doctrines which his troops and the Serb paramilitaries put into practice? In any case, from the time that he used the ethnic disturbances in Kosovo in 1987 to oust his rivals and become the champion of the Greater Serbian dream, his whole existence depended upon the oppression, expulsion and when necessary murder of non-Serbs.

Without Milošević, the wars against the other constituent nations of Yugoslavia would probably not have happened at all. And if they had happened, they would have been far less bloody and prolonged. Milošević was able to give effect to the wildest and most terrible fantasies of the Balkan mind precisely because he was not himself just a frenzied bigot. As a communist boss, he could use all the resources which the Party provided. As a smooth-talking negotiator, he was just the man to persuade a string of vain and gullible Westerners that he was part of the solution rather than the root of the problem.

Milošević had performed his own coup in the Yugoslav Communist Party, and Serbia had performed its coup within Yugoslavia, even before Slovenia and Croatia decided they had to leave. The Slovenes were able to escape and the Yugoslav army's attempts to crush them were ignominiously defeated. But when it came to Croatia, there was a substantial Serb minority whom Milošević and his friends were determined to unite with Serbia. Belgrade thus incited and armed Croatian Serbs to rise up against Zagreb and then sent in the Yugoslav army to 'restore order' – which meant assisting the rebels and driving all non-Serbs from their land.

Faced with this challenge, Western leaders made, as I have mentioned, three key errors. First, they tried to keep Yugoslavia together when it was clearly no longer possible to do so. This gave the Yugoslav army the impression that there would be no outside opposition to its trying to suppress the separatists by force. Second, the international community imposed an arms embargo on all the component parts of the former Yugoslavia.

This deprived the Slovenes, Croats and Bosnians of the means to defend themselves and left them heavily outgunned by the aggressor. Third, the attempt at even-handedness in assessing blame for what was occurring, when the truth was that one side was the aggressor and the other the victim, led the West into something approaching complicity with the crimes being committed. Far from being 'the hour of Europe', as Jacques Poos (the then Foreign Minister of Luxembourg) proclaimed, it was the hour of Europe's shame.

In January 1992 Slovenia and Croatia finally received international recognition. This is still sometimes declared an error and even blamed for the outbreak of the war in Bosnia. But that is nonsense. International recognition of Croatia at least meant that there were now limits to what Belgrade could hope to achieve. The war in Croatia accordingly gradually ground to a halt. And as for Bosnia, the Serbs had begun their campaign of creating Serb enclaves there *before* the Bosnians declared independence in October 1991. The Serb war in Bosnia was not provoked – it was planned.

In any case, by February 1992 when the UN despatched fourteen thousand 'peacekeepers' to Croatia, about a third of the country was in Serb hands. The UN force then presided over continued ethnic cleansing of Croats from Croatian territory and, as Croatia grew stronger, began to act as a force protecting the Serb aggressors. Meanwhile, Milošević and the army chiefs who had obligingly been permitted by the international negotiators to withdraw their heavy weapons from Croatia to Bosnia were now able to set them to work against the non-Serb inhabitants there.

The lessons of the conflict in Croatia were not to be learned for several more years. But they were already clear if anyone had been honest enough to deduce them.

- There should have been no attempt to keep Yugoslavia together, once the constituent nations showed they wished to leave it
- The right to self-defence by those under attack should have been respected
- And the early stages of the aggression against Slovenia and

Croatia should have drawn condemnation, followed by an ultimatum, followed by military action – air strikes, combined with the supply of arms to the besieged, would undoubtedly have saved Vukovar and other Croatian cities.

WAR AGAINST BOSNIA

Looking back at the history of this war, one sees that the real causes of Bosnia's destruction have come from outside Bosnia itself, and have done so twice over: first in the form of the political strategy of the Serbian leadership, and then in the form of the miscomprehension and fatal interference of the leaders of the West.[*]

This judgement by Noel Malcolm, the soundest and wisest commentator on Balkan affairs today, seems to me to be precisely right.

The background to the Bosnian genocide was provided by the same odious doctrine as lay behind the slaughter at Vukovar, but whereas towards the Croats it manifested itself in hatred, towards the Muslims it spoke the language of contempt. Anyone who wants to read the evidence for this need only consult Professor Norman Cigar's profound and disturbing volume, *Genocide in Bosnia*.[†] This kind of Greater Serbian racist thinking was summed up in the words of the West's one-time heroine and now indicted war criminal Mrs Biljana Plavšić about the Muslim Bosnians, whom she described as 'a genetic defect on the Serbian body'.[‡]

But the outside world also played its part in what followed. In particular, the attempt at 'even-handedness', which robbed the West's approach towards Croatia of both moral integrity and practical effect, continued with Bosnia. Thus the international

---

[*] Noel Malcolm, *Bosnia: A Short History* (London, 1994), p.251.

[†] Norman Cigar, *Genocide in Bosnia: The Policy of Ethnic Cleansing* (Texas A&M University Press, 1995). Professor Cigar and Dr Malcolm were among those who provided me with invaluable briefing during the Bosnian crisis.

[‡] Quoted by *The Times*, 12 January 2001.

community deprived the Bosnian Muslims of the chance to arm themselves. Yet it did not itself afford them any serious protection from Bosnian Serb forces, which had been provided with a well-stocked arsenal by the Yugoslav army. The West's equivocation damaged our own interests too. It outraged the Muslim world, which claimed – not without reason – that atrocities on this scale would never have been permitted if they had been perpetrated against Jews or Christians. By the end of the conflict, Islamic extremists had begun to appear in Bosnia, an area where there had traditionally been exemplary tolerance and where Islam had always had a distinctly European flavour. Eventually, the United States – though not the European countries which wavered till the end – recognised these dangers and acted upon them. But by then some two hundred thousand people were dead.

The siege of Sarajevo began in April 1992 and continued until February 1996. During that period the suffering of the population was enormous. But arguably what was happening elsewhere in Bosnia was still worse. Far away from the television cameras, campaigns of violence and terror, involving mass rape, unspeakable torture and concentration camps, were employed by the Bosnian Serb leadership, with support from Belgrade, to achieve the ethnic cleansing of non-Serbs from what its proponents claimed was historic Serb territory. All in all over two million people (out of a pre-war population of 4.3 million) were driven out of their homes. An estimated nine hundred thousand people took refuge in neighbouring countries and in Western Europe, while 1.3 million were displaced within Bosnia.* In Croatia and Bosnia, particularly, the burden of caring for these people was crushing.

These refugee flows were destabilising, and were intended to be so. The arrival of thousands of Muslim refugees in Central Bosnia, shifting the ethnic balance between Muslims and Croats, was an important contributory factor to the open warfare which broke out in March 1993 between the two.†

During this whole period international conferences were held

---

* UNHCR figures.
† Information has also surfaced since the death of President Tudjman confirming Zagreb's involvement in these matters, and more revelations are possible.

and international mediators were appointed in order to try to bring what were called the 'warring parties' to the negotiating table. I have no doubt that the mediators did their best. But mediation could be no substitute for reversing aggression, and without the West summoning up the will to do that the mediators found themselves sucked into a process which steadily entrenched and legitimised the ascendancy of the aggressor. Indeed, sometimes the negotiators unwittingly created the conditions for more bloodshed. So, for example, the plan advanced by Cyrus Vance and Lord Owen – the 'Vance–Owen Plan' – for the division of Bosnia into ten ethnically denominated cantons was the spur to the war which broke out between Muslims and Bosnian Croats. In the circumstances prevailing at the start of 1993 both sides considered the scheme as amounting to partition and were determined to gain control of as much territory as possible – above all, control of the ethnically mixed canton of Central Bosnia. The Bosnian Serbs were the main beneficiaries of the struggle between their enemies. But that did not predispose them towards accepting the Vance–Owen Plan themselves.

In reality, by the end of 1992 the Serbs had seized most of the territory that they thought they could hold. Although constituting just 31 per cent of the population they had thus gained control of over 70 per cent of the land. From that point on, their main purpose was to expel the non-Serbs from it so as to remove all trace of them, their cultures and their religions. The Serbs needed time to proceed with this, particularly in areas where there were large numbers of well-established Muslim and Croat communities to dislodge. The international community gave them that time. Even as the Bosnian Muslims recovered and regrouped, forming a better-trained army and acquiring more weapons, the Serbs were able to hold the Bosnian capital, Sarajevo, to ransom, shelling its population whenever they chose. And the international community's responses were largely ineffectual, and sometimes worse.

What the West should have done was to work out and put into effect a coherent programme to defeat the aggressor and reverse the aggression. Of course, this was never going to be easy. It would have taken time. It would also have entailed abandoning the pretence that 'peacekeeping' was the West's objective. The arms embargo against the Bosnians would have had to be lifted. The Russians would have had to be marginalised and their objections ignored. And the only global power – America – rather than the deeply divided Europeans, would have had to take the lead.

In fact, something along these lines did eventually materialise. But neither then nor since have Western leaders been prepared to draw the right conclusions.

It was, above all, necessary to shift the balance of power against the Serbs on the ground. This meant bringing together the Muslims and Croats. In March 1994 the conflict between them was ended by an agreement brokered in Washington. A Muslim–Croat Bosnian Federation was established and at the same time a confederal agreement between Bosnia and Croatia. The new alliance was also strengthened by the provision of training and weapons for the Croatian army, which was thus turned into an extremely effective force.

Seeing the way the tide was beginning to turn, Slobodan Milošević decided that the time had come to settle. The practical limits of Greater Serbia had been reached. Milošević must also have known that the ill-organised gangsters who controlled the so-called Serb Krajina area of Croatia and the Bosnian Serb 'Republic' were a good deal weaker than the West thought.* Consequently, in the summer of 1994 he tried to induce the Bosnian Serbs to accept what would have amounted to a partition of Bosnia highly favourable to the Serbs, who would have received 49 per cent of Bosnia, while the Muslim–Croat federation received 51 per cent.

The Bosnian Serbs, however, were confident enough of their own position and contemptuous enough of the West's threats to refuse the deal and to carry out new offensives. NATO accordingly responded with air strikes. The Serbs then retaliated by seizing more than four hundred international peacekeepers. The consequences of past follies were never more evident. Western forces in Bosnia were by now not an asset, they were a liability, because they were potential hostages.

1995 was the year of decision. In May the Croatian army retook

---

* I was told this myself at this time by a Croatian and a Bosnian General, and, of course, they were proved right.

Serb-held West Slavonia. The Serbs in retaliation fired rockets at Zagreb, killing six and wounding two hundred civilians. But the rapid success of the Croatian campaign had openly exposed just how weak the Serb rebels in occupied Croatia now were. The Serbs in Bosnia imitated the tactics of their counterparts in Croatia by attacking civilian targets. Thus in June they stepped up the shelling of Sarajevo and, worst of all, in July they overran the so-called UN 'safe haven' of Srebrenica. For the West this was perhaps the most humiliating and disgraceful episode of the whole crisis: and for the Muslim inhabitants of the town it meant expropriation, expulsion and – for about seven thousand of them – death.

There has been much rewriting of history about what now happened. The truth is that Croatia, with support from the largely Muslim Bosnian army and from Bosnian Croat forces, acted to do what the international community for four long, shameful years had failed to do. Croatia and her allies won back much of their land from the Serbs and by their victory created the circumstances for a return to some semblance of peace and order. On 4 August the Croatian army retook Knin and quickly swept through the Krajina area. Having insufficient heavy weapons – because of the West's foolish arms embargo – the Muslims were not able to achieve comparable successes. But the fact remains that had it not been for a new intervention by the West – whose leaders were as always keen to snatch at least partial defeat from the mouth of complete victory – the main Bosnian Serb-held city, Banja Luka, would also have fallen. Had this happened, Bosnia would have been rescued as a united country in which there was some prospect of different ethnic communities eventually being able to live together under a democratically elected central authority. Banja Luka, we should note, had itself been the scene of massive ethnic cleansing by the Serbs who had burnt down the hated mosques and Catholic churches which might serve to remind them of the multi-faith and multiracial past. If anywhere deserved to be liberated from the ethnic cleansers it was Banja Luka.

It is not possible, particularly after years of such brutality, to conduct even just wars without loss to civilians. The Serbs who now streamed out of the retaken areas were some of them fleeing retribution. Some were doubtless intimidated. Many more were falsely persuaded by their leaders that they risked wholesale mass-acre. There were indeed within the reconquered Krajina area epi-sodes of killing, looting and burning by the incoming Croats.

But these culpable incidents do not detract from the fact that the defeat by the Croatians and Bosnians of the Serbs in 1995 was immensely beneficial for the region and indeed for the West. Without that defeat, Balkan genocide and Western humiliation would have continued. To try, as some have done, to equate the operation launched to retake Croatian land with earlier acts of Serb aggression is a travesty.

NATO air strikes against Serb artillery around Sarajevo at this time also provided valuable support for the Croat and Muslim forces. Disproving all the learned nonsense emanating from mili-tary sources, it was shown that air strikes could indeed work without large-scale deployment of ground troops. The task on the ground could be left to local not international forces – as long as the former were sufficiently armed. And just in case anyone imag-ines that this analysis is merely hindsight, perhaps I could quote myself three years before the event:

> It is argued by some that nothing can be done by the West unless we are prepared to risk permanent involvement in a Vietnam- or Lebanon-style conflict and potentially high Western casualties. That is partly alarmism, partly an excuse for inertia. There is a vast difference between a full-scale land invasion like Desert Storm and a range of military interventions from lifting the arms embargo on Bosnia, through supplying arms to Bosnian forces, to direct strikes on military targets and communications.

I went on to argue that in the event of continuing support for Bosnian Serb aggression by Serbia itself

> ...military retaliation should follow, including aerial bombard-ment of bridges on the Drina linking Bosnia and Serbia, of military convoys, of gun positions around [the besieged] Sarajevo and Gor-aždе, and of military stores and other installations useful in the war. It should be made clear that while this is not a war against

the Serbian people, even installations on the Serbian side of the border may be attacked if they play an important role in the war.*

What happened in 1995 showed that such tactics work. But it was only during the latter stages of the Kosovo campaign in 1999 that my prescription was applied – though still, as I shall describe, with insufficient commitment.

The Dayton Accords which were signed in the autumn of 1995 still provide the framework within which Bosnia functions – or does not function. Like all the previous partition plans they represented an excessive concern for the (now defeated) Bosnian Serbs who had caused the whole problem in the first place. The Serbs were given a separate autonomous entity, the Republika Srpska. It was to be part of Bosnia-Hercegovina. But the names of the institutions themselves betrayed the thinking: while the Serb entity was called a 'republic', Bosnia-Hercegovina itself lost that title.

The Dayton Accords are enormously detailed, and this also is significant. Different and contrary trends and tensions were involved. The Muslims stressed those aspects which reinforced the territorial and institutional integrity of the state. The Serbs and to a lesser extent the Croats emphasised those which devolved power locally. The undertaking which was fundamental to the whole settlement, though, was that the refugees should be allowed to return to their homes. If this did not happen Dayton meant partition and victory for the ethnic cleansers and their sponsors in Belgrade.

And that is exactly how it has so far turned out. While progress has been made in returning refugees to the territories of the Muslim–Croat Federation, the authorities in the Republika Srpska have remained determined to prevent members of the minority communities coming back to the homes from which they were driven. Thus of the 715,000 refugees who have returned, 80 per cent have gone back to the Federation and only 20 per cent to the Serb-controlled areas.† It is sometimes argued that these figures

---

* My article in the *New York Times*, 6 August 1992. For an account of my involvement in attempts to rescue Bosnia, see *The Path to Power*, pp.514–17.

† Bosnian government figures, as of 30 January 2001.

do not matter. 'You cannot force people to live together if they don't want to,' the saying runs. And that much, of course, is true. But it is not acceptable that people who *do* want to return should be stopped from doing so.

In fact, the position is worse than that. While it is certainly true that the years of war will leave deep and enduring scars on Bosnian life, a Bosnia which does not have an intermixture of faiths and ethnicity is one which will some time explode again. I am not one of those who sees our goal in Bosnia as the creation of some ideal multicultural state. But I do believe that political arrangements which are based upon violence, intimidation and theft will eventually break down – and will deserve to do so.

The other major condition upon which Dayton's quasi-partition of Bosnia-Hercegovina was accepted was the detention of war criminals. This has still not proceeded very far. True, approaching half of those publicly indicted have gone to The Hague. But many of the worst culprits, such as Radovan Karadžić and Ratko Mladić, are as I write still at large. Although twenty thousand NATO-led soldiers are deployed in Bosnia, some sectors – notably the French – still provide safe haven for these villains. Meanwhile, the Tribunal seems to be extending its activities further than events or the requirements for a period of peace, stability and reconciliation would warrant. It was absolutely right – and overdue – that Milošević as the author of so much tragedy should face trial at The Hague. But from now on the court would be best advised to concentrate on arresting and trying those who have already been indicted, rather than indicting people who played no leading part in the violence. The *quid pro quo* should be that all concerned make a serious and concerted attempt to ensure that the main perpetrators are brought to book; for while they remain on the loose, it will be impossible to return to normality.

There are today widespread calls to revise Dayton. That, though, can mean one of two things. It can be an excuse to forget past pledges, redraw maps, and prepare a quick exit of Western troops. This would presumably entail recognising the Republika Srpska as an ethnically pure mini-state, or even an ethnically cleansed component of Serbia proper. That course, by rewarding the aggressor and penalising the victim, would be morally wrong.

It would also be politically foolish. It would give a green light for the Croats in Hercegovina to try again to create their own ethnically pure mini-state, which would in turn lead to conflict and in all probability to the creation of a virtually landlocked, economically unviable and increasingly radical Muslim state. No one should welcome that prospect. Not for the first time, doing the wrong thing would rebound on the West's interests as well.

On the other hand, a review of Dayton could involve a serious attempt to compel the leaders of the Republika Srpska to honour their commitments to take back those whom they and their predecessors expelled. The Bosnian Serbs could be told that unless they make serious provision for ensuring the return of refugees, they will lose the right to their own autonomous entity. And the government in Belgrade could be warned that there will be no more help from the West until the Bosnian Serbs comply.

If the Bosnian Serbs realise that the West is serious, they will probably reluctantly accede to our demands in order to avoid that loss of autonomy. And so will Belgrade, which has always had far more influence over the Bosnian Serb leadership than it admits. The departure of Milošević and his cronies from the scene has made this plan more achievable.

So I believe that one last, determined push is now required. There would be strong opposition from the remaining Serb extremists. But there is no possibility for peace unless these people are defeated. And it is only when they are, that the international community can scale down and in due course end our military deployments. The aim must be to create the broad social and political conditions for peace, and then leave it to local people to enforce. That also means, of course, that we have to ensure that the government in Sarajevo has the military capability to resist new challenges to its authority. It is still not too late to give Bosnia and its peoples a chance.

I conclude that:

- **Abandoning Bosnia, after so much suffering and so much effort, would be both morally wrong and politically foolish**
- **The aim must be to make the Dayton agreement work in such a way that Bosnia remains a single state, albeit with a large**

measure of devolution, and that the mass expulsion of people from their homes is reversed
- We need also, though, to be realistic. We should not be in the business of utopian nation-building. Our aims should be to create the broad conditions for peace and stability and then let local democratic forces take over
- And the time is ripe for one last vigorous effort to achieve this.

WAR IN KOSOVO

While I was in Zagreb in September 1998 I delivered a lecture at the end of which I spoke of 'the terror and oppression which flow not now into Croatia or even Bosnia, but to Kosovo, where again the ethnic cleansers are at work. Who knows where and when the madness will end?'*

We do now know. The West finally stood up to Slobodan Milo-šević and he crumbled. I have many criticisms of the way in which the Kosovo campaign was conducted, but I believe that it was a just and necessary war, and I believe too that Prime Minister Tony Blair – of whom I also have many criticisms – in this case showed real determination in conducting it.

When doubts began to grow about whether the NATO campaign could succeed, a number of critics came out of the woodwork. Since some of these were people on the right of politics I considered it necessary to express publicly the support which I had also given to Mr Blair privately. I therefore used another speech – this one at a dinner held to commemorate the twentieth anniversary of my becoming Prime Minister – to explain why the enterprise in Kosovo had to be seen through to the bitter end.

I asked those who were publicly agonising about the campaign to turn their minds instead to the unacceptable consequences of doing nothing. We had to remember that Slobodan Milošević was not just some minor local thug. In Kosovo he had a calculated plan, which was to use human tides of refugees to destabilise

---

* Lecture to the Economics Faculty of the University of Zagreb, 16 September 1998.

Serbia's neighbours and weaken his opponents – the same plan, in fact, that he had implemented elsewhere in the former Yugoslavia. The surrounding countries simply could not absorb the two million ethnic Albanians he was driving out without risk of an explosion, and this in turn could suck in Greece and possibly even Turkey, both NATO members. These, of course, were strategic considerations of considerable weight. But nor did I duck the moral argument. I described Milošević's regime as sustained by a genocidal ideology and representing a truly monstrous evil. And I concluded: 'Let there be no doubt: this is a war that must be won . . . I believe that the British people will want to see this through – they know our cause is just.'*

There is a certain historical symmetry in that Slobodan Milošević's rise and fall centred on Kosovo. It was there in 1987 that he opportunistically first harnessed Serb xenophobia to oust the leadership of the Serbian Communist Party and take control himself. It was then by exploiting the six hundredth anniversary of the 1389 Battle of Kosovo, around which emotive (if unhistorical) myths were woven, that he raised Serb nationalism to new heights of aggressive frenzy.† And finally it was Milošević's defeat in Kosovo which brought the power-structure he had erected crashing down around him.

While the war was raging in Bosnia, Greater Serbianism was proceeding to the same goal by other means in Kosovo. In April 1995 – shortly before the Serb defeats that led to the Dayton Accords – I had the opportunity to learn from the self-styled President of Kosova, Dr Ibrahim Rugova, about the systematic intimidation of the ethnic Albanians there. Deprived of employment, education and access to medical care by a policy of racial discrimination in favour of the Serb minority, the Albanians – who constitute 90 per cent of the population – had eschewed violence and instead set up a whole system of parallel institutions. They had even elected their own 'President'. Dr Rugova, a moderate, mild-mannered and highly civilised intellectual, had become

---

* Speech at the International Free Enterprise Dinner, London, 20 April 1999.
† Noel Malcolm critically but fairly examines these and other Serb myths about Kosovo in his definitive study *Kosovo: A Short History* (London, 1989).

the centre of this resistance movement. Although demanding full independence, he would probably at that time have been prepared to settle in the medium term at least for a return of Kosovo's lost autonomy – crushed by Milošević's thugs – and guarantees of basic human rights. But at Dayton the fate of Kosovo was almost entirely ignored. As a result, and in the face of continuing harassment by the Serb authorities, Kosovar resentments took more radical and violent channels, and so the Kosovo Liberation Army (KLA) was born. Tensions escalated, incidents multiplied, and the Serbs at some point resolved that the time had come for a 'final solution'. This was the background to NATO's increasing concern to prevent a political and humanitarian crisis, which resulted first in the Rambouillet peace talks in February/March 1999 and then – after Belgrade's rejection of the proffered terms – in the initiation of the NATO bombing campaign.

NATO's success should not obscure the serious shortcomings of the operation which now followed. There was over-optimism about our ability to coerce Milošević without inflicting serious damage upon Serbia. This meant that in its early stages the campaign was not pursued with sufficient vigour. For his part, Milošević used this opportunity not to seek terms but rather to expel over one million of the 1.7 million-strong ethnic Albanian population. Even after the first week of April, when the rate of air strikes was substantially increased and a wider range of targets in Serbia itself hit, the fact that our aircraft were not (as a rule) permitted to fly below fifteen thousand feet meant that progress was slow. A reading of the Serbs' traditional aims in Kosovo, which from the nineteenth century have been rooted in the obsession with altering the ethnic balance in their favour, ought to have prepared Western planners for what happened. Even then, the expulsions themselves would have been almost impossible to prevent – but it should have been feasible to plan ahead to cope with the refugees.

These are serious criticisms. There were also important technical deficiencies exposed by the campaign, which I have described earlier and which need to be remedied. But some of the *ex post facto* analysis which seeks to damn the whole venture is very wide of the mark.

There has, for example, been debate about the real extent of atrocities committed by the Serb forces in Kosovo before and during the campaign. But almost daily new evidence surfaces. Indeed, it had already begun to do so before Milošević's departure for The Hague, and doubtless the pace will now quicken. Yet the most important consideration is, of course, that we already know from Bosnia how the Serbs treat those of other nations. The rhetoric which they employed against the Kosovars was the same as that used against Muslims in Bosnia. I have no doubt that Milošević and his collaborators intended similar genocide in Kosovo. That intention was quite enough to justify acting to prevent its execution.

Again, it is frequently pointed out that although NATO spokesmen and others claimed that the purpose of the campaign was to prevent a humanitarian disaster, the immediate effect was to accelerate and broaden it. I did not and do not like attempts to justify military interventions in purely humanitarian terms – for reasons which I have outlined earlier.* But we should surely bear in mind that the mass expulsion of ethnic Albanians from Kosovo by the Serbs had begun *before* the first NATO bomb dropped. Indeed, by May 1999 approximately seven hundred thousand Kosovars had been driven from their homes and had fled to neighbouring states such as Bosnia-Hercegovina, Albania, Macedonia and Montenegro. In addition an estimated six hundred thousand Kosovars had been internally displaced.† The logic of Milošević's policy required removal of a substantial section of the population. All that NATO's action did was to cause him to accelerate his plans. And let us never forget that *without* NATO's action the refugees would not have been able to return at all.

Finally, it is said that the whole operation was a failure because it has not in fact delivered a multi-ethnic Kosovo, since over 150,000 Serbs (about three-quarters of the original ethnic Serb population) there have fled Albanian retaliation and intimidation. But this argument is also flawed. Wars always create problems

---

* See pp.34–9.
† 'Erasing History: Ethnic Cleansing in Kosovo', US State Department, May 1999.

which the maintenance of a just peace would have avoided. It is unrealistic to expect the Kosovar majority to look kindly upon the Serb minority after barely escaping Serb genocide. It is equally true that the Sudeten Germans in Czechoslovakia suffered disproportionately after the Second World War because of what Germany itself had done. Fighting wars and then losing them has consequences. Only the most cosseted commentators fail to understand that. In fact, as I shall explain, I do believe that an effort should be made to protect the Serbs who remain in Kosovo and to ensure that those who wish to return home are able to do so. But that said, I am not convinced that many will want to live in what is grindingly poor and increasingly alien territory. We can reckon that the Kosovo operation was a success because it prevented a whole people being dispossessed. If the cost of that is some injustice, such are the inescapable fortunes of war.

Having won, we now have to use our victory wisely. There are two courses of action, which unfortunately seem to be widely favoured in diplomatic circles if only through inertia, but which should in fact be ruled out. The first is to try to keep Kosovo within the so-called Federal Republic of Yugoslavia, i.e. Serbia-Montenegro.

Even before the Kosovo campaign, it made no sense to prevent the vast majority of the population exercising self-determination. But once we had to wage war against the Serbs over Kosovo any attempt to force the Kosovars to remain within a Serb-dominated rump Yugoslavia should have become unthinkable. The status of Kosovo within the former Yugoslavia under Tito's 1974 Constitution was not really very different from that of the republics which broke away and whose independence has now been internationally recognised.* Noel Malcolm neatly summarises the position:

> . . .[I]n practice, [Kosovo] exercised the same powers as a republic, having its own parliament, high courts, central bank, police service,

---

* The 1974 Yugoslav Constitution, which gave republics like Slovenia, Croatia and Bosnia the right of sovereign self-determination, withheld it from the autonomous provinces of Vojvodina and Kosovo. These were thus components *both* of the Republic of Serbia and of the Federal Republic of Yugoslavia.

and territorial defence force; it was formally defined (from 1968 onwards) as part of the federal system, and it was represented directly – not via the republic of Serbia – at the federal level. By all normal criteria of constitutional analysis, Kosovo was primarily a federal unit, and only very secondarily a component of Serbia.*

To which I would only add: there is, in any case, no particular reason why we should adhere to every detail of the constitution of a communist state drawn up a quarter of a century ago when assessing what is best now.

There are also those who argue that regional stability requires that Kosovo remain part of the rump Yugoslavia. This case has apparently been lent greater weight as a result of what has been happening in neighbouring Macedonia; but it still dissolves on closer examination.

Macedonia has a large ethnic Albanian minority, comprising perhaps a third of the population, and they have not always over the years been treated well by the Slav majority. The residual tensions became much worse in 2001, and at the time of writing they look as if they might even still lead to outright civil war. Some of the ethnic Albanian rebels have close connections with Kosovo.

These are murky waters. But what is quite clear is that the business of trying to stop a violent break-up of Macedonia in which the West is engaged will not be helped by denying the ethnically Albanian majority in neighbouring Kosovo a referendum on their independence. To the contrary, frustrating that overwhelming desire will further fuel Albanian radicalisation in the region. Dr Rugova and his moderate supporters were undermined once by the West by being left out of the Dayton settlement in 1995: the emergence of the radical KLA was the result. If NATO countries now set their face against Kosovan independence, that can only promote violence, terrorism and militarisation across the borders. This is hardly a recipe for stability.

That leads me to the second widely favoured (and ill-thought-

---

* Noel Malcolm, 'Kosovo: Only Independence Will Work', *The National Interest*, winter 1998–99.

out) possible future for Kosovo – as a kind of perpetual protector-ate ruled by international authorities and NGOs. This is such an unrealistic option that one would not normally take it seriously, and it is indeed more likely to be assumed than explicitly asserted. The truth is that there now exist a very large number of people and interests determined to internationalise every problematic region of the world and thus create a continuing need for their own allegedly indispensable services. This tendency should be strongly resisted, in Kosovo as elsewhere. National democracy may have its faults, particularly in the Balkans, but it certainly offers better hope for the future than international bureaucracy. It is also cheaper, and that too should count. The inhabitants of Kosovo have to know that it is in the end up to them – not us – to determine and take responsibility for their affairs.

We should, therefore, promise that within a fixed period – no more than a year or two – there will be a referendum on Kosovo's future, the results of which the international community will then recognise. Fair conditions for holding it, though, must also be established. The Serb and other minorities must be allowed back.* Only those against whom there is sufficient evidence of serious criminality should be exempted from this right of return. It is important that any referendum take place on the basis of the situation prevailing before the recent upheavals. To do otherwise would be to legitimise ethnic cleansing – and that is no more acceptable when the victims are Serbs than when they are Albanians.

I would, therefore, wish to see in place:

- a practical programme of reconstruction and refugee return
- a clear timetable for a referendum on independence
- the subsequent speedy but orderly withdrawal of international forces from Kosovo
- a continuing guarantee by NATO of Kosovo's security to deter any future Serb adventurism.

---

* There should also probably be explicit guarantees of human rights and of protection for the Serbs' holy places under the proposed new constitution.

THE BALKANS – BEYOND KOSOVO

The most important achievement of the international community in the countries of the former Yugoslavia has nothing to do with diplomacy: it is simply the overthrow of Slobodan Milošević. While it is true that Milošević found many willing collaborators, he was the originator of the Balkan wars and he had the strongest interest in keeping them coming. His departure to The Hague offers the region a new start.

Unfortunately, there seems at present to be limited understanding of how to take advantage of this. That was evident, for example, in the amount of energy expended upon making life easy for Milošević's successor, President Vojislav Koštunica. Koštunica may have a useful role. Although, like other members of the Yugoslav government, he shared Milošević's objectives in his wars against non-Serbs, Mr Koštunica is not a communist – which is an advantage. He is said to be honest, which helps as well. But the European Union was ill-advised to welcome Serbia so quickly back into the world community. Doubtless, it made sense to provide some aid after Serbia showed its willingness to cooperate with the Hague Court. But bribing regimes to comply with requirements which they should have acknowledged in the first place is not a process that appeals to me. Certainly we would be unwise to start pouring money into Serbia until there is real evidence of a change of direction. And, as I have outlined above, the main change must be in Serbia's attitude to Bosnia. But it is also necessary to ensure that the remaining indictees are handed over for trial for the crimes they committed in the name of – and for much of the time with the enthusiastic support of – the Serb nation.

Serbia has been in the grip of an ideology not dissimilar to that which laid hold of Germany in the 1930s. And like Germany it has to be thoroughly purged of that poison. Once the Serbs acknowledge and show remorse for what has been done it will be time to begin to treat Serbia as an ordinary member of the international community. Not before.

Some of the same misconceptions are apparent in international discussion of Serbia and its neighbours as were evident at the beginning of the Balkan disasters of the 1990s. Most of these can be found expressed by enthusiasts for the so-called Stability Pact for South-East Europe, which was drawn up by European Union Foreign Ministers at Cologne on 10 June 1999. This strangely named initiative aims at producing 'lasting peace, prosperity and stability' in the region through fostering regional cooperation, market economies and 'integration into [EU] structures'. All of which sounds plausible. But one must first question the assumptions.

First, is it true that the Balkan wars broke out because of economic underdevelopment? No. Poverty was the result not the cause of conflict. So why will prosperity *of itself* stop future wars?

Second, is it true that the region *as a whole* was disrupted by these wars? No – only those countries of the former Yugoslavia in which there were large numbers of Serbs whom Belgrade wanted to unite under its rule. So how will broader regional cooperation help?

Third, is it true that Europe's role during the conflicts was positive, and that therefore enlarging that role is likely to lead to the right solutions? Actually, no – that is not true either. Peace and stability have returned to the region despite, not because of, the European Union's efforts.

This is not, of course, to say that Europe cannot help. Opening its markets to producers in the whole region will certainly allow those who wish to practise peace to sell their goods and restore their countries. There should also be some well-targeted and tightly monitored aid. But not too much. Bosnia, for example, has probably reached the point at which international aid does more harm than good, by encouraging corruption and dependency. Kosovo could easily go the same way. And, further ahead, so could Serbia.

The real roots of all this international activity focused through the EU upon the Balkans lie in the view which the diplomats still take about the cause of the war – indeed, the cause of all wars – that is, national identity and national sovereignty. Thus Carl Bildt, Special Envoy of the UN Secretary-General to the Balkans, has called for:

> ...the evolution towards structures of layered sovereignty that...should allow for both wide-ranging autonomy and far-

reaching European integration so that over time they might bridge the gulfs that otherwise will forever threaten the region's stability. The necessary alternative to setting up new nation-states in the region is setting up new European and regional structures.*

In the same vein – eerily echoing the warnings against the break-up of the old federal Yugoslavia in 1991 – the European Union has been warning Montenegro against breaking away from Serbia. One really might have thought that international diplomats would had learned by now the lesson of trying to tell other people what is in their own national interest. Montenegrins are inevitably tempted by the thought of a modestly prosperous life without being bullied or bled dry by the Serbs. It is for Serbia – not us – to try to persuade them to stay, by offering suitably favourable terms. And if I were a Montenegrin I know that I would want to get out as fast as possible.

The trouble is that the European Union can never pursue sensible policies towards the countries of the Balkans, for a very simple reason. The EU, or more precisely the class which rules it, cannot accept the validity of nationhood – for that would be to make nonsense of the European idea itself. So rather than try to encourage nation states to develop and advance, the EU will always try to suppress or undermine them. This bodes ill everywhere. But particularly in the Balkans it risks creating more intense and destructive – because vilified and frustrated – national passions.

The West's aim should rather be to encourage a broader vision of nationalism, linking it with democracy and a law-governed liberty. I expressed this thought in my lecture in Zagreb in 1998:

A nation state is not a state in which only one nation lives. It is, rather, a state in which the common ties of blood and history of the great majority of the population provide a special unity and cohesion. But that does not mean that the minorities are deprived of rights they enjoy by virtue of being citizens. The state is not,

---

* Carl Bildt, 'A Second Chance in the Balkans', *Foreign Affairs*, January–February 2001.

after all, merely a tribe. It is a legal entity. Concern for human rights . . .thus complements the sense of nationhood, so as to ensure a nation state that is both strong and democratic.

I believe that this is a vision which a new generation of politicians in South-East Europe – men and women untainted by the totalitarian mindset of the past – will come to share. Incidentally, this philosophy is called conservatism.

CHAPTER 9

Europe – Dreams
and Nightmares

THE PROBLEMS OF EUROPE

During my lifetime most of the problems the world has faced have
come, in one fashion or other, from mainland Europe, and the
solutions from outside it. That generalisation is clearly true of the
Second World War. Nazism was, after all, a European ideology,
the Third Reich an attempt at European domination. Against both,
the resolve of Britain, of the Commonwealth and, decisively, of
America were successfully brought to bear. A great victory for
liberty was the result. The mainland Europeans benefited from an
outcome which, by and large, they had not themselves secured:
some have resented it ever since.

But my opening generalisation is also in a different sense true
of the Cold War. Although it was above all in the Soviet Union,
that is outside a narrowly defined 'Europe', that Marxism became
the ideology of empire, Marxism too had European roots. Karl
Marx was, it should be remembered, a European thinker in a
line of European thinkers; he developed his ideas by studying the
experience of Revolutionary France and, I am sorry to say, he
prepared his works by courtesy of the British Museum, long before
they took political shape in St Petersburg and Moscow; and it
was finally the liberal democratic values of the English-speaking
peoples, spearheaded from Washington, which proved the ultimate
antidote to communism. For a second time – for a third if you go

back further to the First World War, though the issues there are somewhat more complex – salvation came from across the Atlantic.

At a personal level, I am conscious that much of my energy as Prime Minister was also taken up with Europe – and, if I had my time again, still more would have been so. Of course, Britain was not in those days fighting a war against a European power. But there was an increasingly intense struggle, all the same – one which focused on issues of great national and international significance. And, looking forward into the century which has just begun, there is every reason to imagine that this clash of aims and ideas is likely to continue.

I want, therefore, to examine now in some detail what is at stake – in this chapter from a mainly global perspective, in the next from a more narrowly focused British one. Having sketched out the problems, I shall also suggest some possible solutions. These will, however, not by and large be directed at 'Europe'. Too many British and other critics have spent too long trying to do that: it is, to speak bluntly, a waste of time, because, as I shall seek to show, Europe as a whole is fundamentally unreformable. My suggestions will thus be addressed principally to those who are still not fully party to the project, and thus not fatally compromised by it.

NEW STATES FOR OLD

For most of the Cold War period, the boundaries of Western states marked out on our atlases seemed remarkably clear, and seemed likely to last. In Asia, and still more in Africa, the situation was, of course, more fluid and confusing; though even there it was generally new names rather than new borders that appeared, as one after the other European colonies gained their independence. The greatest divide, though, was between communist and non-communist states, with the former, whatever their notional titles and dignities, falling under the sway of the Soviet Union or China, and the latter enjoying political sovereignty under the formal or informal protection of the United States.

Since the end of the Cold War, however, that easily identifiable and comprehensible pattern has radically, and probably permanently, changed. Recent years have seen more new states emerge in Europe than at any time since the 1918–19 Versailles and Trianon Treaties. Not that most of these were 'new' in the sense that they lacked political antecedents. But certainly in the former Soviet Union and in the Balkans the maps have been redrawn in ways that still leave politicians trying to draw breath, and cartographers in profit. This, then, has been one feature of modern times.

Yet over the same period, another and contrary trend has also emerged. While the countries of Eastern and Central Europe, the Balkans and the old USSR have been trying to establish viable national institutions, the countries of Western Europe have been seeking to supplant and replace theirs with international ones. The last pretences that the European Union is an economic organisation of freely collaborating independent states are now being discarded. I very much doubt, for example, whether any of his Continental equivalents would echo Mr Blair's promise that he would 'have no truck with a European superstate' and would 'fight for Britain's interests and to keep our independence every inch of the way' – and then advocate a European single currency.* Only in Britain does anyone still peddle such nonsense and expect to be believed. A fair-minded reading of recent history shows the way events are leading. Each new global development – the reunification of Germany, instability in financial markets, war in the Balkans, the rise of the American superpower – has served as a spur to create a politically united Europe. We are at or very near the point of no return. But Downing Street seems not to have noticed.

Of course, in one sense the confusion about the European Union's true goals is understandable. No one has ever seen anything quite like it before. States, we must admit, are always to some extent artificial creations. After all, without the machinations of Bismarck there would probably have been no united Germany – at least not one based on Prussia. And much the same could be said of Cavour and his project for a united Italy based on Pied-

---

* Tony Blair, 'I'm a British Patriot', article in the *Sun*, 17 March 1997.

mont. Even the oldest nation states – Britain and France – are the result of deals and diplomacy and to some extent remain together because of them. States are thus the work of man, not nature.

This is even more so in the case of empires. They, above all, require able and committed elites employing skills and stratagems to sustain or expand them. Indeed, the fact that they are ultimately based on force not consent (though culture may supply some bonds in time) makes them supremely the fruit of artifice.

But how does Europe fit into this pattern? The emerging federal Europe is not, of course, a nation state.* It is, indeed, based upon the suppressing or, as the enthusiasts would doubtless have it, the surpassing of the concept of national identity. Its actions are often aimed at creating a kind of 'nation' of Europeans – hence the European anthem, flag, cultural and educational propaganda programmes and the like. But this process of nation-building, it is understood by all concerned, will take time. And it will certainly have to follow, it cannot hope to precede, the process of institution-building on which the Euro-enthusiasts have embarked. In fact, the EU's priority is clear: first make your government, the rest will follow.

Is the new Europe, therefore, an empire in the making? Here the parallels are closer, for its elite displays much of the arrogance and introversion of a supra-national ruling class. Yet Europe is clearly not an empire in other traditional and conventional respects. It is not a power possessed of great military might, or of over-arching technological supremacy, or of boundless resources – though again it wants to acquire or develop all these things.

Europe is, in fact, more like a state or an empire turned upside down. It lacks so much that would provide the solid foundations of statehood or imperial power that it can only exist through the satisfaction of accumulated vested interests. You only have to

---

* There are, it is true, debates about what 'federalism' means. The term has been used in America to mean restoring powers to the states which despite the provisions of the US Constitution have passed to the federal government. In Europe, federalism is usually understood in the light of the federalism of the Federal Republic of Germany, i.e. a state in which sovereignty is exercised by the central government with a degree of local autonomy. This is the sense in which I shall be using the term.

wade through a metric measure or two of European prose, culled from its directives, circulars, reports, communiqués or what pass as debates in its 'parliament', and you will quickly understand that Europe is, in truth, synonymous with bureaucracy. It is government by bureaucracy for bureaucracy – to which one might add 'to', 'from' and 'with' bureaucracy if one were so minded. It is not that the actual size of the EU bureaucracy in absolute terms is so staggering – at roughly thirty thousand employees it has a smaller staff than Birmingham City Council, though this figure leaves out the much larger number of national officials whose tasks flow from European regulation. No: what makes Europe the ultimate bureaucracy is that *it is ultimately sustained by nothing else.*

The structures, plans and programmes of the European Union are to be understood as simply existing for their own sake. Europe thus provides a new variation on Descartes' 'I think therefore I am': in its version 'I am therefore I do' – though, like other multi-national bureaucracies, it gets round to doing rather less and less effectively than it intended. Pope John XXIII was once asked by a visitor to the Vatican how many people worked there. He answered: 'About half.' This reflection may be applied to Europe too.

The movement towards a bureaucratic European superstate – for no other term adequately serves to describe what is emerging – has huge implications for the world as a whole. Yet I am repeatedly struck on my travels outside Europe by just how little understanding there is of this. At least until recently, the main attention which the issue received in America or in the Far East related to the nuts and bolts of trade agreements. And when successive British governments – not least that which I led in the 1980s – were seen to be at odds with the rest of Europe, and particularly with the dominant Franco–German axis, that was put down merely to the quirks of history or to the ordinary jostling of national interests.

That perception is now changing, particularly in Washington. And not a moment too soon. It is one of the great weaknesses of reasonable men and women that they imagine that projects which fly in the face of commonsense are not serious or being seriously undertaken. The creation of the new European superstate is a case in point. It is time for the world to wake up to it; if it is still possible, to stop it; if it is not, to contain and cope with it.

THE EUROPEAN IDEA

Bismarck, who makes several appearances in these pages and whose opinions on such matters should be taken seriously, knew exactly what to make of appeals to European idealism. 'I have always,' he observed, 'found the word "Europe" in the mouths of those politicians who wanted from other powers something they did not dare to demand in their own name.'* This too has been my experience.

The concept of Europe has always, I suspect, lent itself to a large measure of humbug. Not just national interests, but (especially now) a great array of group and class interests happily disguise themselves beneath the mantle of synthetic European idealism. Thus we find an almost religious reverence for 'Europe' accompanied by a high degree of distinctly materialistic chicanery and corruption. I shall try to explain the low-mindedness later. But here it is the high-mindedness that accompanies it which concerns me, because it is actually the more disturbing in its consequences.

It is often said that the origins of the European project should be traced back to the post-war determination of a number of Continental European politicians, officials and thinkers to build a supra-national structure within which future wars in Europe would be impossible. To this end, France and Germany would be locked together, initially economically, but by incremental steps politically too. And, of course, this impulse was indeed historically important. It was the basis of the first stage of the European plan – the European Coal and Steel Community established on 18 April 1951 – conceived by Jean Monnet and Robert Schuman. It was then manifested in the famous (or notorious) preamble to the Treaty of Rome, signed on 25 March 1957, which sought 'ever

---

* I am indebted to Jeffrey Gedmin for drawing my attention to this quotation.

closer union'. And it has persisted and grown in strength up to the present day, when a federal European superstate is on the verge of creation. One should add that this was not the *only* impulse at work throughout that period: it was not, for example, my goal, or as I then believed the Conservative Party's goal, in the seventies, eighties and nineties. But the fact is that it is the ideas of Monnet, Schuman, de Gasperi, Spaak and Adenauer – not those of Thatcher (or even de Gaulle and Erhard) which have ultimately prevailed.*

My point here, however, is that the impulse to create a European superstate was not simply that of avoiding war in Europe. It was a good deal older than that. Nationalism is often condemned as providing an excuse for the persecution of national minorities. But *supra*-nationalism should be still more suspect, because it provides a doctrine for the subjugation of whole nations. So it has proved in Europe. At the height of its power in the sixteenth century, the Habsburg Holy Roman Empire, for example, aspired to universal domination. The initials A-E-I-O-U (*Austria est imperare orbi universo* – Austria is destined to rule the whole world), the Habsburg motto, famously summed up that ambition. But, in practice, it was only partially and fleetingly realised. Then for a still briefer period, though with much bloodier thoroughness, Napoleon Bonaparte bestrode the continent of Europe. It is not simply that the language was French which makes the Napoleonic programme for European unity seem so contemporary. For example, among Bonaparte's aims was, he said, to create 'a monetary identity throughout Europe'. He later claimed that his common legal code, and university and monetary systems, 'would have achieved a single family in Europe. No one would ever have left home while

---

* Jean Monnet (1888–1979), French financier and high official, often regarded as the founding father of the European Common Market; Robert Schuman (1886–1963) – as French Foreign Minister he proposed the Schuman Plan which led to the European Coal and Steel Community; Alcide de Gasperi (1881–1954), Italian Prime Minister 1945–53; Paul Henri Spaak (1899–1972), alternately Belgian Prime Minister, Foreign Minister and international high official; Konrad Adenauer (1876–1967), first Chancellor of West Germany (1949–63).

travelling.'* The President of today's European Central Bank could hardly have put it better.

Adolf Hitler can with good reason be seen as following in Napoleon's footsteps in his ambitions for European domination. Indeed, the Nazis spoke in terms that may strike us as eerily reminiscent of today's Euro-federalists. Thus Hitler could refer contemptuously in 1943 to 'the clutter of small nations' which must be eliminated in favour of a united Europe.†

It is not, of course, my suggestion that today's proponents of European unity are totalitarians, though they are not well-known for their tolerance either. What we should grasp, however, from the lessons of European history is that, first, there is nothing necessarily benevolent about programmes of European integration; second, the desire to achieve grand utopian plans often poses a grave threat to freedom; and third, European unity has been tried before, and the outcome was far from happy.

In reply to this, it will certainly be said that the purpose of today's projected European political union is quite different, because it is not to be achieved by force, and because its proclaimed rationale is to preserve peace. But this argument is no longer convincing, if indeed it ever was.

It is surely questionable whether either the European Coal and Steel Community, or the European Common Market, or the European Economic Community, or the European Union – let alone the incipient European superstate – played or will play any significant role in preventing military conflict. A defeated, divided and humiliated Germany was not in any position to cause trouble during the Cold War years – and it is a very long time indeed (since Napoleon, in fact) since any power *other* than Germany ever caused wars in Europe. The threat during the Cold War was, rather, from the Soviet Union, and it was an American-led NATO, not European institutions, which preserved Western Europe's peace and freedom. Even today, it is still true that an American

---

* Quoted by Luca Einaudi, *National Institute Economic Review*, April 2000.
† Quoted in John Laughland's profound and revealing study of the origins of Euro-federalist thinking, *The Tainted Source: The Undemocratic Origins of the European Idea* (London, 1997), p.19.

military presence in Europe is the most important guarantee of the Continent's security, both in the face of threats emanating from the former Soviet Union and from any renewed German ambitions – not that I wish to exaggerate those dangers at present either. Finally, it does seem to be stretching the pacifist credentials of the Euro-enthusiasts beyond credibility to maintain that a united Europe is necessary to keep the peace, when it is energetically seeking to become a major military power.

The idea of Europe would, though, not have as powerful resonance if it was merely associated with cartels, Commissioners and the Common Agricultural Policy. As someone who has come to be profoundly disillusioned with and suspicious of all that is done in the name of 'Europe', I fully recognise this. The European myth is no less powerful for being that – a myth. And its power stems from its association in many people's minds with most of what goes to make up civilised living. For example, the contrast is often made, particularly in France, with the alleged vulgarity of American values. In the eyes of many Euro-enthusiasts, Europe vaguely represents ideas of law and justice that stem from the Greek and Roman eras. For the aesthetically minded, it is Gothic cathedrals, Renaissance paintings and nineteenth-century classical music that hold sway. The European idea is, it seems, almost infinitely variable. Therein lies its appeal. If you are pious, it is synonymous with Christendom. If you are liberal, it embodies the Enlightenment. If you are right-wing, it represents a bulwark against barbarism from the Dark Continents. If you are left-wing, it epitomises internationalism, human rights and Third World aid. But the fact that this portentous concept of Europe is so infinitely malleable means that, in truth, it is simply empty.

'Europe' in anything other than a geographical sense is a wholly artificial construct. It makes no sense at all to lump together Beethoven and Debussy, Voltaire and Burke, Vermeer and Picasso, Notre Dame and St Paul's, boiled beef and *bouillabaisse*, and portray them as elements of a 'European' musical, philosophical, artistic, architectural or gastronomic reality. If Europe charms us, as it has so often charmed me, it is precisely because of its contrasts and contradictions, not its coherence and continuity. It is difficult to imagine anything less likely to be moulded into a successful political unit than this extraordinarily uneven mix of unlike with like. I suspect that in actual fact even the most fanatical Euro-enthusiasts have, in their heart of hearts, understood this. They keep quiet about the fact and would protest the opposite, but actually they do not like the day-to-day human reality of Europe one bit. That is why they want to harmonise, regulate and twist it into something altogether different, rootless and shapeless that can be made to fit their utopian plans.

THE EUROPEAN ECONOMIC AND SOCIAL MODEL

To the extent that there is a 'European' identity it can best be perceived in what is often described as the European economic and social model. This model, though it comes in several somewhat different shapes and sizes, depending upon the politics of the Euro-peans concerned, is clearly distinct from and indeed sharply at odds with the American model. In order to illustrate the philos-ophy behind it, and so as not to confuse it with old-fashioned socialism, one can profitably consider some words of Edouard Balladur, the then French Prime Minister: 'What is the market? It is the law of the jungle, the law of nature. And what is civilisation? It is the struggle against nature.'*

M. Balladur is an extremely sophisticated and intelligent right-of-centre French politician. But he clearly understands nothing about markets. Markets do not exist in a void. They require mutual accept-ance of rules and mutual confidence. Beyond a certain level, only the state, setting weights, measures, rules and laws against fraud, profiteering, cartels and so on, can make markets work at all. Of course, the market – any market – implies limits upon the power of the state. In markets the initiative comes from individuals, the prices reflect supply and demand, and the outcomes are, by necessity, unpredictable. But to describe the operation of markets as barbaric shows a particularly shallow and unrealistic understanding of what constitutes Western civilisation and underpins Western progress.†

---

* Quoted by *Financial Times*, 31 December 1993.
† I investigate the nature and operation of markets more fully in Chapter Eleven.

In France, the hostility to markets – and particularly to the international markets through which nations trade with another – is very deep-rooted. It may be that there is something in the French psyche which reacts better than the British to a large measure of state control and high levels of regulation. Certainly, the quite successful performance of the French economy in recent decades might confirm that.

But the European economic model also has a German variant, and this, given Germany's size and wealth, is the more important one. Whereas the French prefer statism – they invented the word, after all – the Germans incline to corporatism. They are not anti-capitalist, but their conception of capitalism – sometimes referred to as Rhenish capitalism – is one in which competition is limited, cartels are smiled upon, and a high degree of regulation is pro-vided. Another aspect of this system is revealed by the term 'social market'. This expression was coined by Ludwig Erhard,* though I believe that he later came to dislike it because it was used to justify too much state interference and expenditure. For Germans nowadays it implies the provision of more generous social benefits than anyone in Britain, apart from those on the left of the Labour Party, would normally consider appropriate to a 'safety net'. And indeed the Germans are still wrestling with the need to curb that spending.

What both the French and the Germans can agree upon, how-ever, is that the sort of economic policies pursued in America, and to a large extent in Britain since 1979, are unacceptable. Thus, writing in *Le Monde*, the French and German Finance Ministers proclaimed: 'The obsessive insistence of the neo-liberals on the deregulation of labour markets has contributed more to the blocking of reforms than to the creation of jobs. We are con-vinced that the European social model is a trump card, not a handicap.'†

In fact, a number of authoritative studies have quite convinc-ingly proved the opposite. Examining the impact of moves in

---

* Ludwig Erhard (1897–1977), West German Economics Minister 1949–63, Chancellor of West Germany 1963–66.
† Oskar Lafontaine and Dominique Strauss-Kahn, *Le Monde*, 15 January 1999.

France and Germany to stimulate employment by limiting working hours, Keith Marsden noted that at the same time as the average number of hours worked had fallen, the two countries' unemployment rates had risen. By contrast, in the United States where people were working longer, and in Britain where working hours had remained stable, there had been significant falls in unemployment. Similarly, early-retirement programmes in Europe had not made available more opportunities for younger workers: rather, the effect had been to increase social security taxes to support the retired – so burdening business. Finally, Mr Marsden noted:

> There is a clear correlation between higher government expenditure and lower employment. In the US, the government share of GDP was twenty-two percentage points below that of France but its employment ratio was fifteen points higher. Britain's public spending level was eight points below Germany's, yet its employment ratio was seven points higher.*

Another study of Europe's social model by Bill Jamieson and Patrick Minford has highlighted the main economically harmful features of the European model: higher state spending, higher overall taxes, higher social security contributions – noting particularly the damaging burden this places on business – higher corporate taxes and higher levels of regulation, especially of labour markets. The results have been eminently predictable, but as an example of wilful self-damage no less shocking all the same: 'The contrast with the United States is stark. Since 1970 the US economy has created almost fifty million new jobs, while the EU has created just five million.'†

---

* Keith Marsden, *Handicap, Not Trump Card: The Franco–German Model isn't Working* (Centre for Policy Studies, July 1999).
† Bill Jamieson and Patrick Minford, *Britain and Europe: Choices for Change* (Politeia and Global Britain, 1999).

GOVERNMENT SPENDING AND UNEMPLOYMENT

GOVERNMENT SPENDING AS A PERCENTAGE OF GDP/ LEVELS OF UNEMPLOYMENT AS A PERCENTAGE OF THE LABOUR FORCE, 1999

	GDP	Unemployment
Britain	39.1	6.1
Germany	45.9	8.8
France	52.1	11.3
Italy	48.3	11.3
Euro Area	46.8	10.0
USA	30.0	4.2
Japan	38.1	4.7

Source: *OECD Economic Outlook*, December 2000: Annex Table 28

EUROPE'S PENSIONS CRISIS

Another way of describing the difference between the European and the American models is to borrow a rather profound observation of Friedrich von Hayek. In *The Road to Serfdom*, first published in 1944, Hayek wrote:

> [T]he policies which are now followed everywhere [in Europe], which hand out the privilege of security, now to this group and now to that, are nevertheless rapidly creating conditions in which the striving for security tends to become stronger than the love of freedom. *The reason for this is that with every grant of complete security to one group the insecurity of the rest necessarily increases.** [Emphasis added]

The European model epitomises precisely this: it places security above everything else, and in its persistence in eliminating risk it

---

* F.A. Hayek, *The Road to Serfdom* (London: Routledge and Kegan Paul, 1979), p.95.

inevitably discourages enterprise. That is the basis of Europe's pensions crisis, whose full implications are still not widely grasped.

Of course, in one sense the cause of the crisis is demography, the failure of much of Western society to reproduce. One can speculate about the causes for this and what it may tell us of contemporary values, attitudes and institutions. One can also debate whether and how policies might be changed to reverse long-term demographic decline. But such discussions, fascinating as they are, are irrelevant to the crisis much of Europe is facing *now*.

No less a person than the EU Commissioner in charge of the Internal Market and Taxation, Frits Bolkestein, has admitted that Europe faces a 'pensions time-bomb'. He has noted that the ratio of workers to pensioners will decline from four to one to less than two to one by 2040. And he observes that if unfunded pension liabilities were shown up in the national accounts of some member states this would represent a debt of over 200 per cent of GDP.* Italy is the EU country which is facing the worst crisis. It has a fertility rate of just 1.2, the lowest in the world, and also the world's most costly pensions system, amounting to over 15 per cent of GDP – 33 per cent of worker payrolls, expected to rise to 50 per cent by 2030.†

Continental European countries have walked into a trap from which there appears no painless exit. Of course, they could not know just where demography would lead. But they have known well enough for some years that the promises implicitly made to pensioners could not be afforded. It was precisely because we realised the implications for Britain's public finances that in 1980 we ended the connection between the retirement pension and incomes (it now rises in line with prices). And in 1986 we cut back state funding of the State Earnings-Related Pension Scheme

---

* Speech to the Friends of Europe, 6 February 2001.

† Demographers regard the 'replacement rate', i.e. the fertility rate needed to see that the population stays the same, as being 2.1. In Italy Silvio Berlusconi's right-of-centre administration was trying to get to grips with the pensions crisis when it fell in 1994. He and his colleagues will now have the chance to try again: see pp.347–8 below. These figures are drawn from Peter G. Peterson, *Gray Dawn: How the Coming Age Wave will Transform America and the World* (New York: Random House, 1999), pp.77–8.

(SERPS) and provided incentives to opt for private-sector Personal Pension Plans (PPPs). As a result, future state obligations have been curtailed to manageable levels. Britain also now has more money invested in pension funds than the rest of Europe put together. Although other EU countries have made repeated attempts to scale back their social liabilities, none has taken similar substantial steps. As a result, just three countries – the United States, Britain and Japan – possess three-quarters of the entire world's funded pension assets.*

Quite how the countries of mainland Europe are going to cope with their problems is unclear. But someone is going to be disappointed – either pensioners or workers. And it seems that the official figures actually understate the scale of that disappointment. This is because it is not enough to express the problem in terms of national finances: it can only be understood in terms of equity between the generations. There is nothing theoretical about this. If one generation is expected to carry an excessive burden on behalf of another it will seek by every means to avoid it. It will either demand that past promises are broken, or it will not work, or it will not pay its taxes, or the most talented people will leave. Socialist governments which have tried to tax 'till the pips squeak' have ample experience of that. It is the main reason why even left-wing governments today try to keep marginal tax rates down. In the present case, and employing the concept of 'generational accounts' – which 'represent the sum of all future net taxes (taxes paid minus transfer payments received) that citizens born in any given year will pay over their lifetimes, given current policy' – Niall Ferguson and Laurence J. Kotlikoff have made various projections of the changes required to achieve 'generational balance'. The scale of what is implied is illustrated by the conclusion that, for example, nine EU countries would need to cut government spending by more than 20 per cent if they wanted to rely on this means to achieve balance.†

---

* Peterson, *Gray Dawn*, p.164. Actually, the first truly radical steps towards a national system of funded private pensions were made in Chile in 1981 – under the Pinochet government.

† Niall Ferguson and Laurence J. Kotlikoff, 'The Degeneration of EMU', *Foreign Affairs*, March–April 2000.

THE COMMON AGRICULTURAL POLICY
AND PROTECTION

Europe's pensions problem is relatively recent. By contrast, its agriculture problem is of long standing. Although the European Common Market had its origins in a project to create a common policy towards coal and steel, it was the Common Agricultural Policy (CAP) which from the time of the Treaty of Rome was the central pillar of the structure.* Political leaders and their policies come and go. Reform programmes rise and fall. But the CAP goes on for ever. No one seriously seeks to justify it. The days when we were told that without it Europe might be short of food have long since passed. Despite successive attempts at reform, not least those initiated by Britain, the CAP is wasteful, environmentally damaging and extremely costly. It still absorbs some £30 billion – about half of the EU's total budget.† But it continues because it constitutes the most important reason why the less industrially developed European countries put up with other European programmes that diminish their competitiveness, and it is the unspoken reason why so many new countries want to become members.

The CAP puts up the cost of food for EU consumers, thus increasing our costs and reducing our growth. It also depresses food prices worldwide, as subsidised European food exports

---

* The objectives of the CAP were outlined in the 1957 Treaty of Rome. It was designed 'to increase agricultural productivity', 'to ensure a fair standard of living for the agricultural community', 'to stabilise markets', 'to ensure the availability of supplies' and 'to ensure that supplies reach consumers at reasonable prices'. The CAP operates a free internal agricultural market without tariffs or quotas, but with a common system of external protection giving preference to European Community farmers. Farm-product prices are determined by the Council of Ministers, and maintained through export subsidies and intervention. For a full description of the workings of the CAP see Richard Howarth, 'The CAP: History and Attempts at Reform', in Linda Whetstone (ed.), *Reforming the CAP*, Institute of Economic Affairs, June 2000, pp.4–5.
† Howarth, 'The CAP: History and Attempts at Reform', p.5.

deprive farmers in poorer countries of their livelihoods. This is precisely the wrong way round. Industrialised countries need low-cost workforces; agricultural countries need to provide their peasants with incomes. Both lose from the CAP.

The CAP is also a force for global protectionism. It has been estimated that the CAP is responsible for 85 per cent of the world's agricultural subsidies.* Not surprisingly, this prompts widespread resentment. Other countries, aware of this scandalous situation, are thus less willing to make compromises and resolve disputes.

The EU is not the only body which subsidises agriculture and it is not the only trade grouping which is inclined to protectionism. But on both counts it is certainly the most serious global offender. It has been estimated that the total annual cost of the CAP to the world economy is about $75 billion, of which two-thirds is borne by the Europeans in the form of higher prices, inefficient production and economic distortions. The rest falls on non-EU countries through lost agricultural export opportunities.†

Another expert study has found that the EU economy is almost as protected as it was a decade ago. Thus Professor Patrick Messerlin calculates that the cost of this protection, across the board, is equivalent to about 7 per cent of the European Union countries' GDP, some $600 billion.‡

The European tendency towards protection – demonstrated not just in the operation of the CAP but in numerous trade questions: films, bananas, and hormone-treated beef – is inherent in the European project itself. The reluctance to engage in open trade with the outside world only reflects a reluctance to accept the working of open markets at home. The EU and its predecessors were never, it should be remembered, interested primarily in free trade as such. They were and are a customs union – that is a group of countries

---

* Quoted by Graeme Leach, *EU Membership – What's the Bottom Line?*, Institute of Directors Policy Paper, March 2000.
† The estimate is made by economists Brent Borrell and Lionel Hubbard and is quoted by Denise H. Froning and Aaron Schavey in 'How the United States and the European Union can Improve Cooperation on Trade', *Heritage Foundation Executive Memorandum*, 7 March 2001.
‡ Quoted in 'Europe's Burden', *The Economist*, 22 May 1999.

which, while allowing free trade among themselves, charges a common set of tariffs to the rest of the world. The level of these tariffs has fallen sharply from an average of 12 per cent to 3 per cent over the last forty years as part of international trade negotiations. But the concept of global free trade is one to which the European countries have never been wedded, and never will be.

In theory, fundamental reforms of the CAP might, if they ever came about, remove one of the main reasons why the EU is such a force for protectionism. But the combination of high taxes, high levels of regulation and so high costs on the one hand, and the inflexibility resulting from a single currency and interest rate on the other, will in any case press Europe further down the protectionist path. Even within the framework set by the World Trade Organisation, there are many ways in which the EU could provide covert protection for its producers – such as through 'anti-dumping' measures. The EU's trading partners must expect that it will do everything that it can to exploit such loopholes.

As the European superstate emerges on to the world scene, it will be keen to flex its muscles in economic as in other matters. It will seek to combat the 'neo-liberalism', i.e. the belief in free markets, which the French and German Finance Ministers so roundly denounced in *Le Monde*. It will try to substitute a more highly managed, i.e. more bureaucratic, model on international trade and finance. The Europeans will ultimately fail. But 'ultimately' can be a long time. Meanwhile, they spell trouble.

WIDER STILL AND WIDER . . .

In such circumstances it might seem odd that the EU is besieged by countries seeking membership. The shortcomings of the system are, after all, there for all to see. Yet enlargement is still the topic most talked about in European circles – at least in public.

Thus the alleged rationale of the Nice Summit in December 2000 was to prepare for further enlargement of European Union membership. It was argued that increasing the number of member countries from fifteen to twenty-seven required institutional reforms which would allow more streamlined decision-making, i.e. loss of the national veto.* One can see how that fits the federalist agenda. What is increasingly contestable, however, is the sincerity with which EU countries view enlargement.

During the 1980s and most of the 1990s, Britain was in the forefront of those urging a widening of Community membership. As Prime Minister, I was keen to see the former dictatorships of Spain and Portugal given the opportunities and the stability required for democracy to flourish. Both I, and later John Major, were even keener to widen membership to include the former communist countries of Central and Eastern Europe, for very much the same reason. The extension of the frontiers of a free and prosperous Europe to the east was an integral part of the programme of a Europe of cooperating nation states which I had put forward in my speech at Bruges in 1988 – where I reminded my audience that 'we shall [for which read 'should'] always look on Warsaw, Prague and Budapest as great European cities'. After the fall of the Berlin Wall the following year this argument became even more cogent. To prolong the division of Europe by an economic tariff wall once the old political wall dividing West and East had crumbled was manifestly unjust.

Yet this is precisely what the European Community did. Far from welcoming in the former communist countries – with the exception of East Germany, which joined the West with hardly a by-your-leave – they were left to the tender mercies of agricultural dumping under Europe's CAP and a niggling system of trade quotas. Twelve years after the collapse of communism, Poland, Hungary, the Czech Republic and the rest are still waiting.

Enlargement of the Community eastwards has traditionally been attractive to both the British and the Germans, but has been a good deal less so to the French and to the countries of Southern Europe. There is no great secret as to why this is so. Alongside our wish to see the ex-communist countries encouraged to create

---

* The 'next wave' candidate countries are Bulgaria, the Czech Republic, Cyprus, Estonia, Hungary, Latvia, Lithuania, Malta, Romania, Poland, Slovakia, Slovenia.

successful Western-style economies, British governments have hoped that, as the EU jargon has it, 'widening' would be at the expense of 'deepening'. With the prospect of enlargement to include as many as twenty-seven members – counting in all the candidate countries – it seemed to us a plain impossibility to proceed with creating a federal superstate. The differences and potential conflicts between the members would be just too great.

For the Germans, extension eastwards had a rather different attraction and reflected other geopolitical interests. As a revealing CDU/CSU paper, 'Reflections on Europe', of 1 September 1994, put it:

> The only solution which will prevent a return to the unstable pre-war system, with Germany once again caught in the middle between East and West [a somewhat eccentric description of the Third Reich in the thirties!], is to integrate Germany's Central and Eastern European neighbours into the European post-war system and to establish a wide-ranging partnership with Russia ... If European integration were not to progress, Germany might be called upon, or be tempted by its own security constraints, *to try to effect the stabilisation of Eastern Europe on its own and in the traditional way.* [Emphasis added]

By contrast, the French have, with the limited exception of Romania, not sought out friends or clients in Eastern Europe. Moreover, France and even more so Greece, Spain and Portugal have been extremely wary of the impact upon the CAP, and the valuable benefits they receive from it, of the introduction of new members with large, primitive agricultural sectors.

For as long as the Germans continued to be enthusiastic about the entry of the ex-communist countries, some (albeit snail-paced) progress was made. But it is now apparent that resistance within Germany to expansion is growing. The German EU Commissioner for Enlargement, Günter Verheugen, has, for example, suggested that a referendum may be needed in Germany before enlargement goes ahead. German public opinion appears to be quite strongly opposed to the prospect of free entry for goods and services and, above all, workers from the East. In particular, hostility to early full membership for Poland has hardened.*

The present British government is, it seems, still strongly in favour of early expansion. But one may question whether this policy still makes much sense. All that has been seen of developments within the European Union over the last decade confirms that 'deepening' – that is the persistent accumulation of more and more powers by European institutions to override national wishes and interests – will go ahead, however much membership 'widens'. Indeed, as was shown by the decisions made at Nice, even the vague prospect of enlargement provides the excuse for a raft of new measures of centralisation. Similarly, the long-standing British hope that the need to absorb new members would lead to fundamental reform of the European Union's finances, above all the CAP, shows every sign of proving illusory.

For all these reasons, I am now unpersuaded by the case for further EU expansion. And although I fully understand the mix of historical, political and economic factors which account for the enthusiasm of the Central and East European countries for full membership, I also doubt whether they are well-advised to press for it on the terms available. Since leaving office, I have had the benefit of many frank and friendly (and that in the proper not diplomatic sense) conversations with senior political figures from these countries. Most of them, when pushed, are uneasy about what the EU may entail. Having endured the best part of half a century living under socialist bureaucracy, and seeing their national identities and rights overridden, they are not at all keen to be ruled from Brussels. Furthermore, although many of them are deeply uneasy about instability to the east, and so still want the reassurance offered by EU (as well as NATO) membership, they have few illusions about the degree to which Europe is dominated by Germany. And that too worries them, though they are not likely to admit it publicly.

European politicians and officials are wont to talk rather patronisingly of how far the applicant countries have yet to go in modernising and opening up their economies in order to prepare

---

* 'Germany Goes Cool on Polish Hopes to Join EU', *The Times*, 10 October 2000.

for entry. But what really alarms the Europeans is their *own* lack of preparedness in the face of low-cost competition. If as part of their preparations for entry the former communist countries are willing to tie themselves up with all the rules and regulations imposed by Europe, they will finish up by giving away much of the competitive advantage they currently enjoy. At which point, presumably, their slower growth rates could be used in order to justify putting off membership once again. In my view, the applicant member countries would therefore be well-advised to consider long and hard whether full membership of the European Union is what they really want. Negotiating free-trade agreements with the EU and with the North American Free Trade Area (NAFTA) – and, indeed, with Britain (on which, see the next chapter) – might suit their interests better.

So I believe that:

- The old arguments for expansion of EU membership no longer apply
- The EU should be pressed to concede free-trade arrangements with the applicant countries
- It should also be pressed to stop undermining these countries' agricultural sectors by dumping its products at their farmers' expense
- The governments of the applicant countries would be wise to find other ways to modernise their economies and expand their markets – ones which do not involve loss of sovereignty, the acceptance of German dominance, or piling costs on their industries.

DEFYING DEMOCRACY

The EU-applicant countries ought also to be aware of the prevailing style of politics within the European Union. This style is difficult to sum up in one word: it is, in fact, an unusual mix of the authoritarian, the bureaucratic and the interventionist on the one hand, with the compromising, the uninspiring and the ineffective on the other. The European Union is for ever awash with plans, programmes and projects. But the result, more often than not, is an inefficient muddle. Its leaders' eloquence is hyperbolic. But their decisions are characterised by horse-trading. Its ambitions to assert itself as a great power are unmatched. But the means at its disposal are few, and its attempts to play a role on the world stage have been universally embarrassing.

Perhaps the most significant shortcoming of the fledgling super-state is that it is not, will not be, indeed ultimately cannot be, democratic. This has nothing to do with the much discussed 'democratic deficit', which usually refers to the alleged disparity between the power wielded by the Commission and that wielded by the European Parliament. In fact, this is based on a false premise. The Commission and the Parliament share the same federalist agenda – and it is not democratic.

The *real* reason why there can be no functioning pan-European democracy is because there exists no pan-European public opinion. No matter how many attempts are made to create links between the political parties of different European countries, those parties know that they have to campaign upon, and that their fortunes will be determined by, national programmes and issues. The impact of European questions on such elections is most likely to be negative – when something that the European Union favours, such as open borders or more immigration, prompts popular anger.

It is a commonplace, but it is all too frequently ignored, that the European Union nations are extraordinarily deeply divided by language – no fewer than twelve main languages are widely spoken among the present members.* Even those educated elites which speak foreign languages with reasonable facility may well be a long way from sharing the thought patterns of native speakers of those languages. And it is still the case that for the great majority of Europe's population, 'home' is to be described in national, or local, not Continental terms.†

---

* English, French, German, Italian, Spanish (Castilian), Portuguese, Greek, Dutch, Swedish, Danish, Irish (Gaelic) and Finnish.

† For example, a poll of European twenty-one-to-thirty-five-year-olds showed that only one out of three considers himself as European rather than as a national of his own country. There are, though, differences between nations: 40 per cent of young Italians thought of themselves as European first, but

Of course, in time Europeans may all, in any case, speak English (I only half jest).* If that happens, it might be possible to consider seriously trying to make democracy work at a pan-European level. But for the present, and indeed for the foreseeable future, the more decisions which are made at a supra-national rather than a national level, the more remote and thus the less democratic Europe will be.

Moreover, none of the various schemes being put forward to give Europe a new 'constitution' can alter this. It is no surprise to me that the strongest proponents of Euro-federalism today often first cut their political teeth in the infantile utopianism, tinged with revolutionary violence, of the late 1960s and the 1970s. Some people are instinctively wrong about everything – even when they reverse their position. Thus the German Foreign Minister, Joschka Fischer, revelations of whose activities when a young left-wing radical have alternately entertained and shocked the German public, on 12 May 2000 in Berlin gave his views about what he called 'the finality of European integration'. Herr Fischer's answer to current problems was:

the transition from a union of states to full parliamentarisation as a European Federation ... And that means nothing less than a European Parliament and a European government which really do exercise legislative and executive power within the Federation. This Federation will have to be based on a constituent treaty.

He continued by arguing for:

[C]ompleting political integration ... [through] the formation of a centre of gravity. Such a group of states would conclude a new European framework treaty, the nucleus of a constitution of the

---

only 25 per cent of young British people. *Time Magazine* survey, 26 March 2001.

* Besides their mother tongue, 41 per cent of Europeans claim to know English, compared with just 19 per cent French and 10 per cent German. Moreover, some 70 per cent of Europeans consider that everyone in the EU should be able to speak English. *Europeans and Languages*, Eurobarometer Report, 54, 15 February 2001.

Federation. On the basis of this treaty, the Federation would develop its own institutions, *establish a government which within the EU should speak with one voice on behalf of the members of the group on as many issues as possible, a strong parliament and a directly elected president.** [Emphasis added]

And just in case anyone thought that this was merely a little provocative kite-flying, the whole package was later endorsed by others. President Jacques Chirac in a speech to the German Bundestag argued for the establishment of a 'pioneer group' of European countries led by France and Germany, committed to deeper political integration.† Chancellor Schröder went on to call for the European Commission to be transformed into 'a strong European executive' with an elected head – in effect a European government.‡ Then Lionel Jospin, the socialist French Prime Minister, provided his own gloss on the federalising project. Although his ideas differed in some respects from those of the German Chancellor – he wanted more economic regulation and less power for the Commission – M. Jospin was all in favour of a 'European government of the euro-zone'.§ The Franco–German (though now it might be better to call it Germano–French) axis thus clearly remains in good order, despite all hopes and fears to the contrary. And it is an axis which Britain is unable effectively to resist – even if the present British government wished to do so.

The planned erection of this vast federal superstructure would amount to nothing less than the building of a new European super-state. It is empty sophistry to deny this and instead to call it a 'superpower', as Tony Blair insists upon doing.¶ I shall give a copy

---

* Speech at the Humboldt University, Berlin, 12 May 2000. Interestingly, very similar sentiments have been expressed by that other former left-wing revolutionary, and now Green Party MEP, Daniel Cohn-Bendit; *Guardian*, 10 November 2000.

† Speech to the German Bundestag, Berlin, 27 June 2000.

‡ Chancellor Schröder's proposals are outlined in 'Responsibility for Europe', a draft document published by the Social Democratic Party of Germany, 30 April 2001.

§ Speech in Paris, 28 May 2001.

¶ Speech by Tony Blair to the Polish Stock Exchange, Warsaw, 6 October 2000.

of my memoirs to anyone who can provide a credible description of a European superpower which is not a superstate. Somehow I think I shall still have a few volumes in stock.

As I have already explained, unless and until there comes to exist a genuine European-wide public opinion, which in turn would involve the evolution of a genuine European-wide sense of identity, there are deep-seated reasons why Europe cannot be democratic. But if this argument should strike some as a little theoretical, one can turn instead to the ample evidence provided by European politicians' and officials' demonstration of their contempt for ordinary democratic procedures. The following examples should suffice.

The Germans know that perhaps the greatest symbol of their post-war achievements was the Deutschmark, managed with such exemplary skill and integrity by the German Bundesbank. So, not surprisingly, most of the population wanted to keep those arrangements. In 1992 opinion polls showed 84 per cent of the German public in favour of a referendum on the Maastricht Treaty. And almost 75 per cent opposed the loss of their currency.* But there was no referendum, and the Deutschmark was duly abolished in favour of the untried euro. The German political and business elite closed ranks and the wishes of the majority went for naught. They still do: opinion polls taken in March 2001 showed 70 per cent of Germans opposing the introduction of the euro.† But nobody seems to care.

Similarly, when the Danes – who were actually permitted a referendum – voted to reject Maastricht on 2 June 1992, the response from Europe and Denmark's pro-European political elite was that they should keep on voting until they came up with the right answer. For good measure, Britain's Foreign Secretary of the day, Douglas Hurd, warned that voting 'no' once again would result in Denmark's 'isolation' and could provoke a 'crisis affecting Denmark's position within the EC'.‡ The Danes, thus browbeaten,

---

* Findings from polls conducted by the Wickert Institute and *Stern* magazine, reported in *The Times*, 23 September 1992.
† *Daily Telegraph*, 3 April 2001.
‡ *The Times*, 27 April 1993.

dutifully reversed their earlier decision and on 18 May 1993 meekly voted 'yes'.

But Brussels, like all bullies who initially get away with it, kept on threatening the Danes and eventually went too far. The outrageous threat of Pedro Solbes, the European Commissioner in charge of Economic and Monetary Union, in March 2000 to the effect that 'Part-time membership of the EU is not good enough: in the longer term it's not possible to be in the Union and outside EMU [Economic and Monetary Union],' cut no ice with Danish voters in their referendum that September.* Fifty-three per cent of them defied the warnings and rejected the single currency. But we may be sure that the Eurocracy will be back.†

They certainly will in Switzerland. The Swiss have flourished mightily outside the European Union. They have enjoyed prosperity, stability and liberty, and one might be forgiven for thinking that no one would be foolish enough to want to upset that happy state of affairs. But the Europeans and the pro-European Swiss federal government do not see it that way. In a referendum on 4 March 2001 77 per cent of the Swiss voted against membership of the EU. Indeed, not a single canton voted in favour. Nevertheless, the federal government continues to reaffirm its intention of seeking EU membership in the next five to ten years.

Countries like Switzerland and the states of Central and Eastern Europe would be well-advised to study the EU's treatment of Austria – as the Danes did when pondering their vote before the latest referendum. In October 1999 Austrians voted to end the old, corrupt system of power- and perk-sharing between left and right. Fifty-four per cent of voters supported the Austrian People's Party and the Austrian Freedom Party. There was no suggestion that the election was rigged. It was perfectly peaceful. The right-wing Freedom Party, under its then leader Jörg Haider, won its 27 per

---

* *Daily Telegraph*, 16 March 2000.

† The most recent spat between the Eurocracy and democracy is in Ireland, where after a majority voted in a referendum to reject the Nice Treaty the European Commissioner responsible for enlargement, Günter Verheugen, commented: 'Such a referendum in one country cannot block the biggest and most important project for the political and economic future of the united Europe' (*The Times*, 9 June 2001).

cent of the vote fairly and cleanly. However, the left-dominated EU Council of Ministers, with opportunistic support from President Chirac, imposed political sanctions on Austria in the hope that the Austrians would be prepared to put the left back in power. Various insensitive utterances by Herr Haider were adduced to confirm that Europe was faced with a threat from right-wing extremists. But it seems likely that the Freedom Party's scepticism about the merits of European integration was at least as important in earning the EU's disapproval. Doubtless, the Europeans thought that little Austria would quickly buckle. But the imposition of sanctions turned out to have quite the opposite effect. Austrians who had no love for Haider rallied round the government. There was deep anger. The EU saw that it had overreached itself and worried about the effects on the forthcoming Danish referendum – rightly as it turned out. A face-saving formula was adopted and after a report by three 'wise men' the sanctions were quietly dropped on 12 September 2000.*

The bungled attempt to override the wishes of the Austrian people in order to achieve a national government of a political complexion pleasing to the EU member states was a highly significant indication of the shape of the future. Moreover, Chancellor Schröder's cack-handed threat levelled at Italy, at the height of the Austrian crisis, to the effect that similar action would be taken to stop the right winning power there did not go unnoticed – particularly in Italy.†

The truth is that Silvio Berlusconi and his Forza Italia party, with the Northern League and the National Alliance parties, represent everything that the left-wing power-brokers of the EU fear and loathe. Signor Berlusconi is a dynamic businessman, not a recycled bureaucrat. He and his partners are strongly anti-communist. His programme is based upon liberating enterprise from state control. The House of Freedom coalition is a moderate conservative grouping, whose approach is similar to that of con-

---

* The three were: Martti Ahtisaari, the former Finnish President; Jochen Frowein, Director of the Max Planck Institute in Heidelberg; and Marcelino Oreja, the former Spanish Foreign Minister.
† *The Times*, 19 February 2000.

servatives in Britain and the United States. Yet it is too much for the left-of-centre Euro-federalists, who deeply distrust Signor Berlusconi's commitment to their grand project of burying nation states in a superstate. A concerted Europe-wide media campaign of vilification, the like of which I have rarely seen in politics, was launched against Signor Berlusconi to intimidate the Italian electorate into backing the left. I was infuriated by this, and lent my support to him and his colleagues in an open letter I wrote to the Italian press. It concluded: 'This is not the first such Europe-wide attempt to bully national electorates. But it may turn out to be the last – if Italy refused to bend the knee.'

The piece was widely reported and perhaps it did some good. At any rate, Italians voted heavily for the House of Freedom parties, and the Berlusconi government, as long as it keeps together, now has a real chance of turning Italy into an efficient, prosperous, modern state.

In the case of Italy – a major European country, one of the original Six – the EU's predominantly left-wing governments were prudent enough to refrain from direct threats of sanctions. But we should not assume that this would be the attitude if a smaller country – another Austria – dared to vote in parties that the EU thought undesirable. Indeed, the EU has now given itself still more power to undermine or override political parties and democratic choices it does not like. It was at Amsterdam that the Council of EU Ministers was given the authority to decide on 'the existence of a serious and persistent breach' of the principles of 'liberty, democracy, respect for human rights' etc. by a member state, and then to suspend some or all of that member state's rights (Article 7).* At Nice, Europe's power to threaten those whose policies its majority of governments did not like was significantly extended, by qualifying the language used at Amsterdam so that now the Council of Ministers might decide that there was 'a clear *risk* of a serious breach' (emphasis added). Thus, by degrees, the accretion of central powers and the draining of national democratic choice proceed.

---

* Actually, the EU did not quite dare to do this in the case of Austria – knowing that no such breach existed – and so used the device of 'bilateral' sanctions

The counterpart of the EU's lack of democracy is a lack of accountability. There is simply not sufficient public interest in the conduct of European politicians and high officials to place it under continuing effective scrutiny. The resulting remoteness is a recipe for abuse of power, misuse of public funds, and in some cases straightforward corruption.

One has only to read the damning conclusions of the 'Committee of Independent Experts' on allegations of fraud, mismanagement and nepotism of 15 March 1999. They speak of:

> a loss of control by the political authorities over the Administration that they are supposed to run (paragraph 9.2.2)
>
> instances where Commissioners or the Commission as a whole bear responsibility for instances of fraud, irregularities or mismanagement in their services or areas of responsibility (paragraph 9.2.3)
>
> a 'state within a state' . . . allowed to develop (paragraph 9.2.8)
>
> use [of] Community funds (sometimes illegally) to ensure a match between the objectives to be achieved and the resources to be employed (paragraph 9.4.3)
>
> [its] becoming difficult to find anyone who has even the slightest sense of responsibility (paragraph 9.4.25).

None of this is at all surprising. If you combine within a single system centralised decision-making, a culture of secrecy, and the elimination of genuine debate about ends and means you can hardly complain at the ensuing graft and incompetence. This is not going to change even if you seek out and appoint people of the highest morals and deepest standards of probity. And it will not be cured either by technical and procedural reforms of the sort since put forward by European Commission Vice-President Neil Kinnock.

Indeed, as is the way in Europe, the problems created by extensions of unaccountable central power always seem to justify further such extensions in order to deal with them. Thus the response to the scandalous levels of fraud in the EU has been to

---

by all individual EU countries to achieve the same end. A typical European fiddle.

propose the creation of a European system of criminal law and procedure to deal with fraud against the Community budget, in effect the kernel of a federal criminal justice system. This system, known to the initiated as *'Corpus Juris'*, would create a European Public Prosecutor with a delegate in each capital city. A set of special national courts working under common European rules would issue 'European arrest warrants' and could incarcerate potential defendants for extended periods without trial at the request of the Prosecutor.*

Jury trials would be excluded from these special courts, and the proposed Europe-wide definitions of the offences of fraud are both unclear in scope and considerably wider than would be recognised under British law. There is little doubt that this is intended to be the thin end of a very thick wedge. It should be understood in the light of the provisions in the Treaty of Amsterdam which commit EU members to an 'approximation, where necessary, of rules on criminal matters' and to 'common action on judicial cooperation'.† All these proposals are still at an early stage. But with the decision at the Tampere summit in October 1999 to set up EUROJUST – a body of prosecutors, magistrates and police officers detached from each member state – and with the current proposals to create a 'European judicial space', there is little doubt that they will in one form or another materialise.‡ Considered alongside calls for the expansion of Europol into a Europe-wide version of the FBI, this is very much the shape of things to come – when the Euro-federalists eventually get their way.§

---

* The European Commission has opportunistically sought to gain rapid acceptance of these proposals on the back of the events of 11 September. But, as Martin Howe observes, '. . . current proposals for an EU-wide arrest warrant will do little to assist in the fight against terrorism and will serve to undermine the already inadequate substantive safeguards under the European Extradition Convention'. *Tackling Terrorism*, p.20.

† Articles 29 and 31 of the Treaty on European Union, as amended and renumbered by the Treaty of Amsterdam.

‡ Proposal for a Council Regulation establishing a general framework for Community activities to facilitate the implementation of a European judicial area in civil matters, presented by the Commission on 5 June 2001.

§ In the SPD document 'Responsibility for Europe' (30 April 2000), Chancellor Schröder suggested that Europol be developed into 'an operative European

I conclude that:

- There is no way in which the EU can be made 'democratic': the pursuit of this illusory aim is in fact likely further to reduce the power of national electorates
- Equally, there exists no programme of reforms which can make the EU's politicians and officials genuinely accountable
- The best that can be done at present by Britain and those other member states which value their own democracy is to oppose the bullying and abuse of procedure which the EU favours – no matter against whom those tactics are levelled.

EUROPEAN CURRENCY – PROGRAMME FOR A SUPERSTATE

The most substantial manifestation of the design to create a fully-fledged superstate so far is the European single currency.* This project is essentially political, rather than economic. The power to issue a currency is a fundamental attribute of sovereignty, not some symbolic or technical matter. Indeed, it is not for nothing that in past centuries infringement of that right by counterfeiters was reckoned as something akin to treason and punished accordingly. The truth is not concealed by the modern Continental pro-

---

police force, equipped with executive authority'. In the speech he made in Paris on 28 May 2001, M. Jospin endorsed a similar approach.

---

* For a discussion of the specific implications of the euro for Britain, see Chapter Ten. The timetable for introduction of the euro by the twelve participating states – Belgium, Germany, Greece, Spain, France, Ireland, Italy, Luxembourg, The Netherlands, Austria, Portugal, Finland – is as follows: the European Central Bank (ECB) was set up by the end of 1998; conversion rates between the euro and the old national currencies (which alone circulated) were fixed on 1 January 1999, with the ECB setting a single interest rate; between 1 January 2002 and 30 June 2002 there will be dual circulation of both euros and national currencies; by 30 June 2002 national currencies are to have been withdrawn from circulation.

ponents of the euro, who on this as on other related matters have been a great deal franker than their British counterparts.

> We want the political unification of Europe. Without monetary union there cannot be political union, and vice versa (Ex-Chancellor Helmut Kohl)*

> The introduction of the common European currency was in no way just an economic decision. Monetary union is demanding that we Europeans press ahead resolutely with political integration (Chancellor Gerhard Schröder)†

> The introduction of the single currency is not primarily an economic but rather a sovereign and thus eminently political act (German Foreign Minister Joschka Fischer)‡

> The Council of Finance Ministers of the eleven euro-zone nations will become the 'economic government of Europe' (Former French Finance Minister Dominique Strauss-Kahn)§

> The single currency is the greatest abandonment of sovereignty since the foundation of the European Community by the Treaty of Rome . . . When it is asserted that the step must also lead to political union, something logical is being said and something fundamental is being forgotten. The conclusion is logical because it is impossible to leave it at that and take no further steps. It is forgotten, though, that this decision is of an essentially political nature, because it is the abandonment of one of the distinguishing marks of sovereignty which define our nation states (Former Spanish Prime Minister Felipe Gonzalez)¶

---

* Quoted in *The Times*, 6 November 1997.
† Speech at the Bundesbank, Frankfurt, 30 August 1999, quoted in the *Financial Times*, 31 August 1999.
‡ Speech to the European Parliament, 12 January 1999, quoted in the *Daily Telegraph*, 13 January 1999.
§ Interview in *The Times*, 1 January 1999.
¶ Article in *Frankfurter Allgemeine Zeitung*, 27 May 1998.

We now need an economic government of the euro-zone (French
Prime Minister Lionel Jospin)*

All these people ought to know. They should be heeded. Without the power to issue and so to control one's own currency –
and by 'control' I include the generally desirable aim of letting it
float freely – a state can no longer be said to determine its own
economic policy. It can no longer set its interest rates in line with
monetary conditions and other requirements: instead, interest rates
are set for it by a supra-national authority according to supra-
national criteria. A state's ability to cope with economic shocks
or to respond to economic cycles is thus very much constrained.
It is, consequently, forced to rely on fiscal means alone to ride out
difficulties.

But precisely because there has been a fundamental shift of
power and authority to the supra-national (in this case European)
level, individual countries using the single currency are not going
to be allowed to spend, tax and borrow as they and their electors
like. It is an illusion to think that fiscal and monetary authority
can ever in the long run be politically separated – after all, even
'independent' national banks which set interest rates are ultimately
responsible to the political institutions from which they derive
their authority. The Maastricht Treaty's assurance that 'a member
state shall not be liable for or assume the commitment of central
governments, regional, local or other public authorities, other
bodies governed by public law or public undertakings of another
member state' is not where matters will or can end.† There will
not just be a single currency in euro-land: there will be a single
balance sheet. Already we see this in the form of the so-called
Stability Pact, effectively imposed by Germany as a condition for
allowing European economic basket-cases into the euro. The Pact
places limits beyond the Maastricht criteria on what countries can
borrow and imposes heavy fines for those which break the rules.
Combined with the drive for tax harmonisation stemming from a
distorted interpretation of the Single Market, such pressures on

---

* Speech in Paris, 28 May 2001.
† Article 104b.

individual countries to hand major fiscal decisions to the European authorities will eventually turn member states into more or less the equivalent of local authorities. Thus the vision of Maastricht's 'Europe of the Regions' will be fulfilled.

I believe that:

- The European single currency is bound to fail, economically, politically and indeed socially, though the timing, occasion and full consequences are all necessarily still unclear
- It therefore follows that countries which have not already joined the project would be well-advised to keep out
- This failure cannot be rectified by American or other international attempts to rescue the euro, because the fundamentals of euro-land are irremediably unsound
- The most important priority for the non-Europeans is to see that European policies do as little harm as possible now or later to the world economy.

EUROPEAN ARMY – PROGRAMME FOR A 'SUPERPOWER'

As I have noted, the European superstate is also designed by its architects to become a superpower. The roots of this aspiration lie deep in French soil. France has for many years wanted to see an alternative military power to an American-led NATO. The European Union's plans for a separate integrated European defence have provided the French with a unique opportunity to achieve this goal. These plans only saw the light of day, however, because Tony Blair's government has reversed the traditional British – and indeed its own earlier – opposition to them. It did so at Saint-Malo in December 1998, not for any identifiable security consideration but rather in order to burnish its Euro-credentials at a time when the retreating prospect of sterling's entering EMU was calling them into question.

At Saint-Malo the British and French governments broke new ground by agreeing that the EU 'must have the capacity for autonomous action, backed by credible military forces, the means to decide to use them, and a readiness to do so, in order to respond to international crises'. To this end the EU would 'also need to have recourse to suitable military means ... *outside the NATO framework*'* (emphasis added).

In furtherance of these plans, an EU summit at Helsinki in December 1999 established the goal of being able to deploy within sixty days, and to sustain for at least a year, a force of up to corps level (sixty thousand soldiers), with the necessary command, control and intelligence capabilities, combat support services and additionally, as appropriate, air and naval elements. To provide the recruits for this European 'Rapid Reaction Force' (ERRF), a pool of some two hundred thousand troops would probably be required. Needless to say, this was a huge undertaking.

By the time of the Nice summit in December 2000, the project had taken still clearer shape. The Presidency Report on European Security and Defence Policy, whose conclusions were endorsed at Nice, contains some deliberate ambiguities required for British domestic consumption and inserted at British request in order to reassure the Pentagon. Thus on the one hand, the Report notes of the plan: 'This does not involve the creation of a European army.' Yet on the other hand at every stage it makes clear that something very like a European army is indeed involved. It says that the aim 'is to give the European Union the means of playing its role fully on the international stage'. It emphasises that among the Rapid Reaction Force's tasks will be to act as 'combat forces in crisis management, including peacemaking'. It states that there will be established on a permanent basis a European Political and Security Committee, a Military Committee, and a Military Staff. Among the operating principles mentioned are 'preservation of the Union's autonomy in decision making'.

What does all this verbiage really mean? It seems to me to suggest very strongly that far from serving to strengthen the European contribution to NATO, the EU countries under French inspiration have deliberately embarked upon the creation of at best an alternative and at worst a rival military structure and armed forces.

---

* Joint Declaration issued at the British–French Summit, Saint-Malo, France, 3–4 December 1998.

Of course, there are limits to what the Europeans are likely to achieve acting alone. But these limits are ones of practicality, not of policy. Thus it would in practice be impossible for European forces to be deployed effectively in a 'peacemaking', i.e. combat, role – as in the Balkans for example – without depending upon US intelligence, heavy-lift capabilities and high-tech weaponry. In this sense, the European Rapid Reaction Force may well have a short and undistinguished career – neither European (it will be dependent on US support), nor Rapid Reaction (it will not be able to deploy quickly), nor indeed much of a Force. And the old problems of all multinational intervention forces – different languages, decision by committee, divided authority, competing objectives – will be gravely worsened by the absence of what still makes NATO effective, namely American leadership.

Tony Blair, on his first visit to Washington to see the new President, gave Mr Bush (as the latter confirmed) various assurances about the new force, among which were that 'the planning [of ERRF operations] would take place within NATO' and even that there would be 'a joint command'.* Similarly, Geoff Hoon, the British Defence Secretary, has promised that 'the EU will not divert resources from NATO, duplicate its arrangements, create separate military structures, or conduct operational planning'.†

I do not understand how these assurances can be squared with what the text of the agreement endorsed at Nice actually says. Nor do I see how it is compatible with the objectives of the French and other backers of the project. General Jean-Pierre Kelche, France's Chief of Defence Staff, has stated that 'there is no [NATO] right of first refusal. If the EU works properly, it will start working on crises at a very early stage, well before the situation escalates. NATO has nothing to do with this. At a certain stage the Euro-

---

* At the press conference given by President George W. Bush and Prime Minister Tony Blair at Camp David on 23 February 2001, President Bush said: '[Mr Blair] assured me that the European defence would in no way undermine NATO. He also assured me that there would be a joint command, that the planning would take place within NATO, and that should all NATO not wish to go on a mission, that would then serve as a catalyst for the defence forces moving on their own.'

† *Daily Telegraph*, 28 March 2001.

peans would decide to conduct a military operation. Either the Americans would come or not.'* Hubert Védrine, the French Foreign Minister, has called for the EU force to have its own 'elements of operational planning' and 'its own capability', while General Gustav Hagglund, the Finnish Chairman of the EU's permanent Military Committee, has declared the ERRF to be an 'independent body' and not 'a subsidiary of NATO'.†

The French and those who think like them have been so insistent on achieving an autonomous European defence capability precisely because they see it as constituting a vital attribute of a new European superpower which will rival the United States. So how Mr Blair imagines that he can honour the assurances which he gave to President Bush I do not know. But if he fails to do so he will turn out, through one foolish and frivolous initiative, to have done more harm to the trans-Atlantic relationship than anything since the Suez Crisis of 1956.

As for President Bush, I believe that he was wise at this first meeting to take what Mr Blair said at face value. He carefully phrased his 'support for [Mr Blair's] point of view' on the basis of the specific assurances which he had received. But if I had been the British Prime Minister, I would have taken equal note of Mr Bush's answer at the same Washington press conference to a question about China, whose intentions the Americans have, of course, every reason to doubt: 'I think you've always got to begin with trust until proven otherwise.' The operative word is 'until'.

We shall soon see who is right. If the Europeans truly wish to improve their NATO contribution they can show it simply enough. They can increase defence expenditure. They can move swiftly to establish professional armed forces, like those of the UK. And they can acquire more advanced technology. Indeed, unless that happens soon the gulf between the European and US capabilities will yawn so wide that it will not be possible to share the same battlefield.

Alas, I do not think that sharing battlefields with our American friends – but rather disputing global primacy with them – is what

---

* *Daily Telegraph*, 28 March 2001.
† *Sunday Times*, 4 March 2001; *Daily Telegraph*, 12 April 2001.

European defence plans are truly about. And Britain should never have been party to them.

It is already clear that:

- The fundamental impulse towards a separate European defence is political rather than military
- That impulse, stemming as it does from the French, is also one of rivalry not collaboration with an American-led NATO
- The chances of Britain's transforming the initiative into something different are now slim – though we should still try
- Any European army (by whatever name) will be of limited effectiveness and heavily dependent on the US
- But the project could still damage the cohesion of the Alliance, as senior figures in the US administration have warned
- Unless we can be sure of preventing that, Britain must pull out of Europe's misguided military schemes.

A STATE IS BORN?

In their different ways, Europe's plans for a single currency to rival the dollar, its furtive but rapid moves to create its own armed forces to substitute for those of NATO, its ambition to create a common judicial area which will intrude upon national legal systems, and the current project of devising a European Constitution at the centre of which will be an elected European government all betoken one of the most ambitious political projects of modern times. Its authors are fully aware of this. The obvious parallel is with the creation of the United of States of America. Hence the use by Euro-enthusiasts of the expression 'United States of Europe'.*

The parallel is both deeply flawed and deeply significant. It is flawed because the United States was based from its inception on

---

* Helmut Kohl in particular has been at the forefront of calls for a United States of Europe. For example: 'By the end of this century, the foundation stone will have been laid for a United States of Europe' (speech at Harvard University, reported in the *Boston Globe*, 8 June 1990).

a common language, culture and values – Europe has none of these things. It is also flawed because the United States was forged in the eighteenth century and transformed into a truly federal system in the nineteenth century through *events*, above all through the necessities and outcomes of war. By contrast, 'Europe' is the result of *plans*. It is, in fact, a classic utopian project, a monument to the vanity of intellectuals, a programme whose inevitable destiny is failure: only the scale of the final damage done is in doubt.

But it is also, for these very reasons, significant to Europeans and non-Europeans alike. It seems very likely that the drive for a United States of Europe, a European superstate, is now unstoppable. Of course, something may still occur to derail it. The Americans might call the European bluff on plans to provide an alternative to NATO. The single currency might be buffeted by external shocks and internal dissent, and so collapse. There is even a slight possibility that in either France or Germany – the countries that matter in this respect – the rush to abandon national democratic institutions in favour of bureaucratic European ones might be halted by electoral pressures. Nothing is inevitable – even in euro-land. But I very much doubt whether any of these things will in fact occur. The momentum is just too strong.

It remains for the non-European world, above all America, to try to reduce the harm the new Europe is set to do – and then when the folly falls, as through lack of common interests it finally will, to help pick up the bits. The choice that remains for Britain, though, is rather different – as I shall now explain.

CHAPTER 10

Britain and Europe – Time to Renegotiate

BRITAIN'S EUROPEAN EXPERIENCE

It is frequently said, indeed it has become quite a mantra, that Britain missed the European 'train' and thus was unable to exercise the requisite influence upon its eventual destination.* The lesson drawn from this, naturally enough, is that Britain must from now on take part in every new European venture in order to avoid that happening again, and so as to exert maximum 'influence'. Yet the more we learn about and have the opportunity to reflect upon the history of the European project, the less convincing even the first part of that thesis appears.

The story of the modern drive for European integration, although as I have noted above it had significant precedents, has

---

* For example, former British Foreign Secretary Sir Geoffrey (now Lord) Howe in a speech to the Bow Group at the Conservative Party Conference in 1990: 'The next European train is about to leave, for a still undefined destination, but certainly in the direction of some form of EMU. Shall Britain be in the driver's cab this time or in the rear carriage?' (*The Times*, 12 October 1990). Also, Chancellor Helmut Kohl, addressing a meeting of the German Cabinet in 1992 following Denmark's rejection of the Maastricht Treaty: 'Everything must be done so that the European train is not halted' (*Daily Telegraph*, 5 June 1992).

really to begin in the 1950s.* The attitude of the British government towards the European project in the post-war years was, truth to tell, somewhat ambiguous. In particular, the words of Winston Churchill can be subjected to different interpretations.

On many occasions Churchill waxed lyrical about the prospects of European unity. But it was less clear what exactly he envisaged would be Britain's role. At The Hague in May 1946 Churchill thus expressed the hope 'that the Western democracies of Europe may draw together in ever closer amity and ever closer association'. He saw 'no reason why, under the guardianship of the world organisation [i.e. the UN], there should not ultimately arise the United States of Europe, both those of the East and those of the West, which will unify this Continent in a manner never known since the fall of the Roman Empire'. Yet in the same speech he noted that 'the affairs of Great Britain and the British Commonwealth and Empire are becoming ever more closely interwoven with those of the United States, and that an underlying unity of thought and conviction increasingly pervades the English-speaking world'. How were these grand and opposing concepts in practice to be reconciled?†

A year later, speaking in the Albert Hall in London, Churchill again addressed the same theme and indeed talked of the 'spiritual conception of Europe'. He went so far as to say that 'if Europe united is to be a living force, Britain will have to play her full part as a member of the European family'. And, in what must surely be considered a rhetorical flourish from this independent-minded patriot, he even warned that 'without a United Europe there is no sure prospect of world government'. Yet when it came to practicalities, the security architecture which he favoured in his speech turned out to be quite different:

---

* What follows is based upon William Kenway's pamphlet 'European Union – The Moment of Truth', amended reprint from *European Journal*, 5/8–9, 1998, and upon the account of Britain's first application to join the Common Market in 1961 contained in the official papers now reproduced in Lionel Bell, *The Throw that Failed: Britain's Original Application to Join the Common Market* (London: New European Publications Ltd, 1995), pp.140–96.

† Speech to the States-General of The Netherlands, The Hague, 9 May 1946.

In the Constitution [of the UN] agreed at San Francisco, direct provision was made for regional organisations to be formed. United Europe will form one major regional entity. There is the United States with all its dependencies; there is the Soviet Union; there is the British Empire and Commonwealth; and there is Europe, with which Great Britain is profoundly blended. Here are the four main pillars of the world Temple of Peace.*

In truth, even in his most visionary moods, Churchill does not seem to have envisaged Britain's ever being part of the United States of Europe, however much he thought that she should encourage and contribute to it. As early as 1930, writing in the New York *Saturday Evening Post* with regard to then current federalist ideas, he expressed his underlying conviction:

The attitude of Great Britain towards unification or 'federal links' would, in the first instance, be determined by her dominant conception of a United British Empire. Every step that tends to make Europe more prosperous and more peaceful is conducive to British interests ... We have our own dream and our own task. We are with Europe but not of it. We are linked, but not comprised. We are interested and associated, but not absorbed.†

In the post-war years this remained his view. Nor should it be dismissed as short-sighted or unrealistic. Churchill was quite right at this time to see Britain as enjoying a unique international position that also gave her unique strengths. She lay within three interlocking circles – those of the Commonwealth, the Anglo–American relationship, and Europe. And that was an excellent strategic vantage point, exploitation of which required a large measure of freedom of action. Any yielding up of British sovereignty to a federalising Europe was thus necessarily ruled out. So it is doubly understandable that once Churchill returned as Prime Minister in 1951 he toned down his European rhetoric and con-

---

* Speech in the Albert Hall, London, 14 May 1947.
† Quoted in Timothy Bainbridge (ed.), *The Penguin Companion to European Union* (London: Penguin, 2000), p.43.

tinued the approach of the previous Labour government, keeping Britain out of both the European Coal and Steel Community and the European Defence Community. Accordingly, in terms very similar to those of his article of 1930, we find Churchill speaking in the House of Commons in 1953 posing a rhetorical question:

> Where do we stand? We are not members of the European Defence Community, nor do we intend to be merged in a Federal European system. We feel we have a special relation to both. This can be expressed by prepositions, by the preposition 'with' but not 'of' – we are with them, but not of them.*

Nor, incidentally, did Churchill's views towards Europe mellow into nostalgia towards the end of his life. Andrew Roberts, one of the best historians of the period, notes how 'by 1962 Field Marshal Montgomery found [Churchill] sitting up in bed smoking a cigar, shouting for more brandy, and protesting against Britain's proposed entry into the Common Market'.†

But by then the world had changed in three important respects. The first, and most significant, was the jolt that had been given to British self-confidence by the Suez fiasco of 1956. One can argue the pros and cons of the Suez operation, and I well remember taking part in those debates at the time.‡ But the conclusion drawn by most of the British political classes was understandable – that Britain could no longer rely on the United States and that, as the Commonwealth adopted a diminishing political importance, it was necessary instead to join the European Common Market or, more precisely, the European Economic Community (EEC). The second contributory factor was the recognition that the EEC 'Six' (France, West Germany, Italy, Belgium, Holland and Luxembourg) were making greater economic progress than anyone had previously predicted. In retrospect, this hardly seems surprising: national

---

* Speech opening a debate on Foreign Affairs in the House of Commons, Hansard, 11 May 1953, Col. 891.

† Andrew Roberts, 'Lies, Damn Lies', *Sunday Times*, 28 July 1996. I am also grateful to Mr Roberts for helping me locate these various Churchill texts.

‡ See the account in *The Path to Power*, pp.87–91.

economies devastated by war, in which the workforce is well-educated and highly motivated, are almost bound to enjoy very healthy rates of growth as they recover. But at the time, Britain, bogged down by restrictive practices that had increased in wartime, envied the European record. Europe seemed to offer a way out of our difficulties, one all the more attractive because it avoided facing up to the need to make painful reforms. The third factor, following on from this, was that the European Free Trade Area (EFTA), in which we had placed high hopes, was quite soon widely – and fairly or unfairly – seen to be something of a disappointment.

Harold Macmillan, Prime Minister after Anthony Eden's resignation in the wake of Suez, was in any case an enthusiast for Europe. Yet he was a subtle and pragmatic one. His appreciation of geopolitical realities even now deserves respect, whatever one thinks of his conclusion. This is illustrated, for example, by his statement to Cabinet in April 1961 after his return from discussions in Washington. The minutes (thus in indirect speech) record the Prime Minister's sentiments:

> In recent years, the communist bloc had been gaining ground at the expense of the West and, if this was to be checked, the leading countries of the Western world would need to draw more closely together. There was, however, a risk that current developments in Europe would tend in the opposite direction; for, if the countries of the Common Market formed a close political association under French leadership, this would create a further political division in Europe and would also have a disruptive effect within the Atlantic community. This might be averted if the United Kingdom, together with some of the Seven [i.e. EFTA], could join the political association of the Six and help to build in Europe a stable political structure which would prevent France now, and Germany later, from attaining too dominant a position.*

Macmillan encapsulated in these words what might be called the Atlanticist argument for Europe. It was one which had just been pressed on him particularly hard by the United States. And

---

* Quoted by Bell, *The Throw that Failed*, Appendix D, p.179.

it would become the basis of that steady pressure which Britain has faced – at least until very recently – from America to integrate itself ever further into Europe.

In some respects the argument was persuasive. It was true, after all, that the West needed to hold together in the face of Soviet encroachments. A prosperous and cooperative (Western) Europe could from this point of view help to win the Cold War against the East. In Washington it seemed then and later that Britain, by throwing her weight behind that cooperation (and incidentally by benefiting from the resultant prosperity), could be a crucial counterweight to France, then under the wayward and prickly leadership of General de Gaulle. The echoes of that period reverberated until very recently around the American State Department. I strongly suspect that they still do in the British Foreign Office and in Downing Street – long after Anglo-Saxon hopes and Gallic fears that Britain could reshape Europe became largely redundant.

At this time, therefore, Paris almost as much as Moscow was seen by Washington as 'the problem'. But, paradoxically perhaps, it was de Gaulle and not Kennedy, or even Macmillan, who best grasped the fundamentals of the situation. De Gaulle did not particularly like Britain but he understood us quite well. And perhaps because he was less of a Euro-idealist and more of a nationalist than Macmillan, he perceived where divergent national destinies should lead. As he now told the British Prime Minister, he was 'against an integrated Europe; this was neither practicable, sensible, nor desirable, and the result would be a materialist, soulless mass, with no idealism left . . . [T]he national identity of the European nations should be preserved'. And within such a framework of nation states Britain would always be the odd man out. As de Gaulle put it in the course of the famous press conference in January 1963 at which he explained his renewed 'Non' to British entry:

England is . . . insular, maritime, linked through its trade, markets, and food supply to very diverse and often very distant countries. Its activities are essentially industrial and commercial, and only slightly agricultural. It has . . . very marked and original customs and traditions. In short, the nature, structure and economic context

365

of England differ profoundly from those of the other States of the Continent . . . It is foreseeable that the cohesion of all its members, who would be very numerous and very diverse, would not hold for long and that in the end there would appear a colossal Atlantic Community under American dependence and leadership which would soon completely swallow up the European Community.*

De Gaulle was half right – and from Britain's point of view it was the more important half. By her history and her interests Britain is indeed a fundamentally different kind of nation state to those which are involved in 'building' Europe. One would have to add, as de Gaulle himself could not, that it was more than economics that was at issue here. It was Britain's long history of continuous constitutional development, the respect in which her institutions were held, the honesty of her politicians and the integrity of her judges, the fact that not since the Norman Conquest had she known occupation, and that neither Nazism nor communism had ever gained a grip on her political life – all these things marked Britain out from Continental Europe. But, I repeat, the General was right in so far as his pride allowed: Britain *is* different. That is why Britain is still repeatedly at odds with the other European countries, however determinedly cooperative British politicians wish to be.

De Gaulle was, however, wrong in another respect. He imagined that his own principled and patriotic, if sometimes wanton and cantankerous, defence of France's national interests would be matched by his successors. He sincerely believed in a *Europe des états*, a Europe of sovereign states. But federalism, not Gaullism, was the destination to which the Euro-train was bound.

France's veto of Britain's entry into the Common Market seemed a bitter blow at the time. Almost no one in Britain – even those who were somewhat sceptical of the benefits of entry – thought that de Gaulle was right. His action was just deemed childish, insulting and irrational. After the initial annoyance had

---

* Charles de Gaulle, speaking at a press conference, 14 January 1963. Quoted by Charles G. Cogan, *Charles de Gaulle: A Brief Biography with Documents* (Boston: St Martin's Press, 1996), pp.200–1.

subsided, the desire to join the Common Market again began to flourish with renewed vigour among the British political class. It could even be argued that if de Gaulle was so determined to keep us out, was that not proof of the beneficial consequences of being in? What did he know that previous British leaders had not? So it was that Harold Wilson's Labour government made a new application in 1967, which was again rejected by France.

I had become a Member of Parliament at the general election of 1959, so I was in a position to follow these events with an educated if not an expert interest. During the whole of this period, I fully shared the prevailing view that Britain's national interest – particularly our economic interest – required joining the EEC on the best available terms. I also thought that it was important to maintain our links with and obligations to the Commonwealth. As someone who had a warm regard for Reggie Maudling,* the architect of EFTA, I felt that the merits of that modest organisation were insufficiently appreciated. But I was still for membership of the Common Market.

Ted Heath, who beat Reggie Maudling to become leader of the Conservative Party in 1965, and for whom I voted, was a passionate Euro-enthusiast. Like Macmillan, but with greater zeal and perhaps less finesse, he had emerged from his experiences in the services in wartime convinced that European unity was vital for peace and prosperity. Once Ted was in charge of the party, and if he won a general election, it was certain that Britain would strive to join the European Common Market with greater determination than ever. And with the replacement of de Gaulle by President Georges Pompidou in 1969, entry suddenly became possible.

When Britain did actually join the European Economic Community in January 1973 I was a member of Cabinet, as Education Secretary. I continued to view the decision as necessary and right.

---

* Reginald Maudling (1917–79), President of the Board of Trade 1959–61, Colonial Secretary 1961–62, Chancellor of the Exchequer 1962–64, Home Secretary 1970–72. The Maudling Committee, appointed by the Organisation for European Economic Cooperation (OEEC) in 1959, laid the foundations for the establishment of the European Free Trade Association (EFTA) in 1960.

It was clear to all of us that the conditions, particularly as regards fisheries and agriculture, could be criticised. But the wider economic benefits seemed to outweigh the drawbacks, and above all it was imperative to break through the European tariff wall so that our goods could be sold freely to the markets of the Six, with their 190 million consumers.

Yet the forces which would push Europe in a direction other than that which we hoped were in truth much stronger than we then believed. We were, I am afraid it now appears, a little naïve. There is all the less excuse because we were warned. In retrospect, Enoch Powell's assertions during these years that what was involved by entry into the Common Market was not ultimately a matter of economics but rather an unacceptable loss of sovereignty turned out to be absolutely right.*

The most important reason to support EEC entry was, as I have noted, access to European markets. In those days, before the Uruguay Round of trade negotiations in the 1980s and 1990s resulted in large worldwide tariff cuts, the European external tariffs averaged some 12 per cent. So exclusion from the European customs union represented a significant obstacle to British trade. By contrast, other benefits which, it was alleged, would also follow even then seemed more nebulous. It was, for example, argued that our industries would become more efficient as greater competition within the Market helped eradicate restrictive practices, and weakened trade union obstruction. In fact, these benefits did not materialise at all: indeed, Britain never had worse industrial relations than in the years immediately after our entry into the EEC.

Why was there, then, not more and better debate about the merits and drawbacks of entry? There are, I now think, three main reasons. First, as is clear from official documents released under the 'thirty year rule', such debate was considered irrelevant by those with direct responsibility for the negotiations. The basis on which Britain joined was that we could hope to change nothing in Europe: we just had to take what we were offered. In

---

* Enoch Powell (1912–98), Conservative MP 1950–74, Ulster Unionist MP 1974–87, Minister of Health 1960–63, Shadow Minister of Defence 1965–68.

his account of the negotiations of 1970–72, the late Sir Con O'Neill wrote:

> ... the whole of our negotiations were peripheral, accidental and secondary. The general movement of events in 1969 and 1970 revived the opportunity, and was much more important than the negotiations themselves. What mattered was to get into the Community, and thereby restore our position at the centre of European affairs which, since 1958, we had lost. The negotiations were concerned only with the means of achieving this objective at an acceptable price. They therefore had to be concerned with the Community as we found it, as it happened to be. None of its policies was essential to us; many of them were objectionable.*

No doubt those involved behaved honourably by their own lights. But I have to say that such is not in my experience the best way to get a reasonable deal in Europe, or anywhere else for that matter.

Secondly, for all the reasons which had been reiterated since the late 1950s, there seemed no alternative to the EEC – neither the Commonwealth, nor EFTA, nor any other trading partner fitted the bill. In Britain there was, underlying this perception, a strange, largely self-induced sense of impotence and isolation. The country had lost its direction with its mission. Here, it seemed to many, was another chance to find our destiny and to affect the destinies of others.

And third, both in 1970–72 (the debates about entry) and in 1975 (when the referendum was held to decide whether Britain should stay or leave) a series of highly misleading statements were made about what was involved. It would be pleasant to avoid referring to what was said. But an unvarnished assessment makes that impossible. I would just quote three instances:

> There will not be a blueprint for a federal Europe ... What is more, those members of the Community who want a federal system,

---

* Sir Con O'Neill, *Britain's Entry into the European Community: Report on the Negotiations of 1970–1972* (London: Frank Cass, 2000), p.355.

but who know the views of Her Majesty's Government and the Opposition parties here, are prepared to forgo their federal desires so that Britain should be a member.*

The Community is no federation of provinces or counties. It constitutes a Community of great and established nations, each with its own personality and traditions ... There is no question of any erosion of essential national sovereignty ... All the countries concerned recognise that an attempt to impose a majority view in a case where one or more members considered their vital national interests to be at stake would imperil the very fabric of the Community.†

There was a threat to employment in Britain from the movement in the Common Market towards an Economic and Monetary Union. This could have forced us to accept fixed exchange rates for the pound, restricting industrial growth and so putting jobs at risk. This threat has been removed.‡

Each of these assertions has since turned out to be untrue, for reasons that I have described at some length in the previous chapter. Whether those who made these statements believed them to be true at the time I do not know.

Elsewhere I have set out in detail my own dealings with the European Community as Britain's Prime Minister between 1979

---

* Edward Heath, speech to the House of Commons, Hansard, 25 February 1970, Col. 1221.

† White Paper on *The United Kingdom and the European Communities*, HMSO Cmnd. 4715, July 1971, pp.8–9. Interestingly, Sir Edward Heath in a valedictory personal statement to the House of Commons has by implication placed a rather different interpretation on the contents of his White Paper twenty years later: 'My proudest achievement was to have successfully negotiated entry of the United Kingdom into the European Community ... *In the modern world it is only right that we should share our sovereignty with our European neighbours ... I have no doubt that a united Europe is here to stay*' (emphasis added). Hansard, 9 May 2001, Col. 116.

‡ *Britain's New Deal in Europe*, official government leaflet circulated nationally at the time of the 1975 referendum campaign on membership of the European Community.

and 1990.* Here I shall simply reflect on the main issues and their significance.

The terms on which Britain joined the EEC were soon understood to have been unsatisfactory in a number of respects. That understanding – and the unhealed splits in Labour's ranks on the principle of Common Market membership – was why James Callaghan's Labour government sought to 'renegotiate' the terms of Britain's membership prior to putting these to a referendum. In fact, renegotiation secured nothing of note, and not one penny piece reduction in Britain's exorbitant financial contributions. By the time I became Prime Minister in 1979, Britain was losing out across the board.

When I entered Downing Street, Britain was indeed on the verge of becoming the EEC's largest net contributor, even though we were then only the seventh richest nation per head. After several years of bruising negotiations, during which every device of procrastination and obfuscation was employed by our partners, I succeeded at the Fontainebleau summit in 1984 in having Britain's contributions substantially and permanently reduced. We were to receive back as a rebate roughly one-third of our net contributions, and that arrangement was to continue, as it still does. The cumulative value of that rebate between 1985 and 2000 amounted to more than £28 billion.†

This prolonged struggle for a fairer deal for Britain taught me a good deal about the EEC, most of it unflattering. But, odd as it may seem to my critics and even in retrospect to me, I still remained something of a European idealist. I really did believe that the sort of tough talking and hard negotiating which I had practised since 1979 could sharply reduce, if not actually eliminate, the weaknesses which held Europe back, and that it might be possible to shape an agenda that would see it become a force for economic progress. Thus the middle period of my time as Prime Minister, broadly 1984 to 1988, was heavily taken up with the development and implementation of the European Single Market.

---

* See *The Downing Street Years*, pp.60–4, 536–59, 727–67.
† Office of National Statistics and 'European Finances: Statement on the 2000 EC Budget and measures to counter fraud and financial mismanagement', Cmnd. 4771. Figures at constant 1998 prices.

The Single Market was very much a British initiative, though that is not to say that others, with varying motives, were not also keen. Its aim was to fulfil, as we in Britain saw it, the original goals of the Treaty of Rome, which I described at this time as a treaty for 'economic liberty'. The Single Market programme would achieve this by removing 'non-tariff barriers'. These operated, for example, through different national standards on health and safety, regulations and public procurement policies which discriminated against foreign products, and over-elaborate customs procedures.

It was hoped that their elimination would provide a general boost to intra-European trade, growth and employment. Some rather ambitious figures for each were widely floated. The European Commission's Cecchini Report predicted a one-off gain of 5 per cent to Europe's GNP (with an annual increase of 1 per cent thereafter), and 5.5 million more jobs in the longer term.* These projections, however, based as they were upon estimated effects of wider competition and economies of scale, were bound to be speculative.

More important, at least as far as I was concerned, were the potential gains for Britain. With our strength in services, and since we already enjoyed a lighter and more transparent system of regulation than our European competitors, the British economy, it was expected, would specially benefit.

The Single Market programme involved some 280 measures designed to harmonise standards and specification and thus open up markets. In order to see that this ambitious undertaking took effect during the five-year implementation period, we accepted a significant increase in majority voting within the Community. Without this, the programme itself could not have been driven through in the face of vested interests in member countries whose governments would have been under immense pressure to use the veto.

Britain was the originator of and continued to be the driving force behind the Single Market. But I had at first hoped to avoid

---

* Paolo Cecchini (ed.), 1992, *The European Challenge: The Benefits of a Single European Market* (European Commission, 1988).

a new inter-governmental conference to draw up a new treaty – an occasion which I well understood might be used to cause all sorts of mischief. It was only when it was clear that the other EEC members were intent on one that I accepted that there was no other way to bring them fully on board. Even then, I sought to do everything I could to ensure that the extra powers being given to the European Commission were not misused either to pile on regulation or to threaten vital national interests. Thus a 'general statement' was solemnly made at the Luxembourg Council, at which the terms of the Single European Act were agreed, stating:

> Nothing in these provisions shall affect the right of member states to take such measures as they consider necessary for the purpose of controlling immigration from third countries, and to combat terrorism, crime, the traffic in drugs and illicit trading in works of art and antiques.*

The Single European Act can now be assessed with the benefit of a decade's hindsight, and since others have made their – often critical – assessments, I should now add mine. The first question is: did the Single Market programme achieve the economic benefits for which we hoped? On this the experts still differ.† The main difficulty, of course, in making a firm judgement arises from the inescapable weakness in all such hypothetical analyses, namely that we cannot know what might have occurred *without* the Single Market programme. But it seems clear that a good deal of the optimism has proved unfounded.

On the one hand, the Single Market programme may have worked with other independent, global factors to widen competition and open markets. But on the other, the process of harmonisation clearly also resulted in many cases in more harmful regulation – as has been exposed by that indefatigable campaigner

---

* For a fuller account of these and connected events in Europe, see *The Downing Street Years*, pp.546–59.
† For a balanced analysis see Leach, *EU Membership – What's the Bottom Line?*, pp.31–6.

against bureaucratic imbecilities, Christopher Booker.* The importance of this can only be grasped if we recall that, in principle, the new regulations affect the whole of the British economy, not just firms involved in exporting to the EEC. And only 15.5 per cent of Britain's total GDP consists of such exports.† For those firms that are either entirely involved with the domestic market or those doing business with non-EEC countries extra regulation is all loss and no corresponding gain.

In any case, and most seriously, I believe that in negotiating the Single European Act we in Britain made two understandable but undeniable mistakes. The first was to assume that the increased powers given to the Commission would cease to be used to any great extent once the Single Market programme had been completed. After all, if one accepted that the whole purpose of the changes made was to establish a properly functioning market, there was no reason to imagine that the process would be anything other than finite. True, one could not hand back vetoes that had been removed as part of the Single European Act, because governments might subvert the progress that had been made. But there was no reason to think the Commission would need to keep legislating at the same rate, let alone spread its legislative tentacles more widely.

The aim was said to be a 'level playing field'. This phrase has a reassuring ring to it, but it actually encapsulates a fundamental error about trade. Free trade allows firms in differing nations to compete. But because a 'level playing field' stops that part of competition that comes from differing regulative systems it actually reduces the gains from trade. Moreover, as every British schoolboy knows, levelling playing fields does not involve the removal of every minor lump, bump and worm-cast. At some point the reshaping and rolling, the raising and lowering, have to stop so that the game itself can continue normally. This perception, rather obvious to those of us who understood the realities of enterprise, unfortunately proved difficult for Europe's bureaucratic utopians to grasp.

---

* Christopher Booker and Richard North, *The Castle of Lies: Why Britain Must Get Out of Europe* (London: Duckworth, 1996).
† *Economist World in Figures*, 2001.

The second error, which was closely linked to the first, was then and later to take at face value the assurances we were given. I do not now believe that the European Commission or the majority of European governments were ever much interested in economics. They viewed, and still view, policy as equivalent to politics, and politics as about power – and only power. The Single Market thus appealed to these forces, which were already increasingly in the ascendant despite my successes with Britain's rebate, as a device for centralising more decision-making in the hands of Europe. And the idea that these extra powers should be limited to the purpose for which they were actually being given probably never seriously occurred to them.

The European Commission and the European Court of Justice worked together to explore, exploit and widen every loophole. And as they did so, they could rely on the support of most of the member countries and the European Parliament which both shared the federalist dream and were deeply committed to achieving that European social and economic model which I have described at some length in the previous chapter. Indeed, the drive for a 'Social Europe', so beloved of Jacques Delors,* then President of the European Commission and the man who must above all be credited (or blamed) for what has occurred, soon adopted at least as much importance as the 'Economic Europe' which the Single Market sought to create.

Thus the provisions of the Single European Act were abused in order to push corporatist and collectivist social legislation upon Britain by the back door. For example, the Working Time Directive was introduced by the Commission under Article 118a, a health and safety provision which had been inserted into the Treaty of Rome by the Single European Act. Classing the Directive as a health and safety instead of a social measure meant that it could be pushed through under qualified majority voting (QMV), bypassing Britain's veto. This stratagem was then upheld by the European Court in 1996. Such measures may sound innocuous, indeed attractive, in themselves. But they represent an

---

* Jacques Delors (b.1925), French Finance Minister 1981–84, President of the European Commission 1985–94.

unwelcome interference in Britain's affairs, and the underlying purpose is obvious – it is to reduce Britain's ability to compete successfully. Now that the Labour government has misguidedly signed up to the European Social Chapter we can expect much more of this.

Of the phrase 'Single European Market', it has thus turned out that the first two words drained a good deal of the substance from the third. Mutual recognition of standards, and indeed the setting in some cases of a minimum standard, are acceptable, *as long as* they genuinely make trade easier. But if harmonisation goes beyond this, it is merely costly, bureaucratic and illiberal. Above all, if harmonisation is taken beyond technical standards and the like, and is also applied to labour laws, social security and taxation, it is profoundly economically destructive. This is because competition between different countries to provide the most conducive international conditions for enterprise is a powerful engine of economic advance. Once smother that competition, and European governments will have no hesitation in imposing ever-increasing burdens. The result will inevitably be a flight of capital and talent to non-European countries. And on top of all that, of course, is the unacceptable frustration of democracy when an unaccountable supra-national authority decides matters which properly fall to national governments. So, given all these considerations – and given the fact that global forces for free trade have actually proved stronger than those operating within Europe – I cannot rate the European Single Act as other than a disappointment. History does not allow us to retrace our steps. But it does allow us and our successors to learn from what has transpired. This we should now do.

Already towards the end of my time as Prime Minister I was becoming increasingly concerned at the way Single Market measures were being used to impose socialist-style regulation by the back door. It was clear to me that in the struggle to liberalise and decentralise the European Community Britain was fighting a lone and perhaps unwinnable battle. One could forge short-term tactical alliances with other states on particular measures, but Britain alone was exclusively interested in making of the Community an enterprise-friendly common market: the others had different priorities. In the end one had to be unafraid of isolation and simply say 'no'. Of course, that strategy required sufficient political will and sufficient political support from my party: in the event, however, the latter was not forthcoming.

My departure from office ensured that the path to federalism could be trodden more smoothly and swiftly. And so it has been. Under my successor, whose hope it was to place Britain at the 'heart of Europe', the Maastricht Treaty was signed in February 1992. Although this secured Britain an opt-out from the single currency, it also allowed that fraught enterprise to go forward elsewhere. It established a European citizenship and a common defence policy, 'which might lead in time to a common defence'. It also established a 'Committee of the Regions', which marked a complementary approach of trying to undermine the sovereignty of nation states from below. And although Britain opted out of the Social Chapter, as I have already noted above that did not in fact prevent the European Commission from trying with some success to impose higher social costs on Britain.

Britain's attitude towards the European project has, therefore, altered much over the years, depending upon the politics of governments and the personalities of Prime Ministers. And indeed the European issue will, and must, remain one upon which the main political parties offer contrasting approaches. Yet looking back over the years since Britain became a member of the EEC in 1973, I am struck by what all these British governments, including mine, had in common. And this is perhaps as significant as the more obvious differences.

It may sound trite, but it is also true that all of us were doing our best, as we saw it from differing angles, to serve British national interests in Europe. And yet none of us was able to do more than partially improve the otherwise unfavourable terms of our membership – if that.

In 1972 Ted Heath conceded control over our fish stocks, acceptance of an appallingly wasteful CAP and excessive financial contributions in exchange for wider economic objectives. But the gain never materialised, and the pain did.

For my part, I secured a fundamental renegotiation of our financial contributions to Europe, thus righting one major problem

EU MEMBERS, EU CANDIDATE STATES
AND NON-EU MEMBERS

0   600 mil
0   600 km

ICELAND
• Reykjavik

EU states
EU candidate states

ICELAND
• Reykjavik

NORWAY
Oslo •

North
Sea

DENMARK
• Copenh:

NETHERLANDS
BELGIUM
Berlin •

IRELAND   Dublin •
BRITAIN
London •   • The Hague   GERMANY
• Brussles   P.

Paris •   LUXEMBOURG
Vi

Atlantic Ocean
SWITZERLAND   • Bern   AUSTR

FRANCE   ITALY

SLOVENIA

SPAIN   Rome •

PORTUGAL
Madrid •

Lisbon •   Mediterranean
Sea

MALTA

which Ted and Jim Callaghan after him had failed to resolve. But Britain continued and continues to bear an unfair and excessive financial burden. Pressure to reform the CAP and Europe's finances had only limited success. The one positive attempt which Britain made to make the European Community market-friendly, the Single Market, was eventually largely hijacked by the European bureaucracy. And Britain's partners then forced upon Europe an agenda of economic and monetary union against our strongly expressed wishes.

John Major, partly because of his personality and partly because of the circumstances under which he became Prime Minister, tried to defend Britain's interests through gaining special exemptions – on the single currency and the Social Chapter – rather than by holding up in principle the march to federalism, of which I think he probably disapproved. Yet the European Commission relentlessly and successfully pressed unwelcome regulations upon British industry. And the victory that John thought he had won at Maastricht through gaining support for the principle of 'subsidiarity' – which holds that nothing should be decided by an upper tier of authority that can adequately be decided by a lower one – has not actually led to Europe relinquishing one single power to national governments. Nor will it. Another betrayal.

Even Tony Blair's determinedly Euro-enthusiastic New Labour government has found that its attempts to trade on European 'good will' have all been in vain. It is still under siege on the issue of tax harmonisation – notably VAT rates, company taxation and fuel taxes. Problems lie ahead too on labour market regulation and border controls. The attempt to burnish the Blair government's European credentials by signing up to a European defence force has been used by the French to pursue their own anti-American agenda, jeopardising Mr Blair's – I believe genuine – desire to see Britain remain a dependable ally of the United States.

Reviewing all these experiences, we can see that any concessions which Britain makes, or initiatives which she promotes, in Europe are always eventually turned against her and against the original intention. The style, tone and temperament of British governments may change. But attempts to find a *modus vivendi* with Europe in any major policy area always fail sooner or later. Only credible threats of disruption – like mine in the early 1980s – yield results. And these, though they can secure important gains, are still unable to shift the direction in which Europe as a whole is going.

Moreover – and this is the crucial point now – as more and more powers pass from nation states to Brussels, it becomes steadily more difficult to deflect or veto those new measures which harm our interests. Thus over the years the number of measures subject to QMV rather than unanimity has steadily grown. Nor is this the only difficulty, for even as regards measures introduced under QMV our ability to construct a blocking minority is diminishing.* And as for the so-called Luxembourg Compromise – the understanding that if a country declared that its national interests were fundamentally at stake its veto would stand – that has now, it seems, passed entirely into oblivion.†

In recent years the Conservative Party's approach has been summarised in the slogan 'In Europe, but not run by Europe'. That is fair enough as an aspiration. But is it an available option? And if not, where does that leave us? The need now, with the 2001 general election behind us, is for a fresh look at policy towards Europe on a realistic basis, without having recourse either to wishful thinking or to slogans.

KEEP THE POUND

The first priority, though, is to avoid making matters worse. And abolishing sterling to replace it with the euro would make them much worse. The Conservative Party was right to pledge to keep the pound at the last election. But it was judged appropriate to limit that promise only to the duration of a parliament. Unfortunately, while perfectly satisfactory in practice – no one seriously

---

* Under the Nice Treaty, British voting power in the European Council of Ministers will be reduced from 11.5 per cent to 8.4 per cent with enlargement to a twenty-seven-member European Union.
† The Luxembourg Compromise was introduced by the Six in January 1966, and remained in use until the mid-1980s, though it was never officially recognised by the European Commission and the European Court of Justice. I called for its reintroduction in a speech in the House of Lords in July 1992.

thought that a Conservative government led by William Hague would give up the pound – the limited pledge was not very logical. The principal arguments against Britain's joining the European single currency are not, after all, dependent on circumstances: they depend, rather, on matters of fundamental belief which cannot be glossed over or minimised if Conservatives wish to be taken seriously. An illogical compromise on this occasion got the Conservative Party – as in 1997 – into trouble on something which should have been a vital source of strength and support. Unnecessary opportunities were provided for the party's opponents to highlight divisions; the tiny pro-euro minority in the party were not appeased; and votes were lost to the UK Independence Party, which was thought to take a clearer and more principled stand. One can argue about the different possible lessons to be drawn from the election campaign and its outcome. But there is no argument for continuing timidity on the score of the single currency. The Conservative Party should go into any future election pledged to keep the pound sterling – just as it is pledged to keep our freedom and our sovereignty – for good. It can never be right for Britain to abolish its currency. And it can never be right for the Conservative Party to pretend otherwise.*

The reason why that is so is, for a British patriot, self-evident. As I have sought to demonstrate in an earlier chapter, the power to issue and control one's own currency is a fundamental aspect of sovereignty. Sovereignty is a necessary, though not sufficient, condition for freedom and democracy. It is not sufficient, because a government which exercises authority over a nation may, of course, be or become tyrannical or at least authoritarian. But sovereignty is a necessary condition, because unless a government truly has the authority and power to govern – unless it really *is a government* – the constitution cannot be upheld and the democratic mandate becomes a nonsense.

Sometimes arguments about sovereignty are stretched and distorted in such labyrinthine fashion that one would need to be a

---

* I am delighted that the new leader of the Conservative Party, Iain Duncan Smith – a patriot to his fingertips – seems to agree.

genius to understand them.* But it is clear that, alongside the other transfers of power which have taken and are taking place, our transfer to the European Union of the authority to issue currency would move us a long way towards losing our sovereignty. It would, moreover, do this in a way which struck a body blow at our democracy. I made this point in an article which appeared during the May/June 2001 general election campaign:

> Without its own currency, Britain would lose the power to determine its own economic policy . . . There is nothing very complicated about what is at stake. With a single currency, there would be a single interest rate, set not to take account of Britain's needs, but those of a range of different countries – a recipe for 'boom and bust' indeed.† And there would be immense and, in the end, irresistible pressure to allow our budgets to be made by Europe as well. Indeed, with the so-called 'Stability Pact', which limits budget deficits, and with progressive harmonisation of taxes, the direction is already evident.
>
> Add to that the social regulation that will come from Brussels under whatever provision the Commission thinks it can abuse, and the result is clear. The main issues relating to Britain's economic well-being would be removed from Britain's control. And yet it is about these very issues that every British election in modern times has been fought.‡

The abolition of sterling would not, it should be remembered, be merely equivalent to setting up a currency board, by which a country chooses to link its own currency to another, such as the US dollar. It may decide to do this for a variety of reasons – for example, because it wishes to bolster confidence in its anti-inflation

---

* Luckily, one such genius, Noel Malcolm, has demolished the wrong arguments and advanced the right one in his pamphlet *Sense on Sovereignty* (Centre for Policy Studies, 1991).

† This was an allusion to the fact that the Prime Minister and his colleagues had been warning of a return to the Tory years of 'boom and bust'. Actually, there was a great deal more boom than bust, but that is another story.

‡ 'Tony Blair is Committed to the Extinction of Britain', *Daily Telegraph*, 1 June 2001.

strategy, or simply because it does so much trade with the country against whose currency its own is fixed. But such arrangements, however much politicians and bankers may pretend otherwise, are limited. They are entered into voluntarily: voluntarily, too, they can be ended.

By contrast, the Maastricht Treaty, which instituted the European single currency, contains no provision for withdrawal from it. The European Commission President, Romano Prodi, has seemed to suggest that a country could abolish its currency and then, if it changed its mind about the euro, start to issue it again.* In view of the wording of the protocol in the Maastricht Treaty which declares 'the irreversible character of the Community's movement to the third stage of Economic and Monetary Union', this is rather odd. But if Signor Prodi actually knew what he was saying, then he was being disingenuous. Of course it is open to any European country at any stage to declare UDI from the Union or to pull out of the euro. In the case of Britain, as I shall explain, our traditional constitutional doctrine indeed holds that that power can never ultimately be abandoned or lost by our Parliament. But the financial and technical obstacles involved in reissuing a national currency after one's reserves had been transferred to the European Central Bank and one's own central bank had acquired the status of an ECB branch office would be daunting. The then European Commissioner for EMU, Yves-Thibault de Silguy, expressed the commonly accepted view when he bluntly said: 'There is no provision in the treaty for a country which has joined monetary union subsequently to leave. There are no procedures for going backwards. That is why you have to be certain when you join up.'†

I am certain. We should not join.

So there are strong reasons in principle – political and constitutional reasons – why Britain should stay out of the euro. But there are plenty of practical economic reasons too. Not the least of these is Britain's experience when sterling was part of the European Exchange Rate Mechanism (ERM). Shadowing the Deutschmark

---

* Interview with Daniel Hannan, 'Yes, You can Leave', *Spectator*, 27 May 2000.
† *The Times*, 26 April 1997.

from March 1987, what might be called sterling's 'informal' (and by me unauthorised) ERM policy, was responsible for keeping interest rates too low, which in turn allowed inflation to rise. Sterling formally joined the ERM in October 1990, a month before my departure from Downing Street. But I made clear that it was upon monetary policy, based upon assessment of domestic monetary conditions, that we would primarily rely when setting interest rates.*

This subsequently changed. The ERM was now treated as the Europeans themselves had always viewed it, namely as a prelude to economic and monetary union. Maintaining a particular parity of exchange rate took precedence over all other economic considerations. This rigidity was disastrous. When German interest rates rose because of borrowing to cover the costs of East German reunification, those high interest rates were passed on through the mechanism of the ERM to us, for whom they deepened and lengthened the recession. Finally, on Black (or arguably, White) Wednesday (16 September 1992), after some £11 billion of reserves had been spent, and after interest rates had risen to 12 per cent (with 15 per cent announced for the following day), sterling had to withdraw from the ERM. Contrary to the dire warnings received, the pound did not collapse. And far from collapsing, the economy began to recover, even if the then Conservative government's reputation for economic competence did not.

If Britain had been part of EMU at the time, the effects on our economy would have been still more serious because the straitjacket would have been still tighter. There would have been no way to relieve the pressure on British industry by dropping interest rates and the value of the currency. We would have been locked fast into an over-restrictive monetary policy and an inappropriate exchange rate. Subsidies, or emigration, or real wage cuts would have been the only (and deeply unsatisfactory) policy options available to try to cope with worsening recession. What government would have welcomed that? These are matters upon which the dwindling minority of British enthusiasts for the abolition of sterling in favour of the euro should reflect.

There can never, in truth, be a 'right' interest rate, or indeed a

---

* See *The Downing Street Years*, p.724.

'right' exchange rate, for the whole of Europe. The economies of the European countries are simply too diverse. But over and above that there are also particular difficulties for Britain, whose economy is fundamentally dissimilar to those of most of our neighbours.

The British economy is, and for the foreseeable future will remain, much more sensitive to interest rate changes than the economies of mainland Europe. This is because we, unlike them, have a high level of variable mortgage debt due to our traditional emphasis on home ownership. A further reason for suggesting that Britain is economically different lies in the fact that our business cycle does not generally follow that on the Continent: it is far more closely in harmony with that in the United States. Unlike Europe, Britain is a major oil producer. We are also much more dependent than the Europeans on so-called 'invisible earnings', that is services and investment income. Finally, because – as I shall examine later – so much of our trade is with non-European countries and thus not denominated in euros at all, we would have less to gain from removing the costs arising from exchange-rate volatility against the euro. Indeed, locking our exchange rate into Europe's would actually increase the pound's volatility against the dollar, with which sterling has usually moved. And, finally, in answer to those who say that they want a common currency easily available for use throughout the world, this already exists – it is called the US dollar.

The euro is not necessary for Britain to prosper. Participation in a single currency is not necessary for free trade: the North American Free Trade Area (NAFTA), comprising the US, Canada and Mexico, works perfectly well (and, as I shall show, better than the EU) without one. But the euro could certainly harm global free trade, which in turn would disproportionately hurt Britain, in so far as the single currency locked in higher costs and so fuelled Europe's inherent protectionism. Contrary to the gloomy predictions made when it was launched, we can now see clearly that the euro is not necessary for the City of London to thrive: since the euro was born the City has dominated the euro trade and flourished mightily. This is mainly because of the City of London's unmatched skills and its global reputation – and also because of a business-friendly tax and regulatory regime, which exists in Britain despite, not because of, the EU. Finally, the European single currency is not necessary either to attract inward investment to Britain. In 1999 Britain was the most popular destination in the EU for foreign direct investment, with its share rising from 25 per cent to 27 per cent, double that of France and nearly three times that of Germany.* Foreigners invest here because the costs which Britain imposes on business are low, and notably lower than in mainland Europe – hence indignant French protests at so-called 'social dumping'.

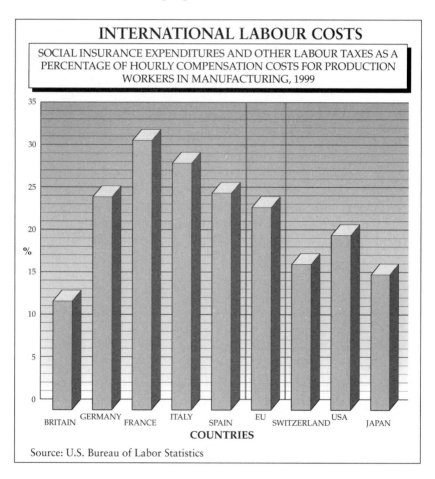

INTERNATIONAL LABOUR COSTS

SOCIAL INSURANCE EXPENDITURES AND OTHER LABOUR TAXES AS A PERCENTAGE OF HOURLY COMPENSATION COSTS FOR PRODUCTION WORKERS IN MANUFACTURING, 1999

COUNTRIES

Source: U.S. Bureau of Labor Statistics

---

* UNCTAD World Investment Report 2000. Sweden, also outside the euro-zone, was the second-largest recipient of non-EU foreign investment.

Abolishing the pound and substituting the euro would be enormously disruptive. It would also be extremely costly – the one-off costs to Britain have been estimated as between £31 billion and £35 billion.* Indeed, prematurely and wastefully, the British government has already embarked upon a programme to 'prepare' British industry for a change-over which the great majority of the British public do not want to see at all. Opinion polls suggest that some 65 to 70 per cent are opposed.† Not that this appears to affect the intentions of the political-bureaucratic elite, which in Britain as elsewhere in Europe believes that it has an overriding mission to achieve European integration by hook or by crook and which is convinced that History (with an extra-large 'H') is on its side.‡

So, in the light of these considerations, I conclude that:

- **Abolition of the pound in favour of the euro would constitute a major loss of Britain's power to govern herself and thus an unacceptable blow to democracy**
- **The alleged economic benefits of the euro are either non-existent, or trivial, or can be achieved by other means**
- **The economic disadvantages are substantially greater for Britain even than for other European countries**
- **Britain should not contemplate giving up the pound.**

---

* *What Would the Euro Cost UK Business?*, House of Commons Trade and Industry Select Committee Report, 7 November 2000. The figures are based on studies carried out by KPMG Consulting and Chantrey Vellacott DFK.

† A May 2001 MORI poll for the *Sun* for example showed 70 per cent of respondents opposed to a European single currency and just 24 per cent in favour. In an ICM poll for the *Guardian* conducted in the same month, 67 per cent of those interviewed declared they would vote 'no' in a referendum on the euro.

‡ This view was exemplified by remarks by the then Foreign Secretary Robin Cook, who on being reminded of the hostility to the euro shown in opinion polls replied: 'I welcome the fact that in those opinion polls which show the majority of the public are against joining the euro, they all show the same two-thirds majority believe joining the euro is inevitable.' *The Times*, 7 July 2000.

EU MEMBERSHIP – LOSSES AND GAINS

It is frequently said to be unthinkable that Britain should leave the European Union. But the avoidance of thought about this, as about other matters, is a poor substitute for judgement. It is only when we honestly weigh up the losses and gains that we can decide which is the sensible course.

A good deal of probably well-intentioned pressure has been exerted in order to prevent this issue being raised at all, at least before any referendum on Britain's joining the euro. I understand why many opponents of EMU feel that that would be the prudent course. They know, as do the proponents of the euro, what the opinion polls show – namely that while a substantial majority of the British public oppose losing the pound, only a large minority at present favour leaving the EU altogether.* The Euro-enthusiasts recognise that probably their only hope of winning a referendum on the euro is to fight it as if it were really a referendum on EU membership. They evidently plan a re-run of the alarmist tactics of 1975, when a large majority voted to remain within the EEC.

This, of course, is dishonest nonsense. Whatever EU Commissioners or Euro-enthusiast politicians may threaten, it is clear that Britain's rights as an EU member, established under the various EU treaties, are unaffected by any decision to stay out of the single currency. There is another factor which the Euro-enthusiasts should consider rather seriously. If they insist on using the argument that rejecting the euro means rejecting Europe as such, then they could find themselves in a very awkward position indeed if the vote went against them. It would widely and with much justification be taken as a mandate for a fundamental renegotiation

---

* A BBC *Today* poll conducted by ICM in January 2001 showed 53 per cent of respondents thinking that Britain should stay in the EU, 30 per cent wanting to leave, and 16 per cent 'didn't know'. A *Sun* poll conducted by MORI in April/May 2001 asked: 'If there were a referendum now on whether Britain should stay in or get out of the EU, how would you vote?' Forty-eight per cent wanted to stay in, 43 per cent wanted to get out, and 9 per cent 'didn't know'.

of Britain's position in the EU, not excluding the option of unilateral withdrawal. I would welcome that approach. But would they? Empty warnings of imminent doom can suddenly become self-fulfilling. I am sure that the story of the little boy who cried 'Wolf!', only then to become the latter's breakfast, must be available in translation in many European languages.

But, of course, there is one thing to be said for what the alarmists allege, though again I doubt it would please them to acknowledge it. The concept of the euro is indeed the clearest expression that we have so far of the direction in which those in charge of Europe want to go – namely, towards a federal superstate. The European single currency is intended to take its place alongside a European legal system, a European foreign policy, a European army, a European Parliament and a European government to create a European superstate. In this sense, the debate about the euro is part and parcel of a growing, necessary and overdue debate about Britain's attitude towards a European Union which is rapidly evolving into something more than a mere Union.

So I return to my starting point. Let us in Britain at last really *think* about what we expect from Europe as it is presently constituted, calculate whether we are getting it, and, if not, consider whether we could do better creating some new trading arrangement.

There have been a number of attempts to work out a 'balance sheet' of losses and gains from Britain's EU membership. The calculation changes, of course, as the EU itself acquires new powers and as conditions alter in the world outside Europe. It is also easier to establish the narrower financial than the broader economic picture.

Even after the rebates which I secured in the mid-1980s, Britain is a large net contributor to the EU budget. In 2000 the figure stood at £2.4 billion. Since we joined the EEC, our net contribution has amounted to £54.7 billion. But it is not enough to look at the net contribution, that is what we pay less what we receive. It is the gross contribution – amounting to £5.9 billion in 2000 alone – which is also important, because this sum represents public expenditure which is in large measure spent on other things than a British government and British electors would choose.* Incidentally, it is really quite remarkable how easily this point is lost and becomes submerged in barrages of misleading figures about how much different regions and localities of the United Kingdom 'receive' from Europe. I agree with the former Chancellor of the Exchequer, Norman (now Lord) Lamont, who has noted that this 'is a bit like the campaign slogan of the Mayor of Sao Paolo in Brazil who said: "I steal, but I give some back." '†

The reason why Britain loses out financially from Europe is now – as ever – the CAP. The CAP leads to bureaucracy and to poor use of our natural resources. But its most damaging impact is that upon the wider economy, by forcing up food prices – something which is particularly damaging for an advanced, urbanised country like Britain.

Like the other economic effects of EU membership, that of the CAP is, though, difficult to calculate. One cannot, for example, simply compare food prices within the EU and those on the world market and say that the difference is the extra we pay. This is because world prices are lower than they would otherwise be because the EU dumps the produce which it has over-produced onto world markets. However, Patrick Minford estimates that the cost of the CAP for a typical year would be some £6.5 billion. This is based upon taking the cost to consumers of paying higher prices for food, subtracting the gain to British farmers, and then adding the loss in real income from reduced consumption of food. The figure rises to £15 billion (roughly 1.5 per cent of GDP) if the UK's net budgetary contribution to the EEC to support the CAP's deficit and running costs is added.‡

---

* Office of National Statistics and 'European Finances: Statement on the 2000 EC Budget and measures to counter fraud and financial mismanagement', Cmnd. 4771. Figures at constant 1998 prices.

† Norman Lamont, *Sovereign Britain* (Bristol: Duckworth, 1995), p.86.

‡ Patrick Minford, *Britain and Europe: The Balance Sheet*, Centre for European Studies and European Business Review, MCB University Press, 1996, p.3. Professor Minford has kindly provided me with an updated figure. A study by Ruth Lea of the Institute of Directors gave a similar figure of £9–£10 billion for the cost of the CAP to the British economy. She points out that in 1999, British taxpayers subsidised other farmers in the EU by about £2 billion (Ruth

The costs and benefits for Britain of EU membership across the board are still more difficult to estimate. For example, do we assume that free trade with EU member countries is a benefit inseparable from EU membership? Or could we negotiate favourable terms of access to those markets from outside? (I shall examine this option later.) Again, though to non-economists this may seem counter-intuitive, there will be some economic *cost* to Britain through being within the European tariff wall. As with the old system of Imperial Preference, privileged access to protected markets, though it may initially be attractive, has the effect of damaging the global competitiveness of one's industries.* But the EU tariff wall is, in any case, now quite low: so the balance of advantage and disadvantage in respect of trade is fairly evenly matched and not very significant.

Where does this leave the balance sheet? On the one hand, in what seems to me a 'worst case' scenario, an analysis by the National Institute of Economic and Social Research has concluded that 'the level of UK output would be about 2 per cent per annum lower outside the EU than inside'. It argues that some jobs would be lost, but adds that 'there is no reason to suppose that the UK will experience mass unemployment outside the EU'. The NIESR accepts that 'outside the EU the UK could take advantage of lower world food prices and could benefit from savings on its contributions to the EU budget'. But it believes that 'these effects would be outweighed by the effects of higher tariffs and administrative costs on exports and by a resulting fall in the number of firms investing in the UK'.†

Although the study emphasises the alleged disadvantages of

Lea, *CAP: A Catalogue of Failure. The Need for Radical Reform*, IOD Research Paper, November 2000, p.6).

---

* This and other connected matters were discussed in illuminating fashion by Martin Wolf, 'Thinking the Unthinkable', *Financial Times*, 18 June 1996. Imperial Preference was a system of preferential tariff rates operated between Britain and her colonies between 1932 and the end of Empire in the 1960s.

† Nigel Pain and Garry Young, *Continent Cut Off? The Macroeconomic Impact of British Withdrawal from the EU*, National Institute of Economic and Social Research, February 2000.

exit from the EU, it also disproves the economically illiterate and socially alarmist warnings from, for example, Keith Vaz, then Minister for Europe, that 3.5 million jobs would be lost if we left the European Union.* I doubt the NIESR's other conclusions, though, because I do not think that it is realistic to suppose that we would be unable to negotiate any special trade relationship with the EU. I do not think either that there would be an adverse effect on investment in Britain, and the NIESR's judgement is heavily influenced by that.† Foreign investors are, evidence suggests, a good deal more concerned about our costs, rather than the mere fact of EU market access, and since we could be even more successful in keeping costs down outside than inside the EU I would expect more not less inward investment. I think, too, that it is unlikely that we would subsidise farming to the same level if we were not part of the CAP. And the fall in the price of food imports – which the NIESR estimates at 20 per cent – could well be greater.

Patrick Minford's judgement, made in 1996 – that is *before* a Labour government signed Britain up to the Social Chapter and pledged to try to take Britain into EMU – seems to me more soundly based: 'There is no balance of advantage to speak of for or against our European membership. It makes sense to try and make a success of that membership, as so much has been invested in it. But in spite of all our efforts if our partners will not tolerate the conditions for that success, then we can walk away in confidence.'‡

There are, though, those who think that the arguments for Britain's membership of the EU are not to be addressed in such matter-of-fact terms. Perhaps because I was a shopkeeper's daughter, or perhaps just because as Prime Minister I developed a

---

* Keith Vaz, interview with the *Daily Telegraph*, 19 February 2000.
† I am grateful to Dr Brian Hindley for allowing me sight of the draft introduction of the revision of the booklet written by him and Martin Howe, *Better Off Out?: The Benefits or Costs of EU Membership* (IEA, 1996). Dr Hindley points out that the adverse effects on inward investment are much exaggerated and notes that the US International Trade Commission report in 2000 describes them as 'small'.
‡ Minford, *Britain and Europe: The Balance Sheet*, p.33.

preference for matters of fact, I cannot agree. If we are receiving an unsatisfactory deal and we have no realistic chance of improving it, and if at the same time we are steadily losing our powers of self-government, that seems sufficient argument against further integration in Europe for me.

I am not, for example, at all impressed by the suggestion that Britain is taken more seriously because we are part of a wider European whole. This view is mistaken because it rests on three fundamental errors.

First, it assumes that the exertion of 'influence', or indeed power, is an end in itself. It isn't. The possibility that Britain might be more successful in bossing other countries around if tied into a multinational colossus is a deeply unappealing, and of course profoundly illiberal, argument for integration with Europe. To be free is better than to be unfree – always. Any politician who suggests the opposite should be treated as suspect.

Second, those who hold this view make an assumption of a necessary and absolute compatibility between the interests of Britain and those of the other countries of Europe. Again, this is simply not true. As I have already sought to demonstrate, Britain really is 'different'. Actually, I believe that if they were willing to investigate the matter honestly and intelligently the politicians of Europe would discover that the interests of their nations were 'different' and conflicting in important ways too; but, of course, in euro-land that would be heresy, and the Euro-Inquisition would soon set political funeral pyres a-smoking. In any case, as de Gaulle realised, Britain's economic and geopolitical interests are unique and uniquely divergent from Europe's. To overlook that and to search instead for the lowest European common denominator is profoundly misguided.

Third, and last, it is highly questionable whether when 'Europe speaks with one voice', as we are so often told it is doing, anyone is really listening. Europe's reputation as a serious player in international affairs is unenviable. It is a feeble giant whose desperate attempts to be taken seriously are largely risible. It has a weak currency and a sluggish inflexible economy, still much reliant on hidden protectionism. It has a shrinking, ageing population and, with the exception of Britain, rather unimpressive armed forces and, not excepting Britain, muddled diplomacy. There are better ways of increasing the country's international standing than through a common European foreign and security policy, let alone common European defence.

OPTIONS

So what should we do? The obvious preference would be to try to retain as much as possible of the existing arrangements, while opting out of present and future mechanisms which harm our interests or restrict our freedom of action. Any sensible person would hope that this approach would yield results, particularly any sensible Conservative – after all, one traditional aspect of conservatism is the unwillingness to make unnecessary changes. I advocated a variant of it in, for example, a speech in The Hague in 1992:

> Why need every new European initiative require the participation of all members of the Community? It will sometimes be the case – especially after enlargement – that only some Community members will want to move ahead to another stage of integration . . .
>
> We should aim for a multi-track Europe in which *ad hoc* groups of different states – such as the Schengen Group – forge varying levels of cooperation and integration on a case-by-case basis. Such a structure would lack graph-paper neatness. But it would accommodate the diversity of post-communist Europe.*

By the time that I came to write at length about Europe, some three years later, I was still more concerned with the direction in which events were leading. I viewed the attempt, which was already mooted and which is again firmly on the agenda, to create a 'two tier' Europe (in which some countries, France, Germany and others, might integrate faster) as offering Britain an opportunity essentially to renegotiate some of our terms of membership. But

---

* Speech to the 'Global Panel', The Hague, 15 May 1992. *Collected Speeches*, no. 51.

this would require determination to see that any attempts to create a 'hard core' of countries respected Britain's fundamental interests. So those countries must not be allowed to impose on other EU members their own priorities on questions like the operation of the Single Market. The price of Britain's agreement to treaty changes might, I argued, be the 'unbundling' of a number of provisions – like those relating to our budget contributions and the CAP – which currently worked to our disadvantage.*

Was this still a realistic option at the time when I put it forward? It is difficult to be sure. Maastricht was by then, of course, on the statute book, and it was already clear that the talk of its being a decentralising treaty was so much hot air. Moreover, Maastricht had provided the treaty basis for a single currency, even though Britain had an opt-out. Once the single currency went ahead, a huge new step towards European federalism would have occurred. At least, though, we still had a Conservative government, so whatever reservations I might have had about its robustness on European issues, I knew that it would remain under heavy pressure from within the party to hold out against federalism.

But I also began to advance an alternative approach, which sought a more fundamental change in our relationship with the EU in order to preserve or (depending upon your viewpoint) to restore Britain's legal sovereignty. Thus I argued for 'amending the 1972 European Communities Act to establish the ultimate supremacy of Parliament over all Community law, making clear that Parliament can by express provision override Community law'. Among other more detailed suggestions, I then called for 'a reserve list of protected matters where Parliament alone can legislate, to include our constitutional arrangements and defence'.†

I believe that, had they been heeded, these suggestions might have formed the basis for a full-scale renegotiation of our terms of membership. But the Major government took a different view, and in any case it lacked a parliamentary majority to give effect to any such approach.

---

* *The Path to Power*, p.502.
† *The Path to Power*, pp.504–5.

There was a change of view when William Hague became Conservative Party leader after the 1997 general election. He understood the need for rethinking and, within what appeared the limits of prudence, sought to practise it. But by then, of course, the Conservative Party was out of power. Tony Blair's Labour government brought with it to Downing Street a determination to take Britain further towards federalism. Thus Britain accepted the Social Chapter, from which John Major had secured an opt-out. Mr Blair declared his support in principle for the abolition of sterling in favour of the euro, though leaving the timing vague. Most seriously of all, perhaps, Britain's long-standing opposition to European defence integration was replaced by support for it. The Amsterdam and Nice Treaties eased the federalist project forward. And for the immediate future Britain will have a government prepared to make further sacrifices of sovereignty and rigidly opposed to any attempts to regain it.

In these circumstances, and given the speed with which the federalist project is now being driven in Brussels and the other European capitals, it is no longer realistic to imagine that a future Conservative government will be able to achieve its goals for renegotiation while pledged to remain a member of the EU under anything like the present arrangements. Even now, it would require a sea change of opinion in France or Germany – and then an unprecedented level of British diplomatic success – to assemble an effective alliance to stop, or slow, let alone reverse the momentum. And to suggest that in, say, five years' time that will be possible is not credible. For these reasons, I do not think that talk of 'variable geometry', 'tiers', 'tracks', 'flexibility clauses' and all the rest is any longer worth the effort. No one is likely to be convinced. And, all things considered, no one should be.

So where does that leave us in negotiating a better relationship with the other member states of the EU? Actually, rather well-placed. The blunt truth is that the rest of the European Union needs us more than we need them. It is just that we have managed to entangle ourselves with Europe in such a way that these strengths cannot at present be used effectively.

Just consider the following three negotiating advantages which we enjoy. First, we are substantial net importers from the rest of the EU – to the tune of $16 billion in 1998.* As a free trader, I understand that trade is not to be considered a zero-sum activity. Trade benefits all who participate in it. But the fact remains that those European imports into Britain are of enormous importance to European companies and their workforces. Many thousands of European jobs depend on them. If we were to seek to change our trading relations with the EU, no matter how ill-tempered EU politicians might become, EU workers are going to bring pressure on them to keep our markets open. And that in turn means keeping Europe's markets open too.† Europe cannot afford a trade war with Britain – even if the WTO were ever to allow one.

Second, Europe will continue to want access to our waters and our fish. We are, as I have described, substantial contributors to the CAP, and the prospect of an end to that bounty might send our partners into a lather. But they have gained one other benefit from the terms of our entry which, to a number of them – particularly Spain – is extremely economically important, namely access to our fish stocks.

Perhaps the worst single aspect of the deal Britain made on entering the EEC related to fishing. Under measures which were dreamt up at the last moment by the Six in order to gain control over the fish of the four applicant countries – Britain, Norway, Ireland and Denmark – the Europeans resolved to regard fish as a 'common resource' to which all member states would have equal access. (The Norwegians were sufficiently angry about this to reject entry as a result in 1972 and again in 1994, and have prospered greatly since – the country now has the third highest GDP per head in Europe.) A few years later, national fishing limits were extended under international law from twelve to two hundred miles. Once Spain with its huge fishing fleet joined the EEC, and once the ten-year transitional period came to an end, the full

---

* *UK Trade Statistics 1998*, Office of National Statistics.

† I am not, though, going to pretend that official free-trade agreements with Europe will ever lead in practice to full free-trade access. Europe's non-tariff barriers, such as anti-dumping duties or their threat, which protect, for example, computers and other durables, would work against us. But then perfectly free trade, like other perfect things, is rarely attainable in practice. I am grateful to Patrick Minford for reminding me of this qualification.

implications of all this for Britain were unpleasantly apparent. There was massive overfishing, and European attempts at conservation were ineffectual. Indeed, they did more harm than good when an absurd system of quotas forced large quantities of dead fish to be thrown back into the sea with damaging environmental consequences. The British fishing fleet shrank drastically – the number of British deep-sea fishing vessels has fallen from several hundred to just fourteen – and the inroads of Spanish fishermen were legitimised in the courts against the express wishes of the British Parliament.*

This cannot be allowed to continue. If Britain were to exert its parliamentary sovereignty and take back control of its waters within the two-hundred-mile limit, there would be an outcry in Brussels – but we would be quite within our rights and we could then regulate entry by bilateral agreement with other countries. This would not only establish an effective means of conservation by the exercise of national sovereignty – for it is an old truth that where no one owns no one cares – it would also ensure that all those European countries which wanted to fish in British waters, from which up to 80 per cent of 'Europe's' fish are taken, would suddenly become very cooperative on this, and indeed on other matters.

Third, however much the Europeans huff and puff about a common European foreign and security policy and a common defence, they know perfectly well that Britain as a European power is in a league of her own. Our language, our links through trade and political influence, our outlook, our closeness with America, our nuclear deterrent – all make us a global power, though not of course a superpower. Not even France, which comes nearest, is any longer a global force in the sense that this is true of Britain. If the EU is to become a global power itself (as it intends) it will

---

* In the 'Factortame' case, ninety-seven Spanish fishermen were awarded £55 million compensation in February 2001 after the European Court ruled that the British government had unfairly discriminated against foreign trawlermen through the 1988 Merchant Shipping Act. The case was brought against Britain by a consortium of Spanish fishing-vessel owners, led by the Spanish-owned company Factortame Ltd, who claimed they had been unable to register their ships to operate in British waters.

need to have cooperative relations with Britain. We may even be called upon to pull its 'rapid reaction' forces out of ill-considered scrapes that arise from an excess of hubris and a lack of advanced weaponry.

Against this background, we should have every confidence that we can achieve a sensible framework within which to defend and pursue our interests – while having cooperative relations with the European countries. How might this be done?

The preliminary step, I believe, should be for an incoming Conservative government to declare publicly that it seeks fundamental renegotiation of Britain's terms of EU membership. The objectives would need to be set out clearly in a White Paper. There would be five.

First, from Britain's point of view, no satisfactory relationship is possible with the rest of Europe which sees us remaining subject to the CAP. Withdrawing from that system would mean both an end to the problem of our net contributions and gaining access to cheaper food imports – both highly desirable and extremely popular. We could at the same time establish a system of support for our agriculture which was environmentally sensitive and suitable for our own particular conditions.

Second, we have also, as I have noted above, to end our adherence to the Common Fisheries Policy. We would establish arrangements for sensible exploitation of our fish stocks which both gave our own fishermen priority and which made for effective conservation. This again would be extremely popular – at least in Britain.

Third, we would need to withdraw from all the entanglements into which we have been drawn by the pursuit of a common foreign and security policy and by common defence. It is likely that by the time of renegotiation substantial British forces will, if Mr Blair has his way, have been placed under a European command with its own planning staff, military doctrine and priorities. Although we would seek to achieve disengagement with the least disruption to any existing missions and commitments, Britain must return to the position in which her forces are under her own or NATO's control – not Europe's.

Fourth, we must seek to achieve as far as possible the basic, sensible objectives of the European Single Market, that is common recognition of standards, and open markets free of subsidies, distortions and non-tariff barriers – but without over-regulation, abuse of powers by the Commission and unwelcome intrusions by the European Court. I say 'as far as possible' because, for all the reasons I have given earlier, it is not at all clear that such an option is available. It may be necessary to negotiate a new relationship which retains most though not all of the benefits of the Single Market, but without the presently accompanying drawbacks.

This in turn leads on to the fifth and final objective of our renegotiation: Britain must regain control of its trade policy. At present the EU negotiates in these matters on our behalf through the Common Commercial Policy. But what suits the EU as a whole, with its bloated agricultural sector, does not suit us. Our interests lie primarily in global not European markets – markets to which at present we have no special access except through the ordinary WTO rules. These markets have also over the years been expanding faster than those of Europe and seem likely in the long run to continue doing so.

We live in a world in which physical distance has become much less significant as a constraint on commerce. This is reflected in the way in which our trade is so great with countries outside Europe. Britain's non-EU trade is the highest as a proportion of total trade of any EU member. Services, the fastest-growing area of our exports, is a particularly important component of this. In 1999, Britain was the world's largest outward investor. The most popular location for British foreign investment is the United States.* America is also by far the single most important source of Britain's inward investment – something which is often obscured by an excessive preoccupation with Japanese investment and so with the well-known advocacy by some Japanese businessmen of British membership of the euro.

Once free to do so, we could reorientate our trade policy in order to take advantage of these national and global trends.

The process of renegotiation on the basis of these five objectives should not be too protracted. It will be evident to our partners

---

* Jamieson and Minford, *Britain and Europe*, pp.73–4.

OVERSEAS INVESTMENT					
BRITISH DIRECT INVESTMENT OVERSEAS, YEAR END 1999			**FOREIGN DIRECT INVESTMENT IN BRITAIN, YEAR END 1999**		
Location	£(billions)	%	Location	£(billions)	%
Germany	10.9	2.6	Germany	38.4	15.3
France	12.9	3	France	19.1	8.4
Italy	3.0	0.7	Italy	1.1	0.5
Holland	69.0	16.3	Holland	37.3	15.7
Ireland	27.2	6.4	Ireland	2.6	1.1
(EU)	(150.2)	(35.5)	(EU)	(103.7)	(45.6)
Switzerland	5.7	1.3	Switzerland	8.0	3.5
United States	185.4	43.8	United States	90.2	39.7
(Americas)	(207.2)	(48.9)	(Americas)	(100.8)	(44.3)
Japan	3.7	0.9	Japan	3.1	1.4
(Asia)	(25.3)	(6.0)	(Asia)	(4.9)	(2.2)
Australia	9.4	2.2	Australia	5.0	2.2
Africa	9.9	2.3	Africa	1.1	0.5
Source: Office of National Statistics, 13 December 2000. Figures are for book value of net assets. Total: £423.3 billion.			Source: Office of National Statistics, 13 December 2000. Figures are for book value of net assets. Total: £227.4 billion.		

that our goals cannot be met by a few marginal adjustments or promises of future reviews.

But it should be made clear right at the start that in order to secure our objectives we would be prepared, if it became necessary, unilaterally to withdraw from EU membership. This might seem at first sight a provocative tactic: but it actually makes good sense. We will never be taken seriously in renegotiation if our partners are allowed to believe that in the end we will settle for whatever we are offered.

But we must then, of course, be willing to have our bluff called. For reasons outlined above, any major changes in the operation of the EU to make it an organisation congenial to Britain are not very likely to be forthcoming. It is only realistic to expect that the outcome may well amount to Britain's leaving the EU as it will have developed by the time of the negotiations, and establishing new links with European and non-European countries on a different basis. We should wish to make any such parting of the ways as amicable as possible – but friendship is a two-way street, and it may be that resolution in the face of a good deal of Continental temperament will be required. Yet reason will eventually prevail, as it so often does in life, by way of self-interest. Once our partners understand that we are serious, they too will talk seriously about how to establish a new and more stable relationship which suits their interests and ours.

There are a range of possibilities open to us. The first is simply to pursue a policy of unilateral free trade. This option is, in fact, a good deal more logical and attractive than it at first sounds. Experience and economic theory alike show that free trade is the best way for a country to exploit its natural advantages. Tiny Hong Kong is a case in point. Hong Kong grew rich as a duty-free port which, levying virtually no import tariffs, and from having an extremely modest standard of living forty years ago, rose to enjoy a GDP per capita higher than that of the UK. Those willing to put their skills and resources to good use on the open international market have nothing to fear but fear itself.

It may be objected that a policy of unilateral free trade by Britain is politically unrealistic. And that may turn out to be right. Producers' interests can never be totally overcome by the interests of consumers. But the option is certainly worth discussing, not least because it exposes the fallacy that outside the EU Britain would be 'alone', 'isolated', 'excluded' and so on. Countries trade with each other – or to be more precise people buy and sell from each other across frontiers – because that is the way to advance their interests. We do not need to beg people to trade with us – as long as we have something that people want, of a quality they expect and at a price they are prepared to pay.*

The second option is to seek to join NAFTA. I have advocated this course of action for some years, not just for economic but

---

* For a fuller discussion of markets and trade see pp.458–66.

also strategic reasons – that is, as a way of strengthening the trans-Atlantic links of NATO. Originally, I envisaged the formation of a NAFTA (rechristened a North *Atlantic* Free Trade Area) in which an enlarged EU would participate, along with the United States, Canada and Mexico (the present NAFTA members). This is, in theory, still a possibility. But I am no longer convinced that it is a serious option. The EU shows no real interest in making the reforms which would be required to qualify. Moreover, Europe's centralising political ambitions have risen to the top of its agenda and seem likely for the foreseeable future to remain there. As a result, the EU and NAFTA look less and less similar as the years go by.

It would, therefore, probably be preferable for Britain to join NAFTA under a separate agreement, something in which there is also serious interest in some quarters within the United States. For example, Senator Phil Gramm, until recently Chairman of the Senate Committee on Banking, Housing and Urban Affairs, has been at the forefront of calls for Britain to be included in NAFTA.*

NAFTA's advantages over the EU are numerous and significant. It has more and, on average, richer consumers than euro-land. Its economies have been growing faster. Its markets are more open and it has stronger links with the global economy. It is much less reliant on subsidies. It is more attractive to outside investors. Finally, it is also much better at creating jobs: since 1992 the number of jobs has risen by 38 per cent in Mexico, 13 per cent in Canada and the US, compared with just 3 per cent in euro-land.†

Perhaps most significant, however, is not just the potential of NAFTA as opposed to that of the EU: it is, rather, the fact that NAFTA is neither a customs union nor a political/administrative entity with grand ambitions. It is simply what it says it is – an association dedicated to free trade. Membership of NAFTA does not therefore inhibit a country from entering into trade relation-

---

* 'Euroland and NAFTA: The View from Across the Atlantic', speech by Senator Phil Gramm to the Centre for Policy Studies, 4 July 2000.
† Keith Marsden, *Towards 'A Treaty of Commerce': Euroland and Nafta Compared* (Centre for Policy Studies, July 2000), p.19.

ships with other countries as and when it sees fit. And this leads to the third possibility – a global Free Trade Area (FTA).

This idea has been advanced by John Hulsman, a scholar at the Heritage Foundation, as constituting a 'new trading agenda for the age of globalisation'.* Dr Hulsman advocates Britain's entry into the FTA of which we and the United States would be charter members – along with Singapore, Bahrain, the Czech Republic and Chile among others. The framework of the organisation would be one within which the freest economies of the world – judged according to the criteria of freedom to trade, freedom to invest, freedom to operate a business, security of property rights – would come together voluntarily. Not only would this arrangement work to stimulate the members' prosperity: it would also act as a beacon and an example to others. And, like NAFTA, it would, of course, leave the member states free to manage their own affairs.

Either NAFTA or the global FTA or indeed any other free-trade organisation would allow Britain the liberty to negotiate a new trade relationship with the countries of the European Union. Ideally, of course, this would take place before Britain formally withdrew as a full member of the EU: no one wants more disruption than necessary. But whatever the circumstances, it would be right to try to keep some aspects of our present trading relationship. For the reasons given earlier, there is no doubt that the EU members would want such links. How *much* they wanted them would, within the overall WTO framework, decide how favourable to us the final arrangement would be.

There are, though, useful precedents. In 1992, Norway, Iceland and Liechtenstein – that is the remaining EFTA countries, bar Switzerland – concluded negotiations with the EU which established a European Economic Area (EEA). These countries now enjoy free trade with the European Union, that is the freedoms of movement of goods, of services, of people and of capital. They also enjoy the unhindered access guaranteed by the operation

---

* John C. Hulsman, *The World Turned Rightside Up: A New Trading Agenda for the Age of Globalisation*, with commentaries by Patrick Minford, Martin Howe, David Davis and Bill Jamieson, Institute of Economic Affairs, 2001.

of the European Single Market. But they remain outside the customs union, the CAP, the CFP, the common foreign and security policy and the rest of the legal/bureaucratic tangle of EU institutions.

The main problem for these countries is that they are effectively required to implement all the EU Single Market directives without having a vote on the form those directives take. There is also a mechanism by which they are very strongly encouraged, if not actually forced, to accept European Court decisions on the interpretation of these rules. This is not a very satisfactory situation because the relationship is skewed in favour of the EU.

But Britain is in a different league from countries like Norway (population 4.4 million) or Iceland (population 270,000), let alone Liechtenstein (population thirty-two thousand). Their negotiating position hardly compares with that which Britain would enjoy with a population of 59.5 million and the second largest GDP in Europe. We could press for Britain to be represented in the drawing up of all Single Market legislation, even though we were not party to other EU functions – like the CAP – where of course we could not be represented.

The existing EEA is not now the only model available to us. A more comparable, and very recent, precedent is that set by Mexico, which is also, of course, a member of NAFTA. In November 1999 Mexico and the EU negotiated a free-trade agreement which is the most comprehensive ever entered into by the Europeans. It covers the free movement of goods (including agriculture) and services, intellectual property rights, investment, public procurement and competition. Like NAFTA, and unlike the EEA, it excludes, however, free movement of people.* The provisions relating to Single Market directives and their interpretation are more satisfactory. Mexico is not subject to the rulings of the European Court of Justice. Trade disputes between the EU and Mexico will be negotiated by officials from each side, and if further resol-

---

* This 'freedom' has in any case always been problematic in view of the need to apprehend terrorists and other criminals and to curb illegal immigration and bogus asylum seeking. In this matter, NAFTA perhaps offers a better model than the EEA.

TRADE BLOCS			
TRADING ASSOCIATIONS: EU, EEA, EFTA, NAFTA			
EU	**EEA**	**EFTA**	**NAFTA**
Austria	Austria	Iceland	Canada
Belgium	Belgium	Liechtenstein	Mexico
Britain	Britain	Norway	USA
Denmark	Denmark	Switzerland	
Finland	Finland		
France	France		
Germany	Germany		
Greece	Greece		
Holland	Holland		
Ireland	Ireland		
Italy	Italy		
Luxembourg	Luxembourg		
Portugal	Portugal		
Spain	Spain		
Sweden	Sweden		
	Iceland		
	Liechtenstein		
	Norway		

ution is required the matter goes for bilateral arbitration through the WTO.

Mexico is a large country (population ninety-five million) with a still larger potential for growth. But its economy is less than a third the size of Britain's. Whatever Mexico can achieve in obtaining a fair deal with the EU struck from outside, Britain can more than achieve from within – given our ability to cause trouble if we are not properly treated.

The Mexican example also provides a further model according to which a member of a dedicated free-trade area (NAFTA) can also enjoy free trade with a customs union (the EU). The theoretical problem of how to ensure that imports from third countries do not pass into the economy of one member of a free-trade area to be re-exported into another – which would undermine a country's ability to govern its trade relations with third countries – is solved. Thus, as with the EEA, agreed procedures will be established to determine 'rules of origin'. Typically, for a product which contains material that originates from outside the EU or Mexico, it must have undergone a significant amount of processing within the free-trade zone if it is to qualify for reduced or zero tariffs.

Such a system, it is true, has some drawbacks for trade; but they can easily be exaggerated. Although the rules relating to Mexico are more stringent on paper than those for the EEA, there is not much difference in practice. Provisions for 'approved exporters' smooth the movement of trade, and over recent years there have been large reductions for technical reasons in worldwide trade bureaucracy in any case.

Anyone who doubts that making a large free-trade area work is a practical proposition need only examine the successes of NAFTA. And, of course, such an approach has one enormous advantage – under it Britain would retain control over her own affairs and could, therefore, adapt her policies to her interests as events unfold.*

Finally, one should mention Switzerland, the only remaining member of EFTA not within the EEA. Switzerland is unique in many ways. But whatever Switzerland has secured in its dealings with Europe Britain too could certainly obtain without great difficulty. Switzerland enjoys free trade with the EU and has reached some 150 bilateral agreements. One of those awaiting ratification by the EU includes free movement of labour. The EFTA model is perhaps not ideal: but it is certainly an acceptable option. Moreover, when discussing the case of the Swiss and the EEA members we must remember that trade with Europe is far more important for them than for us. Britain is a truly global player.

All these matters are basically economic, and no worse for that: those who talk in a superior fashion of 'bread and butter issues'

---

* The details and the implications of this agreement are analysed by Ronald Stewart-Brown in 'The Mexico–EU Free Trade Agreement', *Global Britain Briefing Note*, 8, 2 June 2000. I am grateful to Mr Stewart-Brown for his very helpful explanation of the intricacies of the EU–Mexico FTA.

generally eat something better than bread and butter. Yet at the heart of our relationship with the other members of the EU and the EU institutions is a constitutional fact. However Britain's renegotiated relations with the EU turn out, the British Parliament will have to take back powers which have been lost through the Treaty of Rome, through subsequent treaty changes, and through the operation of the European Court of Justice and indeed the British courts. Without this exertion of parliamentary sovereignty, it would be impossible to recreate our relationship with Europe on a satisfactory basis.

It is sometimes suggested that Britain has no right to withdraw from the EU, if that is the route which – after a referendum – were to be chosen. And doubtless this is something which would be argued, at least in Europe. It is certainly true that neither the Treaty of Rome nor the Maastricht and other treaties contains any explicit secession or denunciation clauses. It is also true that, given the EU's determined acquisition of more and more powers pertaining to statehood, at some stage in the future development of the European Union into a superstate Britain might cease to be regarded in international law as a sovereign state in its own right. This view might even, given current trends in judicial thinking, at this final stage be echoed in British courts.

But we are not at that stage yet. The fundamental point to bear in mind now is that the UK is (in the language used by international lawyers) a 'dualist' rather than a 'monist' state. What this means is that international law is regarded in our domestic law as a separate legal system. International treaties thus do not (except in exceptional cases, and this is not one of them) give rise to legal rights or obligations which can be enforced in British courts of law. It follows from this that Britain does indeed possess the effective legal power to leave the EU – or to change the terms of its relationship with the EU – because Parliament can when it wishes terminate the enforceability of Community law in British courts.*

There is, though, a further point which should not be forgotten. No one has a higher view of law than I do. But laws have to be rooted in the hearts and minds of the people if they are to be

---

* I am grateful to Martin Howe QC for his advice on these matters.

authoritative. Ultimately, what determines where sovereignty lies is whether the authority of a state's constitutional government is sufficient to command the loyalty of its citizens or (in the British system) the obedience of its subjects.

That is not, of course, a hard and fast distinction – which is one reason why it is always a risky business to try to alter long-standing political institutions and shake the habits and attitudes built around them. But it can still be said without any shadow of doubt that the people of Britain believe that they live under the sovereign authority of their own constitutionally elected government rather than that of the EU. As long as this remains the case, the traditional doctrine of the sovereignty of Parliament (or more precisely of the monarch in Parliament) will hold good. Parliament's ultimate ability to make or unmake laws thus also remains.

It sometimes happens that almost overnight a course of action which has previously been dismissed as unthinkable becomes a matter of sheer commonsense. I witnessed just such a turnaround when as British Prime Minister after our 1979 election victory I led a government which up-ended Keynesian economic orthodoxy and substituted monetarist policies deemed unthinkable by the post-war political consensus. Ronald Reagan as US President experienced much the same. As he wryly put it, reflecting on America's economic renaissance: 'The best sign that our economic programme is working is that they didn't call it Reaganomics any more.'

I predict that it will eventually be the same with Europe. That such an unnecessary and irrational project as building a European superstate was ever embarked upon will seem in future years to be perhaps the greatest folly of the modern era. And that Britain, with her traditional strengths and global destiny, should ever have been part of it will appear a political error of historic magnitude. There is, though, still time to choose a different and a better course.

I believe, therefore, that:

- **We in Britain should fundamentally reassess our relationship with the rest of the EU and renegotiate it in order to secure our national interests and sovereignty**

- We should not rule out any particular framework, as long as it meets our stated objectives
- NAFTA seems likely to be the best trading association to join initially, given Britain's historic and continuing trans-Atlantic links, but other complementary free-trade arrangements may also emerge
- We trade globally, and we must think globally – not confined within the bounds of a narrow Europe.

CHAPTER 11

Capitalism and its Critics

FREE-ENTERPRISE CAPITALISM

It is strange but true that free-enterprise capitalism – capitalism for short – is almost everywhere triumphant yet remarkably little understood.* There has never been so much talk about markets. Left-of-centre governments and even, as in South-East Asia, reformed communist governments are keen to introduce market mechanisms. They understand that there is simply no alternative (to coin a phrase) if they want to generate the wealth which, like all leftists, they then want to tax as much as possible. And yet at the same time there is scant discussion of the essential features of capitalism, let alone of the moral and social system which it embodies.

This disjuncture is dangerous. Systems which are accepted merely because they 'work' do not put down deep roots. It is, after all, one of the underlying truths about free markets, indeed about freedom in all its forms, that outcomes are unpredictable. Economies, like human beings, can become sick – the mighty US economy is looking somewhat sickly at present. But, again like human beings, what matters is whether economies have the inner resources to recover. If the only reason for accepting free enterprise as the right basis for economic policy is short-run pragmatism,

---

* The term 'capitalism' was coined and popularised, it seems, by the early socialist theorist Saint-Simon and by Marx: but it is one of the few words which the right have appropriated from the left rather than vice-versa.

sooner or later when political storm clouds gather that policy will be blown off course.

Free-enterprise capitalism is at one level a system so simple that we might be tempted not to describe it as a system at all. It is, in truth, just about the most natural thing in the world. Adam Smith expressed the point succinctly:

> The division of labour, from which so many advantages are derived, is not originally the effect of any human wisdom, which foresees and intends that general opulence to which it gives occasion. It is the necessary, though very slow and gradual consequence of *a certain propensity in human nature which has in view no such extensive utility: the propensity to truck, barter, and exchange one thing for another.** [Emphasis added]

The instinct to better one's lot by trade is common to every human being, in at least some degree. And, as Adam Smith goes on to note, it appears not to pertain to any other species.

This instinct is an application of self-interest, or what Smith called 'self-love'. It is the underlying principle of economic life, because it alone animates exchange between people who are not relatives, friends or even acquaintances. This is plain common-sense. From strangers one cannot expect to gain what one wants just by their goodness of heart. Rather, a man has to show 'that it is for their own advantage to do for him what he requires of them'. And so it remains today, for, as Smith famously notes: 'It is not from the benevolence of the butcher, the brewer, or the baker that we expect our dinner, but from their regard to their own interest.'†

This formulation and the thinking which it encapsulates has never failed to make some people uneasy. Although Adam Smith does not himself elaborate, it could easily be deduced that the most important means for satisfying the wants of mankind is the market, and that the market functions through selfishness.

---

* Adam Smith, *The Wealth of Nations* (London: Everyman's Library, 1991), p.12.
† Smith, *The Wealth of Nations*, p.13.

Actually, this is a misunderstanding. Smith, who was a moral philosopher before he was an economist, did not believe that self-love was the only principle that mattered, let alone the highest one. 'Benevolence' (which we might nowadays call altruism) was the real foundation of virtue. As he put it: 'To feel much for others and little for ourselves ... to restrain our selfish, and to indulge our benevolent affections, constitutes the perfection of human nature.'*

Grasping this has some relevance today. What those of us who believe that free-market capitalism is the only reliable basis for economic progress are saying is not that we believe that there is no place in life for charity or that only material things matter. Rather, we are asserting that in the vast majority of human undertakings it is best to rely on men's pursuit of their own individual good to ensure that the wants of all are supplied. This rule must be assumed to hold true unless we have some clear reason for thinking that it does not. For example, within a properly functioning family we would expect to find that love, duty, sacrifice and other considerations override, or at least tame and reduce, individual selfishness. Doubtless, in closed single-purpose institutions, such as monasteries and other similar religious communities, something of the sort applies too. But when we are dealing with wider groups whose members cannot even know, let alone can be assumed to care about each other's needs, the most realistic and indeed most fruitful assumption to make is that self-interest will prevail.

There is both a negative and a positive deduction to be drawn from this. The negative deduction is that we must go on to assume that anyone who claims special powers, rights or privileges on the basis that he or she can be relied upon to be altruistic rather than selfish, must be viewed with extreme suspicion. Deep scepticism about the motives of those who seek power over others is one of the healthiest and most characteristic features of British democracy. Unfortunately, it required experience of socialism in the

---

* Adam Smith, *The Theory of Moral Sentiments* (New York: Prometheus Books, 2000), p.27. I am grateful to Professor William Letwin who helpfully explained to me the subtlety of Smith's views in a short paper some years ago.

1970s, and then the reforms of the 1980s, to ensure that this scepticism was extended from the political into the economic arena. And indeed, the modern world is still too willing to believe in the high-mindedness of regulators and bureaucrats – hence the great value of what is called Public Choice Theory economics, which assumes that there is a vested interest lurking behind every government act.*

The positive deduction from acceptance that self-interest will generally prevail in the real world is equally if not more valuable. This is that the free market has enormous potential benefits which can be secured *without* making unrealistic assumptions about human nature, and indeed without embarking on coercive attempts to mould or transform it. 'Not from benevolence': these three words thus constitute in their implications perhaps the most liberating phrase in the English language.

As this brief examination of Adam Smith's formulations shows, free-enterprise capitalism is based upon a psychological insight – the human 'propensity to truck, barter, and exchange'. It is through this propensity that what Smith calls an 'invisible hand' operates to shape an economic order, whereby the individual pursuit of profit leads to the material benefit of society as a whole.

But capitalism also involves institutions, and it is here that modern thinkers, above all Friedrich Hayek, have more to teach. Hayek's idea of a 'spontaneous order' in society, which arises without the interventions of some omniscient and omnipotent central authority, and which describes the functioning of a free society within a rule of law, is perhaps the most profound of these insights.† Hayek applies the concept far beyond economics, to the rules and habits which allow modern society to operate at all. Thus he argues 'that our civilisation depends, not only for its origin but also for its preservation, on what can be precisely

---

* Public Choice Theory originates from the ideas of James Buchanan and the 'Virginia school'. It seeks to apply methods of economic analysis to the political process, which it sees as the outcome of individual choices made by voters, politicians and bureaucrats interacting in the political marketplace.

† F.A. Hayek, *The Constitution of Liberty* (London: Routledge and Kegan Paul, 1960), pp.159–61.

described only as the extended order of human cooperation, an order more commonly, if somewhat misleadingly, known as capitalism'.*

I believe that it is possible to identify five conditions necessary for free-enterprise capitalism to work effectively – by which I mean that it serves well the individual and the common interests of all involved.† The first fundamental condition is that there must be private property. Property is essential because it brings stability and confidence. No society in which there is ingrained doubt about who owns what can advance very far. This is such a basic requirement that to assert it at all may seem banal, even superfluous. But the full implications are far from fully accepted. One has only to consider the difficulties there have been in gaining acceptance by the Chinese of proper protection for what are known as intellectual property rights, to grasp how vital the notion of the patent has been in promoting invention.

Similarly, a fascinating recent study by the Peruvian economist Hernando de Soto illustrates the enormous importance of property rights in a highly contemporary fashion. Based upon detailed research in a number of Third World countries, Señor de Soto argues that what holds back these societies is a failure to turn assets into capital. He discovered, for example, that in Egypt the wealth which the poor have accumulated is worth fifty-five times as much as the sum of all direct foreign investment there:

> But they hold these resources in defective forms: houses built on land whose ownership rights are not adequately recorded, unincorporated businesses with undefined liability, industries located where financiers and investors cannot see them. Because the rights to these

---

* F.A. Hayek, 'Was Socialism a Mistake?', in *The Fatal Conceit: The Errors of Socialism, The Collected Works of Friedrich August Hayek Vol. 1*, ed. W.W. Bartley III (1990), p.6.

† Here I am not talking about matters which traditionally concern so many economic historians and policy-makers – the growth of banking, the accumulation of capital, limited liability and the like – important as these things obviously are, but rather the underlying fundamentals which determine whether capitalism takes root.

possessions are not adequately documented, these assets cannot readily be turned into capital, cannot be traded outside of narrow local circles where people know and trust each other, cannot be used as collateral for a loan and cannot be used as a share against an investment.*

In these countries, where property rights remain uncertain and officially unrecognised, we can see all too clearly the importance that private property still has as a cornerstone of capitalist development.

Very closely linked to property is the second essential feature for successful free enterprise, namely a rule of law. This phrase trips so easily off the tongue that we are inclined to forget just how wide and deep are its ramifications. Roger Scruton's definition strikes me as excellent:

> The form of government in which no power can be exercised except according to procedures, principles and constraints contained in the law, and in which any citizen can find redress against any other, however powerfully placed, and against the officers of the state itself, for any act which involves a breach of the law.†

In this democratic age, when basic political rights are generally to be considered safe, the rule of law is of most practical importance because of its implications in the economic sphere. I have already drawn attention to the damage which its absence has done in post-communist Russia and other countries of the former Soviet Union.

The point here is that arbitrariness and unpredictability are profoundly inimical to wealth creation. Workers need to be assured of the fruits of their labour. Investors have to be confident that they will reap whatever benefits accrue to their capital. Businessmen must know that their profits are not going

---

* Hernando de Soto, *The Mystery of Capital: Why Capitalism Triumphs in the West and Fails Everywhere Else* (London: Bantam Press, 2000), p.5.

† Roger Scruton, *A Dictionary of Political Thought* (London: Macmillan, 1996), p.489.

to be subject to confiscatory or retrospective measures. And everyone involved in the country's economic life has to be protected against extortion and corruption. If these conditions go unfulfilled the complex calculations and the nexus of relationships which lie behind economic growth are disrupted, and prosperity accordingly suffers. What economic activity there is will most likely take place in the 'black' or informal economy. So we can see, for example, that in OECD (i.e. broadly free-market) economies the average size of the black economy is 14 per cent of GDP, but in Third World African economies it is 54 per cent.*

Law consists of written rules, but there are also unwritten rules, and these are the third element upon which capitalism depends – what can be summed up by the word 'culture'. Here we are necessarily dealing with something intangible, although as Hayek's earlier observation shows, by no means incomprehensible. It seems clear that some cultures, or at least the dominant values in those cultures, are more conducive to free-enterprise capitalism and thus to economic progress than others.

It is not difficult to list, in no particular order, the attitudes which render a society more rather than less enterprising: curiosity, imagination, ingenuity, application and risk-taking would be among them. These attitudes in turn often reflect different religious and philosophical traditions. Here the crucial difference seems to be between societies which accept a very limited role for free will and a very large role for fate, and those which emphasise the creativity of man and the uniqueness of the individual. The Judaeo-Christian tradition which, in various forms, dominates the West is firmly in the second category. The great Asian religious traditions must be accounted within the first, as must be (insofar as we know about them) the religious traditions of Africa. Jews and Christians share a respect for the value of work. Their religions firmly state that Man is to be the master of his environment – he is not a kind of offshoot of it, as pantheists suppose. Jews and Christians also have a sense of linear time – not a deterministic

---

* These figures come from an address by Professor Friedrich Schneider published by Centre for the New Europe, *Liberty Briefing* 1, 2001.

belief in cycles and repeating stages. All these things have gone to help shape the way in which Western society views itself, its members and the world around it. Albeit with many variations and qualifications, such views are reflected today in economic progress and living standards.

Of course, such an explanation fails fully to explain the successes of non-Western countries, particularly those in the Far East. As I have noted earlier, there is a real if limited sense in which 'Asian values' can be seen as an element in these countries' success. But it is only fair to add that it required a vital inflow of Western techniques and methods to produce these results. As for sub-Saharan Africa, one can only say that no amount of such Western influence so far seems to make much difference – and this, as I shall explain, has nothing whatsoever to do with the alleged ills of colonialism or post-colonialism.

So cultural background goes far to explain the evolution of modern economies. It does so primarily by affecting invention. By valuing individual human effort and accepting the possibility of progress, Western society provided the background for free experimentation.

Admittedly, there have always been people who thought that the scope for inventions had diminished or even disappeared. The Commissioner of the US Office of Patents observed in 1899: 'Everything that can be invented has been invented.'* But, in fact, no one has yet been able in Western society to put a stop to invention. The spur is constant, the pace breathless.

And this leads on to the other, equally important, role of culture – that of allowing a society to realise an invention's potential and so to put it to effective use. The Chinese invented the wheelbarrow, the stirrup, the rigid horse-collar, the compass, paper, printing, gunpowder and porcelain. They were centuries ahead of the rest of the world in the technology of textiles and iron manufacture. But none of these advances was properly exploited. Indeed (perhaps uniquely), 'Chinese industrial history offers examples of tech-

---

* Cited by Christopher Cerf and Victor Navasky, *The Experts Speak: The Definitive Compendium of Authoritative Misinformation* (New York: Villard, 1984), p.225.

nological oblivion and retrogression,' as the foremost historian of the subject has noted.*

It would, though, be erroneous to believe that culture *alone* decides how successfully capitalism takes root. Cultural determinists, like determinists of all kinds, are at once excessively optimistic and pessimistic. Culture is itself malleable. The values it holds may become more or less conducive to initiative and enterprise. And quite obviously preferences change as markets allow new experiences to be gained, new opportunities to be savoured – sometimes literally: witness the expansion throughout Asia of American fast-food outlets, which some see as today's most manifest expression of globalism.†

Culture also reflects the physical and political circumstances in which it grows up. And that brings me to the fourth important condition for successful free enterprise – diversity and competition between states.

I have already touched on this in discussing the benefits which Europe has enjoyed through never having been subject to one single political authority. But the great philosopher of Anglo-Saxon liberty, John Stuart Mill, expressed the point in a fashion particularly relevant here, when he wrote:

> What has made the European family of nations an improving instead of a stationary portion of mankind? Not any superior excellence in them, which, when it exists, exists as the effect, not as the cause; but their remarkable diversity of character and culture. Individuals, classes, nations, have been extremely unlike one another; they have struck out a great variety of paths, each leading to something valuable; and although at every period those who have travelled in different paths have been intolerant of one another, and each would have thought it an excellent thing if all the rest could have been compelled to travel his road, their attempts to thwart each other's development have rarely had any permanent success,

---

* David Landes, *The Wealth and Poverty of Nations: Why Some are so Rich and Some so Poor* (London: Abacus, 2000), p.55.
† This is explored by James L. Watson in 'China's Big Mac Attack', *Foreign Affairs*, May/June 2000.

and each has in time endured to receive the good which the others have offered. Europe is, in my judgement, wholly indebted to this plurality of paths for its progressive and many-sided development.*

Mill was right. And we can go further. Capitalism is the enemy of enforced homogeneity. It thrives on and it also promotes difference and individuality. This characteristic is arguably as important as wider considerations of culture as a factor in the success of the free-enterprise system. It is, for example, illuminating to consider the role of refugees and immigrants in promoting enterprise. The Jews driven from Spain and Portugal in the late fifteenth century, the Huguenots expelled from France in the seventeenth century, the English Nonconformists who emigrated to America, the Chinese communities scattered around the Far East, the East African Asians who came to Britain in the early 1970s – all have been a rich source of enterprise and wealth-creation.

Capitalism may not be culture-blind, but it is colour-blind. Prejudice stands no chance in a free economy, because it leads eventually to poverty. There is nothing mysterious about this. It is simply another way of restating Adam Smith's famous argument. Precisely because we do *not* make economic transactions 'from benevolence', we are most unlikely to refrain from making them 'from malevolence'. Whether manufactured by black, white, brown or yellow hands, a widget remains a widget – and it will be bought anywhere if the price and quality are right. The market is a more powerful and more reliable liberating force than government can ever be.

Private property, a rule of law, an enterprise-friendly culture, and a diversity of independent and competing countries – these four factors must still be supplemented by a fifth if capitalism is really to flourish. This final element is an encouraging framework of tax and regulation. Of course, at one level that is merely an extension of the second factor – a rule of law. And it is certainly true that the arbitrariness of a state ruled by the *ad hoc* commands of politicians or bureaucrats, rather than by a known, predictable and

---

* John Stuart Mill (ed. Gertrude Himmelfarb), *On Liberty* (London: Penguin, 1985), p.138.

universally applicable body of law administered by objective and honest courts, is extremely bad for business. (Just look at Russia and some other countries of the former Soviet Union today.) But in order to get the best out of capitalism the burdens of the state have to be not merely equitable – they have to be *light*.

THE RIGHT WAY AND THE THIRD WAY

This point is nowadays broadly understood even by left-of-centre governments. Increasing marginal tax rates beyond a certain point will eventually be met by a fall in tax revenues, because it becomes no longer worth working or worth making capital work – hence the famous Laffer curve.* Similarly, heavy regulation will diminish production and so inhibit wealth creation. Over-taxation and over-regulation cause talent and capital to flee to more conducive economic climes. And, finally and paradoxically, both excessive taxes and excessive regulations, that is extensions of state control, will actually in the end result in a *reduction* of the authority of the state – as more and more activity moves outside the law and into the informal or 'black' economy. Indeed, much as this process is denounced by law-makers and revenue services, it provides in the last resort a rather unorthodox safety valve against the pressures built up by excessive state power.

Left-of-centre governments, like that in Britain and those in most of Europe, grasp much of all this in general terms. But their understanding is rather like that of performing dogs in a circus. They have been trained by the experts to beg while wearing a hat and howling accompaniment to the band. Yet what these imitated actions signify is quite beyond their comprehension. It is simply that these are the conditions on which they are fed.

The left do not accept the importance of limiting the burden of

---

* Arthur Laffer (b.1940), leading American supply-side economist and highly influential adviser to the Reagan administration. He demonstrated, through the 'Laffer curve', that there is an optimum rate of tax at which government tax revenue is maximised – i.e. tax cuts may not only help the economy, they may even fill government coffers.

the state *as a matter of principle*. This may seem a sweeping assertion but it is, in fact, really a truism – because it is this lack of understanding which is the defining attribute of their politics. Their basic error is to believe that it is the state that creates wealth, which is then distributed (or redistributed) to individuals. Of course, the left do not actually say this quite so crudely nowadays; but they still assume it. And the truth about the economic process is precisely the opposite, because it is individuals who create wealth. They do this by employing their effort, skills and capital in the manner Adam Smith so well described some two centuries ago, and so they generate 'The Wealth of Nations'.

The left-wing politician does not begin by asking: Why should the government take an extra pound (or dollar, or yen, or euro) from the citizen's pocket? He asks instead: Why not? In the eyes of such politicians everywhere, wealth is collective not individual, it is theirs and not ours. The conservative thinker Richard Weaver famously remarked that 'Ideas have consequences.'* Unfortunately, that is also true of bad ideas, and the idea that socialists have about wealth is one of the worst there is. What they will not accept is that capitalism works best with only a bare minimum of regulation. It is, as I have already noted, wrong to suggest that markets can operate in anything but a crude and unsatisfactory form without *some* framework of enforced rules. And these rules will naturally have to become more complex as the capitalist order develops and markets become more sophisticated. For example, while such rules will simply relate to things like weights and measures in the case of primitive markets, they will become more concerned with hidden obstacles to competition and transparency of accounting in more developed ones. Yet the basic fact remains: every regulation represents a restriction of liberty, every regulation has a cost. That is why, like marriage (in the Prayer Book's words), regulation should not 'be enterprised, nor taken in hand, unadvisedly, lightly, or wantonly'.

Public spending and taxation also by their nature cramp liberty, though there are rather few today who seem to consider that a serious objection. It is, indeed, an unfortunate fact that nowadays

---

* It was in fact the title of his classic book published in 1948.

even among many members of right-of-centre parties – particularly in Europe – it is tacitly accepted that public expenditure is essentially good and that private expenditure is either bad, or at best neutral. This is actually not an entirely new phenomenon. Hayek acknowledged it when he wittily dedicated *The Road to Serfdom* to 'the socialists of all parties'. But it is dispiriting all the same. Even politicians should be expected to learn from past mistakes. Thus right-of-centre parties still often compete with left-of-centre ones to proclaim their attachment to all the main programmes of spending, particularly spending on social services of one kind or another. But this is foolish as well as muddled. It is foolish because left-of-centre parties will always be able to outbid right-of-centre ones in this auction – after all, that is why they are on the left in the first place. The muddle arises because once we concede that public spending and taxation are more than a necessary evil we have lost sight of the core values of freedom.

In some cases, taxation is, of course, absolutely necessary – those cases are well known and not, except at the margin, much disputed. Defence and law and order services are obviously, for example, the direct concern of the state and the taxpayer. Basic standards of health and education provision, free for those who cannot afford to pay, and a safety net of benefits for those who genuinely cannot cope are also clearly within that category – though one should avoid the assumption that simply because a service is necessary it follows that it is best provided directly by the state, or without charge.

There will always – and rightly – be arguments about just where the limits between public and private should be drawn at any one time. But there is a much more important argument of principle against *any* particular proposal for increased public spending – that is, that however worthy the objective, it must also risk impoverishing the nation both materially and morally.

To deal with each of these in turn: the material impoverishment comes from the burden placed upon wealth creation. The most successful economies in terms of growth, incomes per head and job creation are generally those whose public expenditure measured as a share of their national income is low. America and the Asian Tigers are the obvious examples. Within Europe, Britain's record also bears this out. This is not to say that there are no exceptions. And it is certainly not to say that low public spending alone is enough to guarantee prosperity, if other economic policies are faulty – witness the recent problems of Japan.* But recent research confirms what first principles and commonsense suggest – namely, the larger the slice taken by government, the smaller the cake available for everyone. Thus one economist, examining the effect of the long-term rise in government expenditure, has concluded:

> It is clear that the effects of the increased public spending experienced over the past forty years have been immense, in terms of the potential output forgone, with the best situated economy, the US, seeing a 37 per cent reduction in national output compared to what it would have been if the 1960 public spending ratio had been maintained and the worst situated country, Sweden, having thrown away a potential extra 334 per cent rise in its living standards.†

That brings us to the issue of moral impoverishment as a result of over-government. A society which was so tightly controlled that individuals had no choice at all – if such a thing could be imagined – would necessarily be one in which they could earn no moral merit. More practically, in a country where it is assumed that the state provides for all, there is no scope for charity and no need for self-sacrifice. We can see the obverse of this principle in action without having to speculate about it. The United States is the richest and freest country on earth; and, not surprisingly, it is also the most generous. Each year Americans give over $200 billion to good causes.‡ Britain too shares in this tradition, where individual

---

* I note, however, that the massive increase in public spending – from 27 per cent of GDP in 1960 to 47 per cent in 1996 – was accompanied by a worsening of Japan's economic performance. There is no evidence that recent large spending increases have helped either. This point is made by David B. Smith – see below.

† David B. Smith, *Public Rags or Private Riches? High Public Spending Makes us Poor* (Politeia, 2001), pp.17–18.

‡ *Giving USA 2001: The Annual Report on Philanthropy for the Year 2000*, American Association of Fundraising Counsel Trust for Philanthropy, Indianapolis.

freedom and individual responsibility are assumed to go together – hence the country's inspiring history of charitable foundations and voluntary effort. The more we rely on remote public authorities to cope with the tragedies of life, the less we will do ourselves – and the more the unpleasing canker of selfish materialism will grow.

I tried to express this thought, some years ago, in an interview with the magazine *Woman's Own*. It stirred up a hornets' nest, but I felt that the hornets were buzzing around the wrong target. I said:

> I think we've been through a period where too many people have been given to understand that if they have a problem, it's the government's job to cope with it. 'I have a problem, I'll get a grant.' 'I'm homeless, the government must house me.' They're casting their problem on society. And, you know, there is no such thing as society. There are individual men and women, and there are families. And no government can do anything except through people, and people must look to themselves first. It's our duty to look after ourselves and then, also, to look after our neighbour. People have got the entitlements too much in mind, without the obligations. There's no such thing as entitlement, unless someone has first met an obligation.*

There are a number of things I have said in my political life which I would have liked to rephrase. These words are not among them. Yet they caused a furore. 'No Such Thing as Society' is still quoted (out of context, naturally) by left-wing politicians, journalists and the occasional cleric to sum up what they think was wrong with the 1980s, and what is still wrong with 'Thatcherism'. Yet they have a problem. If I am wrong, and there are indeed no moral limits to entitlements, how do they themselves provide a moral justification for keeping public expenditure and taxation within limits at all? Why not redistribute everything?

The left has sought to answer this ultimately unanswerable question by coining the phrase and extolling the concept of the 'Third

---

* Interview, *Woman's Own*, 31 October 1987.

Way'. Socialists have always spent much of their time seeking new titles for their beliefs, because the old versions so quickly become outdated and discredited. Interestingly, such self-descriptions acquire a cyclical quality. Thus 'social democracy' was originally a brand of Marxism. It was then dropped in favour of 'democratic socialism'. And then when 'socialism' – democratic and undemocratic – fell out of fashion, 'social democracy' acquired a new respectability. Nowadays we hear so much from the New Left about 'community' – Mr Blair's speeches are liberally peppered with it – that one almost expects the term 'communism' to reappear in its full glory. But perhaps not.

The 'Third Way' might be thought to represent a halfway house between capitalism and socialism. But according to Mr Blair this is not the case at all. It is rather, he explained in a long, dense article on the subject, 'social democracy renewed'.* So that's clear then . . .

As a phrase, the Third Way has probably passed its popularity peak. It never pleased Chancellor Schröder, who preferred the clanking Teutonic 'New Middle'. It seemed thin gruel to M. Jospin, who is the closest thing the West has to a socialist Prime Minister. And it also became an embarrassment in the United States, even under President Clinton, let alone President George W. Bush. As one American journalist observed: 'Now we know where the Third Way leads: onto the fast left lane of an expanded welfare state.'† Apparently the expression 'progressive governance' is now nudging aside the Third Way in well-connected left-wing circles. A new banality is born.

It is easy enough, of course, to laugh at the verbal contortions and intellectual convolutions of the New Left. But they have managed to persuade people in most of Europe and much of the rest of the world that free-enterprise capitalism needs to be tamed, qualified or restrained by state interventions to render it sympathetic. They have succeeded in this because it is still not widely understood that capitalism contains *within itself* the means by which society as a whole progresses. It does not need a touch of

---

* 'Third Way, Phase Two', *Prospect*, March 2001.
† Irwin Stelzer, 'Third Way or U-Turn?', *The Weekly Standard*, 9 October 2000.

socialism on the tiller to help it along. Indeed, insofar as government does intervene, rather than limiting itself to those functions which a successful capitalist economy requires and which I have earlier listed, the results are, unfortunately, bad.

One can demonstrate all this by considering the experience of Britain since 1997 under a Labour government which has achieved a (not wholly justified) reputation for economic competence. Prime Minister Tony Blair and Chancellor of the Exchequer Gordon Brown made no bones about basing their economic policy on the foundations laid by the Conservatives in the 1980s. Inflation has stayed low – and contracting out monetary policy to the Bank of England has helped reassure the City. Marginal income tax rates have stayed down. Although there were some increases in trade union power, the main reforms of the Conservative years remained in place. So there was no return to full-blooded socialism.

But that is only part of the story. There have, for example, been some significant and costly increases in regulation.* And most important there has been a large increase in taxation. These 'stealth taxes' – so-called because they are devised to attract minimum popular and political attention – have been aimed at businesses and at savers. They have discouraged people from starting traditional families (by ending the married couple's tax allowance), from buying their own homes (by ending mortgage tax relief and increasing stamp duty on house purchase), from building up pensions (by taxing the pension funds), and from taking out health insurance (by ending tax breaks for the elderly).† On top of all that the number of people paying the top (40 per cent) rate of income tax has also increased, because the tax threshold has risen in line with prices not earnings.

---

* These have been investigated in a useful pamphlet by Nicholas Boys Smith, *No Third Way: Interfering Government and its Cost to Business* (Politeia, 2001).

† Of these tax increases the most serious and the most surreptitious was that contained in Gordon Brown's first budget, when in the course of changing the system of advanced corporation tax he abolished the pension funds' ability to reclaim dividend tax credits. This meant that retirement savings were henceforth subject to £6 billion tax a year and the amount available to pay out in pensions was thus reduced.

There is worse. As one analyst has noted: 'The tax burden has not only gone up, but the structure of the tax system has increased the economic damage of raising revenue. The tax system is less neutral, more biased against saving and more complicated than it was four years ago.'*

The total net increase in taxation over the course of the last Parliament (1996–97 to 2001–02) amounted to £52.7 billion in cash. Differently put, the tax take has risen by over 50 per cent since the Labour Party took power, and British taxpayers are paying £1 billion a week more for the privilege of having a Labour government.† Tax and social security contributions now take 46.1 per cent of household income, compared with 42.1 per cent in 1996–97. It is not surprising that this large increase has been accompanied by a measurable deterioration in economic performance, notably a slowdown in the levels of economic growth and of productivity growth.‡

It is still unclear at the time of writing just what effect the large increases of public expenditure that have been announced will have on the public finances. These increases were imprudent at the time and now look more so.

The general conclusions, though, are clear:

- Capitalism can work well only if the fiscal and regulatory burdens on individuals and businesses are light
- The left – even the post-socialist left – can only be relied upon to accept this within limits: they still see nothing essentially wrong with tax and regulation as intrusions upon liberty
- It is the duty of conservatives everywhere to argue for low spending, low taxes and light regulation from first principles – and it also makes political sense
- Even limited deviations from the right path of free-enterprise

---

* Warwick Lightfoot, *Labour's Return to Tax and Spend: The Economic Record of the Labour Government* (Politeia, 2001).

† *Inland Revenue Statistics 2000 (Up-dated to 2001)*, Table 1.2. Net Receipts of Inland Revenue Taxes. Figures in cash. These dramatic figures were made public by Ian Cowie in the *Daily Telegraph*, 23 May 2001.

‡ Keith Marsden, *Miracle or Mirage? – Labour's Economic Record in Perspective* (Centre for Policy Studies, 2001).

capitalism have some adverse consequences – and these consequences can only grow insofar as left-of-centre parties and their programmes are electorally successful.

THE MORAL CASE AND ITS CRITICS

It is to me astonishing, but it is also true, that the left, New and Old alike, always manage to contrive an insuperable, and insufferable, sense of moral superiority. Socialists from time to time claim that they are also more competent at managing public affairs – we are in one of those periods again now – but they *always* claim to be operating on a higher moral plane than their conservative opponents. This is manifested in the criticisms which the left make of capitalism.

The first charge against capitalism I have, in fact, already mentioned in reference to the views of Adam Smith. This is the argument that capitalism is wrong, because it is based on self-interest. As Smith shows, the pursuit of self-interest is, in reality, the only way in which a market economy – or what Hayek calls an 'extended order' – can operate at all. But one can go further than that.

The accumulation of wealth is a process which is of itself morally neutral. True, as Christianity teaches, riches bring temptations. But then so does poverty. And in any case it is not, one suspects, concern for the consciences of the wealthy which lies behind the criticisms of wealth creation through capitalism. It is what we do with wealth that renders it – and us – good or bad. As John Wesley put it: 'Do not impute to money the faults of human nature.' And to 'money' I would add capitalism.

But it is mainly the way in which money is accumulated – not just what is done with it – that so annoys the critics. This process seems to them to be fundamentally unjust at two levels. It is unjust to begin with, they think, because not everyone starts off with the same opportunities. And it is unjust in its consequences because some finish up with more than they need and some less. There is a serious error here, which unfortunately conservatives are often too tactful (or too feeble) to point out. The error is to confuse justice with equality, either (in the first case) equality of opportunity, or (in the second case) equality of outcome.

Really, only a moment's reflection should suffice to see what is wrong with this equation. With all respect to the drafters of the American Declaration of Independence, all men (and women) are not created equal, at least in regard to their characters, abilities and aptitudes.* And even if they were, their family and cultural backgrounds – not to mention the effect of mere chance – would soon change that. On one thing, nature and nurture agree: we are all different. If this is unjust, then life is unjust. But, though one hears this expression – usually in the form of the complaint that 'life is unfair' – it really means nothing. In the same vein, someone once said to Voltaire, 'Life is hard.' To which he replied: 'Compared with what?'

This does not mean that the state should do nothing to overcome the disadvantages under which certain groups or individuals suffer. It is right in a developed country, where such things can be afforded, that a good basic education should be provided and proper medical care made available irrespective of families' ability to pay for them. I also favour policies which are aimed at encouraging people to build up some capital and acquire some property. Promoting these objectives was central to the programme of the Conservative government in Britain in the 1980s and 1990s. But policies must be framed so that they neither distort markets nor destroy incentives.

Wherever possible, government action to promote social welfare should be undertaken in ways which maximise individual choice – for example, through the use of education vouchers or credits rather than centrally planned provision, and through tax breaks rather than through blanket subsidies. The same principle should apply in trying to promote racial and cultural harmony in society. Discrimination against people because of their colour, race, sex or beliefs is morally wrong; it also makes for instability – as well, incidentally, as being opposed to the economic interests of the

---

* Actually, of course, Jefferson had a rather restricted view of the matter himself. He never, for example, had any qualms about owning slaves or presiding over a highly restrictive (and exclusively male) suffrage.

431

nation as a whole. But the use of quotas applying to the appointment or promotion of individuals because of their collective identity or background is an unacceptable incursion on freedom, however well-intentioned the motives. Nor does it help those who are its intended beneficiaries. Individuals from these groups may well feel patronised; their professional reputations in posts which they would anyway have attained on merit are diminished, because they are thought to occupy them by special privilege; and they are likely to become the targets of resentment and possibly even ill-treatment.*

In fact, we must remain clear about our goals. There is much to be said for trying to improve some disadvantaged people's lot. There is nothing to be said for trying to create heaven on earth. Governments should thus be very wary of connecting social policies with 'social justice' as it is usually called. As Hayek once pointed out, social is a 'weasel word [which] has acquired the power to empty the nouns it qualifies of their meaning'.†

'Social justice' can take a free society into still deeper and more treacherous waters if it is applied not only to equality of opportunity but also to equality of outcomes. Inequalities are the inevitable price of freedom. If people are left free to make their own decisions, some will respond more prudently and imaginatively than others. And, on top of that, some will have good luck and others won't. There is, in any case, no agreed set of criteria by which wealth and other advantages could be apportioned to the deserving. Even if there were, there is no possibility of government or any other body acquiring all the necessary information to make the judgement. And finally, since governments are only human after all, and politicians are particularly human on this score, there is every likelihood that horse-trading, influence-peddling and old-fashioned corruption will very soon be at work.

All these deficiencies were apparent under communism. Enough

---

* These arguments have been clearly and courageously advanced by Ward Connerley, a black civil rights leader who led the successful campaign for Proposition 209, the law which eliminated the state of California's system of race-based preferences in 1996.

† Hayek, 'Our Poisoned Language', *The Fatal Conceit*, p.14.

books have been written about them to fill, I imagine, a whole wing of the British Library. But what seems to be forgotten is that these drawbacks are present in differing degrees in *all* socialist systems, however mild the socialism is. When the objectives of government include the achievement of equality – other than equality before the law – that government poses a threat to liberty.*

That is why those who value freedom above all other political objectives – as I do – will settle for justice without adjectives, and rely on the rule of law not social engineering to uphold it. As long as all men and women are truly equal before the law, and as long as the law is effectively administered and honestly adjudicated, then however much their fortunes differ they have no right to complain that they are 'unjustly' treated. It is up to them what they do with their lives and their property. They bear the ultimate responsibility for success or failure – and everyone's life consists of a mixture of the two. And the government of the day, if it is a true friend of freedom, will avoid redistributive taxation and other forms of intervention aimed at social planning, because it knows that these things are, for all the accompanying talk of social justice, fundamentally *unjust*.

Traditionally, it has been the clergy as often as politicians who have denounced capitalism as harsh and unfair and called for counter-measures. They have a right to make these points: just as I have a right to disagree. But I do wish that they had been prepared to face up to the full implications of what they were proposing.

Not being a Roman Catholic myself, I can perhaps more easily say that the present Pontiff in this regard (among many) is wiser than some of his predecessors.† His views make abundant sense to people of all faiths and none. Perhaps in his economics as in his philosophy he benefited from having seen the reality of socialism in

---

* This is the theme of a splendid little book by Keith Joseph and Jonathan Sumption, *Equality* (London: John Murray, 1979). As the authors say (p.125): 'There is no greater tyranny possible than denying to individuals the disposal of their own talents.'

† Pope Paul VI, for example, was much keener on systems of global redistribution: he was also keener on cutting deals with communism through the then fashionable *Ostpolitik*.

action in his native Poland. That, at least, is what John Paul II's great encyclical *Centesimus Annus* suggests to me. Reflecting on the fall of communism and the bankruptcy of socialism, the Pope asks:

> Can it perhaps be said that after the failure of communism capitalism is the victorious social system and that capitalism should be the goal of the countries now making efforts to rebuild their economy and society? Is this the model which ought to be proposed to the countries of the Third World, which are searching for the path to true economic and civil progress? The answer is obviously complex. If by capitalism is meant an economic system which recognises the fundamental and positive role of business, the market, private property and the resulting responsibility for the means of production as well as free human creativity in the economic sector, then the answer is certainly in the affirmative, even though it would perhaps be more appropriate to speak of a business economy, market economy or simply free economy. But if by capitalism is meant a system in which freedom in the economic sector is not circumscribed within a strong juridical framework which places it at the service of freedom in its totality and which sees it as a particular aspect of that freedom, the core of which is ethical and religious, then the reply is certainly negative.*

I would not want to enlist John Paul II as an unqualified supporter of the free market – he is not. But I would certainly say 'Amen' to this assessment. I do not, as a matter of fact, know of any advocate of capitalism who thinks that it should not be accompanied by a strong rule of law. For myself I would certainly agree that there is more to freedom – and to life – than economics. And I have no doubt that capitalism, simply because it reflects flawed human nature, cannot of itself be relied upon to produce a good society and a wholesome culture. Irving Kristol expressed the thought neatly almost twenty years ago when he wrote: 'The enemy of liberal capitalism today is not so much socialism as

---

* *Centesimus Annus*: Encyclical on the Hundredth Anniversary of *Rerum Novarum* by Pope John Paul II.

nihilism. Only liberal capitalism doesn't see nihilism as an enemy, but rather as just another splendid business opportunity.'*

But pursuing that trail further would take me beyond the scope of this chapter, or indeed this book.

Those who believe that there is a strong moral case for free-enterprise capitalism must put it – and on moral, not just pragmatic grounds.

We should:

- Point out that money is morally neutral – it's what you do with it that counts
- Draw a clear distinction between the pursuit of equality before the law – which is part of freedom – and the pursuit of other kinds of equality, which generally involve diminution of freedom
- Frame policies to assist disadvantaged groups and individuals so that they do not distort markets or destroy incentives, but rather widen choice and ownership
- Reject in principle concepts of 'social' justice which undermine real justice
- Remember that capitalism is as good and as bad as the people who participate in it.

GUILT, POVERTY AND THE THIRD WORLD

In the passage above from *Centesimus Annus* the Pope specifically alludes to the problems of the Third World. His view and the view of many others is, I deduce, that if free-enterprise capitalism does not work for poor people living in poor countries there is something wrong with it in principle. That is a serious challenge, but I am confident that it can be met. Indeed, the experience of the Third World reinforces, if only negatively, the experience of the developed world, and both show that what we need is more economic freedom not less.

The starting point for any analysis must surely be the facts in as

---

* Irving Kristol, 'Capitalism, Socialism and Nihilism', in *Neoconservatism: The Autobiography of an Idea* (New York: The Free Press, 1995), p.101.

far as we know them. These show that there is a strong correlation between economic freedom and prosperity. In almost every case, the freer a country's economy, the higher its income per head – and the less free its economy, the lower its income per head – as the tables opposite show.

Of course, one cannot definitively prove from this that economic freedom actually makes countries rich and the lack of it makes other countries poor. Doubtless, there are other factors. But the relationship between free enterprise and prosperity is surely strong enough to give those criticising capitalism for keeping the Third World poor pause for thought.*

But probably not for long, unfortunately. Like the Bourbon dynasty, the Third World poverty lobby learns and forgets nothing. Despite all the evidence that collectivism leads to economic decline and capitalism to economic prosperity, these lobbyists advocate in the international arena policies which no sensible national politician – even a left-of-centre politician – would favour applying in their own country. We all talk now about the harmful impact of redistributive policies on the economy and of welfare dependency on society: yet the chatter about new international economic orders in which the poor are to be helped at the expense of the rich never seems to get drowned out by commonsense.

In the late 1970s and early 1980s the Brandt Report called for a 'new international economic order' and interventionist measures to secure a massive redistribution of resources between 'North' and 'South'.† The report, which was widely praised at the time, deemed this redistribution necessary for the preservation of the rich countries' security – overtones here of the left's long-standing yearning for an international uprising of the masses against their masters. And its subtitle, 'A Programme for Survival', echoes the

---

* The definitive and devastating critique of Third World 'development economics' is that by Professor Deepak Lal, *The Poverty of 'Development Economics'*, Institute of Economic Affairs, Hobart Paperback No. 16, 1997 (first published in 1983).

† *North–South: A Programme for Survival – Report of the Independent Commission on International Development Issues* (1980). The commission was chaired by the late Willy Brandt, leader of the German Social Democratic Party 1964–87, Chancellor of West Germany 1969–74.

FREEDOM AND PROSPERITY

THE WORLD'S FREEST ECONOMIES AND THEIR GDP PER HEAD[‡]		THE WORLD'S LEAST FREE ECONOMIES AND THEIR GDP PER HEAD[‡]	
Country[*]	**GDP/Head**	**Country[†]**	**GDP/Head**
1 Hong Kong	$25,257	1 North Korea	$1,000
2 Singapore	$28,460	2 Iraq	$2,700
3 New Zealand	$17,210	3 Libya	$7,900
4 Bahrain	$16,140	4 Somalia	$600
4 Luxembourg	$30,140	5 Cuba	$1,700
4 United States	$29,010	6 Congo, Dem Rep.	$710
7 Ireland	$20,710	7 Laos	$1,300
8 Australia	$20,210	8 Iran	$5,300
8 Switzerland	$25,240	9 Angola	$1,030
8 United Kingdom	$20,273	10 Uzbekistan	$2,500
11 Canada	$22,480	10 Bosnia	$1,770
11 Chile	$12,730	12 Vietnam	$1,850
11 El Salvador	$2,880	12 Turkmenistan	$1,800
11 Taiwan	$11,989	12 Guinea-Bissau	$900
15 Austria	$22,070	15 Azerbaijan	$1,770
15 Netherlands	$21,110	16 Burma	$1,200
17 Argentina	$10,300	16 Belarus	$5,300
17 Belgium	$22,750	18 Equatorial Guinea	$2,000
19 Iceland	$21,970	19 Syria	$2,500
19 Japan	$24,070	19 Rwanda	$720
19 United Arab Emirates	$18,110	19 Haiti	$1,340
		19 Burundi	$730

Figures in US$

Figures in US$

* Ordered by degrees of economic freedom. A country's position in the index is determined by several factors: levels of corruption, non-tariff barriers to trade, the fiscal burden of government, the rule of law, regulatory burdens, restrictions on banks, labour market regulations, and black market activities

† The least free is at the top of the list

‡ Figures are for purchasing power parity

Sources: *Heritage Foundation/Wall Street Journal, 2000 Index of Economic Freedom/CIA World Factbook 2000*

apocalyptic note without which any such lobbying would be deemed deficient. Ronald Reagan and I succeeded in defusing the worst of the report's bombshell proposals at the 1981 Cancún summit.* But just as with Gresham's Law† – which stipulated that bad money drives out good – so it seems a kind of law in international affairs that bad ideas repeatedly drive out sensible ones. Thus Brandt has his worthy successor in the Commission on Global Governance. This august body marked the millennium with a report complaining about the 'inequitable' effects of globalisation and the 'marginalisation of the poor'. It urged the creation of 'stronger and more representative structures of global economic governance'.‡

If one looks at the arguments put forward for all such grand schemes we come across our old friend, believed lost and still unlamented – socialism. Indeed, socialism on the international level, albeit concealed and repackaged under a variety of exteriors, is a far greater danger to freedom and prosperity than many people realise. The reason why discredited arguments of the sort still advanced are met with a respectful hearing can be summed up in one word: guilt. Westerners feel that they are somehow to blame for the undoubted ills and misfortunes of those in poor countries. But actually we are not. That great slayer of economic sacred cows, (Lord) Peter Bauer, has observed:

> Far from the West having caused the poverty in the Third World, contact with the West has been the principal agent of material progress there. The materially more advanced societies and regions of the Third World are those with which the West established the most numerous, diversified and extensive contacts: the cash-crop producing areas and entrepôt ports of South-East Asia, West Africa and Latin America; the mineral-producing areas of Africa and the Middle East; and cities and ports throughout Asia, Africa, the Caribbean and Latin America. The level of material achievement

---

* See *The Downing Street Years*, pp.168–70.
† Sir Thomas Gresham (1519–79), merchant and financier under Elizabeth I.
‡ *The Millennium Year and the Reform Process: A Contribution from the Commission on Global Governance.*

usually diminishes as one moves away from the foci of Western impact. The poorest and most backward people have few or no external contacts; witness the aborigines, pygmies and desert peoples.*

What is true is that while most of the world has made large economic advances during the twentieth century, some countries have been left behind: the question though is 'Why?' In a number of cases there has actually been significant deterioration – notably in African countries which while rejecting traditional Western values have borrowed Western socialist ideas and combined them with locally generated dispositions to tribalism and massive corruption. In fact, to the extent that the West is to blame at all for the ills of the Third World it is to the extent that the West created Marx and his successors, among whom must be numbered many of those who advised the Third World leaders in the post-war years. A statement by the Western-educated and much-venerated late President of Tanzania, Julius Nyerere – an indisputably charming man who did untold damage to the country's economy and much else – will illustrate the problem:

> I am saying it is not right that the vast majority of the world's population should be forced into the position of beggars without dignity. In one world, as in one state, when I am rich because you are poor, and I am poor because you are rich, the transfer of wealth from rich to poor is a matter of right; it is not an appropriate matter for charity.†

It is necessary to be very clear in our minds about what can and should be done to help societies struggling in poverty. My old friend Keith Joseph used to tell us how the great Jewish teacher

---

* P.T. Bauer, 'Western Guilt and Third World Poverty', in *Equality, the Third World and Economic Delusion* (London: Weidenfeld and Nicolson, 1981), p.70.

† Nyerere was speaking on a visit to Britain in 1975. The quotation comes from William L. Scully, *The Brandt Commission: Deluding the World*, Heritage Foundation Backgrounder No. 182, 30 April 1982.

Maimonides had identified eight descending levels of charity.* The highest level consisted of raising the recipient up to the point at which he was self-supporting – a charity that removed the need for future charity. Apart from disaster relief, which will always be necessary some time somewhere, it is this eighth level of charity which should be the driving imperative of all programmes of international aid.

Recognising this has important implications. Clearly, it rules out vast global strategies aimed at achieving equality – or even tackling inequalities – between nations or regions. The world has become more unequal, it seems, over the years. This is a long-term trend. In 1870 the average income per head of the world's seventeen richest countries was 2.4 times that of all other countries; in 1990 the corresponding group was 4.5 times as rich as the rest.† Apparently, the gap has widened further as the advances of the global economy have quickened.‡ This does not in itself, however, concern me, and it should not concern anyone else. Inequalities of wealth are part and parcel of economic advance, whether nationally or internationally. It is arguable that they even promote that advance. But, in any case, the only way of removing inequality directly is by redistribution, and redistribution, however subtly planned, slows down economic advance – nationally and internationally. What *should* concern us is something altogether different. It is whether countries are fulfilling their potential and so increasing the opportunities of their citizens.

In a system of free trade and free markets poor countries – and poor people – are not poor because others are rich. Indeed, if others became less rich the poor would in all probability soon become still poorer.

Some countries have remained poor because of unfavourable natural conditions, such as inhospitable climate, bad communications, water shortages and the like. Such things can be amelior-

---

* Maimonides (1135–1204), Jewish philosopher, known as the 'second Moses'. Chief Rabbi of Cairo and physician to Saladin, ruler of Egypt and Syria. Author of the *Mishneh Torah* and the *Thirteen Articles of Faith*.
† Figures quoted in *The Economist*, 11 September 1999.
‡ Robert Wade, 'Global Inequality: Winners and Losers', *The Economist*, 28 April 2001.

ated but not fundamentally changed. Often the best solution is what the local population are inclined to do anyway: send the most productive individuals abroad to earn a living and repatriate the money to ensure a reasonable standard of life for those that stay behind.

But many, many more countries are poor because of bad government. Misgovernment may be reflected in misguided policies that leave free-enterprise capitalism stillborn. It will usually be reflected in widespread, sometimes all but universal, corruption. It will often be reflected in oppressive or aggressive policies towards groups within the state or towards the state's neighbours – for in such circumstances the aim of power is plunder and the ultimate form of plunder is war. All in all, this is not, for example, a bad description of Zimbabwe under President Robert Mugabe. And here the important question is: why has this state of affairs, not just in Africa but elsewhere, continued for so long?

At least part of the answer – and it is the most important part, since it actually admits of a solution – is that Western countries and Western-led institutions have themselves perpetuated the problems. The West has done this not because of the rapacity of international capitalism, let alone the influence of that other favourite bogeyman, multinational corporations, but rather because Third World misgovernment has over the years been rewarded not penalised.

The World Bank has played an important role in this. Having been set up in 1944 to lend money to the war-stricken countries of Europe, the Bank had, in effect, become redundant by the late 1950s. But, as Alan Walters has put it: 'Unlike old soldiers, international institutions never fade away, they grow ever larger and more powerful.'* So it was with the World Bank (the IMF, too, as I shall explain shortly).

In the 1960s the Bank transformed itself under former US Defense Secretary Robert McNamara from a lender of last resort into an international welfare agency, and such it has broadly remained. Quite apart from the Bank's own activities, it also

---

* Sir Alan Walters, *Do we Need the IMF and the World Bank?* (Institute of Economic Affairs, 1994).

became the main proponent of a doctrine according to which less-developed countries could progress only if sufficient economic resources were transferred to them from the developed nations. Because this doctrine was both widely – at times all but universally – accepted, and because it was so fundamentally flawed, it did enormous harm in three ways. By providing money to finance the needs of incompetent governments, it helped those governments stay in power. By bailing out Third World countries which were pursuing wrong policies, it helped increase their harmful effects. By encouraging the Third World as a whole to think that its problems stemmed from the actions of the developed world, it also encouraged attitudes which militated against the sort of economic reforms that would have raised economic performance and living standards. An independent report conducted several years ago found that of the sixty-six less-developed countries receiving money from the World Bank for more than twenty-five years, thirty-seven were no better off than they had been before they received their loans. Of these thirty-seven, twenty were actually worse off. And of those twenty, eight had economies that had shrunk by at least 20 per cent since their first loan.* No democratic government would have been re-elected if it had turned in such a record. But although international institutions like the Bank may look all too like governments, they bear few similarities to democracies.

I do not, though, wish to be unfair to the various officials of the World Bank. No one forced the developed and developing world to pursue foolish policies. There were quite sufficient numbers of national politicians who went along with the notion that the redistribution of resources, the increase of international aid, the provision of loans, trade protection and import substitution, economic 'self-sufficiency' and the rest provided the answer to international poverty.

I, myself, never thought that; but Britain too had a modest aid programme when I was Prime Minister, and we tried to see that it was targeted as well as possible. Some aid has doubtless done some good. It would be odd if it had not. In many cases, aid has

---

* *The World Bank and Economic Growth: Fifty Years of Failure*, The Heritage Foundation, Backgrounder, 16 May 1996.

also had political and economic strings attached and can thus be seen as an extension of strategic influence – though the practical benefits of this to the donors are probably exaggerated. (One analysis of the effects of US aid programmes concluded: 'US foreign aid has not been shown to benefit the United States either economically or commercially.'* To sum up: the overall consequences of redistribution pursued internationally, like redistribution pursued nationally, are and must be harmful.

Is there, then, a better way? Yes. Step forward Maimonides. A limited amount of assistance strictly targeted at helping to create the right framework for free-enterprise capitalism might yield results. Third World countries need to create a clear and honest rule of law, limited but efficient government, secure property rights and a favourable climate for inward investment. Debt burdens – much of which represent unrepayable loans taken out as a result of foolish lending by the West – can also under the right conditions be alleviated. But there is absolutely no point in providing such assistance to grossly corrupt or blatantly despotic governments. And there is every reason, when in doubt, to let the markets be the judge of whether projects are sound and regimes are trustworthy.

The main way in which the developed world can help the less-developed world to progress is by promoting capitalism in general and opening up its markets and stopping subsidising its export products in particular. On these matters there is still much to do. The European Union could stop bankrupting or impoverishing Third World farmers through the CAP: a third of the cost of the CAP to the world economy falls on non-EU countries. And America could stop putting up barriers against Third World textiles: the annual cost to other – mainly developing – countries of such protectionism runs into billions of dollars.†

Reflecting on the experience of dealing with the problems of the developing world since the Second World War, some lessons are clear:

---

* Bryan T. Johnson, 'Debunking Claims that Foreign Aid Serves US Economic Interests Abroad', Heritage Foundation, *FYI*, 21 July 1997.

† Froning and Schavey, 'How the United States and the European Union can Improve Cooperation on Trade', Heritage Foundation, 7 March 2001.

- Collective guilt, misplaced guilt at that, is a poor basis upon which to devise solutions to real problems
- Policies of global redistribution make as little sense and have as adverse consequences as such policies pursued within individual nations
- The Third World is very much like the First World – just poorer: what works for the West will work for the rest as well
- The West has, though, two blots on its conscience: it educated a generation of Third World leaders in socialism and it then provided them with the means to pursue it – thus impoverishing their people
- Trade, not aid, offers hope of lasting improvement in conditions for the poorest countries.

DOOM AND REALITY

It is an odd fact, perhaps more explicable by psychology than politics, that the better things are and the greater the reason for optimism, the louder the voices prophesying doom seem to become. Just at present, with America reeling from terrorism, our economies stalled, and the international outlook uncertain, it is easy and even reasonable to be somewhat gloomy. But taking the longer perspective, global gloom is out of place. We have so much to be pleased about. We live longer. We are healthier. We are richer. We work less and have many more ways to enjoy our leisure. Of course, there are blips and backward movements. But they are usually only temporary. Was there ever an age when children had better prospects, all things considered, than those born into the world today?*

Yet was there ever a time when pessimism was more fashionable? Perhaps it is a distant echo of our society's all but forgotten religious past: one doubts whether the Old Testament prophets were very cheerful. Yet what marked out the prophets, soothsayers

---

* The facts of our society's material improvement are summarised by Julian Simon, in his Introduction to *The State of Humanity*, ed. Julian L. Simon (Oxford: Blackwell, 1995), pp.1–27.

and oracles of old – or at least those that we still hear about – was that they were proved *right*. Even Cassandra would have been forgotten if Troy had not fallen.

The West, needless to say, has not fallen. Indeed, it has risen inexorably – our enemies never cease to inveigh against the fact. And that is the starting point for consideration of the doomsayers and their warnings. We should be very wary indeed of turning aside from the path which made us rich and free, simply because some group of experts or collection of NGOs advise it.

The modern forerunner of those who still warn that humanity faces catastrophe unless it submits to coercive planning is Thomas Malthus (1766–1834). Malthus, it will be recalled, wrote a famous pamphlet in which he predicted mass starvation, wars and epidemics unless population growth was controlled. The basis of this prediction was the assertion that while population increases 'geometrically' (1, 2, 4, 8, 16, etc.) food supplies increase only 'arithmetically' (1, 2, 3, 4, 5, etc.). This was based on Malthus's observation of what happens in nature where (sometimes) a species goes on breeding until it reaches the limit of the available food supply, and as a result lives in a precarious fashion at the edge of subsistence. Malthus was immensely influential, and still is. But he was wrong. In fact, when he wrote (in 1798) the world was poised on the brink of an enormous advance in *both* prosperity *and* population. In the following century England experienced both a six-fold increase in population and a six-fold increase in income per head. Taking a still longer time-span, between 1820 and 1920, world population increased five-fold and world economies grew forty-fold.*

The fact that Malthus and his many successors are clearly mistaken in general does not, of course, necessarily mean that they are wrong in all particular cases. The tendency, to which a large body of evidence bears witness, is for families to have fewer children as societies become richer and more urbanised. There is no great secret why that is so. In a primitive rural economy it is economically rational to have as large a family as possible to till

---

* Ronald Bailey, 'The Law of Increasing Returns', *The National Interest*, spring 2000.

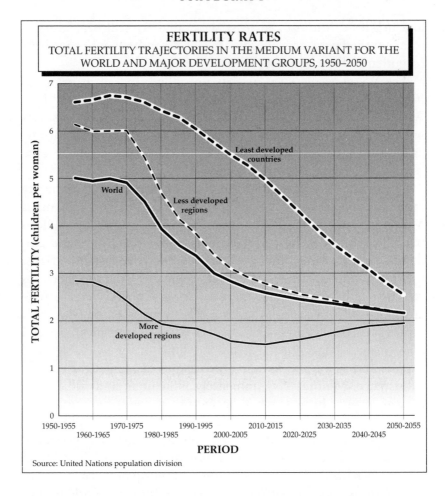

FERTILITY RATES
TOTAL FERTILITY TRAJECTORIES IN THE MEDIUM VARIANT FOR THE
WORLD AND MAJOR DEVELOPMENT GROUPS, 1950–2050

Source: United Nations population division

the land. But in a crowded urban environment, where living space is expensive and where skills are more highly rewarded than physical labour, the economics of childbearing are quite different.

The facts about population in the world today are not really subject to dispute. In the developed world, population is either shrinking or stagnating. In the less-developed world, too, the projected rate of population growth is rapidly slowing.

Perhaps the single most pressing problem for Western economies and societies – as the above table shows – is demographic imbalance, in part reflecting the sharp decline in fertility rates. Underpopulation, not overpopulation, is the West's worry. After years during which it was thought irresponsible to have more than two children, there is even talk of a return to 'natalist' policies to encourage larger families. Actually, it is extremely doubtful whether population policies of any kind are likely to yield much benefit. They may well, indeed, do harm. Governments are no more likely to make sensible judgements about how many people should be born than about how many cars should be produced. It is best for people to be left to make their own decisions. The real challenge for government is to respond intelligently and far-sightedly to the changes that occur.

This is the crux of the matter. Malthus was a pessimist. He underrated people's ability to make sensible choices about their future. He also underrated mankind's ability, given the right framework, to invent and adapt. This is perhaps not a great criticism to make of a thinker living two centuries ago. It is, though, a more serious charge to bring against Malthus's modern equivalents, who should know better.

Today's doomsters have broadened their attack. It is not just population growth but economic growth, not just having babies but having cars, that they dislike. The 1970s was a decade rich in catastrophic predictions – nuclear war, Western political eclipse and energy shortages jostled in the columns of the press, preoccupied economists and obsessed politicians.* Many of the gloomiest warnings were associated with a group of international experts calling themselves the Club of Rome. Their highly influential publication *The Limits to Growth* (1972) extrapolated current trends, assumed finite reserves of natural resources, and predicted that 'the limits to growth on this planet will be reached some time in the next one hundred years'.

The Club of Rome published their conclusions at a lucky moment, at least for the sales of the report. In 1973–74 the world economy was struck by the first Middle East oil shock, with a

---

* The current 'energy shortage/crisis' in the United States is quite different from the scare stories of the late 1960s and early 1970s. The problem, which President Bush and Vice-President Cheney have highlighted, is the result of too many constraints being applied to oil and gas development and to the use of nuclear power. Like most 'shortages' this is man-made; and it can be tackled by deregulation.

second following in 1979–80. From bewailing an excess of plenty and a surplus of economic growth the tone suddenly became one of lament at the onset of a deep recession and corrosive inflation. Of course, the distrust of markets remained constant. I well remember my first taste of economic summits at the tail-end of this sad period, where world leaders pledged ever stricter controls on fuel consumption rather than trusting the price mechanism to do its work.* Only when Ronald Reagan entered the Oval Office did we hear an alternative, optimistic message – that our free-enterprise, democratic system had the moral, intellectual and practical resources to overcome any challenge.

One of the most easily measurable yardsticks against which to judge whether the doomsters or the optimists were right is the price of raw materials. If economic growth were really running up against the buffers of a lack of natural resources, we would expect the price of key commodities to rise steadily as society grows richer. But viewed over the long term that is not what has happened. Indeed, those prices have fallen.†

This is not some statistical freak. It is testimony to the unplumbed depths of human creativity. We are constantly assailed by warnings that we cannot go on consuming. But we hardly seem to reflect upon the extraordinary way in which we get more and more out of less and less. After all, fifty years ago it was an ambitious forecast that 'computers in the future may have only 1000 vacuum tubes and perhaps only weigh 1.5 tons'.‡ And now we have the microchip.

Less farmland is producing more food. There has been a dramatic fall in the number of famines. Food surpluses are a major headache. Far from starving, more and more of the world is threatened by the ill-effects of obesity. There are, of course, still natural disasters. But it is by scientific and technological advance that we predict them, plan for them and cope with them. That advance occurs in free-enterprise capitalist societies, not in sclerotic social-

---

* See *The Downing Street Years*, pp.65–71.
† Julian L. Simon, *The Ultimate Resource 2* (Princeton University Press, 1996), pp.23–37.
‡ *Popular Mechanics*, March 1949, quoted in *The Experts Speak*, p.230.

ist ones. When socialist countries are to be found helping out capitalist countries in their hour of need rather than vice-versa, then – and only then – should we question the system which makes us rich, healthy and secure.

We should, therefore:

- Recall how wrong the doomsters have been and take comfort from the fact
- Learn the lesson that as long as a free political system, a free society and a free economy are maintained, the ingenuity of mankind is boundless.

HOT AIR AND GLOBAL WARMING

The doomsters' favourite subject today is climate change.* This has a number of attractions for them. First, the science is extremely obscure so they cannot easily be proved wrong. Second, we all have ideas about the weather: traditionally, the English on first acquaintance talk of little else. Third, since clearly no plan to alter climate could be considered on anything but a global scale, it provides a marvellous excuse for worldwide, supra-national socialism.

---

* There is a vast amount of highly technical material on these matters. Thankfully, the issues have been clearly analysed and debated by scholars in the United States, though not for the most part in Europe, where tendencies to consensus are once again all too obvious. This section draws mainly upon the following: Kenneth Green, *A Plain English Guide to Climate Change: Explaining the Science of Climate Change* (Reason Public Policy Institute, August 2000); Jerry Taylor, *Global Warming: The Anatomy of a Debate* (Cato Speeches: Presentation before the Johns Hopkins University Applied Physics Laboratory, 16 January 1998); Richard S. Lindzen, *Global Warming: The Origin and Nature of the Alleged Scientific Consensus* (Cato Review of Business and Government, spring 1992); Brett D. Schaefer, *US Foreign Policy and the Environment* (Heritage Foundation, Issues 2000); Fred Singer, *Climate Policy – From Rio to Kyoto: A Political Issue for 2000 and Beyond* (Centre for the New Europe, October 2000); Arthur B. Robinson and Noah Robinson, 'Some Like it Hot', *The American Spectator*, April 2000; Julian Morris (ed.), *Climate Change: Challenging the Conventional Wisdom* (IEA, December 1997).

449

All this suggests a degree of calculation. Yet perhaps that is to miss half the point. Rather, as it was said of Hamlet that there was method in his madness, so one feels that in the case of some of the gloomier alarmists there is a large amount of madness in their method. Indeed, the lack of any sense of proportion is what characterises many pronouncements on the matter by otherwise sensible people. Thus President Clinton on a visit to China, which poses a serious strategic challenge to the US, confided to his host, President Jiang Zemin, that his greatest concern was the prospect that 'your people may get rich like our people, and instead of riding bicycles, they will drive automobiles, and the increase in greenhouse gases will make the planet more dangerous for all'.*

It would, though, be difficult to beat for apocalyptic hyperbole former Vice-President Gore. Mr Gore believes: 'The cleavage in the modern world between mind and body, man and nature, has created a new kind of addiction: I believe that our civilisation is, in effect, addicted to the consumption of the earth itself.' And he warns: 'Unless we find a way to dramatically change our civilisation and our way of thinking about the relationship between humankind and the earth, our children will inherit a wasteland.'†

But why pick on Americans? Britain's then Foreign Secretary, Robin Cook, has observed: 'There is no greater national duty than the defence of our shoreline. But the most immediate threat to it today is the encroaching sea.'‡ Britain has found, it seems, a worthy successor to King Canute.

The fact that seasoned politicians can say such ridiculous things – and get away with it – illustrates the degree to which the new dogma about climate change has swept through the left-of-centre governing classes. It is clearly necessary to place this peculiar phenomenon in context.

As Britain's Prime Minister, I was one of those who in the late

---

* Quoted by Michael Ledeen, 'The Collapse of Clinton Foreign Policy', *The American Spectator*, July 1998.
† Al Gore, *Earth in the Balance: Forging a New Common Purpose* (London: Earthscan, 1992), pp.163, 220.
‡ 'Foreign Policy and National Interest', speech to the Royal Institute of International Affairs, London, 28 January 2000.

1980s followed closely and drew public attention to the issue of climate change. In 1985 the British Antarctic Survey first discovered a hole in the ozone layer – which acts as a kind of shield high in the earth's atmosphere protecting those below from the potentially harmful ultra-violet radiation from the sun. I was soon convinced by the scientific arguments put forward to the effect that the main sources of ozone depletion were chlorofluorocarbons (CFCs), which react with the ozone and destroy it. Use of these chemicals, in aerosol sprays, refrigerators, air-conditioning and elsewhere, therefore, had to be limited. I ensured that the British government was in the forefront of worldwide efforts to cut the use of CFCs – a campaign which has been extremely successful.

It was, however, the 'greenhouse effect' which soon began to assume more importance in the debate. This was a more difficult issue, because the science was much less certain. Although this is an over-simplification, the main effect of the greenhouse gases is to trap reflected radiation from the earth, thus causing the atmosphere to warm.* It was argued that the greenhouse effect was leading to climate change which could have dramatic, and indeed devastating, effects, among which was a rise in sea levels that could swamp low-lying land including whole communities. CFCs were among the greenhouse gases, so action to curb their use would help in this regard too. But the main contributor to global warming, it was argued, was carbon dioxide (CO_2). And the levels of CO_2 were linked to industrial activity. Therefore, the choice might appear to be between preservation of the climate and preservation of prosperity. This is, of course, how left-of-centre opinion wished and still wishes to portray it.

I was more sceptical of the arguments about global warming, though I considered that they should be taken very seriously. At that time there was, in fact, rather little scientific advice available to political leaders from those experts who were doubtful of the global warming thesis, though some doubts were being ventilated in the press. By the end of my time as Prime Minister I was also becoming seriously concerned about the anti-capitalist arguments

---

* Professor Richard S. Linzen describes the process fully in 'Global Warming', *Cato Review*, 1992.

which the campaigners against global warming were deploying. So in a speech to scientists in 1990 I observed:

> Whatever international action we agree upon to deal with environmental problems, we must enable all our economies to grow and develop, because without growth you cannot generate the wealth required to pay for the protection of the environment. We can rely on industry to show the inventiveness which is crucial to finding solutions to our environmental problems.*

Since then, there have been two further developments. First, the anti-capitalism which always lay under the surface of environmentalism has become much more explicit, reflected most recently in an ugly streak of anti-Americanism. This came into full view when President Bush announced in March 2001 that the US would not sign the Kyoto protocol on climate change. France, never easily outdone in this regard, was scathing: the French Environment Minister said, 'Mr Bush's unilateral attitude is entirely provocative and irresponsible.'† The EU Environment Commissioner, Margot Wallström, issued dark if unspecified threats against US businesses. Britain's own Environment Minister, Michael Meacher, described the American decision as 'exceptionally serious', but generously ruled out sanctions against the US, which should not be 'ostracised'.‡ The notion of there being even the remotest possibility of Britain taking action to punish America is so fantastic that it once again demonstrates that in these matters all sense of reality has been left behind.

Actually, President Bush was quite right to reject the Kyoto protocol. His predecessor had supported it for international effect, while knowing that its provisions made it a dead letter at home: the US Senate had voted unanimously on the matter. The protocol would have placed all the burden for reduction of CO_2 on the developed countries, while leaving the developing countries – including India and China – to keep on producing it

---

* Speech to the Royal Society, London, 22 March 1990.
† *Daily Telegraph*, 30 March 2001.
‡ *Guardian*, 30 March 2001.

at a rapidly growing rate. America's target for cuts was totally unrealistic – a 7 per cent reduction of overall emissions of greenhouse gases below 1990 levels between 2008 and 2012.* And all this is before anyone considers the scientific arguments about why and to what extent global warming is occurring. Kyoto was an anti-growth, anti-capitalist, anti-American project which no American leader alert to his country's national interests could have supported.

The other change which has occurred in the debate about climate change since I was in Downing Street is that the science has moved on. And, as is usually the way with scientific advance, the picture looks more rather than less complex.

In matters of public policy it is as important to recognise what we don't know as what we do. Governments, in this respect, are not like private individuals. An individual can most of the time act on hunches or incomplete information without doing any great harm. But governments, whose actions affect millions of individuals, must be much more circumspect. The golden rule is: all government interventions are problematic, so intervene only when the case is fully proven. How then does this affect policy towards the vexed issue of climate change? The answer can be considered in five stages, each of which involves a further question.

First, is the climate actually warming? This may seem so obvious if one reads most of the press and listens to most politicians that it hardly needs answering. But the facts are in some doubt. There seems to be a long-term trend of warming, to be sure; but according to some experts, it is *such* a long-term trend that it is not relevant to current concerns. A warming trend began about three hundred years ago during what is called the Little Ice Age, and this has continued. It is recent developments which are more disputable.

Ground-based temperature stations indicate that the planet has

---

* One American study calculated that compliance with this target would have resulted in a reduction in US GDP of 2 to 4 per cent a year (an annual loss of $100 billion to nearly $400 billion). Margo Thorning, 'A US Perspective on the Economic Impact of Climate Change Policy', American Council for Capital Formation Center for Policy Research, Special Report, December 2000, p.2.

warmed by somewhere between 0.3 and 0.6 degrees Centigrade since about 1850, with about half of this warming occurring since the Second World War. But, against that, the temperatures taken from weather balloons and satellites over the last twenty years actually show a cooling trend. The indirect evidence from rainfall, glaciers, sea levels and weather variability, often adduced to prove global warming, is similarly ambiguous. Some glaciers have expanded, some contracted. Sea levels may have been rising, but it is argued that this may simply be another long-term phenomenon associated with the end of the last Ice Age.

Such complexities though have not discouraged the politicians from claiming, for example, that freak weather conditions show the need for dramatic action. A confusion between the effects of the phenomenon known as El Niño and the broader question of climate change may be part of this.* But political posturing has a role to play as well. Thus Tony Blair has claimed that floods in Britain in recent years were caused by global warming.† John Prescott, the Deputy Prime Minister, has taken to publicly prodding a sandbag at international summits, blaming disasters on climate change.‡ Those faced with the prospect of carbon taxes, deliberate restraints on economic growth and higher unemployment deserve something better than this.

Second, is carbon dioxide responsible for whatever global warming has occurred? Here too the uncertainties are formidable. As noted earlier, CO_2 is not the only greenhouse gas. As well as CFCs, methane, nitrous oxide, aerosols and water vapour – the most abundant greenhouse gas – make major contributions. So exclusive concentration on CO_2 either in analysis or in policy prescription is bound to mislead. Still more important – and still more difficult to assess, as continuing debates confirm – is the role of solar activity. The sun does not burn steadily; it burns hotter and cooler in cycles. Studies have suggested that increased solar

---

* El Niño ('the Christ child') is a phenomenon of widespread weather disruption affecting the equatorial Pacific region.

† See, for example, Mr Blair's speech to the CBI/Green Alliance Conference on the Environment, 24 October 2000.

‡ *The Times*, 22 November 2000.

output may have been responsible for half of the increase in temperature from 1900 to 1970 and a third of the warming since 1970.* And whatever we manage to do about CO2 and other greenhouse gases, we are not likely to be able to do much about the sun itself.

Third, is human activity, especially human economic activity, responsible for the production of the carbon dioxide which has contributed to any global warming? This again might seem naïve if you accept the political rhetoric surrounding the issue. There is now, as always, nothing that the liberal intelligentsia likes to believe more than that 'we are all guilty'. But are we? The facts are unclear.

The widely respected Intergovernmental Panel on Climate Change (IPCC) concluded in 1995 that 'the balance of evidence suggests a discernible human influence on global climate . . . [However,] our ability to quantify the human influence on global climate is currently limited.'† Actually, not all scientists agree even with this view; but in any case it is a great deal more tentative than some alarmist assertions. I can see – as very much a non-expert – why those who are experts employ such nuanced language. Carbon dioxide levels have increased as a component of the atmosphere by nearly 30 per cent since the late eighteenth century, probably because of past deforestation and the burning of fossil fuels. But *in any one year* most CO2 production is not related to human beings. In fact, less than 5 per cent of the carbon moving through the atmosphere stems directly from human sources – again, mainly

---

* The latest research findings on these matters are summed up by Kenneth Green, *A Plain English Guide to Climate Change*.

† *IPCC Second Assessment: Climate Change 1995*, p.22. The IPCC went on to publish its *Third Assessment Report on Climate Change* in July 2001. The Report's 'Summary for Policymakers' was more alarmist in tone than the 1995 study, with warnings that the earth's temperature could rise by between 1.4 and 5.8 degrees Centigrade in the twenty-first century. However, the controversial summary was criticised as misleading by some scientists who co-authored the 2001 IPCC Report, including leading climate change expert Richard Lindzen, Professor of Meteorology at the Massachusetts Institute of Technology. (See 'The Truth About Global Warming', *Newsweek*, 23 July 2001.)

burning fossil fuels and deforestation.* This, of course, strictly limits the impact which any policy aimed at reducing CO_2 by altering human behaviour is likely to have. It is why attention has focused in some quarters on how to absorb (or 'sequester') CO_2 rather than on how to check CO_2 production. The United States, for example, proposed as an additional way of meeting targets for the reduction of CO_2 the planting of forests to sequester carbon dioxide, but this was opposed by the European Union. The more closely one examines specific proposals to reduce CO_2 in the atmosphere by emission controls alone, the more costly and economically damaging they become.

Fourth, is global warming anyway quite the menace suggested? To doubt this is, of course, rank heresy: but one should at least start out with an open mind. In an ideal world we would want a stable climate, or at least those of us who do not live in climatically unpleasant parts of the world would want it. If I were living in Micronesia and was worried about being submerged by the rising Pacific, I would be agitated. And similarly it is easy to see why those living in areas which already suffer from limited water supplies might be alarmed. It is necessary, though, to keep a sense of proportion. The world climate is always changing and man and nature are always, by one means or another, finding the means to adapt to it.

Earth temperatures today are probably at about their three-thousand-year average. And we have known periods of warming before. The Dark Ages and the Early Medieval period – about 850 to about 1350 – for example, saw a quite sharp increase in temperature of 2.5 degrees Centigrade. Although there was some coastal flooding, there were also improvements in agricultural productivity, in trade and in life expectancy. It was, rather, when the climate cooled again that agriculture failed and diseases spread. So when we hear of the dangers posed by encroaching malaria-carrying mosquitoes and of man-eating Great White sharks in the Mediterranean, we should remember that there is only one thing worse than getting hotter – and that is getting colder. Actually,

---

* Green, *A Plain English Guide to Climate Change*. The vast majority of carbon flowing through the atmosphere has natural sources.

some of the commentators should find it easy to remember this. In the 1970s, after two decades of unusually cold weather, there was a minor scare about global cooling – and some of the same people now worrying about global warming offered broadly the same programme of international controls to deal with the problem.*

The answers to each of the above four questions will be directly relevant to the fifth and final one: can global warming be stopped or checked at an acceptable price? At Kyoto the United States answered 'no', at least to the proposals on offer. Perhaps the answer will always be 'no'. On the other hand, perhaps a more realistic package may emerge. But in any case it will be necessary to resolve many remaining uncertainties before risking action that makes the world poorer than it would otherwise be by restraining economic growth. If there were clear evidence that the world was facing a climate catastrophe, that would be different. But such evidence does not so far exist. What is far more apparent is that the usual suspects on the left have been exaggerating dangers and simplifying solutions in order to press their agenda of anti-capitalism. Worries about climate should take their place among other such worries – about human health (AIDS), animal health (BSE), genetically modified foods and so on. All require first-rate research, mature evaluation and then the appropriate response. But no more than these does climate change mean the end of the world: and it must not either mean the end of free-enterprise capitalism.

The lessons drawn from past predictions of global disaster should be learned when it comes to considering the issue of climate change:

- **We should be suspicious of plans for global regulation that all too clearly fit in with other preconceived agendas**
- **We should demand of politicians that they apply the same criteria of commonsense and a sense of proportion to their pronouncements on the environment as to anything else**

---

* For a contemporary report on the 'global cooling' debate in the 1970s, see 'The Cooling World', *Newsweek*, 28 April 1975.

- We must never forget that although prosperity brings problems it also permits solutions – and less prosperity, fewer solutions
- All decisions must be made on the basis of the best science whose conclusions have been properly evaluated.

GLOBALISM AND ANTI-GLOBALISM

Global threats are necessarily a major preoccupation of this book, though the responses I have suggested generally try to avoid over-ambitious global responses. But was there ever so over-used a term as 'globalism'? Almost every aspect of our affairs is deemed to be subject to its – depending on your point of view – baleful or liberating influence. To be for or against globalism turns out on closer inspection to be for or against so many scarcely connected phenomena – financial, technical, cultural, social, judicial, military, political – that the choice becomes all but meaningless.* This has not, however, prevented a large number of people on the left, and – more surprisingly – some who consider themselves on the right, making it. Beginning in November 1999 in Seattle with the mass protests intended to disrupt the meeting of the World Trade Organisation, continuing in April 2000 in Washington where the World Bank and IMF were the target, then in Prague that September (aimed again at the IMF and World Bank), and in July 2001 in Genoa at the G8 Summit, the anti-globalists are now a noisy and often violent force with which governments and police have to reckon.

One can sympathise with the more reasonable opponents of changes sometimes associated with globalisation. After all, it is a strange mentality that welcomes social disruption or cultural transformation in its own right, though one may well conclude that there is nothing one can or should do to stop it. Most of us, whatever our politics, have surely felt on some occasion revulsion at one or other aspect of the modern world. In this sense, every

---

* I have dealt with the real and imagined effects of globalisation upon the power of sovereign states in the Introduction. Trends towards the globalisation of justice are examined in Chapter Seven.

reasonably well-integrated and well-established person is 'anti-globalist', and that must apply particularly to someone of a conservative disposition, attached (as Burke described it) to his 'little platoon'.* But it is the point at which such instincts induce us to try to plan or control the international spread of free-enterprise capitalism that is the point where luddism substitutes for conservatism.

In any case, conservatives (as opposed to socialists) worried about globalism can take comfort from two rather important truths. First, in an important sense globalisation is not new. The world has been here before – at the end of the nineteenth and the beginning of the twentieth centuries. In fact, the share of world production traded on global markets is not much higher now than in the years before the First World War. Many countries had already opened up their capital markets. The outflow of capital from Britain reached 9 per cent of GDP in the Victorian era, with similar figures from Germany and France, whereas in the 1990s the average capital outflow for the world's leading economies was just over 2 per cent of their GDP.†

In the late nineteenth century, just as now, the underlying conditions for economic globalisation were both technical and political. Transport costs fell and transport times shortened in the late nineteenth century as a result of steam power. The first trans-Atlantic telegraph cable was laid in 1866, and by the end of the century the entire world was connected by telegraph – the beginnings of an international communications revolution. Underpinning these developments was a commitment to free trade which spread outward from Britain from the mid-nineteenth century, and more generally the growth of the European colonial empires – especially the British Empire – which brought at least parts of every continent into a global political and economic network.

---

* 'To be attached to the sub-division, to love the little platoon we belong to in society, is the first principle (the germ as it were) of public affection. It is the first link in the series by which we proceed towards a love to our country and to mankind.' Burke, *Reflections*, p.136.

† Ian Vasquéz, 'The Return to a Global Economy', *Ideas on Liberty*, November 2000; Wolf, 'Will the Nation-State Survive Globalisation?', *Foreign Affairs*, January–February 2001.

The renewed onset of globalisation at the end of the twentieth century was similarly linked with both technological and political factors, though the latter were relatively more important. Although the speed of contemporary communications – above all the communication of information – was certainly significant, it is almost impossible to overstate the effects of the conservative 1980s in making the global economy possible. The conservative revolution spearheaded by Ronald Reagan, and pushed forward by me in Britain and like-minded political leaders elsewhere, ensured that national economies were opened up to international competition. Deregulation, lower tax rates and privatisation in our domestic economies were matched on the international level by removal of exchange controls and cuts in tariffs during the Uruguay Round. The triumph of Western values of choice and individual freedom was helped by the information revolution, which made it all but impossible for totalitarian states to brainwash their subjects about worldwide realities. The collapse of communism in Eastern Europe and then in the Soviet Union removed the 'Second World' altogether, and encouraged those parts of the 'Third World' that wanted to improve themselves to do so. The result was the first serious application of free-market policies to underdeveloped countries. In fact, we now have – as at Seattle – the extraordinary sight of protectionist-minded Western countries trying to impose labour and environmental regulations on Third World countries – while the leaders of those countries angrily reject them, knowing that such moves would make them poorer.* All this is testimony to the continuing effects of the conservative revolution without which economic globalisation would have been stillborn.

The second point which should be remembered by those alarmed at the impact of globalisation is that its effects are not by any means universal. Nor am I just referring to the least-developed economies where many still live off the land by subsistence farm-

---

* Commenting on this tendency, Martin Wolf has rightly observed: 'Under the pretence of helping the poor, the industrial countries propose either to undermine their competitiveness or impose protection against their exports' ('Old Wine in New Bottles', *IEA Economic Affairs*, March 1997).

ing. The majority of economic activity and jobs even in most richer economies are not directly affected by trends in global markets. In Britain, for example, 55 per cent of our GDP consists of 'non-tradeables', i.e. goods and services that cannot be traded over long distances. For the United States the figure is 80 per cent, for Japan 76 per cent and France 56 per cent.* So, as always, we should keep a sense of proportion.

All that said, economic globalisation is a powerful force. It is also an immensely beneficial one. Sadly, as the words inside and the protests outside meetings of the institutions that oversee the world economy testify, there is a widespread failure to appreciate just how much free-enterprise capitalism on a global scale has to offer the world's rich and poor alike. For the world's richest country, America, open trade continues to make it richer still, contrary to the warnings of critics of NAFTA. Far from leading to de-industrialisation as a result of capital flowing out to low-wage countries, 80 per cent of foreign direct investment by US manufacturing firms in 1998 went to other high-wage countries like Britain, Canada, the Netherlands, Germany and Singapore. And the US has itself over the last decade been the world's largest recipient of foreign investment.†

It is in the interests of rich and poor alike to trade, because only through specialisation in what we do best, while allowing others to concentrate on what they do best, can productivity be maximised. And the more productive we are, the more prosperous we become. The direct gains for Third World countries from globalisation are several. First, by cutting their own tariffs they will expand the range of goods and services available to their consumers and thus place downward pressure on prices – both of which raise living standards. Second, if cuts in domestic tariffs are part of a global package of tariff reductions, these poorer countries will also, of course, gain new or easier access to the markets

---

* *World Bank Atlas, 2001*. Figures for 1999. GDP measured by purchasing power parity.
† Figures given by Daniel T. Griswold, *WTO Report Card I: America's Economic Stake in Open Trade*, Cato Institute Center for Trade Policy Studies, 3 April 2000.

of other, wealthier, countries. And third, lower prices for their consumers, who are also workers, combined with inflows of investment and new technology, will combine to give a major boost to local businesses. Not surprisingly, the research confirms that developing countries with open economies grow substantially faster than those with closed economies.*

But perhaps the most widely heard charge against global capitalism today is not so much that its gains are uneven or its results unfair, but rather that it is responsible for global instability. Stability, though, must not be confused with stagnation. No political system and no society can exist without change, because change is a source of renewal. And this is above all true of a free political system, a free society – and a free economy. Adam Smith's 'invisible hand' is not above sudden, disturbing movements. Since its inception, capitalism has known slumps and recessions, bubble and froth; no one has yet dis-invented the business cycle, and probably no one will; and what Schumpeter famously called the 'gales of creative destruction' still roar mightily from time to time.†
To lament these things is ultimately to lament the bracing blast of freedom itself. But the instability for which global capitalism is blamed goes beyond this.

The crises in the Far East and Russia in 1997–98 prompted an anguished reassessment not just of the IMF and its lending policies – which was as it should be – but of the operation of global capitalism – which was more dubious. This involved both businessmen and politicians. For example, the international financier and philanthropist George Soros complained that 'the prevailing system of international lending is fundamentally flawed yet the IMF regards it as its mission to preserve the system'. He argued that 'the private sector is ill-suited to allocate international credit'. And he called for 'an International Credit Insurance Corporation [which would] guarantee international loans for a modest fee'.‡

---

* Aaron Lukas, *WTO Report Card III: Globalization and Developing Countries*, Cato Institute Center for Trade Policy Studies, 20 June 2000.
† Joseph Schumpeter (1883–1950), Moravian-born American economist and sociologist.
‡ George Soros, 'Avoiding a Breakdown', *Financial Times*, 31 December 1997.

For his part, the British Chancellor of the Exchequer, Gordon Brown, has proposed, in more general terms, 'a new economic constitution for a global economy'.*

But there is really a prior question which neither Mr Soros nor Mr Brown nor their many equivalents have satisfactorily addressed: that is, are the problems of the global economy the result of how it works, or of the fact that it is prevented from working? Examination of what actually happened in Russia and the Far East shows that in all the most important cases there were very good reasons for investors to take fright, ones which relate to a multitude of shortcomings in the policies of governments of those countries. Lack of transparency, cronyism and corruption, corporatism, exchange rates pegged at unrealistic levels – these and other home-grown factors contributed to the collapse. Those weaknesses were exposed, but they were not caused, by the 'contagion' of which economic commentators wrote so eloquently as, one after the other, currencies and share prices plummeted. They were classically problems of government failure. They were not essentially problems of market failure.†

The question arises, however, of why these problems had been allowed to continue and why so many international lenders and investors were prepared to overlook them for so long. And this brings us directly to the role of the IMF. Like the World Bank, but on an even greater scale, the IMF has very successfully reinvented itself, and one should not assume that the trick will not be repeated. As part of the Bretton Woods system of fixed exchange rates, the IMF was created to assist countries with short-term current account deficits. If the original plan had been implemented, the IMF's modest role would have come to an end in 1973 when the fixed-but-adjustable exchange rate system ended and currencies were left to float. But in the 1970s and 1980s it found a new role. It was entrusted with 'recycling' revenues of oil-producing countries after the oil-price rise; it also became an adviser to developing countries and made loans to ease the burden of adjust-

---

* Speech to the Council for Foreign Relations, New York, 16 September 1999.
† For an account of these events see pp.84–8, 118–23.

ment to the policies it favoured. It involved itself in the Latin American debt crisis of the early 1980s. It then became heavily involved, alongside the US Treasury, in the financial crisis in Mexico in 1994–95.

Although the loans by the IMF and the US to Mexico were repaid and the situation was stabilised – at a large cost to the incomes of Mexicans – an important signal had been given. Foreign banks and financial institutions had effectively been bailed out. They had not been expected to bear the risk they had assumed. As one expert has commented:

> A bad feature of the Mexican program was its contribution to the belief that international banks enjoy a safety net not available to the investors in equities or to purchasers of real assets in foreign countries. The message implicit in these actions was clear to bankers and investors.*

Such was the background to the Russian and Asian crises. The IMF's actions in these crises can and should be criticised. But the most important point to recall is that the problem of moral hazard created by *earlier* intervention was an essential element of what now happened. Similarly, the massive interventions which followed will have increased the risk of future irresponsible lending and investment in unsound environments.

Where, then, does this leave the IMF? Not, surely, as a cornerstone of any new international economic 'constitution'. Nothing in recent years, or indeed in the longer term, justifies broadening the Fund's current role. There is, though, a strong case that it should simply be abolished, as has been vigorously argued by George Shultz, William Simon and Walter Wriston. They point out that while 'loans from the IMF are, in fact, trivial when compared to the size of the international currency market, in which some $2 trillion is traded daily . . . the IMF's efforts are, however, effective in distorting the international investment market', and they conclude that 'the IMF is ineffective, unnecessary and obsol-

---

* Allan H. Meltzer, 'What's Wrong with the IMF? What Would be Better?', *The Independent Review*, autumn 1999.

ete'.* Others favour retaining the IMF, but only subject to fundamental reforms, which would entail ending its long-term lending role, lending at penalty rates so that governments came to the IMF as a last resort, and lending only to countries with minimum pre-established standards of banking.† For his part, Alan Walters suggests stopping the IMF lending money altogether and limiting its role to assessing the credit-worthiness of member governments and perhaps of government agencies.‡ All of these options have their attractions. The proposition which does not attract me at all is expanding the IMF's functions.

This does not mean, of course, that I am hostile to international economic institutions as such. It is important, for example, that the World Trade Organisation (WTO) be made to work effectively. Free trade is the best policy for all, it is even in the long run the best policy for each, but somehow producer interests and the politicians dependent on them are inclined to overlook this. As Adam Smith observed:

> Nations have been taught that their interest consisted in beggaring all their neighbours. Each nation has been made to look with an invidious eye upon the prosperity of all the nations with which it trades, and to consider their gain as its own loss [whereas] . . . in every country it always is and must be the interest of the great body of the people to buy whatever they want of those who sell it cheapest.§

Such is human nature that the siren voice of trade protectionism is never finally silenced.

For all the inevitable disruptions it brings:

---

* 'Who Needs the IMF?', *Wall Street Journal*, 3 February 1998.
† The conclusions of the International Financial Institution Advisory Commission, chaired by Allan H. Melzer, summarised by Allan H. Melzer and Jeffrey D. Sachs, 'Reforming the IMF and the World Bank', *American Enterprise Institute: On the Issues*, April 2000.
‡ Sir Alan Walters, 'Let's Put the IMF out to Grass', *Spectator*, 18 September 1999.
§ Smith, *The Wealth of Nations*, p.436.

- We should celebrate the triumph of global free-enterprise capitalism
- And we must ensure that its benefits are made available through open trade to all the nations of the earth.

Postscript

RUNNYMEDE

Because this has of necessity been a book about power, it may seem rather to have overlooked *people* – those on whose behalf power is wielded. Yet it must never be forgotten by anyone who aspires to lead a nation that political office is, above all, a trust. In fact, it is the highest form of trust. Whether, as in the United States, it is 'We the People' who are formally sovereign, or as in Britain that 'We' is royal, the task of the politician, and thus still more so the statesman, is, first and last, to serve.

To say such a thing nowadays may seem a little obvious, a trifle banal, perhaps a mere concession to the spirit of the times. It is, after all, very much the habit of modern public life to shun all suggestion of pomp and circumstance. Today's political leader will typically pose as the 'man (or, doubtless, person) next door'. But it is indeed a pose. It has to be. Once the man next door moves to Downing Street (or the White House or the Elysée Palace) he ceases from that moment to be the man next door.

In truth, the tendency of politicians to lose their bearings and forget their duties, as they become sucked into closed metropolitan elites, remains undiminished. Indeed, it has probably increased. Political leaders have never mixed so much with their own kind and so little with others. There have never been so many international gatherings; the democratic constraints of parliamentary accountability have never been weaker; and the temptation to forget one's roots and abandon one's principles has never been greater. Presidents and Prime Ministers have to struggle as never before to keep their feet on the ground, and the risk is that many will give up the effort altogether. National electorates should be alert to this.

In the process of holding politicians to account, institutions are, of course, very important. In Britain and America two somewhat different democratic approaches have evolved, and each has more than proved its worth. Yet well-constructed institutions do not of themselves ensure democracy. This lesson is confirmed by all experience in transplanting the seeds of liberty to societies which lack the right conditions for them to grow. The process is futile, and it may well turn out to be dangerous. In order to practise liberty successfully, a nation needs first to have a critical mass of individuals who truly understand it. Such understanding cannot be gained simply by reading books, only by developing the habits and outlooks which make liberty sustainable. Put differently, a free political, economic and social order *first* requires free men and women.

It is not enough, therefore, for the citizens of a free country merely to keep the letter of the law: sullen obedience is an uneasy, and often a fragile, basis for a free society. Free men and women have also to practise those virtues which make freedom possible. They must behave in ways which allow life to carry on without too much intrusion by the state. And they must be capable of thinking and acting for themselves and taking responsibility. They must, in the fullest sense, be individuals.

Individualism has come in for an enormous amount of criticism over the years. It still does. It is widely assumed to be synonymous with selfishness – an argument which I have already examined and I hope successfully dismissed. But the main reason why so many people in power have always disliked individualism is because it is individualists who are ever keenest to prevent the abuse of authority.

A large part of the explanation of why the English have been so successful in making liberty work is, I am convinced, that the nation has bred and nurtured more than its share of these rugged, angular individualists. We all know who they are. They are the people referred to as 'one of a kind', or 'a character', or sometimes and less favourably 'a difficult customer', or even on occasion 'a damned nuisance'. They are not to be consigned to social categories, nor planned into programmes, nor fitted into schemes. They drive socialists wild. We need such individualists in every walk of life. We need them just as oysters need grit. No grit, no pearl.

The sense that it is from the individual not from the group that inspiration and progress should be sought seems to be buried deep in our past. But, of course, individuals have always had to cooperate in order to assert or maintain their rights against the power of government.

In searching out precisely what gave the English, then the British, then the American colonists, and then the wider English-speaking world, characters so irritatingly bent on liberty, so obstinate to right wrongs, so pig-headed in demanding justice, I would go back nearly eight centuries to 15 June 1215. Or, not having a time machine, I would go down to Runnymede.

Denis and I last visited Runnymede Meadow on a hot, still, English summer morning. We walked slowly together up to the Magna Carta memorial. Built in the form of a little Grecian temple, it stands on a gentle slope surrounded by oak trees. It was erected by the American Bar Association more than forty years ago, and you are still as likely to meet American as British visitors there. The memorial is thus a testimony to Anglo–American closeness, but not it seems to historical geography. Although the precise site of the famous meeting between King and barons that led to Magna Carta is unknown, it almost certainly took place somewhere down on the flats of the Meadow itself.

Historians have explored in minute detail what happened there. The place had been carefully selected for that tense parley between a mistrustful King John and his rebellious nobles. It was roughly equidistant from the latter's camp at Staines and the royal castle of Windsor. Amid open country offering security from sudden ambush, it was as safe as anywhere in England could be for such an encounter between foes.

John needed money. The barons needed, for their own security, to return quickly to the King's peace. Yet the rebels were keen to go further than immediate grievances. They felt they had suffered enough misrule by the Plantagenets. They wanted some assurances for the future. Hence those 'Articles of the Barons' which were now agreed and were given solemn and more elaborate form by Magna Carta and then proclaimed throughout the realm.

The Great Charter's contents, as I have noted earlier, dealt largely with practical, even mundane, matters of the day. On the question of doing justice it went somewhat further. But it was the insertion in the text of the document of the word 'freemen', to whom its privileges were accorded, that would make the difference. In centuries to come, that term came to cover most of the population. The baronial programme acquired a significance quite different from superficially similar demands by over-mighty subjects of medieval monarchs elsewhere. And Magna Carta would thus become the supreme and timeless symbol of the liberties of England.

Those barons at Runnymede were more French than English. French not English was their native tongue. They were a brutal, warlike crew not greatly troubled, we may imagine, by the medieval equivalent of a social conscience. But their stubborn awkwardness in bringing a wilful ruler to accept limits to his power, their demand that he henceforth rule by law not force, their inspired reference to the wider community of freemen, began a tradition which has never died. And like all great traditions, it has had more impact on the course of history than the participants in the original events could possibly in their most extreme imaginings have envisaged.*

I am particularly fond of Rudyard Kipling's poetic evocation of the scene:

> At Runnymede, at Runnymede,
> What say the reeds at Runnymede?
> The lissom reeds that give and take,
> That bend so far, but never break.

---

* This is not to belittle Magna Carta – it is rather to extol it; for, as the Charter's authoritative historian notes: 'The "myth" of Magna Carta, that interpretation of it which gives it qualities which the men of 1215 did not intend, was part of the document's potential.' J.C. Holt, *Magna Carta* (Cambridge University Press, 1992), p.9.

They keep the sleepy Thames awake
With tales of John at Runnymede . . .

At Runnymede, at Runnymede,
Your rights were won at Runnymede!
No freeman shall be fined or bound,
Or dispossessed of freehold ground,
Except by lawful judgment found
And passed upon him by his peers.
Forget not, after all these years,
The Charter signed at Runnymede.

And still when Mob or Monarch lays
Too rude a hand on English ways,
The whisper wakes, the shudder plays,
Across the reeds at Runnymede.
And Thames, that knows the moods of kings,
And crowds and priests and suchlike things,
Rolls deep and dreadful as he brings
Their warning down from Runnymede!*

The demand that power be limited and accountable, the determination that force shall not override justice, the conviction that
individual human beings have an absolute moral worth which
government must respect – such things are uniquely embedded in
the political culture of the English-speaking peoples. They are the
bedrock of civilised statecraft. They are our enduring legacy to
the world.

---

* 'The Reeds of Runnymede (Magna Charta, June 15, 1215)'.

Index

Abu Musa, islands, 237
Aceh, autonomy issue, 127
Adenauer, Konrad, 6, 326
Afghanistan: Iran relations, 240; Pakistan relations, 201–2; Soviet invasion, 201; Taliban regime, *see* Taliban; US action, 38
Africa: economics, 419; religion, 418
Ahmići, massacre (1993), 288
Ahtisaari, Martti, 347n
aid programmes, 442–3
al-Qaeda, xxiv, 202, 240
Albania, Balkan policies, 286
Albright, Madeleine, 209–10, 214, 259
Aliev, Haidar, 101
altruism, 414
American Revolution, 24
Amin, Idi, 234
Amnesty International, 273
Amsterdam Treaty, 348, 350n, 397
Andropov, Yuri, 75, 104–5
Angell, Norman, xx
Annan, Kofi, 263
Anti-Ballistic Missile (ABM) Treaty, 53–4, 58, 107
Appleyard, Sir Leonard, 192
Arab–Israeli Wars, 244
Arafat, Yasser, 242
Arbella (ship), 20
Aristide, Jean-Bertrand, 33
Arizona, USS, 47–8

Armenia, government, 101
Asia: economic power, 111–12; financial crisis (1997–98), 83, 119–23, 464; population, 112; powers, 112–13; taxation, 424; values, 113–15, 418, 419
Assad, Hafez al-, 229, 230
Ataturk, Kemal, 223
Aung San Suu Kyi, 114
Austria: election (1999), 346–7; EU relations, 347
Azerbaijan, government, 100–1
Aziz, Tariq, 226

Bahrain, unrest, 237
Balcerowicz, Leszek, 70, 198
Balfour Declaration (1917), 243–4
Balkan region, 282–8; key events (1987–2001), 293–6; *see also* Bosnia, Croatia, Kosovo, Slovenia, Vukovar
Balladur, Edouard, 329
ballistic missile defence system (BMD), 54, 57, 214
Banja Luka, 304
Bank of England, 428
Barre, Muhammad Siad, 31
Bauer, Peter, 438
Belarus, Russian relations, 96
Belgium: jurisdiction, 272n; torture issue, 273

Belgrade, Chinese Embassy bombing, 178

Beneš, Edvard, 3

Berlin Wall, fall, 2, 16, 123, 338

Berlusconi, Silvio, 347–8

Bessmertnykh, Alexandr, 10, 11

Bharatiya Janata Party (BJP), 199, 200

Bildt, Carl, 317

bin Laden, Osama: on Americans, 60; Chechen links, 103; Iraq relationship, 228; objectives, 26; religion, 220; Taliban relationship, xixn, 202; terrorism, xxiv, xxv, 221; UK action against, 266; US action against, 37, 38, 266

Biological Weapons Convention, 50

Bismarck, Otto von, xxi, 6, 282, 322, 325

black economy, 418

Black Wednesday (16 September 1992), 385

Blair, Tony: economic policy, 428; elections (1997, 2001), 269n; ERRF policy, 354, 356, 357, 400; European policy, 322, 344, 380, 397; on global warming, 454; on international community, 34–5; Kosovo intervention, 309; military actions, 266, 309; on Putin, 104; support for US, 37, 356, 357, 380; Third Way, 427

Bolkestein, Frits, 333

Bolshevik Revolution, 23, 74

Bolton, John, 263n

Booker, Christopher, 374

Bosnia: ethnic cleansing, 301; independence, 297; massacres, 259, 261, 288, 293; Muslim–Croat Federation, 303, 306; Serb Republic, 303, 306, 307; US policy, 32, 33; war, 300–9; Western policy, 300–3, 317

Brandt Report, 436, 438

Bretton Woods system, 463

Brezhnev, Leonid, 77, 94

Brezhnev Doctrine, 249

Britain: charity, 425–6; currency, 383–4, 386–8; economy, 386–7, 461; EEC applications, 363–7; EEC contributions, 371, 390; EEC entry, 367–71, 377; EU contributions, 390–1; EU membership enlargement issues, 340; fishermen, 398–9, 400; foreign investment, 401–2; ICC policy, 265–6; investment overseas, 401–2; Kosovo operation, 36; nuclear deterrent, 52; Opium War (1839–42), 163; pensions, 333–4; referendum (1975), 369, 389; single currency opt-out, 377

British Antarctic Survey, 451

British East India Company, 116

British Empire, 25

British Missile Proliferation Study Report, 58–9

Brown, Gordon, 428, 463

Bruges, MT's speech (1988), 338

Buchanan, Patrick, 112

Bukovsky, Vladimir, 13

Burger, Warren, 24

Burke, Edmund, 254, 459

Burma, regime, 123

Bush, Barbara, 7

Bush, George Sr: gift to MT, 24; Gulf War, 28–9, 30; New World Order speech, 208; Prague meeting (1999), 4, 6, 7; Somalia intervention, 31, 32

Bush, George W.: Afghanistan intervention, 37; Blair relationship, 356, 357; defence policy, 59; election campaign, 27, 59; energy policy, 447n; foreign policy, 27, 95; ICC policy, 262–3; Kyoto protocol policy, 452; Putin relationship, 95, 108; Third Way issue, 427; war against terrorism, xxiv, 27, 241

Butler, Richard, 49

Byron, George Gordon, Lord, 9

Callaghan, James, 371, 380
Camp David agreement (1979), 245
Canada, NAFTA membership, 404, 407
Cancún summit (1981), 438
capitalism: free-enterprise, 412–22, 461; global, 462; term, 412n
Carter, Jimmy, 33
Castro, Fidel, 280
Cavour, Camillo Benso di, 322
Ceausescu, Nicolae, 164
Cecchini Report, 372
Central Asian Republics, 96–7, 100
Central Intelligence Agency (CIA), 77
Chang Yung-fa, 148
charity, 425–6
Charter of Fundamental Human Rights, see European Charter
Chechen War, 79, 102–3
Chechnya, 101–3, 108
Chemical Weapons Convention, 50
Chen Shui-bian, 186
Cheney, Dick, 447
Chernenko, Konstantin, 75
Chernomyrdin, Viktor, 82, 83, 84
Chetniks, 287, 291, 292
Chian Ch'ing, 152
Chiang Ching-Kuo, 186
Chiang Kai-Shek, 185
Chile: Falklands War, 267; human rights issues, 268–9, 280
China: Clinton visit (1998), 146, 184, 450; economy, 164–9; history, 160–4, 419–20; India relations, 200; influence, 112; inventions, 419–20; Japan relations, 145–6; military capability, 180; MT's visit (1991), 151–60; MT's visit (1995), 190–1; nuclear capability, 145, 179–83, 200; People's Liberation Army (PLA), 178, 181; politics, 169–75; population, 172; prospects for reform, 175–8; regime, 123, 175–8; religion, 173–5; Russia relations, 107; Singapore relations, 117; Soviet relations, 15; Taiwan relations, 52, 164, 182, 183–5; threat, 178–83; US relations, 25, 26, 47, 52
Chirac, Jacques, 26, 344, 347
chlorofluorocarbons (CFCs), 451, 454
Christianity, 250, 418–19, 430
Chubais, Anatoly, 64, 83
Churchill, Sir Winston: European policy, 361–3; foreign policy, 38; Fulton speech, 20, 55, 253; on Soviet alliance, xxiv; statues, 4–5
Cigar, Norman, 300
Clausewitz, Karl Marie von, 262
climate change, 449–58
Clinton, Bill: administration, 14, 89, 214, 264; China visit (1998), 146, 184, 450; defence policy, 27, 40, 41; on Indian nuclear capacity, 52; interventionist policies, 31, 32, 33, 266; on isolationism, 27; Japan relations, 146; Third Way issue, 427
Club of Rome, 447
Cohen, Eliot, 46
Coke, Sir Edward, 22, 252
Cold War: boundaries, 321–2; effects of, xxi–xxii, 93, 248; end, xxv, 14, 39–40, 160, 208; era, 1; ideology, 320; Japan–US alliance, 145; Reykjavik summit, 11; victory, 8–9, 10, 24–5, 108; years of struggle, 15–17, 327
Commission on Global Governance, 438
Common Agricultural Policy (CAP): British contributions, 396, 398; effects, 335–7, 391, 400, 443; European idea, 328; origins, 335; reform of, 337, 340, 377, 380
Common Commercial Policy, 401
Common Fisheries Policy, 398–9, 400
Commonwealth, 367, 369

Commonwealth of Independent
States (CIS), 94, 96, 101
communism: Asian, 123; collapse of,
460; legacy, 74–9; New Left
stance, 427; social justice, 432–3;
Soviet system, 15, 70
community, international, 34–5
Comprehensive Test Ban Treaty
(CTBT), 50
Congo, Democratic Republic of the,
260, 262
Connerley, Ward, 432n
Conquest, Robert, 12n, 72n
Conservative Party, 381–2
Convention on Genocide, see
Genocide
Cook, Robin, 265, 388n, 450
Council of Europe, 274
Council of Ministers, 348
Cox Report (1999), 180
Croatia: Bosnian victory, 304;
conflict, 299; ethnic cleansing, 301;
independence, 297–300; massacres,
259, 288; MT's visit (1998),
289–92; US policy, 32
Cruise missiles, 10
Cuba, human rights issues, 280
culture, enterprise-friendly, 418–20,
421
Custine, Marquis de, 73
Czechoslovakia, Velvet Revolution, 2,
6

Dalai Lama, 173
Dayton Accords (1995), 33, 306–7,
308, 310, 311
de Gaulle, Charles, 19, 326, 365–7,
394
Delors, Jacques, 375
Deng Xiao Ping: on calligraphy, 154;
government, 161; Hong Kong
discussions, 163, 191–2; reforms,
165–6, 187; successor, 155, 159,
160, 192
Denmark, referendum (1992), 345–6
Descartes, René, 324

détente, 13, 249
diplomacy, xxi, xxii
Disraeli, Benjamin, xix
diversity and competition between
states, 420–1
Djilas, Milovan, 75
Dubrovnik, bombardment, 290
Duncan Smith, Iain, 382n

East Asian financial crisis, see Asia
East Kalimantan, autonomy issue,
127
East Timor, 124, 126
Economic and Monetary Union
(EMU), 346, 354, 370, 384–5, 389
Economic Club of Chicago, Blair
speech (1999), 34
Eden, Sir Anthony, 364
Egypt, economy, 416
Elchibey, Abulfaz, 101
'end of history', xxv, 208
English language, 196–7, 343
Erhard, Ludwig, 326, 330
Estonia, 94–5
ETA, 221
euro, 384–8, 389
EUROJUST, 350
Europe: economic and social model,
329–31; idea of, 325–9, 361–3;
pensions crisis, 333–4
European Bank for Reconstruction
and Development (EBRD), 78
European Central Bank, 351n, 384
European Charter of Fundamental
Human Rights, 278, 279, 281
European Coal and Steel Community,
325, 327, 363
European Commission, 342, 350n,
375, 380, 401
European Communities Act (1972),
396
European Convention on Human
Rights (ECHR), 275–8
European Convention on Extradition
(1957), 274
European Court, 375, 401

European Court of Human Rights, 276, 277, 278, 281
European Court of Justice, 278, 406, 409
European Defence Community, 363
European Economic Area (EEA), 405–6, 407, 408
European Economic Community (EEC), 363, 366–71
European Free Trade Area (EFTA), 364, 367, 369, 405, 407, 408
European Parliament, 342
European Rapid Reaction Force (ERRF), 355–7, 400
European Single Market, *see* Single European Market
European Union (EU): army, 354–8; Balkan policies, 316–18; British relationship with, 281; bureaucracy, 324; Common Agricultural Policy (CAP), 328, 335–7, 340, 443; candidate states, 378–9; currency, 351–4, 358, 383–4, 394; environmental policy, 456; extradition policy, 274; federalism, 323, 344–5; fraud, 349–50; goals, 322–4; human rights, 278; languages, 342; membership, 337–41, 378–9, 389–95, 407; politics, 341–51; population, 394; Rapid Reaction Force (ERRF), 355–7; United States of Europe, 358–9
Exchange Rate Mechanism (ERM), 384–5
Extradition Act (1989), 274

Falklands War (1982), 267
Fall, Sir Brian, 63
Falun Gong movement, 174
feminism, 44–5
Ferguson, Niall, 334
Fernandes, George, 200
First World War, 40, 321
Fischer, Joschka, 343, 352
fishing, 398–9, 400

Fletcher, Yvonne, 233
France: Declaration of the Rights of Man (1789), 253–4; economy, 330, 461; EU membership enlargement issues, 339; Kosovo operation, 36; Revolution, xvii, 23, 254, 320; Rwanda intervention, 261; torture issue, 273; US relations, 25, 26
Frederick II (the Great), King of Prussia, xvii
free trade, 403, 465
Free Trade Area (FTA), global, 405
Frowein, Jochen, 347n
Fukuyama, Francis, 30, 114, 208
Fulton, Missouri, MT's speech (1996), 55

Gadaffi, Muammar, 52, 232–5
Gaidar, Yegor, 82
Galbraith, J.K., 12–13
Gamsakhurdia, Zviad, 101
Gandhi, Indira, 197–8
Gandhi, Rajiv, 197–8, 221
Garton Ash, Timothy, 6
Gasperi, Alcide de, 326
Genoa, G8 Summit protests (2000), 458
Genocide, Convention on, 255, 256–7, 258
Georgia, government, 101
Germany: currency, 345; defence spending, 40, 41; economy, 330, 461; EU membership enlargement issues, 339; interest rates, 385; reunification, 2–3, 7, 338, 385; Weimar Republic, 85
Gladstone, William Ewart, xxi
Glendon, Mary Ann, 255
global warming, 449–58
globalisation, xviii, 438, 458–66
Glorious Revolution (1688), 251–2
Goldsmith, Sir James, 111
Gonzalez, Felipe, 352
Gorbachev, Mikhail: Cold War role, 14; coup attempt against (1991),

Gorbachev, Mikhail – *cont.*
64, 76, 81, 151, 158; defence
policy, 11; Germany policy, 2;
MT's visit (1993), 64; Prague visit
(1999), 4, 6–8, 17; reforms, 70,
75–6, 81, 216; regime, 105;
removal from power, 64
Gorbachev, Raisa, 64
Gorbachev Foundation, 64
Gore, Al, 450
Gothenberg, EU–US Summit (2001),
26
Gramm, Phil, 404
Gray, Colin S., 51
Greece, Balkan policy, 286
greenhouse effect, 451, 454
Grenada, US intervention (1983),
30
Gresham's Law, 438
Group of Seven (G7), 80, 81
Gulf states, 223, 237
Gulf War: Bush's policy, 28–9;
effects of, 29–30, 37, 245; Iraqi
regime, 225–8; origins, 49; US
opposition to, 27; victory, 16

Habibie, B.J., 126
Habsburg Empire, 25, 326
Hagglund, Gustav, 357
Hague, MT's speech (1992), 395
Hague, William, 382, 397
Haider, Jörg, 346–7
Haiti, US intervention (1994), 33
Hamas, 221, 237
Hamilton, Alexander, 22
Harrington, James, 22
Hashimoto, Ryutaro, 146
Hassad, Bashar al-, 229, 230
Hassan I, King of Morocco, 223
Hau Pei-tsun, 188
Havel, Vaclav, 4, 6, 29
Hayek, Friedrich von, 16, 332, 415,
424, 430, 432
Healey, Denis, 43–4
Heath, Edward, 367, 370n, 377
Helms, Jesse, 50, 265

Helsinki: Accords, 249; EU Summit
(1999), 355
Henry, Patrick, 22
Heritage Foundation, 58, 405
Hindley, Brian, 393n
Hitler, Adolf, xxiv, 3, 327
Hizbollah, 221, 237
Holocaust, 244, 257, 258
Holy Land, 241–7
Hong Kong: economy, 120, 403;
handover, 189–94; lease, 163;
regime, 124
Hoon, Geoff, 356
Hormuz, Straits of, 237
Howe, Sir Geoffrey, 360n
Hu Yaobang, 160
Hulsman, John, 405
human rights, xxii, xxv, 248–56
Human Rights Act, 275, 277–8
Hungary: Balkan policy, 286; EU
membership issue, 338
Huntington, Samuel, 30
Hurd, Douglas, 151–2, 345
Hussein, Saddam: Gulf War, 266;
Kuwait invasion, 28, 49, 226,
227–8; Palestinian support for,
245; regime after Gulf War,
29–30, 225–6, 228; religion,
225–6, 235; successor, 229; war
with Iran, 237, 239; weaponry, 49,
91
Huxley, Julian, 12

Ibrahim, Anwar, 121
Ibuka, Masaru, 138
Iceland: EEA, 405–6
Ilarionov, Andrei, 87, 106n
Imperial Preference, 392
income tax, 428
India: British legacy, 194–7; China
relations, 200; conflict resolution,
200–6; influence, 112–13; Kashmir
dispute, xxiii, 202–4; language,
196–7; lost opportunities, 197–8;
military capability, 200; nuclear
policy, 52–3, 56, 179, 200–1;

Pakistan relations, 200; partition, 197, 202; path of reform, 198–200; UN role, 148, 205
individualism, 468–9
Indonesia, 124–7; economy, 121; influence, 113; regime, 123; religion, 222
inflation, 428
interest rates, 385
Intergovernmental Panel on Climate Change (IPCC), 455
Intermediate Range Nuclear Forces (INF) Treaty, 90
International Criminal Court, proposed, 262–7
International Institute for Strategic Studies, 40–1
International Monetary Fund (IMF): Japanese forecasts, 141; protests against, 458; role in Indonesia, 125; role in Mexico, 463–4; role in Russia, 79–82, 84; role in South Korea, 121; role in Third World, 441; status, 464–5
International Red Cross, 292
Internet, 47, 171
intifada, 245
Iran: military capability, 55, 239–40; regime, 235–41; religion, 220, 235–7; rogue state, 209, 220; US relations, 237–40; war with Iraq, 226, 237, 239
Iraq: history, 231; Kuwait invasion, 226–7; military capability, 49–50, 55, 239; regime, 225–6; religion, 220, 225, 226; rogue state, 209, 220; sanctions against, 228; war with Iran, 226, 237, 239
Irish Republican terrorists, 221, 232, 233
Islam, 216–25, 235–7
Islamic Jihad, 221, 237
Islamic revolution, 26
Israel: Gulf War, 245; history, 243–5; *intifada*, 245; Lebanon presence, 230, 245; military threats

to, 55, 56; MT's visit (1998), 242–3; Palestinian relations, 243–6; political leaders, 241–2; population, 245; Syria relations, 229–30; Turkey relations, 230, 239; wars, 244
Italy: defence spending, 40, 41; EU relations, 347–8; pensions crisis, 333

Jakarta, Chinese community, 127
James II, King, 251n
James Bryce Lecture (1996), 23n
Jamieson, Bill, 331
Japan: capitalism, 132–7; China relations, 145–6; economy, 127–8, 131–2, 139–43, 425; history, 129–31; influence, 112, 146; investment, 401; Kobe experience, 148–50; military power, 144–5, 147, 181; Ministry for Trade and Industry (MITI), 133; North Korea relations, 55, 56; politicians, 128–9; religion, 130; Russia relations, 83, 107; UN role, 147–8; US relations, 145, 146–7; as world power, 144–8
Jaruzelski, Wojciech, 6
Jefferson, Thomas, 22, 253, 431n
Jiang Zemin: accession, 155, 191, 192; Clinton's visit (1998), 450; MT's visit (1991), 159–60; Russia relations, 26
John, King, 469–71
John XXIII, Pope, 324
John Paul II, Pope, 433–4, 435
Johnson, Paul, 12n
Joint Direct Attack Munition, 36
Joseph, Sir Keith, 439
Jospin, Lionel, 26, 278n, 344, 351n, 353, 427
Judaism, 418–19

Kaifu, Toshiki, 128
Kalimantan, massacres, 126
Karadžić, Radovan, 307

Kashmir dispute, xxiii, 202–4
Kazakhstan, 97, 100
Kelche, Jean-Pierre, 356
Kennedy, John F., 365
Kennedy, Paul, 111
Kenway, William, 361n
KGB, 77, 79, 104
Khameni, Ayatollah Ali, 235
Khatami, Mohammad, 235, 237, 239
Khomeini, Ayatollah, 236
Khrushchev, Nikita, 75
Kim Dae Jung, 209
Kim Il Sung, 210
Kim Jong Il, 209, 210–11, 213–16
Kim Young Sam, 123
Kinnock, Neil, 349
Kipling, Rudyard, 470
Kiriyenko, Sergei, 83
Kirkpatrick, Jeane, 123n, 125
Kissinger, Henry, xviin, xxiiin, 13n, 152
Klaus, Vaclav, 3, 5, 198
Kobe: earthquake, 149; MT's visit (1994), 148–9; MT's visit (1996), 149
Kohl, Helmut, 4, 6, 7, 352, 358n, 360n
Koizumi, Junichiro, 140, 144
Korean war, 210
Kosovo: ethnic cleansing, 309, 310, 312–13; future, 313–15; NATO intervention, xxiii, 33–4, 35–6, 89, 90, 178n, 179, 306, 311–12; Serb defeat, 261; Serb policies, 286–7, 310, 311–13
Kosovo Liberation Army (KLA), 34n, 311, 314
Koštunica, Vojislav, 316
Kotlikoff, Laurence J., 334
Kristol, Irving, 434
Kuchma, Leonid, 96
Kung-Pin Mei, Cardinal, 174–5
Kuwait: Iraqi invasion, 226–7; MT's visits (1991, 1998), 227–8
Kyoto protocol on climate change, 452–3, 457

Kyrgyzstan, Russian military aid, 97

Laffer curve, 422
Lafontaine, Oskar, 330n
Lake, Anthony, 207
Lal, Deepak, 436n
Lamont, Norman, 391
Laski, Harold, 12
Latvia, 94–5
law, 409–10; rule of, 417–18, 421–2
League of Nations, xxn, 29, 244
Lebanon: Arab–Israeli conflict, xxiii; Israeli presence, 230, 245; terrorist groups, 229
Lebed, Alexandr, 101
Lee Kuan Yew, 114, 117
Lee Teng-Hui, 186
Lenin, Vladimir Ilyich, 74, 75
Li Peng, 152, 155, 158–60, 167, 191–2
Li Zhisui, 161n
Libya: regime, 232–5; religion, 220, 235; rogue state, 209, 220; US bombing (1986), 30, 52
Liechtenstein: EEA, 405–6
Lithuania, 94
Locke, John, 22
Lockerbie disaster (1988), 232–3
Longfellow, Henry, 62
Los Angeles World Affairs Council (1991), 29
Louvre Accord (1987), 139n
Lukashenko, Alexandr, 96
Luxembourg Compromise, 381

Maastricht Treaty: British ratification, 377, 396; Europe of the Regions, 353–4; German referendum, 345; secession provisions, 409; single currency, 384, 396; subsidiarity, 380
Macedonia, 286, 314
Machiavelli, Niccolo, xvii
McKinsey & Company, 134
Macmillan, Harold, 364–5, 367

McNamara, Robert, 441
Madison, James, 22, 61
Magna Carta, 20, 24, 251, 252, 470-1
Mahathir bin Mohamad, 114, 121
Maimonides, 440, 443
Major, John: China visit (1991), 151-2; EU membership enlargement issue, 338; European policy, 380, 396-7; Hong Kong handover, 190; Maastricht Treaty, 377, 380
Malaysia: economy, 120-1, 122; regime, 123
Malcolm, Noel, 300, 313, 383n
Malthus, Thomas, 445, 447
Mandeville, Bernard, 140
Mao Zedong: Cultural Revolution, 159; regime, 161, 164, 169; Stalin relationship, 160; Taiwan policy, 185; wife, 152
Marsden, Keith, 331
Marx, Karl, 74, 320, 412n, 439
Mary II, Queen, 251n
Maudling, Reginald, 367
Meacher, Michael, 452
Megrahi, Abdul Baset Ali al-, 232n
Meir, Golda, 243
Mendeleev Institute, Moscow, 63, 64
Messerlin, Patrick, 336
Methodism, 21
Mexico: EU trade agreement, 406-8; financial crisis (1994-95), 464; NAFTA membership, 404, 407
Mill, John Stuart, 420-1
Milošević, Slobodan: aims, 298; Hague tribunal, 259, 261, 307, 316; Kosovo issues, 309-12; Russian relations, 90; warfare, 286-7, 299, 316; Western action against, 266
Minford, Patrick, 331, 391, 393, 398n
missiles: Chinese, 145-6, 179; Cold War, 50-1; Cruise, 10; global system, 58; Iranian, 239-40;

Libyan, 234; Nodong, 146, 212-13; North Korean, 212-13; Pershing II, 10; PGM, 36; proliferation, 49-50, 55-7, 179; Rodong-I, 55; rogue states, 51-2; role of, 52-3; Rumsfeld Commission, 55-6; Scud, 212, 234; Shehab, 240; Soviet stockpiles, 48-9; SS-27; Taepodong ICBMs, 212, 214; Topol-M ICBM, 91; terrorist threat, 57-8; treaties, 50, 53-4, 58, 90; US policy, 58-9
Mitterrand, Danielle, 4, 6
Mitterrand, François, 2
Mladić, Ratko, 307
Moluccas, massacres, 126
Monnet, Jean, 325, 326
Montenegro, EU policy, 318
Montgomery, Bernard Law, Viscount Montgomery of Alamein, 363
Morita, Akio, 135n, 137-9, 143
Morocco, regime, 222-3
Moscow: MT's speech to Supreme Soviet (1991), 81n; MT's visit (1993), 63-4
Mountbatten, Louis, Lord Mountbatten of Burma, 203
Mrkšić, Mile, 293n
Mugabe, Robert, 441
Muhammad, Prophet, 217
multilateralism, 30, 31
Musharraf, Pervais, 202, 204, 205
Muslim Brotherhood, 229, 236
Mutually Assured Destruction (MAD), 53

Nakasone, Yasuhiro, 128
Napoleon Bonaparte, xvii, 326-7
National Institute of Economic and Social Research (NIESR), 392-3
National Portrait Gallery, 1
nationhood, xxii
NATO: Balkan air strikes, 305; Croat-Muslim action, 32; European contribution, 355, 357;

NATO – *cont.*
expansion, 27, 89, 95, 108;
German reunification, 3, 7; Kosovo
intervention, xxiii, 33–4, 35–6, 89,
90, 178n, 179, 311–12;
membership, 340; military
spending, 40, 42; role, 16, 34, 327;
Talbott on, 14; US leadership, 109,
356
Naumann, Klaus, 286–7
Nazarbayev, Sultan, 151
Nehru, Jawaharlal, 195–6, 197
Nemtsov, Boris, 65, 68, 83
Netanyahu, Benjamin, 241, 242
New Left, 248–9, 427
New World Order, 29, 31, 34, 208
Nice Summit (2000), 337, 340, 348,
355, 356
Nice Treaty, 381n, 397
Niño, El, 454
Nixon, Richard M., 160–1
Nizhny Novgorod, MT's visit (1993),
65–9
non-governmental organisations
(NGOs), 277
Noriega, Manuel Antonio Morena,
31
North American Free Trade Area
(NAFTA), 341, 386, 403–8, 411,
461
North Korea: China relations, 179;
military capability, 55, 56, 146,
212–13, 240; regime, 209–16;
rogue state, 208, 209; South Korea
relations, 215–16; US relations,
214
Norway: economy, 398; EEA, 405–6
Novak, Michael, 17
nuclear weapons, *see* missiles
Numeiri, Gaafar Mohamed al-, 234
Nuremberg Tribunal, 257–8
Nyerere, Julius, 439

oil: British, 386; Central Asian, 100,
101; Gulf War, 226; Libyan, 234;
Middle Eastern, 223, 231, 237

O'Neill, Sir Con, 369
opinion polls, 388, 389
Oreja, Marcelino, 347n
Owen, David, Lord, 302

Pakistan: Afghanistan relations,
201–2; India relations, 200;
Kashmir dispute, xxiii, 202–4;
nuclear policy, 52, 56, 179;
partition, 197, 202; religion, 201,
204
Palestinians: guest-workers, 226; Gulf
War, 226, 245; *intifada*, 245;
terrorist groups, 232
Panama, US intervention (1989), 31
Papua, autonomy issue, 127
Parkinson's law, 43
Parliament, British, 396, 409–10
Patten, Chris, 190–1, 192
Paul VI, Pope, 433n
Pearl Harbor, 47–8
pensions: European, 333–4; taxation,
428
Peres, Shimon, 241
Perry, Matthew, 129
Pershing II missiles, 10
Philippines, economy, 120–1
Pinochet Ugarte, Augusto, 204,
267–74, 280
Pipes, Richard, 14, 72n
Plavšić, Biljana, 300
Pol Pot, 256–7
Poland, EU membership issue, 338,
340
Pompidou, Georges, 367
Poos, Jacques, 299
population growth, 445–7
Portugal, EU membership, 338
Powell, Enoch, 368
Prague: meeting (16 November
1999), 2–9; protests (September
2000), 458
precision-guided missiles (PGMs), 36
Prescott, John, 454
pressure groups, 16
Primakov, Yevgeny, 83, 84

Prodi, Romano, 384
property rights, 416–17, 421
Public Choice Theory, 415
public spending, 423–4, 429
Putin, Vladimir: accession, 84, 104; advisers, 87; Bush meeting, 95; career, 104; character, 103–4, 104–5; Chechen campaign, 102; defence policy, 59, 90, 91; foreign policy, 107–8; Korean relations, 213–14; regime, 105–6, 109–10

Qaddafi, *see* Gaddafi
Qian Qichen, 153, 159
qualified majority voting (QMV), 375, 381

Rabin, Leah, 243
Rabin, Yitzhak, 241–3, 246
Rabkin, Jeremy, 257, 266
racial discrimination, 431–2
Radić, Miroslav, 293n
Raffles, Sir Thomas, 116
Rambouillet peace talks (1999), 311
Rao, P.V. Narasimha, 198
Reagan, Ronald: Berlin Wall policy, 2; conservative revolution, 460; defence policy, 10–11, 14, 40, 58, 59; Doctrine, 249; economic policy, 410, 438, 448; foreign policy, 7, 8, 30–1, 38; Japanese policy, 128; Libya bombing, 30, 232; old age, 9
regulation, 421, 422, 428
religion: in China, 173–5; economic role, 418–19; human rights concept, 251; in Iran, 220, 235–6; in Iraq, 220, 225, 226; in Ireland, 221; in Japan, 130; in Pakistan, 201, 204; in Russia, 72–3, 74–5; in Syria, 220, 229, 235; terrorism, 221; in Turkey, 222, 223; in US, 21, 61–2; world religions, 218–19; *see also* Christianity, Islam, Judaism

Republika Srpska, 303, 306, 307
Revolution in Military Affairs (RMA), 46
Reykjavik Summit (1986), 11
Riau, autonomy issue, 127
Richelieu, Cardinal, xvii
Rights, Bill of (1689), 251–2
Rights, Bill of (1789), 252, 253
Roberts, Andrew, 363
rogue states, 207–9
Roman Empire, 25
Rome, Club of, *see* Club
Rome, Treaty of (1957), 325–6, 335n, 372, 375, 409
Rong Yren, 153–4
Rugova, Ibrahim, 310, 314
Rumsfeld, Donald, 55
Rumsfeld Commission, 55–6
Runnymede, 469–71
Russia: Bolshevik Revolution, 23, 74; Chechen War, 79, 102–3; China relations, 107; Communist legacy, 74–9; corruption, 77–8; coup attempt (1991), 64, 76–7, 81; crime, 78–9; economic reform, 79–84; economic reform failure, 84–8; Federal Security Bureau (FSB), 104, 106; financial crisis, 464; health, 85–6; history, 71–4; Japan relations, 83, 107; military power, 89–92; MT's visit (1993), 63–9; nationality problems, 93–103; nuclear capability, 71; nuclear sales, 55, 179; predictions, 69–71; Putin presidency, 103–10; religion, 72–3, 74–5; US relations, 25, 26, 107
Rwanda, genocide tribunal, 258, 259, 260–62

Sacks, Jonathan, 242
Sadat, Anwar, 232, 245
Said, Muhammad Farah, 32
Saint-Malo Summit (1998), 354
Saint-Simon, comte de, 412n
Sarajevo, siege, 301, 302, 304, 305

Saudi Arabia: religion, 237; Western ally, 223
Schröder, Gerhard, 344, 347, 350n, 352, 427
Schuman, Robert, 325, 326
Schumpeter, Joseph, 462
Scruton, Roger, 417
Seattle, WTO meeting and protests (1999), 458, 460
Second World War: end, 39–40; Indian role, 200; influence, 248, 320; Japanese role, 130–1; Singapore, 117; Yugoslavia, 287
September 11 terrorist attacks, xxiii–xxiv, 19, 38, 57, 60, 62, 97
Serbia: EU policy, 316; NATO bombing, 36, 90; see also Kosovo
Shaw, George Bernard, 12
Shining Path, 221
Shultz, George, 464
Sidney, Algernon, 22
Silguy, Yves-Thibault de, 384
Simon, William, 464
Singapore, 115–18; economy, 120, 122
Singh, Maharajah Hari, 203
Singh, Manmohan, 198
single currency, 377, 386–8, see also Economic and Monetary Union (EMU), euro
Single European Act, 373–5, 376
Single European Market, 371–6, 380, 396, 400–1
Šljivančanin, Veselin, 293n
Slovenia, 297–300
Smith, Adam: on capitalism, 413, 415, 421, 423, 430, 462; on free trade, 465; on self-love, 413–14, 430
Smuts, Jan, 29
Soames, Rupert, 5
Social Chapter, European, 376, 380, 393, 397
social justice, 432
socialism, 438, 449
Solbes, Pedro, 346

Solidarity movement, 6
Somalia, US intervention (1992–3), 31–2
Sony, 138
Soros, George, 462–3
Soto, Hernando de, 416
South Korea: economy, 121, 122; regime, 123, 175, 176; North Korea relations, 215–16
sovereignty, 382–3, 409
Soviet Union: China relations, 15; Cold War, 13–15; collapse, 16, 101; history, 71–4; in 1980s, 69–70; nuclear capability, 48–9, 53
Spaak, Paul Henri, 326
Spain: Armada, 271–2; defence spending, 40; EU membership, 338; fishing fleet, 398–9; Pinochet case, 271–2; torture issue, 273
Spratly Islands, disputes over, 182
Srebrenica, massacre (1995), 261, 304
SS-27 Topol-M ICBM, 91
Stability Pact for South-East Europe, 317, 353
Stalin, Joseph: achievements, 12; Chechen deportations, 101; Churchill on, xxiv; Mao's admiration for, 160; regime, 75, 93, 164, 257; Zil limousine, 155
Starovoitova, Galina, 79
START II and III treaties, 51, 91
Steffens, Lincoln, 12
Stepashin, Sergei, 84
Stone, Norman, 72n
Strategic Defense Initiative (SDI), 10–11, 14, 58
Strauss-Kahn, Dominique, 330n, 352
subsidiarity, 380
Sudan: religion, 220; rogue state, 209, 220
Suez crisis (1956), 363
Suharto, Thojib N.J., 123, 124–7
Sukarno, Achmad, 124
Sukarnoputri, Megawati, 126

Switzerland: EFTA membership, 408;
  EU membership issue, 346
Syria: Israel relations, 229–30;
  military capability, 230–1; regime,
  229–31, 235; religion, 220, 229,
  235; rogue state, 209, 220; Turkey
  relations, 230
Szamuely, Tibor, 72n

Taiwan: China relations, 52, 164,
  182, 183–5; economy, 120, 122,
  186–7; elections, 186; MT's visit
  (1992), 187–9; regime, 175, 176;
  US relations, 184–5
Tajikistan, 97, 100
Takeshita, Noboru, 128
Talbott, Strobe, 14
Taliban regime in Afghanistan: drug
  trafficking, 221; Iran relations,
  236, 240; neighbouring states, 100;
  Osama bin Laden relations, xixn,
  202; rogue state, 209n; US action
  against, 37, 38, 97, 201, 266
Tamil extremists, 221
tax: harmonisation, 380; increase in,
  428–9; role of, 421, 422–30
Taylor, A.J.P., 3
television, influence of, 35
terrorism, xix, xxiii–xxv, 19, 26,
  37–8, 51–2, 57–8, 97, 107,
  220–1, 266n, 273n, 277; see also
  al-Qaeda, bin Laden, rogue states,
  Taliban
Thailand: economy, 120–1; regime,
  123
Thatcher, Carol, 65
Thatcher, Denis, 64–5, 469
Thatcherism, 426
Third Way, 426–7
Third World, 435–44
Tibet, Chinese rule, 173
Tito (Josip Broz), 287, 313
Tocqueville, Alexis de, 16–17, 62, 118
Torture Convention, 272–3
trade unions, 428
Tudjman, Franjo, 289, 301n

Turkey: Balkan policy, 286; Israel
  relations, 230, 239; regime, 222,
  223–5; religion, 222, 223; Syria
  relations, 230
Turkmenistan, 97, 100

UK Independence Party, 382
Ukraine, future of, 96
United Arab Emirates, territory, 237
United Nations: Balkan peacekeeping
  forces, 299; Charter, 37, 254–5;
  Commission on Human Rights,
  172, 264n; conventions on human
  rights, 255–6; Sanctions
  Committee, 228; Security Council,
  30, 33–4, 52, 147–8, 179, 205,
  208, 265; Somalia operation,
  31–2; UNSCOM, 49
United States of America: aid
  programme, 443; British
  investment, 401; character, 21–2,
  60–2; charity, 425; Constitution,
  24, 252; currency, 386;
  Declaration of Independence, 20,
  252–3, 431; economy, 331, 412,
  461; environmental policy, 452–3,
  456, 457; European policy, 364–5;
  foreign policy, 24–5, 207–8;
  Founding Fathers, 22, 61; freedom,
  22–4; Gulf War, 28–30; hostility
  towards, 25–6; idea of, 19–20;
  interventionism, 27–8, 30–9; Iran
  relations, 237–40; isolationism,
  26–7; Japan relations, 145, 146–7;
  military policies, 43–6; military
  spending, 40–3; military
  technology, 36; missiles and missile
  defence, 48–60, 181; NAFTA
  membership, 404, 407; National
  Intelligence Estimate (1995), 55;
  North Korea relations, 214; Pearl
  Harbor, 47–8; protectionism, 443;
  religion, 21, 61–2; RMA, 46–7; Russia
  relations, 25, 26, 107; Suez
  crisis, 363; Taiwan relations,
  184–5; taxation, 424

Universal Declaration of Human
  Rights (1948), 255
Uruguay Round, 368, 460
Uzbekistan: ethnic issues, 97; security
  cooperation treaty, 97; US bases,
  100

Vance, Cyrus, 302
Vance–Owen Plan, 302
Vaz, Keith, 278n, 393
Védrine, Hubert, 357
Verheugen, Günter, 339
Versailles Treaty, 322
Vietnam: China relations (1979),
  181; regime, 123
Vogel, Ezra, 132
Voltaire, 431
Vukovar: destruction, 290–3, 300;
  MT's visit (1998), 288–92

Wahid, Abdurrahman, 126
Walesa, Lech, 4, 6
Wallström, Margot, 452
Walters, Sir Alan, 81, 441, 465
Wang Dan, 170–1
war, xix–xx, xxiii, 53–4
Warsaw Pact, 51
Washington Agreements (1994), 32
Washington protests (2000), 458
weapons of mass destruction
  (WMD), 49, 60, 209, 231
Weaver, Richard, 423
Webb, Sidney and Beatrice, 12
Wei Jingsheng, 170–1
Wells, H.G., 12
Wesley, John, 430
William and Mary College,
  Williamsburg, 22
William III, King, 251n

Wilson, Harold, 367
Wilson, James Q., 22
Winthrop, John, 20–1
Wolf, Martin, xixn, 392n, 460n
Woman's Own, interview with MT,
  426
women: in China, 172; military role,
  44–5
Working Time Directive, 375
World Bank, 83, 441–2, 458, 463
World Trade Organisation (WTO):
  arbitration, 407; China's
  membership, 165, 177, 183; EU
  relationship, 337, 398, 401, 405;
  role, 465; Seattle meeting (1999),
  458
Wotton, Sir Henry, xxi
Wriston, Walter, 464
Wu, Harry, 161n, 170
Wu Jie, 171

Yeltsin, Boris: advisers, 79; Baltic
  states policy, 94; Chinese
  relationship, 26, 71; defence policy,
  71, 89; Gorbachev relationship,
  151; IMF relations, 80; Kosovo
  intervention, 90; leadership, 76–7,
  105; reforms, 63, 81–3, 84–5;
  successor, 104
Yugoslavia (former): creation, 297;
  genocide tribunal, 258–9, 262;
  Western policy, 283, 298–9

Zhao Ziyang, 158, 160, 192
Zhivkov, Todor, 164
Zhu Rongji, 166–8, 198
Zia ul-Haq, Mohammed, 201
Zimbabwe, government, 441
Zinoviev, Alexandr, 77